THEOLOGY FOR THE TWENTY-FIRST CENTURY
CENTER OF THEOLOGICAL INQUIRY

Theology for the Twenty-first Century is a series sponsored by the Center of Theological Inquiry (CTI), an institute, located in Princeton, New Jersey, dedicated to the advanced study of theology. This series is one of its many initiatives and projects.

The goal of the series is to publish inquiries of contemporary scholars into the nature of the Christian faith and its witness and practice in church, society, and culture. The series will include investigations into the uniqueness of the Christian faith. But it will also offer studies that relate the Christian faith to the major cultural, social, and practical issues of our time.

Monographs and symposia will result from research by scholars in residence at the Center of Theological Inquiry or otherwise associated with it. In some cases, publications will come from group research projects sponsored by CTI. It is our intention that the books selected for this series will constitute a major contribution to renewing theology in its service to church and society.

WALLACE M. ALSTON, JR., ROBERT JENSON,
AND DON S. BROWNING
SERIES EDITORS

What Dare We Hope?
by Gerhard Sauter

The End of the World and the Ends of God
edited by John Polkinghorne and Michael Welker

God and Globalization, Volume 1:
Religion and the Powers of the Common Life
edited by Max L. Stackhouse with Peter J. Paris

God and Globalization, Volume 2:
The Spirit and the Modern Authorities
edited by Max L. Stackhouse with Don S. Browning

God and Globalization, Volume 3:
Christ and the Dominions of Civilization
Edited by Max L. Stackhouse with Diane B. Obenchain

Redemptive Change:
Atonement and the Christian Cure of the Soul
R. R. Reno

GOD AND GLOBALIZATION:
THEOLOGICAL ETHICS AND THE SPHERES OF LIFE

MAX L. STACKHOUSE, GENERAL EDITOR
WITH PETER J. PARIS, DON S. BROWNING,
AND DIANE B. OBENCHAIN

Sponsored by
The Center of Theological Inquiry
Princeton, N.J.
1999–2001

The world is presently going through a monumental social, political, and economic shift that has implications for faith, ethics, human understanding, and for human well-being. It is clear that the categories of analysis by which most of us have understood the social worlds around us are at least partially obsolete. How are we to understand the new, complex global civilization toward which we are being thrust? What are the ways that religion, theology, and ethics, in close interaction with our social, political, and economic situation, can help guide globalization?

The contributors to this set of four volumes have sorted the "powers and principalities," "authorities and dominions" that are shaping the multiple spheres of life in our world and have proposed creative new perspectives on a massive range of pertinent issues that lie at the intersection of religion and globalization. The four volumes provide insights into ethics, religion, economics, and culture that will interest not only theologians, ethicists, and clergy of many traditions but also academics, social scientists, professionals, and those in business and technology who seek to understand the move toward a global civilization from a social and ethical point of view.

GOD AND GLOBALIZATION: THEOLOGICAL ETHICS AND THE SPHERES OF LIFE

Vol. 1: *Religion and the Powers of the Common Life*
Edited by Max L. Stackhouse with Peter J. Paris

Vol. 2: *The Spirit and the Modern Authorities*
Edited by Max L. Stackhouse with Don S. Browning

Vol. 3: *Christ and the Dominions of Civilization*
Edited by Max L. Stackhouse with Diane B. Obenchain

God *and* Globalization

VOLUME 3

CHRIST AND THE DOMINIONS OF CIVILIZATION

Edited by
Max L. Stackhouse
with Diane B. Obenchain

TRINITY PRESS INTERNATIONAL

Trinity Press International, P.O. Box 1321, Harrisburg, PA 17105
Trinity Press International is a division of the Morehouse Group.

Cover design: Tom Castanzo

Library of Congress Cataloging-in-Publication Data

God and globalization : religion and the powers of the common life / edited by Max L. Stackhouse with Peter Paris.

    p. cm. – (Theology for the twenty-first century)
    Includes bibliographical references and index.
    ISBN 1-56338-311-X
    1. Christian ethics. 2. Globalization – Moral and ethical aspects.
3. Globalization – Religious aspects – Christianity. I. Stackhouse, Max L.
II. Paris, Peter J., 1933. III. Series.

BJ1275 .G63 2000
261.8 – dc21

                                                 00-020203

Volume 3: Christ and the Dominions of Civilization ISBN 1-56338-371-3

Printed in the United States of America

02   03   04   05   06   07   10 9 8 7 6 5 4 3 2 1

CONTENTS

CONTRIBUTORS

KOSUKE KOYAMA is the John D. Rockefeller, Jr., Professor Emeritus of Ecumenical Studies at Union Theological Seminary, New York. He was born and raised in Japan and became a minister of the United Church of Christ in Japan after World War II. He earned his master's and doctoral degrees from Princeton Theological Seminary, and joined the faculty of the Thailand Theological Seminary in Cheingmai before becoming, almost a decade later, dean of the South East Asia Graduate School of Theology. For half a decade, he became the senior lecturer in religion at the University of Otago in New Zealand. In addition to some 120 articles, four books in Japanese, and six books in Thai, he has published six books in English, including the widely quoted *Waterbuffalo Theology, Mount Fuji and Mount Sinai,* and *Three Mile an Hour God.*

JOHN MBITI has for many years been among the most respected scholars of tribal traditions. He has served as professor of theology at Makerere University, Kampala, Uganda, as director of and professor at the Ecumenical Institute of Bossey of the World Council of Churches, and as pastor of the Reformed Church parish in Burgdor, Switzerland, while also teaching missiology at the University of Bern. Born and raised in Kenya, he studied also in England and the United States. His pioneer work, *African Religions and Philosophy,* has extensive sections on African views of time and space. He has been a visiting professor at several universities and seminaries, and in 1997–99 served as the John A. Mackay Professor of World Christianity at Princeton Theological Seminary and in 2001, professor of Anglican studies at the General Theological Seminary in New York. Among his many books are *Concepts of God in Africa, African and Asian Contributions to Contemporary Theology, Poems of Nature and Faith, New Testament Eschatology in African Background,* and *Bible and Theology in African Christianity.*

DIANE B. OBENCHAIN, with master's degrees from Stanford University and a doctorate from Harvard, is a specialist in the comparative history of religion. She was associate professor of Eastern religions at Kenyon College before moving to southeast Asia, where she taught Confuciansim at the National University of Singapore for three years. Since 1988, as visiting professor at Peking University, she has helped introduce the study of religion to China. She is co-author of a textbook for the study of religion to be published by Peking University Press. She is also project director for the "Small Dictionary for the Study of Religion in English and Chinese," funded by The Henry Luce Foundation. She edited *Selected Papers on the Thought of Feng Youlan,* and her *On the Meaning of Ru* and *For China: Essays on Moral Leadership* are forthcoming.

LAMIN SANNEH went to school in his native Gambia before coming to the United States to study history. Later he spent several years studying Arabic and Islam, both in the Middle East and at the University of London, from which he obtained his Ph.D. He taught at the World Religions Center at Harvard for several years before being appointed professor of history at Yale College and simultaneously as the D. Willis James Professor of World Christianity at the Yale Divinity School. He is also an honorary research professor in the School of Oriental and African Studies, University of London, and a life member of Clare Hall, Cambridge University. His publications include *The Crown and the Turban, Piety and Power, Faith and Power: Christianity and Islam in "Secular" Britain,* and the widely acclaimed *Translating the Message,* a comparative study of Islamic and Christian ways of communicating their messages in new contexts.

MAX L. STACKHOUSE is the Stephen Colwell Professor of Christian Ethics at Princeton Theological Seminary. Educated at DePauw, Nijenrode (Holland), and Harvard Universities, he taught at Andover Newton Theological Seminary and Boston College for many years before moving to Princeton. For much of his academic life, he has been involved in international education, having served as a guest lecturer in Japan, China, Korea, Singapore, and Indonesia, and a visiting professor in India, the Philippines, Fiji, and East Germany. His several books include *Public Theology and Political Economy* (also published in Korean and Japanese); *Creeds, Societies, and Human Rights: A Study in Three Cultures; Christian Social Ethics in a Global Era; On Moral Business: Classical and Contemporary Resources for an Ethic for Economic Life;* and, most recently, *A Dialogue on the Value of Modernity,* with Bao Limin, published in Chinese.

M. THOMAS THANGARAJ is the S. W. and Ruth Brooks Professor of World Christianity at the Candler School of Theology, Emory University. He taught for many years at the Tamilnadu Theological Seminary in the famous South Indian temple city of Madurai. He was born and raised in India, and earned his early degrees from leading colleges there before studying for his doctoral degree at Harvard University. His thesis on the Hindu philosophical tradition of Saiva Siddhanta in comparison and contrast to Christianity has been acknowledged as outstanding. He is much in demand as a lecturer, has been deeply involved in interfaith dialogue in the West as well as in India and Burma, and is a musician and composer as well as a theologian. His several books include *The Crucified Guru, Relating to People of Other Religions,* and *The Common Task: A New Theology of Christian Missions.*

SCOTT M. THOMAS is a professor in the Department of Economics and International Development at the University of Bath in the United Kingdom. An American by birth, he earned his B.A. from the School of International Service at the American University in Washington, D.C. He then earned his M.Sc.

and Ph.D. from the Department of International Relations at the London School of Economics, where he was deeply involved in the "Millennium Conference" on Religion and International Relations. He also earned a master's degree in advanced Christian studies from New College, Berkeley, associated with the Graduate Theological Union. His book, *The Diplomacy of Liberation: The Foreign Relations of the ANC of South Africa,* with its accent on the roles of the World Council of Churches and the World Reformed Alliance, led him to focus on the role of religion in world politics, and he has published numerous essays on this topic in both academic and church-related journals.

SZE-KAR WAN was born in China and lived in Hong Kong for some years before coming to the United States. He earned his bachelor's degree from Brandeis University, his master's from Gordon-Conwell Theological Seminary, and his doctorate in biblical studies from Harvard University, where he was awarded the Sinclair Kennedy Fellowship. Since then he has cultivated his interests in Judaic and Christian traditions as editor of the *Review of Biblical Literature* and in philosophical and religious developments in China as the director of the Chinese Hermeneutics Project. He is the editor of the new translations of Philo's works into Chinese, and of *The Bible in Modern China: The Literary and Intellectual Impact.* His newest book is *Power in Weakness* (on conflict in the book of Corinthians) as a part of the New Testament in Context series.

INTRODUCTION

Max L. Stackhouse

Since we began this four-volume project on God and globalization in 1997, a host of notable studies have appeared on the topic of globalization. None so far is more complete than *Global Transformations: Politics, Economics, and Culture* by the British team of scholars, David Held, Anthony McGrew, David Goldblatt, and Jonathan Perraton.[1] Called by some commentators "the definitive work on globalization," it identifies three major, competing views of the phenomenon. The "hyperglobalists" hold that economics has set a developmental trajectory toward a global civilization that will encompass the world, create plenty for all, and bring about the end of all older hierarchies and nationalisms. Some hyperglobalists are more "liberal" and evolutionary in the tradition of free market capitalism, and others are more "radical" and revolutionary in the residual socialist tradition. Some on both sides take these options in a more idealist direction, following the tradition of Hegel, and others more in the conflictual direction, following the tradition of Marx. These orientations mix in various ways, but they share the conviction that a re-ordering of human life is underway in modernizing economic forces and that, on the whole, it will benefit humanity.

The "sceptics," by contrast, point out that regionalization, especially among cultures that are internally quite homogenous, is taking place more dramatically than globalization and is doing so in ways that increasingly marginalize some portions of the world's populations, especially minorities

---

1. Stanford, Calif.: Stanford University Press, 1999.

within larger cultural units. Thus, we find a new European commonality, with evidence of hostility to Turkish, Algerian, or other minorities and a reassertion of nationalist identity by Balkan tribes; a new Chinese nationalism, with attempts to homogenize Tibetans and others into Han culture; attempts to Islamicize Malaysia, Indonesia, and other areas; and the Hinduization of India, with overt mistreatment of religious minorities. These efforts breed resentment, inequality, and alienation, which in turn prompts increased cultural resistance to any forces, internal or external, such as globalization, that further threaten particular cultural identity.

Moreover, the sceptics argue, the world is actually *less* linked in an elaborate system of interdependence than it was in critical periods of the past. Complex political systems attained a balance of power that dominated most of Western and much of Eastern Europe in the eighteenth and nineteenth centuries and that reached also to the colonies around the world. Nations rooted in these patterns still use global links essentially to advance their own national interests, and whatever internationalization that is taking place remains heavily dependent on the policies of nation-states. Indeed, local or regional cultures reassert themselves against the eroding of their political power at the hands of globalizing pressures in ways that could well lead to new, very dangerous, clashes prompted by what some call "retribalization."

In contrast to the hypermodernists and sceptics, the authors of *Global Transformations* believe that a third view, a "transformationalist" one, offers the better interpretation of the matter. They recognize that historically unprecedented levels of interconnection that are less colonial than in the past are being reached and that a significant reordering of the world order is underway. But they argue that in different parts of the world, different aspects of societies are undergoing change in distinct areas of life at various paces. The nation-state is more changing its role than fading away, even as it reasserts its sovereignty to regain cultural identity. All this, they argue, is taking place due to the changing shape of power, or as the subtitle implies, "political, economic, and cultural patterns of determinative influence."[2]

In certain respects, this third volume of *God and Globalization* extends major arguments that we have made in our first two volumes, and our analyses partly support and partly challenge the arguments of *Global Transformations*. That volume is surely correct in these respects: The evidence is already clear that we should not all become unreservedly enthusiastic advocates of economistic hyperglobalism. Indeed, some will remain hostile sceptics, suspicious of the apocalyptic dangers of cultural imperialism on one side and reactionary cultural reassertions on the other. Certainly, there are insights and clusters of evidence on both sides of this debate, for the world is being changed by the impact of economic forces, and there are perils to some cultural options. But the preponderance of evidence rests with the transformationalists. Indeed, as the authors of that volume argue, the changing shape of power does make a great difference. However, just at this point, a substantive reservation must be inserted, one already encountered in the analysis of the primary "authorities" and secondary "regencies" of modernity in the previous volumes of this set: Is the basic analytical framework, specifically the use of a threefold conception of power — political, economic, and cultural — sufficient? A central point of *God and Globalization* as a set of volumes is that it is not. It is surely a marked improvement on the binary forms of social analysis that treat every question in terms of a two-class analysis (bourgeois/ proletariat, rich/poor, powerful/weak, North/South, central/ marginal). Still, neither of these binary nor the three-fold analyses of *Global Transformations* are adequate, even if certain agreements between this study and the views of the transformationalists are sufficiently strong that it is not out of place to cite their definition of globalization as we continue our extended argument. They write that globalization is:

---

2. Ibid., 1.

first and foremost, a *stretching* of social, political and
economic activities across frontiers such that events, decisions and activities in one region of the world can come
to have significance for individuals and communities in
distant regions of the globe. In this sense, it embodies
transregional interconnectedness, the widening reach of
networks of social activity and power, and the possibility
of action at a distance. Beyond this, globalization implies
that connections across frontiers are not just occasional
or random, but rather are regularized such that there
is a detectable *intensification,* or growing magnitude,
of interconnectedness, patterns of interaction and flows
which transcend the constituent societies and states of
the world order. Furthermore, the growing extensity and
intensity of global interconnectedness may also imply
a *speeding up* of global interactions and processes as
the development of worldwide systems of transport and
communication increases the potential velocity of the
global diffusion of ideas, goods, information, capital and
people. And the growing *extensity, intensity,* and *velocity* of global interactions may also be associated with a
deepening enmeshment of the local and global such that
the *impact* of distant events is magnified while even the
most local developments may come to have enormous
global consequences. . . . By acknowledging these dimensions a more precise definition of globalization can be
offered . . . : *a process (or set of processes) which embodies a transformation in the spatial organization of social
relations and transactions — assessed in terms of their
extensity, intensity, velocity, and impact — generating
transcontinental or inter-regional flows and networks of
activity, interactions, and the exercise of power.*[3]

We can learn from such analyses in the social sciences, as
we have already seen in volumes 1 and 2. Although normative
considerations pervade these works, the social sciences take

---

3. Ibid., 15–16; italics in original.

little from religion, theology, or ethics. Even at the descriptive level, as we can see at the very end of the above definition of the key dynamics of globalization, which the rest of *Global Transformations* seeks to explicate, a chief difference between this set of volumes and that study appears. It has precisely to do with the nature and character of power. They understand the powers to be the socially constructed patterns of economics, culture, and, especially, of politics, each of which must be understood historically as well as structurally. This threefold analysis of the powers is widely used in contemporary scholarship. It points to the sphere of political authority, which regulates many dimensions of society by the accumulation, organization, and deployment of coercive force. It also points toward the economic organization of society, wherein human communities gain the capacity to transform the resources of the biophysical universe into usable products that enhance the material condition of human life. And it points to the ways in which economic and political life both shape and are shaped by culture.

These three levels of social power, however, do not take account of that which transcends these realities. What, for example, accounts for the ways in which people will make sacrifices for their families, or for a wider community of loved ones, or for their cultural values, or for their faith? Is this a matter of cultural, economic, or political power? And what of science and technology? Is it not the case, for example, that they are radically reordering both the means of communication and the very fabric of nature and are laden with the moral and spiritual assumption not only that we may do so but that all who are not to be left behind must be enabled to participate in such efforts? In most historic cultures it was held that humans were supposed to fit into nature and culture as given; only a few thought they were obligated to change them due to a supra-natural and transcultural spiritual commission. As a consequence, now, every culture in the world is changing, and new synthetic consolidations of communicative possibility are at hand as new forms of technological transfer are taking place, both fragmenting older patterns of conventional meaning and generating the prospects of a new global interaction. Is that process a function of political, economic, or cultural power, or is it an independent variable involving a diffusion of "worldview"? Is it not the case that the formation and rise to dominance of the corporation as a basic form of social organization is fundamentally changing not only the economy but the fabric of trust and friendship, the structure of civil society, as well as the habits of work, household interaction, education, and healthcare, and thus also politics and culture? Is the corporation as a mode of social organization thus to be considered political, cultural or economic? Such questions raise the issue of whether the "spheres" that theological ethics have long discussed could give a more adequate framework by which to order the questions, because they give a more complex analysis of the institutional patterns that constitute the sectors of civil society in which people actually live. Such questions also raise the issue of whether the social sciences on which many draw reach deeply enough into the very structure of power itself.

In fact, people become devoted to their family members, to their culture, to their institutions of governance and economic life. Moreover, they become committed to various modes of science, technology, medicine, corporate organization, or theories of development, and not only because they serve their political, economic, or cultural interests but because they point toward principles and purposes that are held to be holy or divine or of transcendent worth. At this point, the decisive issue is not only whether there are other powers and spheres of life that should be considered but whether a study that presumes to identify the decisive powers that are driving, and at points resisting, globalization could or should examine religion in the analysis of the global processes it studies. At a deeper level, it is at least arguable that the political, economic, and cultural values to which they point are always nested in moral and religiously held perspectives, and these are subject to ethical and theological analysis. Otherwise, it would seem that these three forms of power had no ethical principles behind them, no interest-guiding spirit in them, and nothing more governing them than the struggle to get and keep political power, economic wealth, and cultural sovereignty.

We might, of course, turn to other, contemporary social scientific efforts that explicitly do take into account such issues. The new book *Principled World Politics* contains a fascinating collection of essays dedicated to Richard Falk, the noted Princeton University professor who has been an outstanding contributor to and advocate of the normative treatment of international relations for many years.[4] The editors and authors, like their mentor, are deeply committed to social justice, have an extensive familiarity with the issues that appear on the soft underbelly of our present global context, and view scholarship as both an exercise in critical and interpretive understanding on the one side and an occasion for the exposé of wrong and the illumination of right on the other. Moral commitment overtly enters these pages as it does not in *Global Transformations*.[5] For these reasons, several essays follow Falk's injunction to heed the voices of those outside the mainstream of social scientific scholarship and political influence, for, the authors hold, these voices offer criticisms of the injustices lurking in the shadows of modern civilization's developments. To be sure, these scholars do "not understand such voices as realistic candidates for global governance — indeed, dissident expression often calls for distancing particular communities from the dynamics of economic and political globalization... (in ways that could be damaging for these communities over time and for human life more generally)."[6] But even these perspectives are to be drawn into dialogue so

---

4. Paul Wapner and Lester Edwin J. Ruiz, eds., *Principled World Politics: The Challenge of Normative International Relations* (Lanham, Md.: Rowman & Littlefield, 2000).

5. One of the contributors to *Principled World Politics* is David Held, an author of *Global Transformations*, but his essay remains in the less overtly principled and passionate mode. This indicates what many might suspect, that social scientific perspectives on the issues of globalization are often laden with moral presuppositions and are not entirely "value neutral" but often block their presuppositions from view.

6. Paul Wapner, introduction to Wapner and Ruiz, *Principled World Politics*, 15.

that all may participate in the process of generating common values, establishing common ideals, and forging progressive strategies to reach them.

Moreover, these scholars are alert to current treatments of ethical principles posed in several forms of postmodern philosophical thought and cultural criticism. For example, Lester Edwin J. Ruiz seeks to identify global capitalism, democratic participation, and governance as cultural practices that can be subject to an "analytic of power" that draws on Marx, Gramsci, and Foucault for its interpretive tools and on Heidegger's understanding of the *poiesis* of human life that "brings forth" the constitutive dimensions of "human dwelling." In other words, the values to which this set of essays turns are viewed as human artifacts that must be constantly constructed, deconstructed, and reconstructed. Indeed, any principles of justice and truth that are to be found are themselves understood to be "productions" of the dialogues.[7]

Such approaches are widely followed in contemporary communities of discourse, and they are suspect of any notion that moral principles or purposes are scripted into human nature or the fabric of the universe, or stand over and against the way things are. Some take objective values seriously at two points — in regard to environmental issues and in regard to human rights. But they do not inquire into the reasons why we should consider nature normative, for ideas of nature are, surely, also socially constructed, or why we might recognize any innate dignity in humans when it is suggested that people create the values they hold. Nor do they take into account any view of any possible Creator of the universe or, indeed, those aspects of human nature that suggest a capacity, however modest, to transcend its bio-socio-economic-cultural enmeshments by the reception of transcendent inspiration or an exercise of commitments and covenants beyond interests.[8]

---

7. See Ruiz's essay, "Culture, Politics, and the Sense of the Ethical," esp. 326–38, in the same volume.

8. Ruiz does, in passing, mention Max Weber's understanding of the Protestant

The scholars in this volume, in other words, presume, but do not supply or invoke any comprehensive understanding of humans as creatures having a universal kinship or a capacity to recognize the dignity, spirituality, duties, and rights of others as humans, although they do treat the post–World War II development of a "human rights regime" as a good artifact of political action and legal construction. The volume does not contain any argument for why this artifact ultimately ought not to be deconstructed. It certainly does not include any evidence about the nature or character of spiritual traditions, worldviews, primal visions, ultimate purpose, or fundamental moral order toward which the religions of the world have long pointed. This makes all such matters entirely a function of the power of group interaction, not anything to which oppressed groups can appeal beyond the constructions of groups that would make justice, truth, or compassion more actual. Thus, this volume too ends up not far beyond the two pages in *Global Transformations* that touch on religion. They see religion and ethics as, essentially, a mostly benign expression of cultural development that arises at significant points in history but that has no formative, regulative, interpretive, or guiding role in globalization or in understanding the forces producing it.

In short, nothing in these works, or the innumerable less excellent ones that follow similar modes of analysis, considers or takes seriously the more ultimate issues of the nature and character of God, humanity, and the world, or even the im-

---

ethic as evidence that culture has a place in the analysis of economic matters. He elsewhere mentions poetry, philosophy, and theology as areas of cultural creativity, and he also makes passing reference to the fact that Paul Tillich, Gustavo Gutiérrez, and John Cobb (all theologians, although that is not mentioned) have written on morality in relationship to political and economic issues. Yet neither he nor others in the volume see religion or theology or ethical first principles of the right or good as constitutive for shaping or organizing cultural constructs. Indeed, these aspects of life cannot be, for they too are cultural constructs. Thus, it is not surprising that when contributing scholars treat Israel, the influence of Judaism is not mentioned. India is treated as if neither Hinduism nor Islam had any influence on economics, politics, or culture. Likewise, when Korea is mentioned, no reference is made to its shamanic, Confucian, or Buddhist heritage or to the rapid growth of Christianity and the roles these traditions play in Korea's economic and political affairs.

pact of beliefs about them on global changes — specifically on those changes that have led us to globalization or to changes that could or should bring about an ordering of an emerging global civilization in the future. It is not the intent here to demand that these scholars set forth their personal beliefs, convert to this or that brand of religion, become scholars of comparative religion, or become professional theologians. Nor is it the intent to offer an extended critique of these specific volumes or their authors. Rather, the intent is to identify a substantive deficit in even very good examples of analytic-interpretive and advocacy-oriented contemporary scholarly analyses of our global situation. Such studies are to be studied and, in many respects, commended, but they are also subject to criticism because the range of their vision is artificially narrowed by their studied exclusion of matters that bear on their topics. It is simply intellectually mistaken to hold that we can understand the generation and reception, the resistance and the adaptations of globalizing realities without reference to the formative influence of primal religions in Africa and elsewhere, Confucianism in East Asia, Hinduism in South Asia, Buddhism in Southeast Asia, Islam in the Mideast, Catholicism in Latin America, and Protestant forms of Christianity in Northern Europe and North America, all with overlapping and interpenetrating characteristics. In its present form, such scholarship simply does not see major aspects of the world it seeks to study. It is thus necessary to take a wider, deeper, longer, and higher view.

Beyond Religious Blindness

This set of volumes differs from even the best available social science and political advocacy that is available on this point. It differs because it seeks to do much of what these other works do from a standpoint that invites them to extend their vision. Their command over selectively interpreted data partly informs, but also dogmatically excludes, issues that would more adequately help us all understand and guide the transformations they seek to explain and influence. The moral and spiritual architecture of every civilization is grounded, more than any other factor, in religious commitments that point to a source of normative meaning beyond the political, economic, and cultural structures themselves. Neither these spheres of life nor the dynamics of the modern professions and the transnational, transeconomic, and transcultural movements for, say, ecology or racial justice can be understood without grasping the religious dimension of moral convictions and social history.

The contributors to this volume are convinced that this acknowledgment of the religious dimension is one of the most important issues of every age — one recognized by serious theological ethicists even if it is rarely recognized today by social scientists and historically by those ordinary believers who find encouragement or consolation in their personal faith but seldom think of the systematic or sociocultural implications of what they believe and think they should do. But the cumulative effect of hundreds of thousands of personal religious commitments, decisions, and actions plays a determinative role in historical development. Moreover, the leaders of the institutions of the various powerful spheres in society finally must make their decisions with reference to the frameworks of great traditions on which ordinary believers also depend, or lose their legitimacy.

Of course, dealing with the deeper forms and kinds of power is more complicated in an era of globalization than it was when our horizons were more limited, for all of the religions now must encounter each other, and the prospect of something approximating a global civilization is developing among us in which religious beliefs and practices are blended by many. Not only does every society find its boundaries permeable but so does every institution in the various spheres of society's life. Such is also the case with regard to religion. Closed societies — those which seek to limit the contact, whether competitive or cooperative, of their own internal institutions, beliefs, and practices with those outside their borders — find themselves not only more isolated but less able to develop the spheres of life that enhance development and loyalty. Thus, many find that they must increase police and military control to keep power. Let it be stated once more as a summary of the main arguments of our two previous volumes: The sociocultural forces that are most often identified with globalization — corporations that generate efficient production, constitutional democracy that protects minorities, family patterns that ensure rights for women and children, communications networks that invite cultural creativity, complex professionalism, advanced technology, awareness of global ecology, the formation of transnational institutions to facilitate or regulate international interaction, the acknowledgment of common principles and virtues beyond diversity, and even the rise of global financial institutions and regulatory agencies — were formed in societies fundamentally stamped by Christian theological ethics. If we do not understand this, we will not understand whence globalization came, what is driving it, how it works, and what it would take to alter, reform, redirect, or channel it.

We must also acknowledge that both Christianity and various globalizing forces have been sometimes allied with colonialism, imperialism, hegemony, forced migrations, slavery, patriarchy, sexual exploitation, conquest, and genocide. None of these, however, was generated by Christianity, is unique to it, is characteristic of its ethics, or is distinctive of its theology, although its theology of sin may help account for them. Still, the development of globalizing forces within Christian-influenced cultures has sometimes been associated historically with these totalistic developments, and the tradition has been subject to critical analysis by critics both of Christianity and of globalization. There is enough complicity in Christian history that honesty demands that its heirs and devotees not become hyperglobalists, even if they distrust also the sceptics. They must also become self-reflexive transformationalists by seeking to penetrate to the deeper levels of analysis of how their own religion has shaped civilizations.

At least, they must acknowledge that the formation, cultivation, and sometimes blessing of those sociocultural forces that are today bearing fruit in globalization have not taken place without contested paternity, a good bit of moral ambiguity, and no small amount of travail.

As we saw especially in volume 2, many of the spheres of authority in modern life saw the European "religious wars" between various Christian divisions — each one legitimating a nation-state and being employed by the nation-state to secure solidarity and legitimation of its laws, customs, culture, and economic arrangements — as evidence of the vacuity of religion in general. In the face of this, many centers of authority declared their independence from the influence of religion and, indeed, subsidized studies to show that purely immanent, nontranscendental forces generated and sustained religion. These autonomous centers of authority, however, became the sources of more devastating forms of colonialism, imperialism, hegemony, forced migrations, patriarchy, slavery, conquest, sexual exploitation, and genocide than the world had previously known.

In recent years, some branches of the Christian tradition have become convinced that their forebears were so complicit in the pathologies of modernity, which they felt betrayed the faith, that they have disowned their progeny. But the deep traces of their legacy remain in them and are being rediscovered by a number of scholars who find it intellectually dishonest to treat the issues of these "secular" spheres of life as if they had no rootage in the commitments that gave them birth.[9] At the same time, other religious traditions and religiously saturated philosophies, cultures, and societies doubt at least some of the claims or the morality of Christianity and are suspicious of the kinds of secularity that have grown in

9. A sampling includes Robert William Fogel, *The Fourth Great Awakening and the Future of Egalitarianism* (Chicago: University of Chicago Press, 2000); Don S. Browning, general editor, *Family, Religion, and Culture Series,* 10 vols. (Louisville, Ky.: Westminster John Knox Press, 1997–99); and Robert H. Nelson, *Economics as Religion* (University Park: Pennsylvania State University Press, 2001).

the West.[10] They know that many of the powers of the globalization that throws them into encounter or conflict with
"foreign influences" are driven by Christian impulses that are
also influenced by Judaism. This is true even if these other traditions selectively adopt the sociopolitical and cultural forces
behind globalization, make them their own, and find their
own contributions to human civilization selectively adapted
into Jewish and Christian-influenced secular cultures.[11]

We do not approach Christianity or any of the world religions in a vacuum. People have thought about them and their
relationship time and again. For several hundred years, it has
been held that one of the highest forms of moral witness is to
call for toleration of other people's religion in both personal
attitude and social policy, and all the great world religions
have acknowledged — although each has sometimes also vi-
olated — the principle that people must be free to believe in
their hearts what they think is ultimately true.[12] Further, the
long-held historical view that each people or land should be
allowed to have its own religion, undisturbed by any attempt
of outsiders to change it, was not only held in one way by
the ancient world but also held in another way by the countries of Europe and the many lands shaped by its influence
in modernity. The ancients held that each people and every

---

10. Ng Kam Weng, the leader of a Christian center for dialogue with Islam in
Malaysia, has drawn my attention to the work of Ismail Faruqi, who exemplifies
this critical view. See his *Al Tawhid: Its Implications for Thought and Life* (Lon-
don: International Institute of Islamic Thought, 1992); and Muhammed Shafiq, *The
Growth of Islamic Thought in North America: Focus on Ishmail Raji al-Faruqi* (New
York: Amana Publishers, 1994). Ng's apologetic response is in his *Perfect Revelation*
(Jalan, Malaysia: Pustaka Sufes, 1995), especially chap. 3.

11. One of the most discussed volumes in the debates over globalization is Samuel
Huntington's *The Clash of Civilizations: The Remaking of World Order* (New York:
Simon & Schuster, 1996), which several of the authors below take up. A new collection of essays, edited by Huntington and Lawrence Harrison, *Culture Matters: How
Values Shape Human Progress* (New York: Basic Books, 2000), refines the central
point of that thesis with a view to the fact that "culture" is deeply shaped by religion
and is not only a by-product or epiphenomenon of it.

12. This is one of the most important legacies of John Locke, especially his often
reprinted "Letter Concerning Toleration." See the new treatments of Locke by David
Lowenthal and Peter MacNamara in Bradley C. S. Watson, ed., *Liberalism in the
New Millennium* (Latrobe, Pa.: Center for Political and Economic Education, 2000),
1–34.

land had its own gods, and a Christian approximation to that pagan consensus was codified for modernity in the treaties of Westphalia, which brought a relative peace after years of "religious wars" in Europe from the Crusades and the Inquisition through the conflicts between Christian denominations after the Reformation. Still, indeed, as a part of this legacy of Christendom, we often speak of Lutheran Germany and Scandinavia, Catholic Italy and Iberia, Reformed Holland, Scotland, and New England, and Orthodox Greece and Eastern Europe. Indeed, all of the great and enduring religions of the world dealt with here have given long and subtle distinctive stamps to large and enduring civilizations in several geographical and historical environments.[13]

Today, as several of our authors emphasize, the world's religions, including Christianity, are in resurgence in one form or another after some years of eclipse by postreligious and often antitheological perspectives and the development of various efforts to achieve viable theories of secularization — each one, ironically, a by-product of the kind of religion against which it reacted. So far as we can see into the future, both the great religions and the various forms of secularism dependent on them will continue to influence the consciousness and behavior of millions and the ways in which a global society develops. They will borrow from and react against each other, sometimes converging and sometimes diverging, sometimes finding common ground and sometimes drawing lines

---

13. We do not have separate chapters on Judaism or Christianity, for they are present in every chapter, as mentioned earlier. The former was widely held to be the paradigmatic tribal or traditional religion by many early anthropologists precisely because it grasped the significance of the worship of one God who was the moral lawgiver for the world and saw itself as a people obligated to bear witness to that transcendent reality and to the ethical order it implied. This view has been indispensable not only for other tribal religions who find much in the scriptures of the ancient tribes of Israel with which they can immediately identify and accept but also for Christianity and for Islam. Indeed, some scholars over the last century have advanced the idea that since the great traditions of Asia, such as Hinduism and Confucianism, contain universalistic values able to engender enduring societies but tend to apply these especially to a people, they are analogous to ancient Judaism or to Greek philosophy. They thus stand as indigenous "Old Testaments" or as profound metaphysical-moral dialogue partners for future global, social, and theological-ethical developments.

in the sand. As discussed in volume 1, the economic interests of Mammon, the political-military ambitions of Mars,
the psychosexual drives of Eros, and the cultural pretenses
of the Muses will again and again seek to set aside or uti-
lize the power of religion for ends that are not central to the
religions themselves. Moreover, the *scientia* of academia, the
jus of law, the *salus* of medicine, as well as the *techne* of en-
gineering, the *Angst* of ecological concern, the *askesis* of the
regulatory "regencies" of the contemporary global scene, and
the *virtu* of heroic figures honored worldwide will be used
to interpret, explain, and channel religious meaning in ways
compatible with their ends, as we saw in volume 2. But in
each of these cases, as was noted, the inadequacy of a secular perspective is palpable. The subordination of religion as
a guiding factor in life and thus necessary to the interpretation of globalization has brought a certain superficiality to
the analysis of globalization and to the kinds of resistance
we find in various places. In this volume, therefore, we look
explicitly at what various authors have already hinted in the
two previous volumes: that religion can and does shape those
principalities and powers, authorities and regencies as much
if not more than they shape religion, and that in the final
analysis religion cannot be reduced to the influence of these
realities.

Behind the design of this volume is the presupposition that
something deeper than the religions themselves stands beyond
every religion. Indeed, the divine reality to which the religions
seek to point is present not only in religion but in all the
spheres of life, and the specific way in which the spheres are
formed and the ways in which they interact are influenced by
the specific kind of religion. Those who follow some particular lord, Lord Jesus for example, will make many similar but
also many distinguishable life decisions compared to those
who follow Lord Krishna or Lord Buddha and those who
follow the ways viewed as "noble" by the heirs of those seeking to follow the Elders, the Prophet Muhammad, or Master
Kong (Confucius). Simultaneously, the fundamental presump-

tions about the right order of things and the principles of wrong that limit behavior and policy (which can be studied by the ethical discipline of deontology) and the goods to be pursued and the evils to be avoided, about why it is that things are distorted in life and what it takes to overcome the distortion (which can be studied by the discipline of teleology, especially as informed by eschatology), will become attached to the operating values that have come to be shared by those who participate in a common historical experience. Together these form the specific patterns of particular institutions in the various spheres of social life (which are studied not only by the social sciences but also by ethology).

In brief, religiously sanctified orientations bend the institutions of society and become incarnate in the ethos of the common life. Behind these more empirically discernable factors stands a commanding image of what, or who, is the source and norm of ultimate truth, justice, and beauty. Each distinctive "religiously sanctified orientation" can be most clearly identified by asking who, or what, is Lord — what divine person or spirit, or what metaphysical-moral law or purpose, is held to have "dominion" in the decisive powers and spheres of life (Latin: *dominus;* Hebrew: *'adôn;* Greek: *kyrios* (or *karios*); German: *Herr;* Sanskrit: *prabhu;* Chinese: *zhu;* English: Lord). A "lordliness" or "dominion" is always directly connected with the concept of that which has ordered reality from the beginning (Greek: *arxē*), the organizing principle or central reality or personal agent by which the world has come into being and from which the world has become separated yet will be the final reality when all the accidental aspects of life are either finally rightly ordered or left behind. In the meantime, in human life and history, life involves a constant attempt to bring the various powers and principalities, authorities or regencies of life into greater convergence with the intent, law, or purpose of the true Lord, of that which should — and really does at the deepest level — have dominion but does not always appear to on the surface of things. The term "should" reveals that what is at stake is normative, simultaneously an ethical and a theological issue as well as an analytic or descriptive matter.

From this point of view, to speak of "Lord Jesus Christ" is socially and religiously similar in an analytic or structural way to what can be found in the devotion to the Spirit Elders of the tribes, to the Lords Krishna, Ram, or Vishnu among the Hindus, and that toward which Lord Buddha, the Prophet and Model Muhammad, and the Sage Confucius are said to point by those who follow them. Moreover, those who claim Jesus Christ as Lord must recognize that those who have followed other Lords have generated distinctive ways of organizing the principalities of the common life and, often, the authorities and regencies of complex civilizations into enduring social systems as well. In brief, all the traditions indicated by this list have had to contend in the loyalties and practices of the people with the perennial powers and principalities of the common life and with the historic authorities and regencies as they develop over the centuries. In the process, they have cultivated a religious ethic based in one or another conception of dominion.

Under conditions of globalization, when we appear to be laying the material foundation for what could become a global civilization under the stimulus of one particular religion that has influenced the basic spheres of modernity and postmodernity, a very large question stands before us. Can we affirm all the great religions equally? Can all of them equally contribute to the moral and spiritual shaping of the necessary institutions and spheres of a worldwide civil society or aid in the correction and constraint of them where they appear to have become destructive and disorienting in their effects? Or is it the case that all religions are not equal in this respect — specifically not equal in their capacity to generate, tolerate, accommodate, restrain, or guide complex civilizations in the face of the globalizing powers that are at hand and, in some cases, threaten to swamp the convictions and institutions by which the religions understand themselves? If all religions are not equal in this respect, can we say that one Lord is better than any other? Is there some *dominus* we should seek to make the universal dominion? Can one better accommodate the contributions and insights of the others? How, if we must do so, shall we assess their comparative worth — recognizing that many who adhere to this or that religion for personal integration or support, or for social solidarity and cultural formation, will not be interested in having any comparative assessment at all and are likely to resist having their own profound commitments and comprehending view of what gives meaning to life subjected to critical comparison? And if we are going to evaluate these powers, to what framework or reference point shall the world turn, on what ground, and with what ethical effects in mind? After all, the governing "Lord" and all that term can stand for must not only be existentially convincing to the heart to have the capacity to form, sustain, or extend its domain and to live with its neighbors, it must also be compelling to the mind and conscience and be capable of constructively shaping the fabric of a viable civilization in the face of changing historical conditions and threats to meaning that come from inside and outside the civilization it shapes. Whether one or another religion is most likely to do that turns out to be not only a covert but an open and decisive question posed by this volume. It is a question that is inevitably theological, for theology, as we have argued earlier, is the discipline that evaluates the degree to which this or that claim of ultimate religious sanction can and should be acknowledged as appropriate for the human condition, fundamentally true, and able to provide a valid ethical stance.

Posing such questions does not imply that the authors of these essays hold that one given religion will or should triumphantly conquer all the other possibilities, should become the exclusive reference point in the convictions of a reader, or will, in the due course of history, ultimately prove its superiority beyond dispute. For one thing, one dimension of every religion has to do with faith, which does not admit of conclusive proof, at least within the course of human history. For another, a dimension of faith is trust, which is always subjective even if some things are more trustworthy than others. No knock-down arguments could prove the superiority of any one religion over any other until all the data of existence are in. Besides, not all religions want to defeat others; they may well, as is true of most of the authors in this set of volumes, want to learn from others, even if what they learn would most likely be interpreted through the filter of the religion or worldview to which they give primary loyalty. Furthermore, we must recognize that religions change (although they seldom alter their own deepest core, and usually die or morph into a new religious constellation if and when they attempt to). Nevertheless, any theological-ethical assessment must be conducted as honestly and impartially as possible, with an eye to what best enhances the possibilities of integrity in personal life, justice in social life, and truth in the understanding of the whole, or else the theology and its ethic will be understood to be little more than an intellectually deceptive amplification of privileged prejudice.

How Shall We Treat the Religions?

In fact, we do assess other religions. Most Christians today see the assigned role of women in Islam as intolerable, although similar patterns have existed in parts of the Christian tradition as well.[14] Similarly, many view the caste system of Hinduism as immoral, although the linked social hierarchies of ethnicity, status, and class have not been foreign to Christianity. In addition, most identify the nationalist loyalties of tribal religions as well as of the Han, Korean, and Shinto traditions as dreadfully chauvinistic, although nationalism has infected wings of Christianity as well. Buddhist monasticism seems irresponsible and Daoism seems romantic to many, although both monasticism and romanticism are well-known

---

14. In a remarkable paper given at the 1999 meeting of the American Academy of Religion, a comparison of Judaism and Christianity as well as Islam on this question was related to issues in Buddhist cultures in Southeast Asia. See Lucinda Joy Peach, "Buddhism, Human Rights, and (Sexual) Slavery" (forthcoming).

to Christian life. Of course, we also find that these traditions offer sharp critiques of Christianity; each of these other religions has its own historical ways of viewing and evaluating Christianity.[15] Partly because of such variations of perspective and valuation, the contemporary way of dealing with religion is to speak of diversity and pluralism. There is wisdom in this, for in the whole of human history religion has been quite diverse and pluralistic in its orientations. That decisive form of postmodernity which we call globalization has not produced religious pluralism, but it has expanded the horizons of many to the pluralism and diversity that always existed. The key question is how to deal with the reality of pluralistic diversity, and we shall quickly find that there are two predominant views of this matter, with various implications and reservations.

Historian of religion Diane B. Obenchain, a specialist in East Asian traditions and a visiting professor at Peking University for the past twelve years, has been a collegially disputatious dialogue partner on the issues in this volume. In spite of her discomfort with indisputably Western terms in which much of the current discussions continue, she traces a major body of literature and learning that has developed in those Protestant circles that helped generate and remained most open to Enlightenment influence over the last couple of centuries and, indeed, has become established in many university departments of religion as a proper approach to the academic study of religion. These views have also deeply influenced contemporary popular opinion. Observing that we can use the term "religion" only if we insist that it be understood as including certain cultural traditions, worldviews, and

---

15. My new colleague, Richard F. Young, has discovered, edited, and published a series of texts that document long-held positions of criticism against Christians by non-Christian traditions. See, e.g., *Resistant Hinduism: Sanscrit Sources on Anti-Christian Apologetics in Early Nineteenth Century India* (Vienna: Institüt für Indologie, 1981); and *Vain Debates: Buddhist Controversies of Nineteenth Century Ceylon,* trans. with G. P. V. Someratna (Vienna: Institüt für Indologie, 1991). These are supplemented by a more recent series of essays: *Perspectives on Christianity in Korea and Japan,* ed. with M. Mullins (Lewiston, N.Y.: Edwin Mellen Press, 1995).

metaphysical-moral sensibilities that are quite obviously not theistic in the Western sense, she is well aware that many traditional cultural beliefs and some newer Western movements are found to be dogmatic, moralistic, and stodgy by scholars and students alike. Moreover, she knows that the fields of phenomenology of religion, comparative religions, and history of religion, as they are called, with nuanced differences, were born in a reaction against the Crusades and European Wars of Religion and, later, aspects of the missionary movements (with, ironically, the children of missionaries at the vanguard) that are still viewed, in some contexts, as imperialist or colonialist. In this regard, she recognizes the dependence of these fields on an attempt to overcome the exclusivist and dogmatic claims of some Christian traditions by turning to the Enlightenment trajectory of scholarship that has cultivated an inclusivist and empathetic appreciation of non-Western traditions. She suggests that such fields of study have made many strides in understanding and have helped overcome contemptuous or dismissive interpretations of the great world religions, advanced the cause of tolerance, and evoked a reconsideration of the arrogant claims of some religious advocates.

Her own perspective reflects many, but decidedly not all, of the themes that are present in the scholarly approaches that she reviews. She does not offer a treatment of the distinctive teachings, ritual practices, or moral content of the various great traditions, which would in any case be available in dozens of introductory texts. Nor does she focus on comparative evaluation of the traditions, ethically or theologically. In fact, the school of thought that she critically represents tends both to acknowledge the pluralism of religious traditions, even to celebrate the diversity, and to understand each one on its own terms, without being judgmental of them as total traditions, even if it is critical of inhumane practices. But the variety and multiformity that appear in historic cultural traditions are viewed as secondary to the common, ultimately universal, human quest to point to, identify, acknowledge, discover, and find a relationship to the transcendent ultimate reality that each seeks to be discerning of the "more than meets the eye" that is transempirical yet everywhere present to the sensitive soul.

In the course of her overview and analysis, however, Obenchain acknowledges that this school of thought has been subject to critique from those who are convinced that the view can become entirely contentless, a formal, abstract concept of existential faith or a kind of love of diversity that loses all rootage in any theological orientation.[16] According to this critique, the empathetic efforts employed to understand traditions other than those of the scholars themselves may well allow a deeper understanding in certain respects, but they can also block the capacity to discern distinctions that advocates of these various traditions hold dear and that have major ethical consequences. For this reason, this tradition of scholarship has come under periodic hostile attack for speaking of "religion in general" as if some form of spiritual Esperanto is what is really the case. Indeed, some religious leaders have held that this position fundamentally compromises the truth-claims of particular faiths.[17] In a bold move, Obenchain challenges both such critics and those who subscribe to this school of thought to recognize how dependent the Enlightenment view of reason is on the biblical, theological, and ethical Judeo-Christian faith — a matter not always acknowledged, and sometimes obscured or denied, by both scholars in this field and religious authorities of particular traditions that have been challenged by the Enlightenment. At least, she implies, the presuppositions of these studies must be seen as compatible and not in conflict with specifically Christian teachings. At most, she

16. This is among the sharp critiques, for instance, posed by S. Mark Heim in his *Salvations: Truth and Difference in Religion* (Maryknoll, N.Y.: Orbis Books, 1999), especially chap. 2.

17. A sharp rebuke to the emerging pluralist school of thought was recently set forth by Cardinal Ratzinger, head of the Congregation on the Faith in the Vatican. In *Dominus Jesu*, a statement approved by the pope and issued in August 2000, the tendency to downplay distinctive Christian doctrines and the centrality and exclusive particularity of Jesus Christ as taught by the Roman Catholic Church was severely criticized.

demands a recognition that the Enlightenment, which generated the quest for a more universal understanding, did not
derive from anywhere else than those strands of Christian
faith that also gave rise to Locke, Kant, Schleiermacher, and
others whom we identify as modern "liberals."

This way of understanding the relationship of various traditions is surely correct in some key areas of the human
understanding of religion. It helps us account for the fact that
we can recognize the integrity of another person's or another
people's conviction, even if we find their specific beliefs unfa-
miliar and unbelievable for ourselves. It thus opens the way to
mutual understanding, tolerance, and the acceptance of difference — in part because it holds that behind the difference
is a human "faithing," the most genuine human phenomenon
that relates us to a transcendent reality which no one knows
perfectly and which we could not otherwise grasp. Indeed,
this view suggests a certain sadness in regard to those who
claim that they have no such faith or sense that there is or
could be such a common, ultimate reality beyond the sensi-
ble world. It understands people who cannot grasp what all
this "religious stuff" is about as persons similar religiously to
those who are tone-deaf and thus cannot appreciate music, or
color-blind and see all as grey, or frigid and can find no joy
in sexuality. They see the world as flat in a moral and spiritual sense, as confined to a narrow range of human emotion
and thought. Thus, to put this in another way, the scholarly schools of thought in this cluster of disciplines recognize
both the profound humanity involved in, and ultimately the
human-transcending ground of, highly pluralistic and diverse
religious experience, even if they do not accent, or even approve of, particular theological systems or dogmatic claims
that make exclusivist emphases.

Obenchain's essay and the school of thought it presents are,
at another level, seldom explicit about ethical matters. On the
one hand, the basis for an ethic of toleration and human solidarity is clearly present, and it points toward self-sacrifice
for the neighbor. It would be quite possible on these grounds

to seek out and give priority to those general principles that seem to be universal in character and to articulate why every great world tradition has a set of first principles that are not unlike those Jews and Christians know as the "Ten Commandments." Certain deontological principles of right and wrong, such as those also accented by philosophers of the Enlightenment, from Locke's "self-evident moral truths" to Kant's "categorical imperatives," are also honored by this kind of thought and see in them tracks of a divine reality that no one fully comprehends. Even more, this perspective leads to a sense of humility in the face of the "other," a willingness to dialogue with, learn from, and live in peace with those who believe differently and who express their faith in distinctive rituals. This implies a deep presumption of common human logic that stands behind our differences alongside faith. It also implies an eagerness to share that which is held to be true, with the presumption that it can be and should be understood and tolerated even by those who do not share that faith.[18]

A number of leading ethicists have, in the last generation, developed this mode of thought on the basis of presuppositions not unlike those articulated by Obenchain. In two studies, for example, Ronald Green shows that a careful reading of Kant illumines both rationality and faith.[19] Religious ethicists David Little, Sumner Twiss, John Reeder, Gene Outka, and Bruce Grelle have also used similar traditions to work out methods of analyzing apparently divergent ways of resolving problems of cooperation by clarifying action guides that not only can be formulated into moral or legal principles, but are legitimated by appeals to multiple religious

---

18. This view has become influential in the World Council of Churches under the leadership of Stanley Samartha of India, Wesley Ariarajah of Sri Lanka, and Diana Eck of Harvard. It is stated as "Guidelines for Dialogue" with other religions. See, e.g., S. J. Samartha, *One Christ, Many Religions: Toward a Revised Christology* (Maryknoll, N.Y.: Orbis Books, 1991).

19. Ronald M. Green, *Religious Reason: The Rational and Moral Basis of Religious Belief* (New York: Oxford University Press, 1978); and *Religion and Moral Reason: A New Method for Comparative Study* (New York: Oxford University Press, 1988).

faiths and are simultaneously both rationally justifiable and "other-regarding."[20]

In defending the tradition of faith and learning that also shapes this explicitly ethical treatment of comparative religious ethics, Obenchain clarifies the metaphysical, logical, and theological roots of the view, especially as these appear to be systematically neglected in contemporary academia by many scholars of religion and of ethics. She argues that an unacknowledged foundation stands behind these disciplines, one that itself could be subject to critical or apologetic argument, for it entails a specific religious and ethical conviction hidden in it that requires overt and systematic acknowledgment. Behind the interpretive attempt to recognize the formal validity of the truth-claims and the ethical sensibilities of the other religions is the profound presupposition that a coherent *logos* stands behind all of existence and history — a basic, ultimate structure of meaning, capable of being experienced in pluralistic ways, susceptible to reasonable discourse between culturally divided peoples, and sustaining of efforts to find coherent, loving, and integrative ways of living together. All the various faiths may participate in, contribute to, and become fulfilled by the recognition of this reality.

According to Obenchain, Christians rightly understand that this deep logos is Christ, the one in whom logos became incarnate and present to human experience. Christians can thus both contribute to the fuller understanding of its nature and seek to learn more about their own faith by studying the many manifestations of that logos as it appears in other traditions.[21] It is not "religion" as a set of abstract doctrines that

---

20. See David Little and Sumner B. Twiss, *Comparative Religious Ethics: A New Method* (New York: Harper & Row, 1978). An effort that anticipated this one but contains essays that depend more on Schleiermacher can be found in Gene Outka and John P. Reeder, Jr., eds., *Religion and Morality* (New York: Anchor Books, 1973). See also the more recent collection, Sumner B. Twiss and Bruce Grelle, eds., *Explorations in Global Ethics: Comparative Religion Ethics and Interreligious Dialogue* (Boulder, Colo.: Westview Press, 1998).

21. It is this factor that allowed both the early Jesuit missionaries and the later Enlightenment philosophs to recognize profound similarities between Confucianism and their own predispositions to endorse "natural law" arguments and

serves as a genus, of which the various traditions are species; it is more that each of the great religions and traditions is itself an expression of that deep logos to which all humans have access in principle, with which persons seek to relate in a variety of ways, by which it is possible to understand one another, and in whom it becomes historically actual in Christ.

It is surely the case that the development of this perspective of "inclusive pluralists" has often led Christians to seek zones of overlapping consensus with others and has rendered a number of common moral statements. In a demure way, Obenchain has argued that Christ is the *dominus,* the nondominating, universal, servant Lord behind the faiths of the world. On this basis, our common humanity as seeking, faithing creatures can be recognized. It is quite compatible with her argument to say that practical implications of the study of religion would include also efforts to develop a global ethic, such as the one that was developed out of the 1993 Parliament of World Religions and drafted by Hans Küng.[22] It declares "a fundamental consensus on binding values, irrevocable standards, and personal attitudes" shared by representatives of more than one hundred religious traditions. Similarly, a Millennium World Peace Summit of Religious and Spiritual Leaders declared a common "Commitment to Global Peace" in a meeting at the United Nations.[23] Moreover, in hundreds of personal, inter-

to develop concepts of "natural theology," even if it sometimes meant exaggerating convergences. See the remarkable, if controversial, volume by Lionel M. Jensen, *Manufacturing Confucianism: Chinese Traditions and Universal Civilization* (Durham, N.C.: Duke University Press, 1997).

22. Hans Küng, ed., "Parliament of World Religions' Global Ethic," *National Catholic Reporter,* September 24, 1993, 11. See also his *Global Responsibility: In Search of a New World Ethic* (New York: Crossroad, 1991); and *A Global Ethic for Global Politics and Economics* (New York: Oxford University Press, 1997). These are deeply related to his earlier works, one with Josef van Ess, et al., *Christianity and the World Religions: Paths to Dialogue with Islam, Hinduism, and Buddhism* (New York: Doubleday, 1986), and another with Julia Ching, *Christianity and Chinese Religions* (New York: Doubleday, 1989). This striking approach will be discussed more fully in vol. 4.

23. Bawa Jain, ed., published in the *New York Times,* September 5, 2000, A13. Another example comes from Orthodox, Islamic, Jewish, and Buddhist leaders meeting in Moscow in November 2000: "Believers have a right to make their lives

personal, local, and regional conflicts, religious leaders of
various backgrounds, faiths, and traditions are the voices of
reason and appeal together for toleration, mutual understanding, and respect. There is a theological reason for that, and
the philosophical and historical study of religions can see that
it is best if they acknowledge the theological ground for it.

A Socially Embodied Pluralism

Obenchain shows how one major stream of modern scholarship has encouraged the study of religion across confessional
lines, and she has suggested a theological basis for doing
so. In a global age, the need for such dialogues is critical.
But in discussions about the shape of this entire volume, she
has acknowledged that she has not traced out the ways in
which particular religions, in varying degrees and with differing effects, influence the various spheres of life in civil
society, establish an ethos with legitimated common meanings, provide the resources to guide new authorities and
regencies, and thus potentially form and sustain a civilization — vital questions in our global era generally and in
this set of studies particularly. If we look at the question
of how to view and assess the world religions from this
angle, we see the reassertion of specific religions as political and cultural forces, and emphatic attempts to establish
or reestablish societies based on particular religious traditions. Indeed, in parts of Africa, Latin America, Northeast
India, and the Pacific Islands, those rooted in traditional
"primal" religions are attempting to gain their autonomous
rule, after having been swept into artificially created nation-
states by colonial governments. Moreover, resurgent Islam
from the Mideast to Malaysia and Indonesia, Hindu na-

---

conform with their beliefs. But no one has a right to use their beliefs to take the
lives or violate the rights of others. No religion allows for that" (*Agence France-
Presse*, November 15, 2000). This is also the sort of thing that, in this view, makes
possible studies in UNESCO. See Yersu Kim, "Philosophy and the Prospects for a
Universal Ethic," in vol. 1.

tionalism in India, and Buddhist-sanctioned militance in Sri Lanka and Burma are evidence of a new particularism that seems also to accompany our era. Further, one can point to Christian liberation movements on the Left or Christian nationalist movements on the Right that seek to exclude other perspectives.

Thus, we turn to a second example of religious pluralism, one written by Scott Thomas, a scholar who is convinced that the specifics of each religion must be an active part of the picture if anything is to be accomplished at the concrete levels of social development and political interaction. The fact that certain strands of Christian theology shaped modernity and now globalization in fuller ways than any of the other traditions is not appreciated by some traditions. Several are sharply critical of everything "modern" and opposed to anything global, an unavoidable fact when we encounter other heritages that also have shaped civilizations and had their own impact on human history. Some, indeed, argue quite explicitly that modern religious scholarship in this area does not, in fact, point to what is universal about religions at the concrete level and that it is nothing more than a "liberal Protestant" Western perspective pretending to be universal and projected onto an Eastern and Southern context that is opposed to such an effort.[24] To be sure, if we interact with such scholars and such societies, it becomes necessary not only to believe, as Obenchain argues, that we can find points of convergence and contact, but also to have to acknowledge that agreement has not been found on an enormous number of decisive social, political, and economic questions, and that we are unlikely to find it soon. Besides, it becomes clear quickly that we cannot only stay at the level of universal religious dimensions of commonality and mutual respect, or with those principles that ethicists usually identify as deontological in

---

24. See, e.g., Luis Dumont, *Homo Hierarchicus: The Caste System and Its Implications* (Chicago: University of Chicago Press, 1970); Edward Said, *Orientalism* (New York: Vintage Books, 1978, new ed., 1994); and Wm. Theodore De Bary, *Asian Values and Human Rights* (Cambridge: Harvard University Press, 2000).

character. Instead, we have also to encounter what contemporary scholars in comparative religions and history of religion are less likely to discuss than anthropologists, comparative sociologists, political theorists, and development economists — that institutional forms of life have been organized in many cultures on the basis of differing faiths and are not likely to blend into a single pattern. If we are to interact with other societies, we shall have to see how primal religious patterns of life, Confucian wisdom, Hindu devotion, Buddhist teachings, and Islamic revelations work out their implications in the various spheres of society. Indeed, we may find that some may only awkwardly be able to engage analytically and constructively the patterns and dynamics of globalization. Others may, indeed, be more likely to contribute to the forces of resistance against them and run the risk of either being crushed by them or being forced to modify their own faith heritage if they chose to enter the discussion about our common future. Thus, another view of pluralism is presented by our second essay.

Scott Thomas, one of the "revisionist" scholars of international relations and economics in Great Britain, explicitly shows that increasing numbers of scholars in his field are beginning to recognize factors previously ignored in order to grasp and influence what is going on. Unlike Obenchain's understanding of the Enlightenment as a significant extension of the theological heritage that gave articulation in secular philosophical and historical terms to profoundly Christian perspectives and principles, many social scientists and political theorists, including those who train diplomats and political leaders, have viewed the philosophies and sciences developed by the Enlightenment as a repudiation of the public pertinence of theology and a subordination of religion to an optional private concern or to a deistic background belief that plays no active role in understanding, life, or social policy. However, Thomas shows that the religions of the world have refused to be privatized and subordinated and are not convinced that the divine reality that once brought the world into being has retired from all vital activity.[25] Directly or indirectly religious claims, religious behaviors, and religious powers continue to influence public affairs with shocking vigor — shocking at least to those who think of themselves as having surpassed that more "primitive" (or "medieval") stage of "mythical" speculation. Moreover, as morally concerned Westerners and indigenous leaders of the "underdeveloped" regions of the world seek to extend the alleged benefits of the Enlightenment — democratic government, human rights, access to technology, efficient economic productivity, decent medical care — they find that the potential capacity of cultures to adopt and adapt these possibilities, or the tendency to resist them as too socially disruptive or "dehumanizing" according to their own standards, depends on religious factors.

In response to this, Thomas argues, many professionals in the social sciences are beginning to recognize that they need greater familiarity with the specific social implications of religions.

Moreover, he identifies a reality that many postmodernists, whether radical or conservative, now see. Religions may have much in common, so that we can treat them all under a general perspective in some respects, but in other respects we must acknowledge difference. It is not clear to the postmodernist, or for that matter to the radical advocate who sees all thought and belief patterns as a function of social location and interest, or to the conservative believer who thinks that the religion or philosophy to which he or she adheres is clearly distinct from and superior to every other religious tradition, that some underlying, universal logos underlies all

---

25. Modern views of religion are stamped deeply by the competing understandings of religion as they are on the one hand sympathetic to, and even a generator of, those parts of the Enlightenment that are inclusive in their attitudes toward non-Christian religions, and simultaneously hostile to those parts of the Enlightenment that deny the dynamic pertinence of religion due to its deistic humanism. This can be seen in the striking study in historical theology by Gerald R. McDermott, *Jonathan Edwards Confronts the Gods: Christian Theology, Enlightenment Religion, and Non-Christian Faiths* (New York: Oxford University Press, 2000).

religion at this level. Rather, particularity and incommensura-
bility characterize the multiplicity of traditions. Each has its
own logic that leads inexorably to distinctive sociopolitical
policies, and it becomes the responsibility of those who are
engaged in diplomacy and development to work with each
on its own terms. Thomas shows us how, in many contexts,
concretely in diplomatic and political life, we in fact accept
without judging, at least overtly, the reality and influence of
religious traditions other than our own, even if we think them
to be quite wrong. He leaves open, as did Obenchain, the
fact that we do, in fact, evaluate, for he too wants to avoid
religious triumphalism or cultural imperialism.

Not all contemporary scholars are so reticent. Some do
evaluate, as we can see in the work of Paul Knitter and his
many allies who not only treat positions such as that presented here by Obenchain with great sympathy, but who
also recognize the concrete pluralism in social formation that
is implied by the various concrete traditions, as presented
by Thomas. Indeed, Knitter is one of the leaders of those
who link the universalistic, Enlightenment-approving "logos"
view of "pluralistic inclusivism" with a concrete sociopolitical
postmodern recognition of "pluralistic diversity" of particular religions.[26] He does this by establishing a single ethical
standard by which every religion, theology, worldview, or cultural practice can and should be assessed. That standard is
liberation[27] — the process of overcoming poverty and suffering by bringing those who are marginalized, oppressed, or
exploited, and thus in socially induced painful situations, to
a condition of freedom in which they, as persons, and the
social groups of which they are a part (a class, race, caste,

26. See his *The Myth of Christian Uniqueness: Toward a Pluralistic Theology of
Religions,* ed. with John Hick (Maryknoll, N.Y.: Orbis Books, 1987).

27. See also his justly influential *No Other Name? A Critical Survey of Christian Attitudes Toward the World Religions* (Maryknoll, N.Y.: Orbis Books, 1985);
One Earth, Many Religions: Multifaith Dialogue and Global Responsibility (Maryknoll, N.Y.: Orbis Books, 1995); and *Jesus and Other Names: Christian Mission and
Global Responsibility* (Maryknoll, N.Y.: Orbis Books, 1996). Critiques of this view
can be found in Gabriel Fackre, Ronald Nash, and John Sanders, *What of Those
Who Have Never Heard?* (Downers Grove, Ill.: InterVarsity Press, 1995).

or sex) can be their own agents, their own subjects, and no longer be treated as objects by dominant groups. This, indeed, is a standard shared by many Christians, Enlightenment philosophers, including the now few remaining Marxist social theorists, and postmodern advocates of pluralism, multiculturalism, and diversity. None want systemic injustice to be perpetrated and all would approve of efforts to overcome human distress — nor, we may presume, do believers in any of the great world religions or philosophies. But, as one of Knitter's sharpest critics, Mark Heim, has argued, to take this criterion as the only one establishes a single social view of salvation as a kind of political religion in itself, one by which all religions and their claims about truth, justice, the human condition, and the laws and purposes of life are to be evaluated. Not only does this view of salvation imply that the fundamental sin from which humanity needs to be saved is a socially created one amenable to a social solution, but it denies pluralism in that it dismisses any religious orientation that does not agree.[28]

Several religious traditions are suspicious of other implications of this view. It not only manifests a great confidence in human freedom but presumes that the political effects of religion are its most important parts. Further, it is a view embraced by recent advocates of the neonationalism of independence movements or of those groups within various political orders who oppose the domination of minorities and see the autonomy of individuals as the implication of enlightened existence. Indeed, this is the fruit of those heirs of the Enlightenment who have abandoned any sense of holiness or transcendence or ultimate fulfillment beyond history and see instead the maximization of freedom in history as the highest goal and end of life.[29] Knitter needs a deeper sense of

---

28. I have depended in several of these formulations on the striking work by Heim, *Salvations*, 115–17.

29. It is widely held that this view was part of the target of the Vatican statement, *Dominus Jesu*. I have written my own critique of this "liberationist" view from a different perspective in *Christian Social Ethics in a Global Era* (Nashville: Abingdon

what are the ultimate purposes of his faith and of the world religions.

The reason why the religions differ is that they have different assessments of why it is that life in this world is fraught with so much difficulty and distress, conflict and anxiety, disease and death. The unity that religions have in pointing to that which is transcendent brings about an awareness that there are other standards, norms, and ideals that ought to govern life than the ones that often do govern it. Religions may have common, or at least quite similar, knowledge of what ought to be universally binding: Humans ought to honor that which is truly holy and respect just authority. They ought not murder, rape, torture, deceive, exploit, or bring wanton harm to other humans, to society at large, or to the biophysical universe that sustains life. Thus, they know that some things are wrong and that it is right to form character and social institutions that will avoid these wrongs. In these respects, there are "universal absolutes" about which religions, together, can remind wayward humanity. Yet the religions explain differently why it is that humans are inclined to do wrong and what it takes to overcome that inclination.

It is the key insight of Mark Heim, whose work is now under lively discussion, that religions and philosophies fundamentally differ over what it is that we need to be "saved" from and hence promise different "salvations." Indeed, he claims that each religion does, in fact, recognize something valid that is a fundamental problem and that each is presumably authentic insofar as it does deliver on what it promises. Let me extrapolate his argument this way: If the underlying difficulty of our existence is that we break community with our ancestral ways and its harmony with nature and thus lose our identity, we must recover and enter into the spirituality of the primal or traditional religions of our forebears. If the fundamental problem of the human condition is that we are

Press, 1995), in dialogue with contributions from Peter Berger, Dennis McCann, and Douglas Meeks, in a study that attempted to clear the ground for the present series.

too much attached to the things of the world, Buddhism can offer a way of becoming detached. If the basic issue is that we do not obey the law of God as delivered to humanity through the prophets, Orthodox Judaism and Islam offer patterns of life that could well encourage us to more nearly approximate those laws. However, this argument forces the discussion between religions to another level — what is the fundamental issue and what has, does, can, or could overcome it?

In facing the issues of globalization, we cannot fail to deal with the diversity of eschatological visions that seek to portray the ultimate normative destiny of humanity and the cosmos. It appears that the idea of the kingdom of God (and "the New Jerusalem") preached by Jesus according to the Christian eschatological vision is distinct from the harmonious communion with nature and the spirits of the ancestors in several primal religions; the notion of *moksha*, with its vision of the integration of Brahma and Atman, as advanced by Hinduism; the concept of *nirvana* as taught by the Buddha; or the understanding of paradise as Muhammad was inspired to announce in the Islamic view. Indeed, it would seem that even every religiously sanitized way of pointing to some ultimate hope, expectation, or belief in a ultimate destiny — the classless society of Marx, the perpetual peace of Kant, the happiness in contemplation of Aristotle, or the cultivated virtuous person in a family-ordered, comprehending empire of master Küng — is in fact a quasi-religious vision. In brief, the teleologies of religions differ, even if the deontology can be said to be basically comparable.

In a study such as ours, however, it is not enough to point out the different eschatologies and their possible theological assumptions and ethical implications. We are especially interested in how these ultimate metaphysical and deontological commonalities and these ultimate teleological and soteriological differences are combined in specific ways over time to form the general contours of complex civilizations.[30] But since the

---

30. I have treated several of these relationships in "The World Religions and Po-

powers of globalization have largely escaped the control of any society and since religion is the only normative force able to shape and interpret them, it becomes critical for us to compare and contrast the ways in which the various religions are likely to shape persons and societies, to structure the interaction of the complex spheres of life, to aid humanity, and to form a moral response to globalizing conditions. Fortunately, we have a wonderful team of scholars to do so.

Dominions of Identity and of Conversion

For our purposes, we can group religions into two broad types, although this, like every typology, oversimplifies the complex reality of that which it seeks to portray. One type of religion essentially gives stabilizing expression to and repeatable guidance to the religious customs, dominant narratives, and cultural identity of a people. It roots this identity in the belief that life and its proper meaning and order are, and ought to be, grounded in the organic harmonies of the eternal cosmic order. Another type of religion is essentially converting and intentionally proselytizing. It seeks to offer its insights to the whole of humanity and to reach beyond any people to invite those who are not part of the tradition to join it. It roots its mission in the belief that the cosmic order is temporal as given. It will pass away, and a more ultimate truth, reality, and moral existence will or can be found on the far side of that demise. One type is intentionally local and context specific, while the other seeks to be universal and context transcending; one forms stable solidarity, while the other forms transforming differentiation. One locates the divine essentially within the self as a part of a specific community of identity, the community as a part of a specific sacred tradition, and the tradition as a part of the timeless cosmic order. The other sees the holy as quite other than either the self or

litical Democracy: Some Comparative Reflections," *Religion and Society* (India) 29, no. 4 (December 1982): 19–49; and "Politics and Religion," in *Encyclopedia of Religion,* vol. 11, ed. Mircea Eliade et al. (New York: Macmillan, 1987), 408–23.

the community of origin, and both are to be altered over time. When the old is transcended, the self joins with others to form new associations to serve the holy and the new companions, near and far, and to reconstruct even the natural environment so that it may better serve what is holy to aid all of humanity in its transformation to the new. In one, religion is decisive for interpreting and integrating life into Being as it is; in the other, religion is the spur to change and the transmutation of existence, for the true reality is not of this world. To be sure, each religion has elements of both and combines them in a distinctive way, but each is also weighted more in the direction of one than the other. As we shall see, they have quite different responses to the issues of unity and pluralism, to the ethical overtones of deontology and teleology, and to the dynamics and effects of globalization.

We begin this stage of investigations into the specific characteristics of distinctive traditions with an essay from John Mbiti, one of the world's renowned scholars of primal religions, particularly in their tribal forms. While his earlier studies focused almost entirely on African religions, he has been influenced by globalization in a way that has brought him to see similar characteristics in traditional groups elsewhere. These groups have been most subject to shock at the hands of colonialism and most receptive to missionary activity. More important, he has recognized analogous concerns, life-orientations, and responses to technology, commerce, and environment-altering activities that modernization has brought, even though they differ widely in the contexts in which these societies developed. Some live in tropical forests, others in vast deserts; still others live on the northern tundras, on the high mountains of great landmasses, or on low atolls in the oceans.[31] Each has a highly distinctive culture and often a

---

31. I am personally very grateful to Wati Longchar, editor of the *Journal of Tribal Studies,* for giving me many issues of this wide-ranging journal, and to his colleagues at Eastern Theological College, Assam, India — principally Ezamo Murry and Mangkhosat Kipgen, whose hospitality, writings, and conversations also gave me a modest firsthand glimpse into this world.

unique language and specific religious beliefs accompanied by practices that shape their societies in very particular ways; but the common features are as striking as the differences. As they are drawn into wider and wider contact with outsiders, many tribal peoples feel besieged by the same pressures, and many have in comparable ways taken elements of their traditional life into the missionizing religions to which they convert.

Of course, conversion is not without selective resistance and a sense of loss in certain regards, but conversion is not at all unusual, for with it usually comes more extensive education, increased access to useful resources, a wider capacity to live in peace with immediate neighbors, and a discovery of deeper understandings of truth and justice — sometimes from within the deontological recesses of their own tradition and sometimes from the new teleological purposes that come with conversion. Still, the old is seldom entirely abandoned. It is more often modulated, adapted, and transformed. For those who become Christians, for example, Christ lives in, among, and with the spirit world of the elders as well as with the living community of identity that now sees itself in a network of world-transforming orientation. Something comparable is true as well for those forms of traditional healing and shamanism that have shown up in Buddhist traditions of Asia, Islamic traditions of the Mideast, and Christian traditions as they are contextualized in Africa, Latin America, Northeast India, and elsewhere. To put it another way, the loyalties and commitments of traditional religions, including aspects of their political, economic, familial, and cultural ways of ordering life, are not only present in "animist" or "primitive" traditions but are taken into other religions as well. Not only persons but the traditions are converted, and the older identity of neither is entirely blotted out.

In the Christian case, one feature that has been particularly attractive to those who were previously non-Christian members of identity traditions has been the legacy of Judaism as it is present in the Old Testament. Key patterns of that earlier tribal society have great analogues to the communities in which they live. Moreover, that particular tradition included elements of universal moral law, which they also discovered anew in parts of their own traditions and which helped prepared them for international interaction and an acceptance of certain principles of human rights, and it included an eschatological expectation that allowed them to imagine a fundamental transformation of life, community, and cosmos, something that, Mbiti writes, is ordinarily "not . . . clearly represented in tribal religions." It is likely that if Christianity had not preserved the Old Testament as a part of its tradition, the Christianization of tribal peoples around the world, which has procccdcd at trcmendous speed during the last two centuries, would not have taken place. In some places, Islam has made comparable gains for similar reasons.

In other ways, tribal peoples feel locked out, excluded from, and threatened by many of the dynamics of globalization. For instance, as Mbiti points out, the whole idea of the world becoming a "single place" does not sit well with members of traditional societies. That is not where people can feel at home, and it is not where they want to die and spend eternity. Instead, the greater focus of traditional religion is on a particular place where one can be familiar with the patterns of community that include the departed Elders, and includes specific niches in nature where one can participate in the spirit-filled character of human interactions with known flora, fauna, and geologic characteristics. Indeed, this sensibility to the natural order, to the deep sacredness of the biophysical environment, and to the threat to it brought by technology and economic development poses an opportunity and a danger for those from traditional religions and cultures. On the one hand, as Mbiti argues, the almost mystical attitude toward nature provides a warning against those globalizing forces that would destroy the ecological order. In this, the insight of traditional peoples "lends itself to transfer onto the global level." On the other hand, suspicion of technology, of corporate economic methods of production, exchange, transportation, and distribution, and the complex patterns of civil society that sustain democracy are disruptive of traditional patterns of community, culture, and nature. When they become established, they are likely to mean that people from tribal backgrounds will be ill-equipped to participate in the management of ecological systems when they are under strain, to overcome the perils of poverty relative to other population groups who are developing rapidly, and to form viable civil societies that give inner shape to democratic politics that are acceptable in the community of nations.

Mbiti does not here extensively discuss the fact that tribal religions and traditional cultures have often been bulldozed, annexed, or marginalized by larger, more complex cultures and civilizations, although it is clear that he shares with most tribal peoples the knowledge that they have been and are being pushed around by forces that they did not generate, do not understand, and do not fully wish to embrace — even if in some ways they want to be a part of the larger picture, to have a voice in it, and to reap at least some of the benefits. This inclines people from these cultures to take up the ideologies of resistance and opposition to outside forces and, in this regard, to avoid the questions of what reconstructive visions of society they think should be developed. This reaction, of course, invites the question of why that is so, why it is that some cultures seem able to organize vast numbers of people and mobilize material and moral resources over great territories and to form dynamic civilizations that not only endure but expand, while others seem to be ever on the defensive and threatened as potential victims.

That leads us to some of our other contributions, for it does seem that at least two great examples of religio-cultural "identity" traditions with certain structural parallels to the traditional patterns Mbiti identifies have become enduring and expansive civilizations that have organized vast systems that have often absorbed minority tribal peoples into them, leaving many of the deep assumptions found in tribal societies largely intact.

The largest, most comprehending tradition that has gener-

ated and sustained a rich, long-lasting, and complex civilization is Confucianism, or, as called by the experts, "Ru" —
the classical heritage of Dao-influenced cosmic and heavenly
order (*tian dao*) that Confucius notably helped systematize
and integrate.[32] As it developed, it was also able to include elements from later Buddhism and to contribute to
what some call "Chinese Religion," the core of a rather
vast array of popular beliefs, as well as the highly cultivated
patterns of values and loyalties that serve as the cultural genetic code of Chinese culture. While we can thus identify this
philosophical-religious complex broadly as one of the "identity" traditions, it has become in the wake of Confucius and
Mencius as much a subtle ethical system and a theory of social
order as a religion, although it also clearly contains extensive patterns of ritual and dogma. This heritage, of course,
has been deeply disrupted by two Western imports — one
in politics and the other in economics. They came first from
abroad at the hands of colonialists and traders in one form,
and they arose internally in another form with the Maoist
revolution and subsequent government and, after the collapse of the economies of Eastern Europe, the adoption of a
rather raw form of capitalistic economic developmentalism —
both of which resisted traditional religions and philosophies
as well as foreign incursions. These disruptions have moved
the more ontocratic loyalty to the past toward a conversion-
ist orientation toward the future. Yet there are also elements
of continuity between the ancient centralized systems of the
great dynasties to which the Confucian literati served as
advisors, agents, and officials, and the administrative bureaucracies of the present, just as there are continuities between
the ancient Confucian ideals of family, status, and virtue that
are held by large portions of the population today. Indeed,
a number of contemporary scholars have suggested that a
renewed form of Confucian ethics is manifest in both the so-

32. See Diane B. Obenchain, "Revelations of the Dragon: Observations on Christianity and 'Ru' (Confucianism) in China Today," *Princeton Seminary Bulletin* 21,
no. 2, new series (2000): 161–95.

cieties around China — Korea, Japan, Taiwan, Singapore — and among the rather large number of overseas Chinese who have become influential in business and the professions as minorities in nearly every part of the world where they are freed from the imperial tyranny to which the older dynastic system is held to have degenerated.[33] These influences could eventually revitalize Confucian thought in China.

In the meantime, China itself seems to be facing an extremely serious crisis. The old traditions of Confucianism are held to be little more than medieval superstition or feudal residue by the government, in spite of this tradition's historic record of high learning — comparable, in the view of many, to the Thomistic traditions of thought in the West. In consequence, the number of institutions that continue to cultivate the heritage and the capacity of the tradition to address current issues in civil society overtly are severely limited. Smaller and smaller percentages of the population know much about it in any detail. At the same time, by all reports, fewer and fewer people believe in the ideology of the Communist Party — although in this area as in regard to Confucianism, residues of its ethic continue to have effect. Many, for example, would assess private motives and public policies accordingly as they "serve the people." Yet, relatively few participate in grassroots organizations for the well-being of the society unless they are mobilized by the state or some faction for some specific political reason. Increasingly, to put it bluntly, both Confucianism and Communism, which each claimed a total and defining loyalty able to shape personal morality and social order in the past, are being left behind, and the society is left without an inner, coherent

---

33. See, for example, Kim Kyong-Dong, "The Distinctive Features of South Korea's Development," in *In Search of an East Asian Development Model,* ed. P. Berger and H. Hsiao (New Brunswick, N.J.: Transaction Books, 1988); "Confucianism and Capitalist Development in East Asia," in *Capitalism and Development,* ed. L. Sklair (London: Routledge, 1994), 87–106; "Confucianism, Economic Growth and Democracy," *Asian Perspective* 21, no. 2 (Fall 1997): 77–97. Cf. Robert Bellah's somewhat dated *Tokugawa Religion* (Glencoe, Ill.: Free Press, 1962) and the more recent S. G. Redding, *The Spirit of Chinese Capitalism* (New York: Walter de Gruyter, 1993).

"metaphysical-moral system." Moreover, this is happening precisely at the time when all sorts of independent economic, cultural, technological, and social dynamisms are at work.

Those familiar with contemporary China as it is found in the universities, in the bureaucracies, in the growing industrial sector, in the villages, or in the exploding cities, and even in its families, uniformly report a quest for meaning and for new ways of morally and spiritually organizing their lives and human relationships beyond the older Confucian heritage and outside the constraints of Communist ideology. That is reinforced by the fact that neither the Confucian tradition nor Communist thought developed a vibrant view of civil society as a range of creative activity outside the control of family and regime. They have nurtured a highly diverse society but not a pluralistic one, and it has neither a historic nor a currently governing vision of the good life that, at its depths, appears to be capable of generating one. Yet globalization, in which China is one of the most recent and enthusiastic participants, is bringing all the pressures to form just such a civil society.

It is in the context of this crisis of meaning and civil society that Sze-kar Wan, a scholar originally from China who has specialized in the comparative study of how various traditions use their classical texts and resources to shape the present and future, takes up the question of current developments in China. His historical work on Judaism, on Christianity, and on Confucianism, as well as his familiarity with the contemporary crisis at the heart of China, equip him to identify basic resources that could very well aid the more promising and transformative undercurrents in contemporary China. He is well aware of how fluid the situation is, and he illuminates the critical role that religion can play in the formation and transformation of civilizations. The expansion of Islam, especially in the minority regions of Western China, may be relatively tolerated because it is treated as a manifestation of ethnic identity not central to the identity of China as a whole; but the virtual apoplexy of the regime over the quasi-religious cult the Falun Gong, its hostility to the Dalai Lama, its attempt to control Christian bishops, and its intermittent repression of the rapidly growing local evangelical, Pentecostal, and fundamentalist prayer groups and "house churches" reveal an awareness that alternative patterns of thought, morality, and organization are partly transforming, partly displacing, and partly being adapted into ancient Confucian and remaining Communist loyalties. To put it another way, the society is presently without an inner Lord that can claim the heart and mind of the people and is thus, for all its deep traditions and solidarity and its modern commitment to revolution, also threatened by loss of moral legitimacy and thus the chaotic unleashing of the powers that we have called Mars and Mammon, the untethering of Eros from its deep moorings in the traditional family, and the cultivation of "Asian values" in the direction of a chauvinism that could sever China's growing ties to international human rights. That could bring the degeneration of learning into nationalist ideology, order into lawlessness, medicine into magic, and technology into catastrophic manipulations of the environment, as has happened in the twentieth century in China already.

Wan recognizes that new and dramatic religious developments have the potential to give the society a fresh inner direction, but he is not convinced that the religious communities that are developing very rapidly in China always have the deepest theological and ethical resources well enough in hand creatively to form the new inner core of Chinese society. Thus, he not only interprets the situation but shows how the ancient Jewish idea of covenant, modified in Christian thought, might well be adopted by this dynamically changing post-Confucian and increasingly post-Communist society in a way that could give inner spiritual coherence and structural moral guidance — and, by forming a new synthesis with profound Chinese traditions, influence theological-ethical thought throughout the world.

The third tradition to which we turn, beyond the primal, traditional religions and the now-challenged traditions of China, is Hinduism. This too can be called an "identity"

religion, and it likewise has given shape to great and enduring social and cultural traditions. Hinduism has ordered its
internal life in a way that is different from either of these traditions, however. It is currently responding to globalization
and reforming its own society in distinctive ways. This is made
clear to us in the essay by Thomas Thangaraj, a theologian
and critical observer of global developments who has lived in,
worked on, and written about the boundaries of Hindu and
Christian thought and culture most of his life. In general we
can say that whereas Confucianism accented the relationships
of husband-wife, parent-child, brother-sister, master-servant,
and regime-household, and wove the duties and responsibilities of these, as nurtured by a religiously held Confucian
ethical philosophy, into an inclusive imperial system that was
partly overthrown and partly replicated by the Communist
Party, Hinduism took similar relationships, as they had been
worked out in various primal ethnic communities and tribes,
and wove them into a highly pluralistic hierarchy of castes,
governed spiritually by a myriad of deities. It did this less
by subordinating the whole to a single imperial system supported by a subordinate, learned literati, as did Confucianism,
than by cultivating a caste of priests at the top of the system who produced subtle and complex rituals, philosophies,
and legal codes to guide an extraordinarily diverse system of
warrior-ruler castes, artisan-trader castes, farming-producing
castes, worker-servant castes, and outcastes, each with its own
cluster of divinities to which the subcastes and extended families in each region gave homage. Together, these formed a
different kind of complex civilization, perhaps the premier
example of hierarchy (*hier*=priest, *arche*=primal order). The
deep logic of this system involves a profound, ontocratic cosmos of social locations, which the individual soul (Atman)
may past through in a series of rebirths as it works its way
back to its original home in the divine oversoul (Brahman).
Thangaraj argues compellingly that every aspect and region
of this society is historically governed by a "bio-piety" linked
to a "geo-piety."

While the primal traditions of primal peoples have often been disturbed by contact with outsiders, and the older Confucian society was fundamentally shocked not only by opportunistic traders with weapons from the West and, even more, by the Communist revolution, traditional Indian society was most disrupted by the fact that much of India was conquered by the Muslim Moguls in the late medieval period and taken over by Christian Englishmen in the modern period. These developments served to centralize the political order more than had been the case under the traditional political pluralism of the maharajas, ruling under the supervision of the Hindu priests. Simultaneously, it served to exemplify the power of a less diversified, more integrated religious and philosophical view and to introduce some wider cosmopolitan ideas from the Islamic and Christian worlds that became internalized in parts of Indian life. Thangaraj points out that this has accelerated in recent times due to the fact that Western education has become increasingly standard. Many Indians have gone abroad for study or economic opportunity and developed new patterns of interaction, which they bring (or send) back to India, and that increased accent has been put on the subtle and quite universalistic theology of "Vedanta" and on highly personal, lay patterns of devotion known as *bhakti*. In addition, the British brought what was intended to be a secular government. These developments challenged the sovereignty of the priestly caste over society, and, thus, Hinduism has had to face intellectual, spiritual, and moral challenges from within as well as from without.

In the wake of independence from colonial rule, a resurgent form of Hinduism has become increasingly influential and, in effect, revised its "geo-piety" into a new form of religious nationalism different from that brought by the Moguls and the British.[34] It has turned "rehinduization" into a religious

---

34. See Mark Juergensmeyer, *The New Cold War? Religious Nationalism Confronts the Secular State* (Berkeley: University of California Press, 1993); and Peter van der Veer, *Religious Nationalism: Hindus and Muslims in India* (Berkeley: University of California Press, 1994), to which Thangaraj refers.

and political crusade, opposed to the secularist and humanist "westernized" programs that dominated Indian political
movements during and immediately after the struggle for
independence. In its more militant social forms, it has threatened Islamic, Buddhist, and Christian minorities and seeks to
bring tribal and outcaste groups into (or "back into") a common Indian-Hindu identity, often by bringing the host of local
and group-focused gods into an integrated henotheism.[35]

Moreover, it is well known that Hindu-based religious
movements have sent their gurus to peoples and areas who
are not historically related to India's spiritual traditions. For
example, various forms of Hindu-based meditation and yoga
have been introduced in the West, and many Westerners know
the names and at least part of the epics of Krishna, Vishnu,
and Shiva. Novels about life in India and movies about such
figures as Gandhi have become internationally famous. At
the same time, modern India has shown that it can maintain
the world's largest democratic government with a constitution that has been a model to many emerging lands, and that
in technology, commerce, and the arts it is open to external
influence and eager to become a partner in globalization — in
spite of several protests in India that this is but another, more
indirect, form of colonialism.[36] The developments are nevertheless modulating the rigidity of the caste system, reinforcing
prospects for human rights, creating a dynamic new set of
middle classes, and generating new possibilities for an emergent civil society.[37] Thangaraj offers an insightful analysis of
Hinduism both in contemporary India and in its international

35. See, e.g., the widely discussed report from Satyakam Joshi, "Tribals, Missionaries and Sadhus," *Economic and Political Weekly* (Mumbai) 34, no. 37,
2667–75.

36. This is true in the minority Christian communities as well as in some Hindu
and Muslim ones. See, e.g., Jesudas M. Athyal, *Relevant Patterns of Christian
Witness in India* (Thiruvalla, India: CSS Publisher, 2000), esp. part 1.

37. My own efforts to identify some of these key issues and trace their development can be found in "The Hindu Ethic and the Ethos of Development," *Religion
and Society* (Bangalore; December 1973), 4–33; *Creeds, Society and Human Rights*
(Grand Rapids, Mich.: Eerdmans, 1984), especially chaps. 7–9; and "Observations
on Globalization in India," in *Dialogue on Globalization,* ed. John Mohen Razu and
Moses Paul Peter (Bangalore: SCM Press, 2000), 13–29.

manifestations with an acute sociotheological interpretation of new prospects.

The fact that Hinduism is already reshaping a complex society that is genuinely pluralistic in new ways in the midst of globalization, and is now apparently more of a proselytizing religion than it was in the past, indicates that it may be more likely to be a force in defining the future of globalization than are either the traditional religions or the residual patterns of Confucian ethics. Neither of these is disappearing, but these and Hinduism are undergoing transformation. All religions, as Obenchain has clearly argued, have universalistic elements in them, and Hinduism has been more focused on the universal motifs, at least in its claims, than the others. Moreover, the forces of moral and spiritual change are coming to the identity religions that do not claim to be universalistic in their aims. Meanwhile, religions that have shaped large civilizations, overtly claim universalistic purposes, form a more integral theological ethic, and reach new populations in new locales are more likely to play a formative role under global conditions. Hinduism is surely to be among these.

Buddhism, Christianity, and Islam are historically the great converting world religions, and they have been instrumental in changing the identity-based religions in distinctive ways. They do not only stay in the lands of their births and shape the identity of their people and culture, but they are always going out and seeking to extend the message that they bear to other peoples in other places, inviting them to change their inherited inner religious and moral identities and, inevitably, their outer social ethic. They include insights about the relation of their deepest convictions to the primal order of the universe, but they are essentially less ontocratic than historical. They know that they were begun at a specific time, were inaugurated as a movement by a historical figure — the Buddha, Jesus Christ, Muhammad. Their disciples teach what they believe to be the fundamental insight into the problem of historical existence and the best salvific way to overcome it and move toward the ultimate destiny of all life.

While we have briefly dealt with Christianity as it is encountering and influencing the primal religions, Confucianism, and Hinduism, we have only mentioned Buddhism and Islam in passing. Yet it is quite possible that these two will have a greater influence in the global future, pose challenges to and interact dramatically with Christianity, and, in some ways, serve as potentially great allies and simultaneously possible great enemies of the globalizing forces that were primarily launched out of an ethos shaped by Christianity. We must attend to them and are fortunate to have two internationally renowned scholars to do so.

A few preliminary observations may be in order. Buddhism is often held to be essentially an epistemologically focused philosophical religion that developed as a protest movement within and then beyond the basic metaphysical-moral, caste-hierarchical, ontocratic, and "polytheistic" assumptions of Hinduism — most especially as the Buddha is believed to have discovered the way to escape from the unalterable and eternal law of rebirth into the various hierarchical levels of cosmic-social status according to the karmic consequences of one's behavior in a previous life. Buddhism claims to have broken the hegemony of bio-piety and geo-piety present in Judaism, many tribal religions, aspects of Confucianism, and more elaborately in Hinduism, but it selectively adopted and rearranged rather than fully denied many of the presuppositions of its parent. Indeed, as Buddhism in its various branches moved north and east through Tibet and China to Korea and Japan, and south and east through Sri Lanka, Burma, Thailand, and Indochina to Java and Bali, it carried modified export versions of Hindu morality, mythology, and political theory to much of Asia.

Within a few centuries, however, Buddhism was practically extinct in India, although it has reappeared there as a reform movement on the heels of India's independence movement, following the brilliant former outcaste author of India's new constitution, Ambedkar, who trusted neither the tradition of the Hindu caste system nor the "foreign" religions of Islam or

Christianity.[38] This relative defeat in India was due not only to the absorbative power of resurgent Hinduism but to several intrinsic characteristics of Buddhism. It developed an intense focus on the capacity of individuals to liberate themselves from the fate of karmic destiny by conquering the desires, attachments, and illusions of the mind that keep them trapped in anguish and misery. It provided, in other words, a highly individualist, intensely subjective, and methodologically precise new eschatological vision that captured the hopes and reshaped the behavior of millions of troubled souls. However, many suggest that it had, and has, no inherent capacity to shape a polity. It has tended to subordinate itself to, and legitimate, the royal political order of which it has been a part ever since its early adoption by King Ashok.

Rather extensive arguments have developed among scholars of Buddhism over whether its substantial dependence on Hindu concepts of social and political order (especially as found in the *Arthashastra*), its creation of the monastic orders (*Sangha*), its cultivation of the bodhisattva ideal in Mahayana sects especially, its consistent advocacy of peace, or its challenge to the theory of inevitable reincarnation into caste status engendered a new social philosophy able to influence the basic institutions of life as well as the inner consciousness of persons. For the most part it appears that Buddhism had the capacity to adapt to many social environments precisely because of its relative lack of a distinctive social message. This has meant, to be sure, that devotion to Lord Buddha has been welcomed by royal traditions, from King Ashok through the theocracies of Tibet and War Lords of China, the long-term imperial houses of Thailand, Japan, and even to the modern "socialist lords" of Sri Lanka and Burma.[39] Buddhist

---

38. See Christopher S. Queen and Sally King, eds., *Engaged Buddhism: Buddhist Liberation Movements in Asia* (Somerville, Mass.: Wisdom Publications, 1996).

39. See my review of some of the key arguments and evidence in "The World Religions and Political Democracy: Some Comparative Reflections," *Religion and Society* 29, no. 4 (December 1982): 19–49. I have been much influenced by my experiences in Burma, and by the works of Medford Spiro, *Burmese Supernaturalism* (Englewood Cliffs, N.J.: Free Press, 1967) and *Buddhism and Society* (London: Blackwell,

monks, often considered to be "jewels in the crown of the king," recognize that in the world of the laity, the ignorant and unliberated do all sorts of evil and that rulers have the dharmic responsibility to keep law and order. Otherwise, it would be difficult to find a distinct, positive vision of social organization in Buddhism that could shape the global future.

Nevertheless, it is quite possible that as forms of Western post-theistic humanist thought moved from thinker to thinker and enclave to enclave, and was preserved by personal discipline, self-examination, and compassionate example in restrictive social circumstances such as medieval Europe and, in other forms, among the intellectuals of the former Soviet Union, Buddhism may well have demonstrated an appeal to the soul seeking liberation from the troubles and cares of life wherever it is practiced. Moreover, it may be that its relative deficit of social theory allows it to fit into multiple cultures. Indeed, it, like Evangelical Christianity, is growing rapidly in China. Moreover, its critical epistemological reflections have elements that might well be compared to secular enlightenment and even more to postmodernist thought. It does not really hold to eternal essences or perennial existents, such as God or gods or souls or even what we have here identified as "the Powers." Thus, if globalization brings us a world that consists of a temporal collage of co-arising and falling appearances that take shape basically in virtual reality as constructed by the mind of the perceiver, Buddhism will have great affinity with those forms of deconstructive, poststructuralist thought that are presently under discussion among the more radical Christian theologians, secular philosophers, and historians of religion in academia today.[40]

Moreover, if it turns out that globalization is to be exposed,

1970); and Bardwell L. Smith, ed., *Religion and the Legitimation of Power in Sri Lanka* (Chambersburg, Pa.: Anima Press, 1978) and *Religion and the Legitimation of Power in Thailand, Laos, and Burma* (Chambersburg, Pa.: Anima Press, 1978).

40. See, e.g., Duncan Ryuken Williams and Christopher S. Queen, eds., *American Buddhism* (Richmond, England: Curzon Press, 1999). Buddhism becomes more activist in the West, as can be seen in Christopher S. Queen, *Engaged Buddhism in the West* (Boston: Wisdom Publications, 2000). See also the overview of five other new

as some claim, as nothing more than a manifestation of the most rapacious, possessive, commodification of the world at the hands of an unfettered capitalism that is destroying the environment, Buddhism's accent on the overcoming of greed, desire, and attachment is likely to have compelling attraction to those disgusted with the consumerism and materialism they see around them. Indeed, one can find some adoption of Buddhist motifs by some Christian theologians who have global concerns.[41]

With such matters in mind, we turn to the striking contribution on Buddhism by the Japanese theologian Kosuke Koyama, who spent a number of years in Thailand before coming to the United States and becoming one of the international leaders in crosscultural and interfaith dialogue. On the basis of long-term dialogues between Christians and Buddhists, he argues that Buddhism is specifically a tradition of observation, of seeing what the fundamental character of reality is and adjusting mind and attitudes to its deepest truth. This method of knowing what is ultimately true and just is different from that of Islam, which has the most strict view of divine revelation of any of the great religions, and it is different from Christianity, which has a profound understanding of divine inspiration but acknowledges the role of human insight and authorship in both the discernment of truth and the actualization of justice. This latter position, common to Judaism and Christianity, has a twofold implication. It suggests that ultimate truth and justice are simultaneously transcendent and intimately present in the time, space, and flesh of life, and that whatever we can come to know about them must be both disclosed and received, observed and enacted — lovingly incarnated in earthen vessels.

---

studies by Michelle Spuler, "Buddhism in the West: An Emerging Genre," *Religious Studies Review* 26, no. 4 (October 2000): 343–50.

41. Perhaps John Cobb, who has helped generate and sustain a dialogue between Buddhism and process theology, is the most outstanding example. See, e.g., his *Talking about God in the Context of Modern Pluralism*, ed. with David Tracy (New York: Seabury Press, 1993). Cf. Russell Sizemore and Donald Swearer, *Ethics, Wealth, and Salvation* (Columbia: University of South Carolina Press, 1990).

This could well be, to Buddhist eyes, evidence of a false perception of reality. The Buddhist wants us to recognize that the universe operates by reasonable moral laws, and wants us to have a compassionate view of reality. The laws of *dharma* have to do with the ways in which the inner spiritual and psychic perceptions of reality operate in relation to highly fluctuating, rising and falling, external phenomena, while compassion has to do with an empathetic awareness that we and our neighbors each tend to become tragically attached to those ephemeral phenomena. We are attracted to and want possession of objects; indeed, we consider the self itself as an object that, we think, might be stabilized or satisfied if it is attached to some other reality. But such attachments are illusory; they do not satisfy. As Koyama spells out the logic and implications of such convictions, we find possible clear commonalities and sharp differences between the spiritual and moral principles behind globalization and those of Buddhism.

In a sharply contrasting way, Islam also poses direct challenges to the prospects of globalization insofar as this process is generating the material infrastructure for a pluralist global civil society. It is itself a globalizing religion, and some historians argue that its rootage in the drive to overcome the fractious conflicts of tribal and clan hostilities of the earlier pagan polytheism of the old Mideast gave rise to a universalizing warrior cult of intense discipline that must fulfill its destiny by unifying the world and establishing a universal reign under a single law.[42] But this is not how Muslims understand their origin. The profound rootage of this tradition is explicitly not found in observation but in revelation — in fact with a basic theory of revelation that is often called in the West "fundamentalism" when it is applied to the Bible. This view holds that a transcendent personal God revealed His will, in teachings and commands, which were inerrantly spo-

---

42. I have traced some of these arguments in "Public Theology, Islam, and the Future of Democracy," in *The Church's Public Role,* ed. Dieter Hessel (Grand Rapids, Mich.: Eerdmans, 1983), 63–83.

ken to Muhammad, recited by him, and recorded by inspired scribes. This is the resource for knowing universal truths that we ought to study and obey without remainder. When we submit to this true Lord, as so known, we are called to spread the truth that is now finally and fully available, empowered to fight the principalities and dominions of life that humans have constructed on the basis of their false speculations, and promised an immediate place in paradise if we faithfully carry out our duties or die in the effort. This fight takes the form of a militant defiance of idolatries, relativisms, and immoralities of all kinds, so long as portions of the world's population deny or oppose the truth and justice that this movement knows. However, it is believed, once a person or some segment of the world's population converts to Islam, a peaceful, learned, graceful, and plentiful life is the result.[43]

Lamin Sanneh, born in a Gambian Islamic family and, after a long intellectual and spiritual pilgrimage, now a Roman Catholic, has been at the forefront of the scholarly investigation of the historical interactions of Muslim, Christian, and tribal traditions in both Africa and the Mideast, and is a frequent participant in a number of ecumenical dialogues between Muslims and Christians. He concludes this volume with a discerning analysis of the ways in which Islam, the most recent of the great world religions, provides a quite overt portrait of social and political life that it promises to and for the world. He points out that while the Qur'an is the chief source of decisive revelation, and the Shariah is seen to be the normative guide in moral, religious, and social law, Muhammad himself is often taken to be a kind of exemplar and model of how the implications of faithful belief could and should work out. While the obedience to the one true god, Allah, is necessarily individualist, there is a collective social and

---

43. See the contrasting views of Islam presently under discussion in, for example, Abdullahi Ahmed An-Na'im, *Toward an Islamic Reformation* (New York: Syracuse University Press, 1990); Dale Eickelman and James Piscatori, *Muslim Politics* (Princeton, N.J.: Princeton University Press, 1996); and Paul Fregosi, *Jihad* (New York: Prometheus Books, 1998).

cultural image as to how life is to be lived in Islamic solidarity, one that echoes not only ancient Hebraic tribalism but also certain features of Christian conversionism. Muhammad was not only the prophet of the tradition, as Sanneh shows. He is also taken to be a model husband, successful merchant, ideal jurist, and heroic warrior on whose life many aspects of Islamic family, business, law, and conquest are based. He was the first theologian and commander king, who "combined in his person the functions that Paul and Constantine" played out in the Christian West. He spread the faith, nurtured its new adherents, and established a regime with Islam as its integrating ideational core.

Of course, there are divisions within Islam, both because of disagreements between Shi'a and Sunni and other schools of thought within the faith, and because of cultural differences that appear in distinctive ways in, say, Turkey as compared to Afghanistan, Sudan as compared to Indonesia, and Morocco as compared to Harlem. Nevertheless, a certain unity exists. In contrast to the opposition of Buddhism to, and the sometimes ambivalence of Christianity about, sexuality, wealth, law, and the place of force in the "pure" life, at least for "true believers," but also in concert with features of primal religions, Hindu nationalism, and imperial Confucianism, Islam offers a radical affirmation of the direct public role of religion, enforced by integrated political authority. Fundamentally opposed to any kind of secular humanism, as it can be found in both Marxist and liberal forms in modernity, and alike dubious about many forms of "soul-cultivation" as it is found in Hindu *bhakti,* Buddhist meditation, Christian devotionalism, and usually even Sufi mysticism, Islam has also had episodic periods of involvement with highly cosmopolitan philosophies and sciences of the Greek and Indian traditions and profound engagement in dialogues with Jewish and Christian thinkers. These features suggest that if Islam becomes the dominant force in guiding the globalization process, it will take the process in a very different direction than now appears to be the trajectory. It is not likely to be fully hospitable to other religious traditions or to a genuinely pluralistic global civil society.

Concluding Observations

Human history is not preprogrammed in such a way that we can predict how globalization will turn out. But we can begin to chart some of the possible and probable directions — if this or that dominant influence, if this or that Lord, becomes the governing model in and for the whole. The scholars in this volume know that religion is decisive as a unifying and universally human reality, giving rise to certain common ethical insights among peoples, and that it has also the capacity to divide precisely because it sees different ultimate ends for human life. These deontological and teleological normative realities combine, often only awkwardly, with each other and with the spheres and powers of human societies amidst the contingencies of history to form civilizations. What we have done in this volume is to investigate how things do and might well look as we try to sort the unifying and diversifying factors when religion and the world religions are taken into account as a force shaping our emerging and increasingly common life on earth.

All of the authors have treated Christianity in relationship to the non-Christian traditions that they have had under investigation, both because Christianity and these traditions directly complement each other at some points and challenge each other at others, and because globalization is, indirectly, bringing certain of the fruits of the Christian impact on civilization to the adherents of these traditions — sometimes in ways they can approve and adopt and sometimes in ways they only disapprove and resist. In this volume, we have not dealt extensively, historically, or systematically with Christian theological and ethical probabilities or possibilities as they may, or should, influence globalization in the future. That must await volume 4, the final one of this series. Certainly, many of the compelling suggestions that have been made in the first two volumes as well as in this one will be taken into account. In the meantime, the authors of the essays in this volume have contributed to the discussion of globalization — they present data, perspectives, and interpretations that leading contemporary academic analyses of the political, economic, and cultural dimensions of globalization seldom take into account. The issues that these authors define, however, point toward factors and perspectives that are fateful for our common human destiny and perhaps for our salvation.

– Chapter 1 –

THE STUDY OF RELIGION AND THE COMING GLOBAL GENERATION

Diane B. Obenchain

Christians hold that when received, thc gospel changes how people live.[1] From its earliest reception until today, two concerns persist with Christians: (1) how to live in accordance with the gospel and (2) how to share the gospel with others, that is, how to relate the gospel to what others are already doing.[2] Each concern entails the other, for living truly in accordance with the gospel is embodied in customs of knowing and living — transformed by the gospel to be sure — present in people's lives before the gospel is received. Christian life has always been a mixture of the gospel and the ways of living that came before that now through transformation newly incarnate the gospel.[3]

When the gospel reached Roman ears, later arrived on Roman soil, and was lived and taught by persons in that context, a Latin concept, known in English today by the term "religion," became associated with it, a concept that continues to be associated with it today.[4] Under Christian influence

---

1. "The kingdom of God is at hand. Repent and believe the good news!" (Mark 1:15).

2. Theologians and preachers continue the tasks of "prophets and teachers" (Acts 3:1–3).

3. See Andrew Walls, *The Missionary Movement in Christian History* (Maryknoll, N.Y.: Orbis Books, 1997); Lamin Sanneh, *Encountering the West* (Maryknoll, N.Y.: Orbis Books, 1993); and M. Thomas Thangaraj, *The Crucified Guru* (Nashville: Abingdon Press, 1994).

4. Karl Rahner states that the English term "religion" derives, probably, from

in the Roman and medieval periods, some change in the meaning of "religion" took place. However, under the reforming Christian, secular, and non-Christian influences of the Reformation, Enlightenment, and post-Enlightenment periods, the concept of religion became a center of focus, change, and development as never before.[5] These were times of (1) protest against "failures of distortion"[6] in ecclesiastical authority, (2) tremendous suffering caused by warring factions of the church, (3) vast new crosscultural exchanges, (4) far greater availability of printed information, and (5) rational systematizing of knowledge that both deepened and hastened what we call "globalization" today.

Contemporary Christians and many scholarly studies of culture are deeply influenced by modern liberal thinkers such as Immanuel Kant and Friedrich Schleiermacher. They shaped our contemporary encounter with other traditions, for they gave a larger role to reason within Christian faith. In so doing, the concept of religion became central to their reflection upon how to live the gospel truly and how to relate it to customs and practices of others. For other liberals, who rejected most or all traditional knowledge and gave exclusive authority to reason and science, the concept of religion referred to those ways in which humans attempt to connect with what

three Latin roots: *relegere* (to express careful respect and honor for a specific god), *religare* (to bind), or *reeligere* (to choose to reorient one's life, as in a conversion). Karl Rahner, ed., *Encyclopedia of Religion* (London: Burns & Oates, 1975), 1358.

5. See Wilfred Cantwell Smith, *The Meaning and End of Religion* (New York: Macmillan, 1963), esp. chap. 2 and notes; Michel Despland, *La Religion en Occident: Evolution des ideés et du vecu* (Montreal: Fides; Paris: Cerf, 1979); and Ernst Feil, *Religion: Die Geschichte eines neuzeitlichen Grundbegriffs von Frühchristentum bis zum Reformation* (Göttingen: Vandenhoeck & Ruprecht, 1986) and *Die Geschichte eines neuzeitlichen Grundbegriffs zwischen Reformation und Rationalismus (ca. 1540–1620)* (Göttingen: Vandenhoeck & Ruprecht, 1997). See conference papers in Michel Despland and Gerard Vallee, *Religion in History: The Word, the Idea, the Reality* (Waterloo, Ont.: Wilfrid Laurier University Press, 1992). See also Nicholas Standaert, "Christianity as a Religion in China," in conference volume of "Religion and Chinese Society" (Hong Kong, May 29–June 2, 1999). Standaert argues that the *Ru* (Confucian) ethics had significant influence on the meaning of our term "religion" today.

6. Paul Tillich, *Christianity and the Encounter of World Religions* (Minneapolis: Fortress Press, 1994), 65.

they imagine is a divine power for assistance in solving life's problems. These attempts were deemed mistaken, for reason and science are far more effective in solving these problems. In either case, for Christian liberals or secular liberals, in a growing protest against "failures of distortion" on the part of religious institutions and leaders, reason was increasingly engaged to understand religion; in the process the modern academic study of religion emerged.

The study of religion has passed through a series of stages as scholars from various liberal and secular persuasions have debated intensely over approach and method. Looking at the overall development from a Christian liberal perspective, one discerns two main groups: (1) those who are guided primarily by faith (engagement with transcendence through a received tradition) and secondarily by reason in understanding religion and (2) those who are guided primarily by reason and secondarily by faith in understanding religion. For the first group, the supportive role of reason is extremely large and very influential. For the second group, the supportive role of faith is often small and, in some cases, almost negligible, although always in some way present in one's thinking. In either case, as Lucien Levy-Bruhl (1857–1939) argued persuasively in *Carnets,* all humanity shares one common mentality in which both participative and ratiocinative thinking are present.[7] This suggests that there is no "rational knowledge"

---

7. In his earlier work, Levy-Bruhl distinguished between what he called "primitive mentality" (or "mystical participation") and "civilized mentality" (or "modern systematic thought"). Primitive thought discerns one's self, other persons, and things as interconnected "mystically" beyond space and time. One simultaneously participates in several aspects of a single mystical unity. Mythic thinking, for Levy-Bruhl, is mystical participation narrated in images. Rational systematic thought, by contrast, is ruled by the principles of noncontradiction, inductive cause and effect, and measurement. In Levy-Bruhl's later discernment, participation is always present even when ratiocinative, systematic thinking is highly developed. The difference between the primitive and modern mentality is one of nuance, in other words, of predominance of mystic participation or rational system, not the absence of either mystic participation or rational system. See Lucien Levy-Bruhl, *Primitive Mentality,* trans. Lilian A. Clare (New York: Macmillan, 1923) and *Carnets* (1949), discussed in Jacques Waardenburg, *Classical Approaches to the Study of Religion* (The Hague: Mouton & Co., 1973), 47 and 334. American anthropologist Stanley Tambiah has similarly argued that participation is a universal aspect of human thinking along

apart from faith, which is participative, however eroded the
foundations of the latter may be in some cases, and there is no
participation without ratiocinative thinking, for interacting
involves thought and communication.

In debates between these two groups and subgroups, we
have learned a great deal about religion. However, reasoned
discussion of religion has become so highly sophisticated that
in the view of an increasing number of scholars, the demands of enlightened reason have caused a gradual eclipse,
both in fact and in explanation, of the role of faith in
guiding discernment of religion. For example, heeding the
demands of enlightened reason has constructed the concept
of religion in such a way that it is difficult to discuss the
gospel and its relationship with other received traditions of
knowledge without getting caught in a series of irresolv-
able problems. This seems particularly true when Christian
liberals defend "religious pluralism as dialogue" using an enlightened rationalist approach to the universal essence and
particular instances of religion. In this approach, normative
demands for change are not permitted. Yet Jesus announced
and demanded such a change, and the gospel when received
changes how we live and think. Moreover, it is precisely openness to such changes that have enabled a particular kind of
social-economic-political order, called constitutional democracy, wherein religious pluralism as dialogue, and the entire
study of religion, thrives.

Thus, although rational discussion of religion set out to
correct "failures of distortion" on the part of religious in-

---

with the rational-logical aspect. See Stanley J. Tambiah, *Magic, Science, Religion,
and the Scope of Rationality* (Cambridge: Cambridge University Press, 1990). Phenomenologist of religion Mircea Eliade makes a similar point when he argues that
the profane world bears traces of the sacred cosmos. See Mircea Eliade, *The Sacred
and the Profane* (New York: Harcourt, Brace & World, 1959). Protestant liberal
theologian Paul Tillich discerned the secular as "leaving the ecstatic, mysterious fear
of the Holy for the world of ordinary rational structures." However, for Tillich, the
secular is yet within the sphere of religion as it exercises its "critical religious function" to fight against "demonic implications of religion." See Tillich, *Christianity
and the Encounter,* 73–74. Postmodernists who argue that reason always functions
within an embrace of personal narrative make a similar point but argue this point
to different ends in literary and artistic theory.

stitutions, that very rational discussion seems to have led to new such failures as enlightened reason becomes increasingly dominant in setting the rules for understanding religion and engaging in interreligious dialogue. The latter fact has caused neo-orthodox Christians to urge against associating the term "religion" with Christian life and teaching, as Christians of an earlier period once did.[8]

Since we now face new issues in an age of globalization, the time has come for a new rally from the liberal side. The purpose of this essay is to argue for a new move on the part of liberals to recognize and acknowledge participatory faith as significantly active in highly reasoned study of religion. To explicate how this is so, the essay has four parts. The first part presents a brief history of the concept of religion. The second part presents four stages in the developing rational study of religion from the Reformation until today. The third part offers a condensation of what we have learned about religion in reformed and enlightened times and a presentation of major Christian pluralist views that seek to account for this new knowledge. The fourth part, while underscoring strengths in the Christian pluralist approach, identifies four difficulties in that approach and a possible way out of these difficulties through fuller recognition of the role of Christian faith in constructing the Christian pluralist position. Finally, the conclusion encourages, with greater acknowledgment of links in faith between liberalism and orthodoxy, that an enlightened Christian perspective in interactive religious dialogue, including evaluative exchanges, has yet more to offer the global era.

The Concept of "Religion" in Western Thought

We can perhaps best grasp the emergent use of the meaning of the concept of religion by reviewing one of the major studies

---

8. Karl Barth (1886–1968) and Hendrik Kraemer (1888–1965) are outstanding examples.

of the term, as found in *The Meaning and End of Religion* by Wilfred C. Smith.[9] He traces the meaning of the Latin term *religio* in its pre-Christian and historic Christian usage. Smith observes that modern scholars are divided as to its earliest use. Some scholars indicate that *religio* initially referred "to a power outside of man obligating him to certain behavior under pain of threatened awesome retribution, a kind of *tabu.*" The *religio* of a specified god or goddess designates the traditional cultic pattern at his or her shrine. From this use, religion as "rite" or "outward ritual observance" continues today. Other scholars, according to Smith, indicate that *religio* referred to a "feeling in man vis-à-vis divine power." This latter sense was set forth early on by Cicero, whose use of *religio* was to refer to something interior, "something within men's hearts." Smith notes a third usage of *religio* in the first century B.C.E. wherein *religio* is "a generalization, abstracted, of something in which other people are involved." Such was Lucretius's usage of the term to refer to something "out there" having to do with what *others* do.[10]

Smith summarizes that in its Latin usage, prior to the Christian takeover of the term, *religio(nes)* referred to "multitudinous congeries of religious practices" relating to a "diversity of gods, places and occasions." With the coming of the Christian *ecclesia* (church), diverse *religiones* that initially were not construed as rivals became rivals, that is, rival *religiones,* with the Christian *religio* being one among the plural rivals. As Christians deemed their *religio* as correct or true, other *religiones* were deemed "astray" or "false."[11] In the Middle Ages, the leading Christian term was "faith" (Latin *fides*), meaning, according to Smith, "a dynamic response of the person to the living reality of God." *Religio* as "rite" referred to monastic orders.[12] However, beginning with the

---

9. The following summary draws from Smith, *Meaning and End,* chap. 2 and accompanying notes.
10. Ibid., 20–23 and notes.
11. Ibid., 24–28 and notes.
12. Ibid., 31–32 and notes.

Renaissance and continuing to the present time, *religio* came to center stage in Christian discussions of how to live the gospel truly and how to relate the gospel to what others are doing.

Regarding the period of the Renaissance onward, Smith highlights the fifteenth-century work of the Italian Renaissance scholar Marsilio Ficino, a translator of Plato into Latin and author of *De Christiana Religione* (which is usually translated *On Christian Piety*). Ficino, in the Platonic rationalist tradition, used *religio* to refer not to rites but rather to a "universal" attentiveness to the divine that renders human beings human. What is universal is a "perception and worship of God." While *religio* is innate, ideal, and universal to humanity, its actual occurrences in human history, as with all "particulars," are imperfect, "in differing degrees of genuineness." Yet all particular *religio* to some degree is good. For Ficino, the best perception and worship of God is that exemplified by Christ. Thus, Ficino follows Augustine's neo-Platonic rationalist approach to *religio* as the ideal inner piety that Christ's piety exemplifies. Smith's own interest in inner piety as faith continues this approach as he spotlights the Reformers (Ulrich Zwingli [1484–1531], John Calvin [1509–64], and others) whose purpose it was to distinguish between faith (inner piety) and false *religio,* that is, those external rites and institutions that draw one's attention away from God. The title of Calvin's major work, *Christianae Religionis Institutio,* is better translated today, according to Smith, as *Instructions in Christian Inner Piety* not as *Institutes of the Christian Religion.*[13]

Smith concludes his survey of the meaning of the term "religion" by explaining that Ficino may or may not have been correct that humanity is endowed with a universal inner piety that directs perception and worship toward God, and that the Reformers may or may not have been correct in directing our attention to inner piety rather than space-time ritual institutions; nonetheless, human systems and institutions of worship

---

13. Ibid., 32–37 and notes.

are diverse and plural. By 1600, the term "religion" referred
to a plurality of systems or institutions of worship.[14] Later
in the seventeenth century, "religion" came to refer to both
doctrines and practices pertaining to worship. By the mid–
eighteenth century, for some, "religion" referred to beliefs
that one did or did not hold. For others, "natural religion"
referred to beliefs about God deemed attainable by reason
alone.[15] Putting these several uses of *religio* together, Smith
enumerates four meanings of the term that came to prevail
and continue to prevail today: (1) personal inner piety in the
singular; (2) outwardly manifest ritual, ethical conduct, belief
statements, and institutions (related to regional communities);
(3) the ideal of one's own inner piety (in contrast with actual
practice); and (4) "religion-in-general," the lump whole of all
human inner piety *and* outwardly manifestations in feeling,
thought, word, deed, and institutions.

In Smith's assessment, as a pietistic Calvinist, the meaning
of the term "religion" has been misleadingly transposed from
a oneness of universal inner piety to a plurality of "systems
of externalized doctrines and practices." Smith laments this
transposing and suggests that the term "religion" be dropped
altogether, as it no longer means inner piety but rather reified
systems of belief, practices, and the like. Instead of "religion,"
Smith suggests adapting the Christian term "faith," by which
he means "a dynamic response of the person to the living reality of God," to substitute for the older, lost meaning of *religio*
as universal inner piety. He suggests the term "tradition" for
the plurality of outwardly manifest systems or patterns of
faith. In Smith's later work, he strongly emphasized that interactions among traditions or patterns of faith have been
constant and mutually transforming. In Smith's discernment,
there is one interactive, human religious history, that is to say,
one plurally diverse, mutually interactive living sacrament to

---

14. Ibid., 38–39 and notes.
15. Ibid., 39–44 and notes.

God, spanning the length and breadth of human life on the earth.[16]

In the medieval period, scholars began to explore the extent to which, in Christian faith, reason could know God's presence in the universe and in human nature without the aid of special revelation. Knowledge of God's presence in his plenitude of created things by the use of reason was called "natural" knowledge of God and was deemed to be different from "revealed" knowledge of God in divinely inspired scripture. Natural knowledge of God was yet another development in a long trend known as "naturalism" in the West, a view that all can be known by natural reason, of which scientific inquiry is the modern form. Medieval naturalism had antecedents in the naturalism of Plato and Aristotle, who moved away from mythological thinking about the divine to rational thinking about ideas.

As the term "religion" emerged from Christian life in the Renaissance and Reformation periods and came to mean a plurality of systems of worship, Christian and other scholars of the Enlightenment period began to employ natural reason not only to know God through creation but also to know God in religion and the "religions of the world," a new expression that quickly gained dominance in constructing how modern people think about plurality. Scholars called this investigation "natural theology." Enlightenment efforts to use natural reason to understand religion echoed earlier Stoic efforts to understand "natural religion."[17] As Enlightenment interest to use natural reason to investigate and to explain any inclination toward the transcendent intensified, the Judeo-Christian understanding of humans as "created in the image of God" and, therefore, naturally inclined toward God, served as presumption and guide. Two of the most outstanding and

---

16. Wilfred C. Smith, *Towards a World Theology* (Philadelphia: Westminster Press, 1981), 18, 20, 38–44, 53, 113–15, 117, 164–68, 173–75, 178, 194. Smith's primary theme is that through meaning in lives of faith, we participate in the life of God and God participates in ours.

17. Eric J. Sharpe discusses the development of this term in his *Comparative Religion: A History* (Chicago: Open Court, 1975), chap. 1.

influential of these scholars are Kant and Schleiermacher, to whose natural theologies we now turn.

Immanuel Kant (1742–1804), particularly, employed "the light of natural reason" to understand religion. While some see him as an enemy of faith, it is more likely that he was guided subtly yet profoundly by an understanding of the Christian faith. Kant was born and raised in a German Pietist home.[18] Pietism, a Protestant reform movement of the mid-seventeenth century, responded to the "creed-bound theological and sacramentarian institution" of the established churches by a demand for firsthand experience of justification and rebirth, not just belief in orthodox doctrine. In addition, emphasis was placed on the practice of care and concern for others, on sincere devotional life, and on kindly treatment of those whose views differed from one's own. For Pietists, one's inner experience was the true basis of faith. For Kant this meant a profound respect for the Jesus of history and the "religion of Christ," as distinguished from the "Christian religion" with its emphasis on salvation through belief.[19]

Kant's revolutionary philosophical contribution was recognition of the human mind as an active agent (the "subjective turn") that organizes experience according to a priori categories. In practical reason, as with theoretical reason, Kant discerned regulative a priori structure. The regulative structure of practical reason, what he called "the moral law" or "categorical imperative," is present in and universal to all rational beings, and provides a sense of the good and one's duty

---

18. The influence of Pietism "on Kant's life and teaching was profound." The indirect influence of Pietism "through men like Kant continued long after [Pietism] had ceased to be an important element in the religious life of Germany" (after the mid-eighteenth century). See Theodore M. Greene, "Introduction: The Historical Context and Religious Significance of Kant's *Religion within the Limits of Reason Alone*," in Immanuel Kant, *Religion within the Limits of Reason Alone* (New York: Harper & Row, 1960), xiv, xxii.

19. Theodore M. Greene notes considerable similarity of historical context between G. E. Lessing (1729–81) and Immanuel Kant. Greene adopts Lessing's distinction between the "religion of Christ" and the "Christian religion," that is, between "the religion that Christ, as a man, recognized and practised" and "that religion which holds Christ to be more than a man, i.e. an object of worship." Ibid., xii–xxii and note 2.

to perform the good. Kant viewed all human beings as participants in a "kingdom of ends," each person potentially a free, responsible, moral agent.

Less well-known or fully explored is Kant's impact upon the concept and study of religion by combining (1) a kind of Christian faith with a strong emphasis on behavior in accordance with the moral law and (2) reasonable demonstration in a manner open to anyone. Having come from a Pietist home, Kant was not interested in Christian "doctrines, dogmas, creeds, liturgies, theologies, prescribed rituals, traditions, and perennial speculations of others."[20] Rather, Kant discerned within the human moral predisposition, a "mystery," something "holy," which subjectively is "capable of being known from within adequately for practical use, and yet, as something *mysterious,* not for theoretical use," as it cannot be made known objectively, publicly. Insofar as one finds within oneself a duty to work for the highest good, one is "impelled to believe in the cooperation or management of a moral Ruler of the world, by means of which alone this goal can be reached." Therefore, religion is "not so much to know what God is in Himself (His nature) as what He is for us as moral beings."[21] In Kant's mature years, he discerned "immediately present in man's moral experience a God who reveals Himself to man in and through the moral law."[22]

On this awareness of God subjectively within as a mysterious, possible cause or ground of moral action in every person, Kant affirmed "the universal true religious belief" that is "conformable to this requirement of practical reason." Universal religious belief is "belief in God 1) as the omnipotent Creator of heaven and earth, *i.e.* as holy Legislator, 2) as Preserver of the human race, *i.e.* as benevolent Ruler and moral Guardian, 3) as Administrator of His own holy laws, *i.e.* as

---

20. Walter Capps, *Religious Studies: The Making of a Discipline* (Minneapolis: Fortress Press, 1995), 7.
21. A mystery is not an "object of knowledge" and cannot be known "objectively." Kant, *Religion within the Limits,* 129–30.
22. Ibid., lxvi.

righteous Judge." Kant further affirmed that "this belief really contains no mystery, because it merely expresses the moral relation of God to the human race: it also presents itself spontaneously to human reason everywhere and is therefore to be met with in the religion of most civilized peoples." Yet more, the "threefold quality of the moral Governor of the human race...can be thought of as combined in one and the same Being." The civil state gives expression to the moral Governor in its necessary division of three different departments of government (legislative, executive, and judicial) which yet form one government. Kant draws examples from the religion of Zoroaster and from the Hindus, Egyptians, Goths, and Jews.

Moreover, this "universal religious belief" is demonstrable not only through reason, but it "was first set forth in a particular (the Christian) body of doctrine and only there made public to the world." While "that great mystery can be made comprehensible to each man through his reason as a practical and necessary religious idea," "in order to become the moral basis of religion, and particularly of a public religion," that great mystery was "first revealed when it was *publicly* taught and made the symbol of a wholly new religious epoch." The public setting forth of Christian doctrine "on behalf of religion in general, has cleared the moral relation of men to the Supreme Being from harmful anthropomorphism, and has harmonized it with the genuine morality of a people of God." Therefore, for Kant "the objective rule of our behavior" is not revealed in reason only but "is adequately revealed to us (through reason and Scripture), and this revelation is at the same time comprehensible to every man."[23]

To understand Kant's notion of "true religion" as he would have, we may use Jesus' metaphor "I am the vine; you are the branches" (John 15:5). For Kant, true religion is behavior in accord with the moral law. The unity of true religion is the one moral law (the vine) expressed in different ways and to different degrees in practice (the branches). God is true religion's

<hr>

23. Ibid., 131–35.

hidden, unprovable source operative in human practical reason. Reason knows it; Jesus Christ has revealed it. Now all Christian and other religion can come to this light of reason and revelation in Christ to be illumined and reformed. There is no sense of separate religions in competition here but a sense of one spiritual vine, the moral law, now better understood in light of reason and revelation in Christ. Because the life of the vine is to be that of the branch, with this new clarity on true religion as behavior in accord with the moral law, a new religious epoch has begun.

Kant's natural theology is highly influenced from the Christian side. One could argue that because of his Pietist moral upbringing, Kant was propelled to represent the truth Jesus had to offer by redefining "true religion" as behavior in accord with the moral law. One acknowledges that Kant's Christian faith was not based on a Christocentric soteriology in the way that dogmatic treatments in Catholic, Lutheran, Calvinist, or Barthian traditions are. Still, Kant's arguments are grounded in Christian piety and teachings that profoundly influenced his discernment of the categorical imperative and use of practical reason.[24] Although Kant has sometimes been considered a deist, Theodore M. Greene makes very clear that Kant had "an understanding for, and a sympathy with, Christian dogmas far deeper than that commonly found in the deistic literature of the period."[25] In spite of current critiques of Kant and of Enlightenment liberalism generally in some theological circles, it can be fairly argued that his discernment of Jesus Christ as moral, of Christian community as moral, of "true religion" as moral, and of the moral law as a key indicator by which we can see the connection of reason with the teachings of Jesus Christ, means that Kant should be seen as a Christian reformer of all religion, including Christian religion.

---

24. Any careful reading of Kant's *Religion within the Limits,* together with his notes, cannot fail to convince one that Kant was not only a Christian but a devout Christian. Jesus' commandment to love one's neighbor as one's self finds clear parallel in Kant's moral categorical imperative of practical reason that is natural to man. Kant makes no effort to hide this parallelism.

25. Kant, *Religion within the Limits,* lxxiv

Like Kant, Friedrich Schleiermacher (1768–1834), a practicing Christian of Pietist background, was influenced not only by modernist Enlightenment philosophy but also by the historical-critical study of textual sources and recorded observations of Christianity and other religions and, more so than Kant, by the humanistic return to literature and the arts characteristic of later Romanticism. When Christian faith in Schleiermacher's day was subject to contempt and mockery, Schleiermacher, in his *On Religion: Speeches to Its Cultured Despisers*, urged taking Christian faith and all religion seriously. To start his second speech, rather than ask, "What are the gods after all?" Schleiermacher asked, "What is religion [after all]?"[26] As with Kant, so also with Schleiermacher: In Christian faith, use of natural reason to know God shifts to the use of natural reason to know "religion" or "religions of the world." However, in contrast to Kant's emphasis on the moral aspect of religious experience that caused Kant to place religion in the category of practical reason, Schleiermacher emphasized the sensitivities of religious experience and placed religion in the category of aesthetics.

Like Kant, Schleiermacher began with nonconceptual intuition: "All intuition proceeds from an influence of the intuited on the one who intuits, from an original and independent action of the former, which is then grasped, apprehended, and conceived by the latter according to one's own nature."[27] However, unlike Kant, who focused on noumenal forms of thought incipiently active in intuition, Schleiermacher focused on the noumenal contribution of the intuited, that is, the one universe, or God, directly encountered in intuition. In short, unlike Kant, who focused on the divine in the intuiter and gave preference to ideal form in moral practice, Schleiermacher focused on the divine in the intuited and gave preference to the ideal of revelation.

While Kant found mystery present in the categorical form

---

26. Friedrich Schleiermacher, *On Religion: Speeches to Its Cultured Despisers*, ed. Richard Crouter (Cambridge: Cambridge University Press, 1996), 18.
27. Ibid., 24–25, n. 9.

of intuition, Schleiermacher was less influenced by the rationalist impulse than the romantic one. Hence, he found mystery "in every sensory perception, before intuition and feeling have separated, where sense and its objects have, as it were, flowed into one another and become one." This mysterious flowing into one, although "fleeting" and "quickly passing away," is "the higher and divine religious activity of the mind." In childlike passivity (what Schleiermacher later called "absolute dependence"), one feels and knows the mysterious totality of the universe and is filled with immediate influences of God.[28] In true religious experience, every individual person, thing, or event is a revelation, a miracle, a representation of the infinite in the finite.[29] Whereas Kant sought to develop intuition through rational activity of the mind, Schleiermacher lamented that rational articulation of these intuitions (revelations) "dissolves" or "desecrates" their "religious sensibility." One ends up with "imitation," "formula," or "caricature," not true religion.[30]

As with Kant, Schleiermacher's approach to "true religion" was influenced by his Pietist Christian background, more deliberately so, perhaps, in Schleiermacher's case. In his later theological writings, Schleiermacher affirms that Jesus Christ "is like all men in virtue of the identity of human nature [the finite]." Yet Jesus was distinguished from all other human persons by "the constant potency of his God-consciousness which was a veritable existence of God [the infinite] in him." The redemptive work of Jesus Christ is his enabling others to be assumed into his God-consciousness by "a creative pro-

28. Friedrich Schleiermacher, *The Christian Faith,* trans. H. R. MacKintosh and J. S. Stewart (Edinburgh: T. & T. Clark, 1928), 12–18, 31–39; cited in *Friedrich Schleiermacher: Pioneer of Modern Theology,* ed. Keith Clements (Minneapolis: Fortress Press, 1991), 100–104, 272–73.

29. Schleiermacher, *On Religion,* 25–36.

30. Ibid., 32–33. See also Francis Schüssler Fiorenza, "Religion: A Contested Site in Theology and the Study of Religion," *Harvard Theological Review* 93, no. 1 (January 2000): 7–33. Fiorenza illumines Schleiermacher's views not only on revelation as religion's "originating individual moment" but also on the "creativity and individuality" of religion in "concrete religious communities with concrete historical language, beliefs, and practices."

duction in us of the will to assume him into ourselves, ... our assent to the influence of his activity." This assent is "conditioned by the consciousness of sin" as "we contemplate his sinless perfection." Therefore, "the Redeemer is best conceived as a pervasive influence which is received by its object in virtue of the free movement with which he [the object] turns himself to its attraction."

Those who freely assent enter into a shared, corporate fellowship in Christ "making them one with himself in the "fellowship of an activity solely determined by the power of God-consciousness." Just as this "activity solely determined by the power of God-consciousness" manifested in the first creative act by which Christ's person was established as "the being of God in him," so "his every activity," his assuming of any believer into his fellowship, is "a continuation of that person-forming divine influence upon human nature." And just as the Redeemer is new-person-forming, he is new-world-forming "in the totality of which the powerful God-consciousness is to be implanted as a new vital principle." Moving from one person to the next and from persons to the natural order, "the creative divine activity out of which the Person of Christ arose" makes the whole creation new and one in him.[31]

As with Kant, we want to understand Schleiermacher's intention in his time. Again, Jesus' metaphor of the one vine with many branches is instructive. Just as in Schleiermacher's discernment the person of Jesus Christ assumes all persons into his God-consciousness, so one also notices that for Schleiermacher, the whole of religion "cannot be completely given except in an unending multitude of thoroughly determinate forms."[32] The plurality of actual relations of human persons to God, each revealing something slightly different of God, are the branches of one vine of true religion that is "inner piety" or "absolute dependence," wherein

31. Schleiermacher, *Christian Faith,* 377–89, 425–48; cited in Clements, *Friedrich Schleiermacher,* 209–34.
32. Schleiermacher, *On Religion,* 100.

God is revealed. Moreover, just as believers receive the mediating, higher activity of Jesus Christ, so also all religion, in Schleiermacher's view, receives, potentially, mediation through Christianity: "the fundamental idea of Christianity about divine mediating powers has developed in many ways, and all intuitions and feelings of the indwelling of the divine nature in finite nature have been brought to perfection within it."[33] In other words, true religion is one vine, Jesus as mediator has accomplished in that vine that which perfects all religion, and Christian religion, ideally, embodies that perfection of religion.[34]

The approaches of Kant and Schleiermacher are similar. In summary, both were grounded in Christian faith, Scripture, and Pietist practice. Both wanted to evaluate religious institutions of their time and to reform Christianity and other religion so as to encourage better human community. Both were trained in the use of enlightened, natural reason to understand the religions of the world. To make their critique, Kant and Schleiermacher used reason to redefine "true religion," taking as their model that which each, differently, discerned as distinctive about Jesus Christ (for Kant, "moral action"; for Schleiermacher, "absolute dependence"). Both found what is distinctive about Jesus Christ present in a natural human capacity. Both encouraged giving attention to that capacity, for leaving that capacity untended impoverishes humanity. Importantly, for both Kant and Schleiermacher, there was a guiding Christian foundation to their use of natural reason to know and to redefine true religion, a foundation often missed or left tacit in assessment of the enlightened, modern views on religion as predominantly or entirely based on reason.[35]

---

33. Ibid., 121.

34. Ibid., 116–22. See particularly p. 116, n. 19, which discusses the idea that Christianity is "religion...raised to a higher power" and the relationship of this idea to romantic literary theory of the time.

35. The same is true for the contemporary Christian pluralist approach, as we shall see.

In their redefining of true religion in order to evaluate religious institutions of their time, each developed, Kant taking one side and Schleiermacher the other, one of two mainstream, scholarly meanings of the term "religion." On the one hand, the direction of Kant's redefining of true religion propelled the study of religion in the direction of transcendence present in formal aspects of human knowing and acting that are deemed innate, are shared in common, and are constant to all humanity. On the other hand, the direction of Schleiermacher's redefining of true religion propelled the study of religion in the direction of transcendence present in the content of what is revealed to one of deep "absolute dependence" or "inner piety," a content which is ever new, rich, and different. Some scholars attend to both directions. These two directions are the wings of what is known today as the phenomenology of religion.

Each direction yields an ideal of religion that renders possible evaluative judgments of religion. But these have been judgments of two different kinds. On the one hand, Jesus overturned the tables of money changers in the temple because of their social injustice. So Christian scholars of a Kantian bent, who define religion in terms of normative moral action, will judge actions and institutions for their lack of social justice. On the other hand, Jesus called the Pharisees hypocrites because their actions and institutions opposed God himself. So Christian scholars of Schleiermacher's bent, who define religion as inner piety wherein revelation takes place, will judge not revelation but actions and institutions for their reducing, polluting, or betraying the content of revelation. Notice that for both ideals of religion, evaluative judgment is of actions and institutions; this was precisely the purpose of Kant's and Schleiermacher's critiques of religion.[36]

---

36. On both types of evaluation, see Tillich, _Christianity and the Encounter,_ particularly "Christian Principles of Judging Non-Christian Religions" and "Christianity Judging Itself in the Light of Its Encounter with the World Religions." See also Wilfred C. Smith, "Idolatry: A Comparative Perspective," in _The Myth of Christian Uniqueness: Toward a Pluralistic Theology of Religions,_ ed. John Hick and Paul F. Knitter (Maryknoll, N.Y.: Orbis Books, 1987), 53–68.

Significant to both Kant's and Schleiermacher's approaches is their shifting of the locus of the essence of religious faith from doctrine or belief to experience. This shift to experience of religion that is based in a natural capacity of human beings and open to anyone enabled two possibilities. First, reason could be employed to fathom the "essence" of "true religion," or "religious experience," especially its categorical or moral form. Second, all varieties of religious experience could be investigated and compared. With this shift, a liberal movement took hold as theologians in Christian faith relied increasingly upon some or all of the following: (1) reasonable, scientific analyses of sacred texts and practices, especially investigation of the historical origins and contexts within which these texts and practices were understood; (2) scientific explanation of human nature or the human condition, with or without interpretation from what they held to be revealed traditions; and (3) scientific explanation of the origins of the universe and all therein.

In the eighteenth and nineteenth centuries, with working definitions of religion along the lines of Kant or Schleiermacher (or both), a great train of linguists, ethnographers, and scholars of folklore and myth, followed later by anthropologists and sociologists, went out from the West to every place on earth they could get to in order to make a rational case for and an empirical record of "religious experience." (Some of these scholars of world religious experience were children of missionaries who developed a great love for the people and cultures in which they were raised.) The study of religion developed quickly and with considerable complexity, as we shall see, as the connection between Christian liberalism and the study of religion was challenged by several varieties of anthropological naturalism.

Natural Evolution:
Hegel, Comte, Durkheim, Spencer, and Tylor

A second major intellectual trend developed in the last half of the eighteenth and the first half of the nineteenth centuries.[37] Evolutionism is the view that "the universe and some or all of its parts have undergone irreversible, cumulative changes such that the number, variety, and complexity of the parts have increased."[38] A version of evolutionism is "progressionism," the view that all is ascending in a unilinear movement toward greater perfection. Combined interest in both progressionism and naturalism influenced understanding of religion in various ways. In the views that developed under this influence, it was less an anthropological naturalism than a historical developmentalism.

On the one hand, some liberal Christian scholars of religion discerned progressive development of religion leading to Christianity. Outstanding among these was G. W. F. Hegel (1770–1831), who discerned a dialectical, progressive revelation of absolute Spirit that is expressed in reason, actions, and religious institutions ever progressively renewed. From primitive forms in which Spirit is revealed in cosmic forces, religion progresses toward "absolute religion" in which Spirit is revealed in human form, Jesus Christ, who, in turn, is progressively revealed in the freedom of human reason as thinking spirit, whereby actions and religious institutions are reformed.[39] Whereas for Kant and Schleiermacher engagement in a certain style of Christian piety was foundational to their employment of reason to redefine "true religion," for Hegel and a growing number of other philosophers of religion, Christian faith seems less foundational (although some themes in Judeo-Christian teachings may contribute a lead-

---

37. The historical survey of Western approaches to the study of religion, in this and the following sections of this chapter, draws from Jacques Waardenburg, *Classical Approaches to the Study of Religion* (The Hague: Mouton, 1973); Frank Whaling, *Theory and Method in Religious Studies: Contemporary Approaches to the Study of Religion* (New York: Mouton de Gruyter, 1995); Eric Sharpe, *Comparative Religion: A History* (Chicago: Open Court, 1975); and Walter Capps, *Religious Studies: The Making of a Discipline* (Minneapolis: Fortress Press, 1995).

38. Thomas A. Goudge, "Evolutionism," *Dictionary of the History of Ideas* (New York: Charles Scribner's Sons, 1973), vol. 2, 174.

39. See Quentin Lauer's "Hegel, G. W. F.," *The Encyclopedia of Religion*, ed. Mircea Eliade (New York: Simon & Schuster Macmillan, 1995), vol. 6, 144–48.

ing motif), and Enlightenment rationalism seems increasingly dominant in defining religion.

On the other hand, a large number of scholars countered the Christian liberal approach that desired to reform religious institutions by redefining religion in terms of true religious experience. Some of these scholars, inspired by the mushrooming trend of evolutionary progressivism, sought the reform of institutions by moving beyond religion altogether. Generally, in a growing secular trend, these scholars turned to the question of the origin and development of religion. They formed two schools, one located in France and one located mainly in England and Scotland. Members of the French school emphasized social evolution, religion's part in that evolution, and often the surpassing of that religious influence. Several were founding contributors to the new academic discipline of sociology. Members of the British and Scottish school emphasized the evolutionary development of religion itself and contributed greatly to the formation of the academic discipline of anthropology.

On the French side, mathematician and philosopher Auguste Comte (1798–1857) furthered both Antoine-Nicholas de Condorcet's (1743–94) view of history as unilinear progress from superstitious barbarism to an age of enlightened reason and Claude-Henri de Rouvroy, Count de Saint-Simon's (1743–94) view that humanity had already passed through polytheism, monotheism, and metaphysics to the next stage of positive science. Comte discerned a progressive historical development of the sciences, from the simple and abstract to the complex and concrete — from mathematics to sociology. Correspondingly in society, Comte discerned an inevitable progression from a religious or theological stage, through a metaphysical stage, to the stage of positive science. Religion belongs to the infancy or childhood of human development and performed a useful function when human beings were attempting to make sense of their world for the first time. Now, however, religion is superseded by science. These reductive assessments of religion on the part of French social scientists later gained supporters among German philosophers Ludwig Feuerbach (1804–72), Karl H. Marx (1818–83), Friedrich W. Nietzsche (1844–1900), and Sigmund Freud (1856–1939), each with his own contribution.

Contemporary with Freud, and influenced by the Scottish scholar W. Robertson Smith's (1846–94) studies of totemism and social integration, Émile Durkheim (1858–1917), one of the French founders of sociology, proposed that "religion is something eminently social." Indeed, for Durkheim, religion is the creation of or "caused by" a society that has symbolically formed and institutionalized its discernment of the sacred. The sacred is narrated in mythic story and ritual and is set apart from the profane that contaminates it. Through ritual, myth, and other symbolic events, religion functions to give a social group its collective, or "we," consciousness by forming the social group's intellectual categories of time, space, class, number, cause, and so forth. In this manner, religion conforms the individual to society, uniting all into a moral community. Thus, although illusory, religion has its origin in that which *is* real: social reality.

The British and Scottish school also was taken by evolutionary theory. Charles Darwin's (1809–82) unified theory of organic evolution, based on empirical science, explained the development of living things on natural rather than divine causes. Herbert Spencer (1820–1903) drew out cosmological, philosophical, ethical, and political implications. As differentiation and complexity increase, integration that re-forms differentiated processes into new inclusive "wholes" also increases. The same is true in society and religion: all evolve.

Spencer discerned religion as a mode of intelligence that recognizes "unknowable" mystery and attempts to translate it into something explainable by making transempirical generalizations deemed to refer to that which is real. The earliest stage of religion was belief in ancestral spirits or ghosts (manism). Acts of propitiation in funeral rites gave rise to other kinds of religious ceremony as human discernment of ancestral spirits developed into discernment of divine beings.

In more advanced societies, humans discern a monotheistic divine being with attributes of volition, intelligence, and personality similar to humanity itself. While science and religion are at war, both will recognize that each offers explanation of a certain kind that enables control: religion over social organization and science over the physical domain. Yet both religion and science are nonabsolute and humbled before the great unknowable that remains mysterious, even as humanity learns increasingly more about the unknowable all the time.

Like Spencer, Edward B. Tylor (1832–1917), the founder of anthropology as the scientific study of humanity and culture, was interested in the natural evolution of human civilization. He traced that evolution by going from the present back to the past, by discovering earlier stages of what was known in Tylor's time. Defining religion as "belief in spiritual beings," Tylor posited the earliest stage as belief in the soul (animism), a belief that develops into belief in higher spiritual beings. In proposing his animistic theory of nonliterate and higher civilizations, Tylor argued against nonreligious, materialistic philosophy and received approval from scholars of religion in his time. Still, Tylor understood religion to be solely the product of human reason; that is, religion is in no way aided by anything deemed "supernatural" (transcendent). In his investigation and study of religion, he explicitly did *not* want to work with the philosophies or creeds of the Christian religion. Employing inductive reasoning, Tylor investigated the non-Christian religion of others.

Tylor was soon challenged. On one side, Scottish folklorist scholar Andrew Lang (1844–1912) argued that belief in a supreme being and/or belief in a soul is the source of religion that does *not* necessarily develop unilaterally. On another side, comparativist James G. Frazer (1854–1941) attempted an even more unilinear evolution of the religious mind, with magic preceding religion. More convincingly, Robert R. Marrett (1866–1943) argued that discernment of the "supernatural" as both *tabu* ("not to be lightly approached") and *mana* ("wonder-working power") is the origin of religion and

is primarily an individual, psychological experience. Rudolf
Otto and Gerardus van der Leeuw would follow Marrett's
lead. In his descriptive rather than evaluative approach and
his argument that the key to religious evolution is in social evolution, Marrett pointed the way forward in both
phenomenological and sociological research on religion.

The Phenomenology of Religion: Two Approaches

Christian liberals of the nineteenth and twentieth centuries
have opposed the reductive assessments of religion pro-
pounded by philosophers, sociologists, anthropologists, and
psychologists who have taken science and rational thought
as an external standard to judge religion as "childlike" or
"in error." In this counter move, Christian liberals take seriously human engagement with "more in life than meets
the eye" (transcendence) *and* reason and science. In so doing, they offer a new approach, called by different names,
with slightly different purposes: the "science of religion,"
"history of religions," "comparative religions," or "phenomenology of religion." The approach has developed into two
camps: one that deliberately intends that faith (engagement
with transcendence through a received tradition) has a role
in understanding religious phenomena and one that does not.
In addition, Christianity and Judaism come into the sphere of
comparative work that challenges any view that one instance
of religion is altogether unique, self-sufficient, and absolute.

This new approach counters theorists of natural evolution
in several ways. First, following Hegel's and Schleiermacher's
lead, phenomenologists of religion discern religion as having
a unity and ultimacy that necessitate the study of religion
in itself and not reductively as part of other human phenomena studied by other academic disciplines, especially if
these other disciplines seek to explain away religion's distinctive character. A combination of disciplines is needed to
comprehend religion. Second, religions are not discerned in
natural evolutionary sequence. Rather, religions are discerned

as composites of elements with inherent coordination and history. These elements and their particular interrelationship in each instance can be studied empirically and documented descriptively. Interest in development shifts from evolutionary succession of religions to change and history within a religion and within the interactive history of religion globally. Third, accurate description and comparison bar external standards of evaluation.

Max Müller (1832–1900), a Christian, Kantian idealist, student of Friedrich Schelling's *"Natur-philosophie,"* scholar of Indo-European philology, post-Hegelian historian, prolific author, and editor of the still valuable *Sacred Books of the East* (fifty volumes, 1879–94), was the first to plead for the science of religion as an autonomous discipline. As a science, the study of religion (1) follows "the rules of critical scholarship," (2) is based on "impartial and truly scientific comparison," (3) treats the history of Christianity "in the same spirit in which we treat the history of other religions," (4) "assigns to Christianity its right place among the religions of the world," (5) offers in the "wider view of the religious life of the world...many a useful lesson" for resolving difficulties that "have troubled the hearts and minds of men as far back as we can trace the beginnings of religious life," (6) restores "to the whole history of the world...its true and sacred character," and (7) constructs "the true *Civitas Dei* on foundations as wide as the ends of the world."[40] As a Christian, Müller discerned the future of Christianity in a new incarnation, deriving not only from Christian roots but also embracing "all religions of the past."[41]

Rudolf Otto (1869–1937), German theologian and historian of religions, traveled to Asia to investigate non-Christian religions, particularly those of India. A follower of Martin

---

40. Max Müller, *Chips from a German Workshop*, vol. 1, *Essays on the Science of Religion* (London: Longmans, Green & Co., 1867), xviii–xxviii, and *Introduction to the Science of Religion* (London: Longmans, Green & Co., 1873), 4–17, 24–35; cited in Waardenburg, *Classical Approaches*, 86–95.

41. Sharpe, *Comparative Religion*, 44–45.

Luther and influenced by Kant and Schleiermacher as well as his travels abroad, Otto argued for a fourth category of human experience unique to religion — the category of the "numinous" or "holy" that has two simultaneous, opposing aspects: (1) fear-filled awe (*mysterium tremendum*) and (2) immense attraction (*mysterium fascinans*).[42] Numinous experience, while nonrational in essence, becomes rational to some extent in "ideograms," that is, in symbols, concepts, and doctrines not admitting total logical explanation. Otto's category of a numinous experience common to all human beings provided a hermeneutic device for interpreting and connecting seemingly quite different religious experiences. His purpose was to relate Christian theology to the whole of the world's religious experience.

While heartily greeted by Christian liberals in the phenomenological study of religion, Otto's category of the numinous was criticized by anthropologists for its "lack of empirical evidence." There are interesting parallels between Otto's numinous category and anthropologist Robert R. Marrett's (1866–1943) *tabu-mana* description of human discernment of the "supernatural" (notice the difference in term). American anthropologists Alexander A. Goldenweiser (1880–1940) and Paul Radin (1883–1959), in their fieldwork with North American Indians, also discerned ambivalent human responses to the "supernatural." The latter two scholars attributed the human response of fear or awe to human struggle for survival, not to some aspect of God, as is implied in Otto's approach. Here the striking difference between the Christian liberal, phenomenological approach and the anthropological approach to religion is laid bare: The former works theologically from within faith while the latter endeavors intentionally to work apart from faith. Both use empirical methods of science to discern and describe religious phenomena. The former find in phenomena an understanding

---

42. Rudolf Otto, *The Idea of the Holy,* trans. John W. Harvey (Oxford: Oxford University Press, 1923).

of religion that enhances their own religious faith. The latter find that religion serves a biological, social, or cultural end, and are viewed as reductionists when they insist that some such function is all that the religion is about.

Phenomenologists of religion want to understand religion fair-mindedly, without bias and distortion. Their approach is threefold: (1) factual description, (2) arrangement of the descriptive data to reveal patterns inherent in the data, and (3) connection of patterns to yield fuller comprehension of what religion is. Although some kind of working definition of religion is needed to orient one toward the facts that one seeks to describe and understand, one expects, even seeks, that one's working definition will be revised and expanded by what one learns in this approach. The purpose of the phenomenology of religion is to enable the phenomena of religion to inform one as to the essence of religion in itself. This contrasts with earlier Christian liberal approaches, such as those of Kant and Schleiermacher, who allowed their understanding of what was distinctive about Jesus or Jesus Christ to inform them as to the essence of religion, which then served as a guide to discerning "religions of the world." Both this Christian bias and the bias of the natural evolutionists were to be avoided in the new science or phenomenology of religion.

Making a Kantian distinction between noumenon, "religious reality-in-itself" which cannot be directly known, and phenomena, the empirical appearances of religions, phenomenologists hold that phenomena are constructed expressions of that which cannot be directly known. In order to become aware of religious phenomena as they are for those actively engaged in a religion, a scholar must free herself or himself from prejudices of belief, unexamined presuppositions, causal explanations, and judgments. The scholar is to intuit essential meanings of phenomena as those phenomena are meaningful to believers. To assist in intuiting these essential meanings, phenomenologists of religion borrow two devices from philosophical phenomenology, especially that of Edmund Husserl (1859–1938): *epoche* and *eidetic* vision. *Epoche* (Greek: "to hold back") is to exclude from one's mind all presupposition and to suspend judgment.[43] *Eidetic* (Greek: "that which is seen") is to discern the essence of a phenomenon.[44] Husserl followed Plato's meaning of Greek *eidos* to refer to "universal essence." To intuit the universal essence of something is to recognize those necessary elements of a phenomenon that enable one to classify a phenomenon as a phenomenon of a certain kind. Using *epoche* and *eidetic* vision, fair-minded discernment and description of factual data, categories of religion, and religion itself is deemed possible.

Yet the approach is not so straightforward and easily applied. In the phenomenological study of religion, one seeks to understand the meaning phenomena have for believers. Yet as scholars of hermeneutics such as Schleiermacher, Wilhelm Dilthey (1833–1911), Max Weber (1864–1930), and in other ways, Martin Heidegger (1889–1976) and Hans-Georg Gadamer (b. 1900) have set forth persuasively, in any act of understanding, we project our prereflective assumptions, expectations, and categories, known as a "horizon," on that which we seek to understand. How then can one know the meaning that some action, book, dance, drawing, or person has for another? Whereas Schleiermacher and Dilthey regret that historical, cultural, and personal distance can lead to misunderstanding, Gadamer, following Heidegger, contends that prereflective assumptions precondition and enable understanding as well as misunderstanding. This is so because of our shared human nature. Kant, Schleiermacher, Marrett, Müller, Otto, and others have argued, differently in each case, that human beings share in common a religious capacity or sensibility of some sort.

Here matters are delicate. Phenomenologists of religion, countering the reductive theories of religion, take faith (en-

---

43. John Macquarrie has offered the English phrase "put into brackets" for *epoche,* the intention of which is to enable consciousness to attend to pure phenomenon, abstaining from every kind of value judgment such that one is present to the phenomenon impartially, without questions of truth or falsehood. Sharpe, *Comparative Religion,* 224, n. 8.

44. Ibid., 224.

gagement with transcendence) very seriously both for persons whose meaning one seeks to understand and for oneself. On the one hand, the specifics of faith of the scholar are not to intrude in understanding the specifics of the faith of other believers. On the other hand, it is precisely faith that enables insight into the inner, personal, and social meaning of specific religious phenomena. While there is no agreed upon explanation, phenomenologists have settled on "empathy" (*Einfühlung*) as that by which one feels or intuits the meaning that phenomena have for believers. But what is the role of faith in empathy? Is faith put into brackets (*epoche*), along with presuppositions, causal explanations, and evaluative judgments? Or can one demonstrate empathy without suspending one's faith?

Different answers to these questions separated for a time (mid-1960s to early 1990s) into two schools of phenomenological study in the United States. At Harvard's Center for the Study of World Religions from the 1960s to the early 1990s, led by Wilfred C. Smith and later John B. Carman, the discernment was that one does take faith in empathy to understand another. One brackets evaluative judgment but not faith. This approach follows a line of predominantly Dutch-Scandinavian scholarship of the nineteenth and twentieth centuries. In contrast, the "Chicago School" is heir, to considerable degree, to German scholarship in hermeneutics, sociology, and phenomenology of religion. While members of this school openly acknowledge that faith is surely vitalized by the historical and phenomenological study of religion, matters of faith are theological concerns. Phenomenology, by contrast, concerns critical, reasoned reflection on methods; thus, method defines this school.[45]

The approach of the Center deemphasized the "essence-instance" model, whereby a particular religion is considered a manifestation of a "universal essence" of religion. While cer-

---

45. Nowadays scholars of both approaches are present in most religious studies programs around the world.

tainly not abandoning this model, more important and of far greater interest is the "meaning" religious phenomena have for persons. In the end, empirical description and classification of religious phenomena do not conclude with greater understanding of religion but with greater understanding of persons, communities of persons, and our common human personhood. Since persons are persons of faith of some sort, logically one's own faith, Christian or otherwise, provides clues to the faith and ways of living of other persons.

Earlier in this line of approach, Cornelius P. Tiele (1830–1902), who once stated, "Our religion is ourselves, in so far as we raise ourselves above the finite and transient," urged that impartial scientific investigation of religious phenomena does not require that one be "a sceptic"; one is not disqualified from impartiality if one has "earnest religious convictions of one's own."[46] In faith, Nathan Söderblom (1866–1931), archbishop of the Church of Sweden and a person of deep piety whose descriptive study of holiness remains classic in the field, recognized revelation in all religion such that at the end of his days, he confided, "There is a living God, and I can prove it by the history of religions."[47] A scholar of many languages and the religions of the ancient Near East, as well as successor to Tiele, W. Brede Kristensen (1867–1953) "sought sympathetic and loving understanding" of the faith of others through learning the language of others, by avoiding rational extremes of modernity, by giving priority to the particular rather than the general, and by putting aside "praise

---

46. Cornelius P. Tiele, *Elements of the Science of Religion, Gifford Lectures 1896 and 1898* (Edinburgh and London: William Blackwood & Sons, 1897), cited in Waardenburg, *Classical Approaches,* 99.

47. Cited in Capps, *Religious Studies,* 275–76. Söderblom, following a Lutheran theological principle that Christianity is marked by God seeking humanity while other religions are marked by humans seeking God, distinguished between two main types of religion: natural/cultural religion and revealed/historical religion. As with many other Protestant theologians of his time, Söderblom discerned Christianity as "the highest religion." Other scholars have made similar distinctions between "types" of religion: Max Weber (priestly/prophetic), Ernst Troeltsch (church/sect), Robert R. Marrett (natural/ethical), Victor Turner (hierarchy/communitas), Andrew Walls (primal/universal), David Tracy (manifestation/proclamation).

or blame."[48] In this manner, predisposed by one's own faith, one may empathize with and learn from the faith of another.

It was Gerardus van der Leeuw (1890–1950), student of Kristensen, who put matters most clearly: "[F]aith and intellectual suspense (the *epoche*) do not exclude each other." He observed further that the Catholic Church "recognizes a *duplex ordo* of contemplation, on the one hand purely rational, and on the other wholly in accord with faith." Influenced by the hermeneutics of Wilhelm Dilthey and Eduard Spranger (1882–1963), he argued that "understanding religion" is more accurately "religion becoming understood." Affirming "the ultimate ground of understanding lies not within itself, but in some 'other' by which it is comprehended from beyond the frontier," he concurred with Spranger that "all understanding 'has a religious factor. . . . [W]e understand each other in God.' " Hence, "faith is that upon which all comprehension is grounded."[49] Thus, phenomenology is not separate from theology in van der Leeuw's work.

The Chicago School under the direction of Joachim Wach (1898–1955), honored as the "second" founder of the "science of religion,"[50] takes method as the focal point. A student of Husserl, Otto, and Friedrich Heiler (1892–1967), Wach brought the German school of phenomenology to Brown University in 1935 and to the Divinity School at Chicago University in 1945. In Leipzig in 1924, Wach worked to bolster the still young "science of religion" (*Religionswissenschaft*) as nonnormative, separate from theology and philosophy.[51] Following Dilthey's approach to "understanding" and culture, in

---

48. This is the assessment of John B. Carman, Kristensen's one translator into English, who studied under Kristensen. See W. Brede Kristensen, *The Meaning of Religion: Lectures in the Phenomenology of Religion*, 2d ed. (The Hague, 1960). See also John B. Carman, "W. Brede Kristensen," *The Encyclopedia of Religion,* ed. Mircea Eliade (New York: Simon & Schuster Macmillan, 1995), vol. 8, 383–84.

49. G. van der Leeuw, *Religion in Essence and Manifestation*, vol. 2 (New York: Harper & Row, 1963), 683–84.

50. Waardenburg, *Classical Approaches,* 64.

51. Joachim Wach, *Religionswissenschaft: Prolegomena zu ihrer wissenschaftstheoretischen Grundlegung* (1924), 68, cited in Joseph M. Kitagawa, "Joachim Wach," *Encyclopedia of Religion,* vol. 15, 311–13.

a three-volume work on hermeneutics in the nineteenth century, Wach insisted that the science of religion stand on the hard ground of hermeneutic theory. Wach's second methodological emphasis was sociology, drawing from both German and American schools. Like Max Weber (1864–1920), who correlated economic, social, and ethico-religious spheres but argued against the materialist view of Marx, Wach was interested in social forms of religious experience and, in this regard, desired to connect the science of religion with the social and human sciences.[52] Wach's later methodological emphasis sought a rapprochement of phenomenology of religion with normative philosophy of religion and theology. Whereas "it is the task of theology to investigate, buttress, and teach the faith," the comparative study of religion "guides and purifies" faith.[53] "The sense of the numinous is not extinguished by [the comparative study], but on the contrary, is awakened, strengthened, shaped and enriched by it."[54] In all, Wach demanded that method in the study of religious experience "be adequate for the subject matter"[55] and that it thus include mental, behaviorial, and institutional dimensions.

Wach's successor, Mircea Eliade (1907–86), a Romanian historian of religions and enthusiast of the Italian Renaissance, Greek philosophy, Indian religion (particularly yoga), peasant cultures, and creative writing, emigrated to Paris in 1945, where he settled on the concepts, such as *homo religiosus, axis mundi,* hierophany, and many others, that became the hermeneutic structures of his phenomenological study of religion. After coming to Chicago in 1957, Eliade continued Wach's disciplinary concerns for hermeneutic method, historical description, and systematic analysis of different types of

52. Joachim Wach, *The Sociology of Religion* (Chicago: University of Chicago Press, 1944).

53. Joachim Wach, *The Comparative Study of Religions* (New York: Columbia University Press, 1958), 6–15, cited in Waardenburg, *Classical Approaches,* 494.

54. From Kitagawa, "Joachim Wach," 1–15, and in Waardenburg, *Classical Approaches,* 510.

55. Wach, *Comparative Study of Religion,* cited in Waardenburg, *Classical Approaches,* 493.

religious experience. Yet Eliade's work went in new directions:
(1) morphological interpretation of religious symbolism,[56]
(2) Jungian psychological interpretations of the structure and
function of myth,[57] and (3) metaphysical interpretation of
man's existential religious condition.[58] A distinction between
the sacred and the profane and between archaic and historical (linear) world views runs through his writings.[59] As
programs in religious studies at North American universities proliferated in the 1960s and 1970s, faculty and students
were immensely attracted to Eliade's nontheological style and
his metaphysical speculation concerning the "fall of man"
from the archaic and cyclical into the historical and biblical. Eliade hoped that the history of religions would lead to
a "deeper knowledge of man" and "a new humanism."[60] His
monumental work gives witness to great religious passion in
a nontheological mode.

Both the Harvard and Chicago schools of the phenomenology of religion evince faith and reason at work in the study
of religious phenomena, past and present, worldwide, for the
purposes of better understanding what religion is and who
we are as human beings. The former has been more willing
to admit a leading role of faith in phenomenological work,
while the latter has preferred a methodological separation of
phenomenological historical and systematic work from theological issues of faith. Scholars of both schools recognize
that phenomenological studies of religion, with or without
faith intentionally involved in the scholar's approach, have
the effect of deepening one's personal faith.

---

56. Mircea Eliade, *Patterns in Comparative Religion* (New York: Sheed & Ward,
1958).
57. Mircea Eliade, *Myths, Dreams, and Mysteries* (New York: Harper & Row,
1960).
58. Mircea Eliade, *Cosmos and History: The Myth of the Eternal Return* (New
York: Harper & Row, 1954).
59. See, especially, Eliade, *Sacred and the Profane.*
60. Mircea Eliade, "History of Religions and a New Humanism," *History of
Religions* 1 (Summer 1961).

Religion and Christian Pluralism

Through all of these approaches to the study of religion, we have learned much about religion. First, we have learned that religion involves a human capacity that engages in or responds to "more in life than meets the eye." Second, we have learned that religion involves both critical forms of reason and a point of contact wherein religious experience takes place. Third, we have learned that religion is expressed creatively in individual emotions, thoughts, words, ceremony, ethical conduct, art, and social institutions. Fourth, we have learned that religion functions to create community, an interpersonal cohesion that extends not only to the social whole but to the natural order and the cosmos as a whole. Fifth, we have learned that religion is ever changing through interaction of people. Putting all five points together: in religion a human capacity that discerns, engages in, and responds to "more in life than meets the eye" is activated and finds expression in all spheres of life as human beings link with "more," with each other, and with all things to form a oneness that gathers all into mutual interaction and transformation. In general, this is what the study of religion has taught us to this point in time.

One important understanding about religion not gleaned from the study of religion is that true religious living transforms us into better human persons, persons who realize more of the best we can humanly be. While the study of religion can make a record of claims to this effect on the part of believers, the discernment that true religion moves humanity in the direction of the good comes not from the study of religion but directly from the faith of the scholar.

A second understanding about religion not gleaned from the study of religion is that persons of one expression of religion "ought" to connect positively with persons whose religious expression is different. This knowledge also comes directly from the faith of Christians, Jews, Muslims, Zoroastrians, Buddhists, groups of Hindus, Sikhs, *Ru* (Confucians), Daoists, and primal groups who seek to interconnect constructively with each other to heal broken relations due to warfare and past mistakes of mission that were harmfully associated with imperialism. While the study of religion can report aspirations, discernment that these efforts for positive linkage, interaction, and transformation "ought" to succeed comes directly from faith.

Knowing this, several scholars of religion have endeavored to overcome the (1) "failures of distortion" in religious institutions, (2) broken relations in the world's religious community, and (3) a preoccupation with rationalistic methods in the study of religion to the detriment or even exclusion of faith in understanding religion. Thus, they have developed a view of "religious pluralism," a move based on the phenomenological study of religion and interreligious dialogue. Several liberal Christian scholars of religion have sought to live their own faith truly while interacting with others whose faith is expressed differently. These scholars address the two persisting concerns (living the gospel truly and relating the gospel to what others are already doing) that prompted Christians to take up the Latin term *religio* in the first place. Notable among these pluralists are Wilfred Smith, John Hick, Paul Knitter, and Diana Eck, each with a distinctive contribution to the pluralist approach.

Subsequent to the work of W. C. Smith, as already discussed, John Hick, in a deliberate Kantian approach, argues for "an ultimate ineffable Reality which is the source and ground of everything." The "infinite Real, in itself beyond the scope of other than purely formal concepts, is differently conceived, experienced and responded to from within the different cultural ways of being human." While the Real as noumenon may be plural in some sense, the Real is transcendentally one — identical, ineffable, ultimate — in response to which the multiple phenomenal religious traditions give different conception, along with correspondingly different "forms of experience" and "forms of life." In each of the traditions, "a transformation from self-centeredness to Reality-centeredness takes place." Against relativism, Hick

argues that persons should evaluate different religious traditions by their moral fruits, which reveal the salvific quality
of a religious tradition. Hick qualifies further by observing that religious traditions "as long-lived historical entities"
are "complex mixture[s] of valuable and harmful elements."
When a religious tradition aligns with the one ineffable, ultimate Reality, it is a "context of salvation/liberation" and
bears soteriological fruit.[61]

Paul Knitter, following a more radical, historicist view as
it developed from Hegel through Marx to contemporary lib-
erationism, discerns liberation from social injustice as the
foundation of our evaluation of any theology and the critical
mark of religious pluralism. Poverty, oppression, and nuclear
and ecological disaster are problems common to all humanity.
Traditions offer a plurality of ways of recognizing and remov-
ing social evils and injustice. Moreover, a religion that does
not seek to remove poverty and oppression "is not authentic
religion." Like Hick, Knitter affirms that "from their ethical,
soteriological fruits we shall know them." In other words, we
can judge whether and to what degree a religion is salvific by
the degree those of a religion actually work to remove social
injustice. Knitter affirms further that recognizing liberation
from social injustice as the center for the evaluation of religions is the first step toward dialogue among the religions.
Moreover, that dialogue has a mission: to transform each religion in such a way that it becomes a greater actual source
of healing rather than a source of exclusive claim to superiority in healing. The encounter of one religion with another
is an opportunity for self-critique and correction, moving a
religion in the direction of "the mystery of Soteria" and thus
the centrality of practice over doctrine.[62]

61. John Hick, *A Christian Theology of Religions* (Louisville, Ky.: Westminster
John Knox Press, 1995), 11–30. See also his "The Non-absoluteness of Christianity,"
in *The Myth of Christian Uniqueness,* ed. John Hick and Paul F. Knitter (Maryknoll,
N.Y.: Orbis Books, 1995), 16–36; and "A Religious Understanding of Religion:
A Model of the Relationship between Traditions," in *Inter-religious Models and
Criteria,* ed. J. Kellenberger (New York: St. Martin's Press, 1993), 21–36.
62. Paul F. Knitter, "Toward a Liberation Theology of Religion," in Hick and

Diana Eck also emphasizes that religious pluralism means religious dialogue. Eck carries forward Wilfred Smith's views on religious diversity as a plurality of patterns of faith in the singular. In Eck's terms, faith is lived through commitment to a particular community and, hence, we can speak of a plurality of communities of faith whose members are committed to the "struggles of that community, even as restless critic[s]." Moreover, Eck states, "pluralism is not the sheer fact of plurality alone, but is active engagement with plurality." "The task of a pluralist society...is to create the space and the means for the encounter of commitments" or life orientations. "Meeting, exchange, traffic, criticism, reflection, reparation, renewal" bring one or a group out of isolation and exclusivity into a shared world household (*oikoumene*), which is the first purpose of dialogue. The second purpose is "to understand ourselves and *our* faith more clearly" such that understanding of others brings mutual self-transformation, a process shared on the part of all those engaged in dialogue. Each person, each group, as a member of the one inhabited earth family, is on a pilgrimage of "truth-seeking" to know God and to live one's particular faith commitment to God better.[63]

For Christian pluralists such as Smith, Hick, Knitter, and Eck, pluralism begins with a discernment that religions share a oneness in common (transcendence, the Real, Soteria, God, respectively). Human beings and groups of human beings engage with, respond to, and express this oneness in a plurality of ways. Yet, given religious oneness, there is a oneness of humanity even among the diversity of religion. Interaction among different ways of engaging this oneness deepens that engagement, whether that engagement be discerned as "transcendence-orientation" or "faith" (Smith), or "transformation from self-centeredness to Reality-centeredness"

Knitter, eds., *Myth of Christian Uniqueness,* 178–200; and "Inter-religious Dialogue: What? Why? How?" in *Death or Dialogue?* ed. Leonard Swidler, John B. Cobb. Jr., Paul F. Knitter, and Monika K. Hellwig (London: SCM Press, 1990), 19–44. See also his *No Other Name?* (Maryknoll, N.Y.: Orbis Books, 1996).

63. Diana L. Eck, *Encountering God* (Boston: Beacon Press, 1993), 91, 188, 195–98, 203.

(Hick), or "liberation of others from social injustice" (Knitter), or "expression of the presence of God within one" (Eck). One may put these four points into familiar Christian terms: God transcends us; God is more real than what is temporal; God saves us from sin and death; God engages us and we respond, and the collective whole of these engagements with God forms one communal human body with one history; as members of the same body, interacting and influencing each other, we honor, serve, and help one another. Clearly, there is a distinctive Christian perfume to this pluralist approach to religion.

From Pluralism toward the Global Era

Four difficulties exist with the explication of the work of the pluralists, difficulties that must be overcome if these perspectives are to make an enduring contribution to the global era now upon us. First, those engaged in interreligious dialogue seem always to be talking about the interrelationship of "religions." Using this term does not make clear the important distinction between the gospel and Christian religion. As our review of the study of religion has disclosed, "religion" consists of many aspects: human religious capacity, religious experience, religious expression, religious community, the social and ethical functions of religion, and interactive religious history. If interreligious dialogue must now be a more self-conscious and deliberate engagement in interactive religious history, we need to ask ourselves not just what we share in common but also what we are offering to each other that is different. Seldom is a whole religion transmitted. A careful look at religious interactive history indicates that what has been offered and received across religious traditions has been some gift, insight, or practice that has been taken up into the religious life one already has and that has restructured that religious life, sometimes substantively, and often has reflexively influenced the religious life of those from whom the gift, insight, or practice is borrowed. The religion one lives combines "pieces" of religious living taken from more than one source and woven together meaningfully in the fabric of individual and community life. Hence, in interreligious dialogue as a deliberate field of religious interaction, we need to work more flexibly with religion's several aspects and not just with religion as a whole. Bearing in mind religion's several aspects, we need also to consider what we offer each other that is different.

Second, after Kant and Schleiermacher, as philosophers, sociologists, anthropologists, and psychologists took reason as the be-all-and-end-all in the study of religion, Christian liberal scholars in the secular university endeavored to keep the pace by offering explanations for their approach to and discernment of religious phenomena and religion itself in terms of "reason alone." In so doing, a "secular flip" has occurred for many Christian liberals, whereby reason and science have become dominant in explaining how we approach, understand, and assess religion, while personal faith takes a secondary role. Since Müller and Otto, and often using a Platonic distinction between "universal essence" and "particular instantiation," the liberal Christian phenomenological study of religion has searched for the "universal essence" of religion, of which particular instances of religion are deemed to be variations. A universal essence of particular religions is something quite different from the "true religion" that Kant and Schleiermacher in their own ways discerned as a living vine with many branches.

While liberal Christian pluralists often evince in spirit a "living vine in the branches" approach, they have sometimes allowed rules or normative demands of a Platonic "universal essence-particular instance" approach to construct the way in which religions relate to each other and the role of evaluative judgments. Accordingly, all religions are deemed particular and equal — in the sense of "equidistant" from the universal that is absolute (transcendence, the Real, Soteria, God).[64]

---

64. See, e.g., Langdon Gilkey, "Plurality and Its Theological Implications," in Hick and Knitter, eds., *Myth of Christian Uniqueness,* 37–50.

Logically, as "equal" particulars, no particular religion is absolute and, therefore, none is permitted to judge another. Yet it is possible, or so Hick and Knitter argue, to judge the extent to which a particular religion or instance of a particular religion aligns or does not align with the universal or absolute. But who but God is in position to judge this? Platonic constructions of a plurality of particular religions "equidistant" from the universal or absolute bears its own "failures of distortion." And it aggravates further the first difficulty presented above in disallowing helpful, evaluative judgment and contribution to take place interactively among different aspects of religion. For example, a Buddhist may want to say that the genocide of Jews in the Holocaust was wrong and that he or she has a contribution to those Christian ways of life that allowed this to happen. Likewise, a Christian may want to say that a Buddhist's self-immolation in passivist rejection of war is wrong and that she or he has a contribution to the Buddhist way of life that could help. But the Platonic presumptions of a dialogue among particular religions as whole entities that cannot evaluate and make judgments of each other inhibit helpful exchanges between particulars of what Jesus Christ has to offer, what Buddha has to offer, what the Qur'an has to offer, and so on.[65]

For example, Jesus offers the gift of forgiveness of sins. This gift demands the recognition of distortion within oneself and one's own way of life as well as the need of a gift to overcome that distortion. Forgiveness of sin thus changes our self-assessment and how we live. The forgiven person is a new creation, a child of God, a member of God's household, brought out from the old into a new family — a family interconnected by the same Spirit and expressing one and the same divine love: "Just as I have loved you, you also should love

---

65. Others arguing a similar point but in different ways include S. Mark Heim, *Salvations: Truth and Difference in Religion* (Maryknoll, N.Y.: Orbis Books, 1997); Joseph Runzo, "God, Commitment, and Other Faiths: Pluralism versus Relativism," *Faith and Philosophy* 5, no. 4 (October 1988); and Frank W. Klos, C. Lynn Nakamura, and Daniel F. Martensen, eds., *Lutherans and the Challenge of Religious Pluralism* (Minneapolis: Augsburg Fortress, 1990).

one another."[66] As a child of God, one puts off ways of feeling, thinking, and acting that are not of God.[67] Does this mean putting off every manner of custom, ceremony, and instruction? Paul, perhaps the first to work out the ways in which Christ encountered the great traditions beyond the Hebraic roots of Christianity, answers "No!" All can put off whatever human philosophy, instruction, custom, ceremony that is deceptive, hollow, and false. Then, in compassion, kindness, humility, gentleness, patience, and forgiveness, wrapped in love and ruled by peace and thankfulness, we can offer back to God the new life we have received and seek to use the provisions that we have received to provide for others.[68] In this manner, participating in God's creative-redemptive action, persons express God's self-offering love in received traditions of ceremony, custom, teaching, and philosophy that are reformed day by day in Christ. These choices are not made lightly but are guided by the Spirit, and they matter vitally. One's actions have new ethical intention and significance. By choices, individually and collectively, what is of Christ in the received tradition is taken higher and what is not of Christ is "put off" with the old self.

Collectively, Paul calls this new family in multi-incarnational form "the body of Christ." The shared "head" is Christ, God's self-offering love that gathers, orders, and integrates all into a peaceful and harmonious one. Interlinking this unity are different strengths (portions of grace): God's "gifts to men."[69] In short, the gift of Christ receives all gifts: This is precisely what the Epiphany portrays and means. In receiving these gifts, the gift of Christ is also augmented by them.[70] Each person as co-

---

66. Mark 1:15, 2:5, 10; John 1:12–13; 3:5–8; 15:12; Eph 2:19; Jas 1:18; 1 Pet 1:23.

67. Rom 6:1–14; 2 Cor 6:17; 7:1; Eph 2:14–15; 4:14–31; 5:3–18; Col 3:5–10; 1 Thess 4:3–8.

68. Phil 2; Col 2:6–23; 3:12–17.

69. Eph 2:24–18; 4:7–8.

70. When the gospel is received, God's self-offering love often incarnates yet more radiantly and instructively in the person receiving the gospel in older customs now being reformed in Christ than perhaps in the missioner.

partner with God contributes to the building up of the body of Christ through free, reasoned, and loving choice. In transformed, diverse, multicultural and subcultural forms, moral covenant community, the just and righteous society, incarnates Christ, not perfectly, but in the process of being perfected and sanctified.[71] How is the gift passed on? As Paul describes, not by one's own effort but by the power of the gift itself. This is to say, not for profit or commending anything of themselves, persons made competent by God himself serve as ministers of a new covenant of the Spirit of the living God. This Spirit is "a light shining out of darkness," a "treasure in jars of clay to show that this all-surpassing power is from God and not from us."[72] Those sharing the gift are not commending themselves or their religion but the gift.

Nothing here even hints that Jesus thought of himself as starting a religion. Nor does he tell his followers to start a religion or to pass on a religion.[73] Rather, Jesus was concerned with healing and reconciling. If we loosen up our "lump" concept of religion a bit, we discern that what the gospel brings to religion — all religion — is a healing of the human capacity for religion. Christ's self-offering love by which sin is forgiven and remembered no more heals the human instrument by which the grand symphony of humanity is played to the glory of God. This is the gift of forgiveness of sins. By the gift of healing, persons are drawn into one whole, one person, the family of humanity (the incarnate Christ).[74] From the self-offering love, who is Christ, that originates on God's side through obedience to love others as we are loved from our side, healed and reconciled, we are called into a new covenant of holy intimacy and friendship with God and one another.[75] Each person, each group, each culture, each

---

71. On perfection, see Matt 5:48; Phil 3:12; Col 1:28. On sanctification, see John 17:17–19; 2 Thess 2:13; 1 Pet 1:2.

72. 2 Cor 2:17; 3:1–5; 4:6–7.

73. Schleiermacher makes a similar point; see his *On Religion,* 112–22.

74. 2 Cor 5:16–21.

75. John 15:12–15.

religion, healed in Christ, provides a strength to the one reconciled body of humankind.[76] Now we see more clearly God's purpose in human interactive religious history:[77] Jesus comes to fulfill, not to destroy.[78] As Christians we know the gospel to heal, fulfill, and reconcile all religion. But this is not to say that Christian religion fulfills all religion. Nor is it to advise that one convert to the Christian religion. Rather, it is to urge that one receive the gospel and incarnate that healing and reconciliation in all that one has known before, now transformed in Christ. It is the whole of that transformation of older customs around the world in Christ that is Christian religion today.

Christians are not the only ones with something to offer in the deliberate interaction of religion known as interreligious dialogue. Every religious group has something unique to offer. The swapping of offerings, gifts, and contributions to religious life across different groups has been going on from the beginning of time. What is offered is not precisely the same. Christ offers from the side of transcendent power a healing of the human religious capacity, a healing that restores that capacity to proper functioning. Contributions from other religions may also involve the human capacity for religion but in different ways. As an example, the *Ru* (Confucian) cultivation of the human person offers a unique contribution to the maturing of humanity as one family body — a cultivation process Christians surely can receive and engage in the Spirit of Christ. The point is that contributions from different received traditions may well be called to interact and mutually assist each other in the perfecting of human life in God's image. These interacting contributions need not be considered in competition, nor need religions. Rather, we have a new way of

---

76. The Christ (Word of God) of creation is also the Christ (Word of God) of resurrection. On Chinese contributions to the body of Christ, see K. H. Ting, *Love Never Ends,* trans. Janice Wickeri (Nanjing: Amity Press, 2000), esp. 378–91.

77. On this point, S. Mark Heim, in honoring his friend George Peck, concurs with the latter's words: "I have committed my life to Jesus Christ; *therefore* I am open to other religions." Heim, *Salvation,* x.

78. Matt 5:17.

conceiving of and engaging in interactive, "nonimpositional" mission.

A third difficulty with the explanation of Christian pluralist dialogue as that explanation now stands is that it does not give a full account of how faith invisibly guides reason in Christian liberal discernments of religious phenomena and religion itself. We need not lament that faith is actively engaged in the study of religion, as it was Christians in faith who adopted the term "religion" as a means for living the gospel truly and relating the gospel to what others are doing. Christians intended that Christian faith would transform the Latin concept *religio,* as was the case with Greek *logos* and a host of other key terms and symbols. This being the case, we need attend more fully to how personal Christian faith, as with Kant and Schleiermacher and the entire history of the study of religion, is guiding our discernment of religious phenomena and religion. Because all discernment of religious phenomena begins with a working definition of what religion is, whatever our faith is influences our working definition of religion and our initial discernment of what religious phenomena are. Obviously, no Christian phenomenologist has defined religion in a way contrary to Christ. Thus, in a sequence that many scholars of religion have denied, theology comes before phenomenology of religion and not merely after. In fact, theology comes before, during, and after.

To take Christian liberals as an example once again, the content of Christian faith differs from person to person, scholar to scholar. What Christians believe is not all the same. By admission on the part of many Christian pluralists, their faith is "theocentric," not "Christocentric." Nonetheless, there are markedly Christocentric-like themes in their views: restorative healing, reconciliation, ethics of self-offering love, denying of self (and sometimes even Christ and the Christian gospel?) to lift up the other, trusting, covenant community of friendship and mutual help, among others. Clearly, profound knowledge of and faith in Jesus Christ constructs the main frame of the Christian pluralist view. If Christian pluralists do not *say* that Jesus Christ is the full revelation of God, they argue just below the surface as if it were so. One may go a step further to suggest that not only is a Christocentric-like faith present in the working definition of religion with which Christian liberals start their study of religion but it is present also in their discernment of the meaning of religious phenomena in the lives of others. Too little attention is given to these facts in pluralist writings.

The same would be true for any person of faith. A Buddhist phenomenological study of religion would be guided by Buddhist faith (engagement with "more in life than meets the eye"). So also for the Hindu, Muslim, Daoist, *Ru* (Confucian), and so on. Faith, articulated in a tradition, is inevitably involved in the phenomenological method. What then is bracketed in order that one may understand another? As a Christian working in Christian faith and theological terms, one suggests that what is put into brackets is not one's faith but the cultural or subcultural incarnation of the faith with which one is most familiar — that is, one's religion. What one discerns or recognizes in the other is another incarnation (new, informative, with power to transform one to be sure) of that which one already knows and holds dear.[79] One then begins the process of relating what one learns in a very different incarnation to the incarnation one already knows. Christians do this all the time when talking with Christians of different backgrounds; so do Buddhists, Muslims, and others. One would suggest that it is happening as well when we meet persons of other religions. In this Christian explanation, the phenomenological method is an important means for connecting with and incorporating all that is of the Word

---

79. Effective missioners are doing this all the time. See three insightful responses to the Hendrik Kraemer–William Hocking debate of 1938 (Tambaran, Madras): Antony Ellenjimittam, O.P., "A Christian Monk in a Hindu-Buddhist World"; William Temple, "The Case for Evangelization"; and Padipeddi Chenchiah, "Christianity and Non-Christian Faiths." These essays appear in Moses Jung, Swami Nikhilananda, and Herbert W. Schneider, eds., *Relations among Religions Today* (Leiden: Brill, 1963). See also Eric J. Sharpe, *Karl Ludvig Reichelt* (Hong Kong: Tao Fong Shan, 1984).

in creation into the multiply incarnated, worldwide body of Christ. If this is the case, then phenomenological study of religion is inclusivist and has theological purpose. This does not render a Christian phenomenologist in error but rather more accurate in assessment and explanation of what he or she is doing.[80]

Does this mean then that the Christian or any liberal phenomenological study of religion does not belong in the university today because it is based in faith and not in reason alone? As we have emphasized in discussion of four difficulties in the development of the academic study of religion, even those who reject religion altogether are quite obviously guided in their scholarly work by a residual faith. Consider, for example, Hegel's interest in spiritual liberation, Durkheim's interest in the social collective, Weber's interest in "charisma," or James's interest in "a sense of ease in response to the necessary."[81] One could argue that in every case, what is said by a Westerner about religion, positively or negatively, borrows a theme from the Judeo-Christian heritage. Here we encounter again Lucien Levy-Bruhl's insight that all thinking is both participative and rationative, with difference of emphasis on one or the other in different persons, cultures, or periods. Hence, even secularists are in some way guided by faith even if they have given up on religious institutions altogether. This also would be true in any culture.[82]

Once it is recognized that all knowledge is inclusive and that aspects of one perspective, religion, or culture have always been evaluated and adapted by those of others, then the so-called secular university ceases to be quite so secular as it pretends, and is recognized as the place it always has been, a place where faith commitments are shared in rational dis-

---

80. See Raimon Panikkar, *The Intra-religious Dialogue* (New York: Paulist Press, 1999), especially his "Critique of the So-Called Phenomenological Epoche in the Religious Encounter."

81. William James (1842–1910), *Varieties of Religious Experience* (New York: New American Library), 57.

82. See Tillich, *Christianity and the Encounter,* 63–79 ("The Significance of the History of Religions for the Systematic Theologian").

course according to certain cooperative rules. But what are these cooperative rules and what is their source?

A fourth difficulty with the Christian pluralist explanation of its approach is that it does not offer an adequate account of its own Christian institutional grounding. The cooperative rules of the university that enable exchanges of teachings, perspective, culture, and even religion are grounded, to a far greater extent than usually acknowledged, in what Jews and Christians have termed "covenant." Martin Buber has poetically suggested that "I" and "thou" meet each other in the eternal Thou.[83] Made in the image of the eternal Thou, the meeting of I and thou incarnates the eternal Thou, whose inclusive compassion, justice, and righteousness are to find expression in the pattern of interpersonal relations. When this happens, we are in covenant relationship with another and with the eternal Thou.[84] Covenant relations yield an intimacy, a friendship, as we have said, with Thou and with one another that is manifest in morality that is marked by denying oneself and lifting up the other. The result is covenant community in which no one person or point of view shouts or shuts down any other.[85]

Constitutional democracy, that is, democracy with guarantees of human rights, is a political order based in covenant community and supported by enlightened reason. It is precisely this covenant community, with its Judeo-Christian roots articulated by enlightened reason, that provides the cooperative rules wherein exchanges of teachings, perspective, culture, and religion take place within the modern university. It is precisely these cooperative rules, grounded in the Judeo-Christian covenant tradition, that construct the Chris-

---

83. Martin Buber, *Ich und Du,* German text published in 1923. First English translation by Ronald Gregor Smith, *I and Thou* (New York: Charles Scribner's Sons, 1958).

84. On "covenant" as human interrelations under a higher law, see Max L. Stackhouse, *Creeds, Society, and Human Rights* (Grand Rapids, Mich.: Eerdmans, 1984), 33.

85. See Sidney E. Mead, *The Nation with the Soul of a Church* (New York: Harper & Row, 1975).

tian pluralist approach. The fair-minded, descriptive work of Christian liberal phenomenological study of religion thus stands upon normative ground.

We bring this fourth point alongside the previous three. Recognizing that (1) what we call "religion" has several aspects that need careful, individual consideration, (2) religions need not be constructed as "lump" wholes in a Platonic rationalist construction that disallows evaluative judgment of particulars by particulars. Rather, interreligious interaction and evaluative sharing of aspects of religion have always been taking place. Moreover, recognizing that (3) faith is always a guide to reason in the phenomenological study of religion, (4) covenant community is not only the ground of democratic institutions and their continual reform but also the ground of the phenomenological, pluralist approach to religious dialogue.

This being the case, we would suggest that despite lack of adequate, explicit explanation in approach and method, Christian liberal, pluralist scholars of religion have tacitly been offering Christ, God's self-offering love, and Christian covenant community in interreligious dialogue and in efforts for ethical reform of political and social institutions around the world. Christian, universalizing, new covenant teachings, having enlisted the aid of enlightened reason, have transformed the levers of political power in an ethical direction with some success. Knowing this and desiring to share the good news, Christian liberal, pluralist scholars of religion reach out to the world with "interreligious dialogue" — a positively helpful, contemporary expression of the multi-incarnational covenant body of Christ (self-offering love).

Conclusion

The global era now upon us is a new *kairos* with new demands. In the late eighteenth century, Kant and Schleiermacher employed the light of reason to "true" religion in an effort to transform corrupt, misleading, and, in their view, harmful religious institutions of their time. Their efforts were part of a liberalizing trend that led not only to the academic study of religion as we know it today but to the very democratic institutions subtending and enabling that study.

In our times, at the start of the twenty-first century, matters are a bit different. The academic study of religion has constructed the concept of religion in such highly rationalist terms that it is distorting how we conceive of and live the gospel as well as share it with others. Members of other received traditions also complain of distortion by the contemporary notion of religion. This does not mean that the concept of religion and its study are not helpful. They surely are. Our argument is that alongside reason, let us recognize, explain, and encourage better the role of faith in the academic study and understanding of religion. One recommends this for every received tradition of religion.

For the marked quality of the younger generation studying religion in our secular age around the world is that these are persons seeking to understand religion in order to engage in religion deliberately for the first time. This is quite different from the days of Kant and Schleiermacher. However, the effect of a highly rationalist construction of religion is that it has rendered forms of religion or particular religions relative, nonabsolute, whereas those engaged in religion know themselves to be engaged in that which is absolute. Young people are thirsty for life lived not in relative terms but absolute terms, and they are painfully unaware of the theological grounding of their political institutions, democratic or not.[86]

The Christian pluralist explanation of its approach as it stands now is not helping a great deal. Many young people, perhaps through no fault of their own, consider the Christian liberal view to encourage relativism. While not all Christian liberals hold the Christological views that this writer does, nonetheless, one suggests that Christocentric-like views have

---

86. See Robert N. Bellah, "Religion and the Shape of National Culture," *America* 181, no. 3 (July 1999).

certainly constructed the Christian liberal and pluralist view far more than is supposed and surely more than is explained. In our times, with the needs of the next generation different from those present when the liberal movement began, rediscovery of the leading role faith continually has had in highly reasoned, methodological study of religion is needed.

In short, we need to take liberal theology, phenomenology, and pluralism to a deeper level of self-recognition for ourselves, for our students, and for our friends of other religions. By allowing, understanding, and explaining better the role of faith in liberal endeavors, we may correct distortions of omission and distortions of commission that have allowed reason to operate without noticing faith. By greater recognition of the role of faith in the Christian, or Hindu, or Muslim, or *Ru* (Confucian) liberal position, scholars may recognize themselves as more continuous with orthodox tradition than perhaps thought. This recognition of links with orthodoxy has the positive effect of encouraging others to reciprocate, with greater willingness to employ highly reasoned understanding of religion and interactive religious history as a means to live in faith more truly and to share better what we have to offer with others.

Liberals of any received tradition have the same purpose to engage reason alongside faith to reform religious, social, and political institutions. As Christian liberals, let us advocate interreligious dialogue for its Christian covenant approach to denying oneself and lifting up the other in mutual trust that allows deep and transforming evaluative assessment and contribution to each other. Such dialogue can render each received tradition of religion, as it is strengthened by contributions of others, an inclusive, ever-being-transformed whole that is better equipped for ethical reform of social and political institutions.[87] In this manner, liberalism continues alive

---

87. Concerning the "central event" to which Paul Tillich referred, see Tillich, *Christianity and the Encounter*, 22, 49–79. See also David J. Krieger, *The New Universalism: Foundations for a Global Theology* (Maryknoll, N.Y.: Orbis Books, 1991).

and well and offers still more to a global era of interconnected oneness with need for dynamic regional and local community.

Each inclusive religious whole will be tested for its ability to receive and to be significantly transformed by other contributions while at the same time continuing to live in terms of its own contribution in ethically reformed social and political institutions. The gospel of Christ, the gift of new covenant community, is a gift that receives all gifts, but it too will be tested. In Christian faith, guided self-consciously and deliberately by the Spirit of Christ, who does not cease to lead us in recognizing God's inclusive, compassionate love and justice wherever it appears, let us offer the gospel and receive the gifts of others in Christian covenant community as we engage in interactive pluralist dialogue. In so doing, we shall ever receive and be strengthened by Christ coming to us in sources and traditions as yet unknown to us.

In the words of Father Iwuchukwu from Nigeria in his eulogy on the Great Commission on Unity Sunday, January 2000: "Go and enlist all who are turning back to God, even in ways you do not fully understand."[88] Father Iwuchukwu had it just right.

---

88. In this eulogy, given at St. Michael's Cathedral in Toronto, Father Iwuchukwu was commenting on the grand passage from Isaiah, "I will make an everlasting covenant with you" (Isa 55:3). At the time of Jesus' teaching, there was a movement already engaged in turning back to God. Father Iwuchukwu explained that Jesus was telling his disciples to go and corporately identify with this movement. Wilfred Smith, who, on this Unity Sunday, I was visiting for the last time, dedicated his life and intellectual work to doing precisely this.

– Chapter 2 –

THE GLOBAL RESURGENCE OF RELIGION AND THE CHANGING CHARACTER OF INTERNATIONAL POLITICS

Scott Thomas

One of the main debates among theorists of international relationships is the nature of the social bonds that hold states together as an international society. This debate has brought together theorists of the otherwise sharply contending schools of neorealist structuralism (the current versions of the traditions of Thucydides, Machiavelli, Hobbes, and Rousseau) and of neoliberal institutionalism (the contemporary forms of the traditions from Grotius, Kant, Bentham, and Rawls). They have belatedly come together, for they increasingly recognize that they both share certain assumptions.[1] First, they both have a functional conception of international politics; second, they both adhere to the "Westphalian presumption" in international relations. The first presumes that there are no normative principles or values that can or should trump those created and imposed by material and social forces, such as the power of the state. The second assumes that religion

---

This essay is related to and partly draws from my "Taking Religious and Cultural Pluralism Seriously," delivered to a conference on Religion and International Relations at the London School of Economics in May 2000. That paper is forthcoming in *Millennium: The Journal of International Studies.*

1. See Michael Doyle, *Ways of War and Peace* (New York: W. W. Norton, 1997).

is not rational and that its truth claims cannot be allowed to gain dominant influence in states or to shape a genuinely international society, for the irrational passions of religion lead to conflict and war. Religion, and its inevitable social and cultural implications, must be privatized, marginalized, or confined to an isolated sphere by the state, or entirely surpassed by scientific or instrumental reason if there is to be any genuine international order.

However, the Western form of modernity and the institutions of international society that these realist and liberal assumptions have embedded in our current culture are being challenged by the global resurgence of religion as well as by a new awareness of cultural pluralism in international relations. As a result of the large-scale religious change now underway, international society is becoming a genuinely multicultural, global, civil society for the very first time. Therefore, a new approach to international order is required, one which acknowledges the global role of religion and its inevitable social and cultural pluralism, and takes it seriously in international relations.

This essay explores the debate over the nature of international society and why it is unlikely that neorealism and neoliberal institutionalism will be able to provide an adequate basis for international order. The one presumes an international anarchy that influences and constrains the behavior of states, and the other emphasizes a rationalistic or utilitarian adherence to laws, rules, and principles that does the same. This essay also expresses doubts about how sensitive to cultural difference a "cosmopolitan" ethic can be if it denies the role of religion in society and if it is based on the highly individualistic culture of a Western modernity at odds with the way most people in the world, which means the developing "two-thirds world," live out their moral lives.[2]

---

2. Although many of the issues in the "cosmopolitan-communitarian" debate in international relations theory are relevant to this essay, it is meant to be more of an attempt to think through the implications of the global resurgence of religion for international relations than a contribution to this debate. On this debate, however,

The final part of the essay suggests how dialogue between social traditions may allow us to take religious and cultural pluralism seriously in international relations.

The Global Resurgence of Religion

The resurgence of religion can be seen in the growing saliency of religion in the politics of countries throughout the world. It is occurring in countries with different religious traditions and in countries at different levels of economic development, so it cannot be explained as a feature of any one religion or of some lack of development that makes people religious.

In some respects, the global resurgence of religion exposes the larger crisis of modernity. This crisis reflects a deeper and more widespread disillusionment with perspectives that reduce the world to that which can be perceived and controlled through reason, science, technology, and bureaucratic rationality, and leaves out considerations of the spiritual or the sacred dimensions of life. Insofar as postmodernism shows a greater sensitivity to the human limits of what Max Weber identified a century ago as the "disenchantment of the world," postmodernists share a basic insight with those theologians, cultural critics, artists, and activists in the so-called new social movements who recognize the limits of this disenchantment and express them through their concerns about the rat race, materialism, the environment, or the commodification of everyday life in a global economy, even though they may not recognize these concerns as religious or spiritual in nature. For these reasons, the twentieth century may be the last modern century; the postmodern world of the global society will be a postsecular one as well.[3]

see the article by Chris Brown, Peter Sutch, and David Morrice, "Communitarianism and Its Critics," *Review of International Studies* 26, no. 2 (April 2000).

3. See Scott Thomas, "Religious Resurgence, Postmodernism, and World Politics," in *Religion and Global Order*, ed. John Esposito and Michael Watson (Cardiff: University of Wales Press, 2000), 38–65; Robert Wuthnow, "Understanding Religion

In other respects, the global resurgence of religion is the result of the failure of modernizing, secular states to produce enduring democracy or genuine development in the most needy lands. Ernest Gellner has argued that since the period of colonial occupation, the developing countries have been confronted with a dilemma: Should they emulate the West in order to gain equality in power (thus spurning their own culture), or should they affirm their own cultural and religious traditions (thus remaining materially weak)?[4] In many countries, the desire for a new identity and rapid development was pursued in the first years after independence by emulating the West. The generation of Third World elites that came to power beginning in the late 1940s (largely following the model of Ataturk's Turkey in the 1920s) — in, for example, Nehru's India, Nasser's Egypt, and Sukarno's Indonesia — espoused a similar "modernizing mythology" inherited from the West. That mythology included a profound trust in the benevolent effects of secularism in culture, participatory democracy in politics, socialism in economics, and nonalignment in foreign policy. These elites believed that strong "development-oriented states" could promote cultural independence, political stability, and economic achievement, and that these would all be undermined if religion, or considerations of ethnicity or faith or community loyalty, dominated politics.[5]

The failure of this modernizing mythology to produce what it promised, and the failure of the modernizing secular states it engendered, is evident in what is identified as "political decay,"[6] the decline of politics into authoritarianism, patrimonialism, and corruption since the late 1960s, and by

---

and Politics," *Daedalus* 120, no. 3 (Summer 1991): 1–20; and "The Last Modern Century," *New Perspectives Quarterly* 8, no. 2 (1991).

4. See Ernest Gellner, *Postmodernism, Reason, and Religion* (London: Routledge, 1992).

5. James Mayall, "International Society and International Theory," in *The Reason of States,* ed. Michael Donelan (London: Allen & Unwin, 1978), 133–36.

6. See Samuel P. Huntington, *Political Order and Changing Societies* (Cambridge, Mass.: Harvard University Press, 1968).

"political collapse,"[7] the disintegration of some states, particularly in Africa, since the late 1980s. Dissatisfaction with the project of postcolonial secular statism and the conflict between religious and secular nationalism was one of the most important developments in politics in the 1990s.[8]

The global resurgence of religion also manifests the search for authenticity and development in the Third World. The global resurgence of religion in developing countries can be seen as part of the "revolt against the West." Hedley Bull, one of the premier theorists of international relations of the post–World War II generation, identified what could be called three "waves of revolt." The first, from the 1940s through the 1960s, was the anticolonial struggle for independence and equality as sovereign states; the second, from the 1970s through the 1980s, was the struggle for racial equality and economic justice; and the third, less clearly defined in time, Bull called the struggle for cultural liberation, the "reassertion of traditional and indigenous cultures" in what was often called "the Third World."[9]

The struggle for cultural liberation could be relabeled as the global "struggle for authenticity and development." It became more powerful in the 1990s. In the Third World, the modernizing, secular state has failed to provide a legitimate basis for political participation or to provide the conditions for basic economic welfare. In many developing societies, secular nationalism and Marxism have failed to produce economic development and viable political participation, sometimes leading to increased poverty. And while the neoliberal pre-

---

7. See I. W. Zartman, *Collapsed States: The Disintegration and Restoration of Legitimate Authority* (Boulder, Colo.: Lynne Rienner, 1995).

8. See Mark Juergensmeyer, *The New Cold War: Religious Nationalism Confronts the Secular State* (Berkeley: University of California Press, 1993); Jeff Haynes, *Religion in Third World Politics* (London: Open University Press, 1994); David Westerlund, ed., *Questioning the Secular State: The Worldwide Resurgence of Religion in Politics* (London: I. B. Tauris, 1996).

9. Hedley Bull, "The Revolt against the West," in *The Expansion of International Society,* ed. Hedley Bull and Adam Watson (Oxford: Clarendon Press, 1984), 217–28.

scription of free markets and open economies has seemingly produced more wealth, it has done so with considerable inequality, both internally in these countries and in comparison with more developed societies. Many feel that they can never catch up. Because of this situation, "authenticity has begun to rival development as the key to understanding the aspirations of the non-Western World."[10] The search for authentic identity as the key to governmental, economic, and cultural policy indicates a new direction in the politics of developing countries. We face multiple attempts to "indigenize" modernity rather than a common effort to "modernize" traditional societies.

As a result of this new "revolt of the masses," states with greater political participation are having to respond to more popular, less elitist, less secular perspectives on politics. This means modernizing political elites have to be more responsive to the religious concerns of ordinary people. This has not only shaped domestic policy, it has more surprisingly influenced the foreign policies of developing countries as well, often in ways unanticipated by students of international affairs. Because the values of religion tend to generate cultures that strongly influence social policy, social policy has become foreign policy. This was mostly clearly seen in the UN conferences on Human Rights, Women, and Population, where the culture of Western modernity (the UN's social development agenda) confronted the new assertiveness of developing countries, some of which sought to protect the privileges of their traditional elites but others of whom wanted greater sensitivity to their religious and cultural values in the formation of social policy[11] and a greater appreciation of the fact that

---

10. See Robert Lee, *Overcoming Tradition and Modernity: The Search for Islamic Authenticity* (Boulder, Colo.: Westview Press, 1997).

11. See John Finn, "Human Rights in Vienna," *First Things* (November 1993); George Weigel, "What Really Happened at Cairo, and Why," in *The 9 Lives of Population Control,* ed. Michael Cromartie (Washington, D.C.: Ethics and Public Policy Center, 1995), 129–48; and Mary Ann Glendon, "What Happened in Beijing," *First Things* (January 1996): 30–36.

one dialect of human rights — the dialect of a rights-based liberalism of a highly individualistic culture that predominated in the delegations from the United States — was being globalized without due regard for what is most human and most right in other countries.[12]

For all these reasons, the global resurgence of religion and the spread of cultural pluralism need to be examined more broadly than by notions of the "clash of civilizations," "fundamentalism," or "religious extremism," as if the global resurgence of religion is an aberration in an otherwise "modern" world. What is happening is that a truly multicultural global international society is being formed for the first time. Therefore, coming to terms with this large-scale religious change, and taking its cultural and social effects seriously, will be an important part of the international politics of this century.[13]

Contending Views of International Society

Common to most definitions of society is the notion of a social bond that holds the units (individuals, city-states, or states) together as a group with common obligations and common purposes all members recognize. The nature of this bond — what is subjective, organic, or traditional about it, and what is objective, functional, or contractual about it — is central to recent debates in the international society tradition. The issue is relevant, for it bears on the basis and nature of international cooperation. Because of the global resurgence of religion and the assertion of cultural pluralism, the nature of this social bond also has been part of the growing debate on ethics and international society over the role of common rules, inter-

---

12. See Mary Ann Glendon, *Rights Talk: The Impoverishment of Political Discourse* (New York: Free Press, 1991).

13. See Esposito and Watson, *Religion and Global Order;* Ken R. Dark, ed., *Religion and International Relations* (London: Macmillan, 2000); and Jeff Haynes, ed., *Religion, Globalization and Political Culture in the Third World* (London: Macmillan, 1999).

ests, or conceptions of justice in any meaningful conception of international society.[14]

A crucial aspect of the idea of international society has to do with understanding the subjective difference between participating in a system as a part, and belonging to society as a member. These imply distinctive views of the rights and obligations that are valued by the whole or by the other members. This subjective aspect, the sense of being bound by certain rules and institutions, was crucial to Bull's understanding because it was for them what distinguished a society from a system.[15]

Most scholars of international relations today recognize that simple compliance with international rules, norms, or laws is not what determines the existence of international society. As Bull pointed out, almost intimating what is now called a "constructivist" understanding of international society, rules and laws are intellectual and social constructs that the states accept as part of the idea of international society. "The element of international society," he wrote, "has always been present in the modern international system because at no stage can it be said that the conception of the common interests of states, of common rules accepted and common institutions worked by them, has ceased to exert an influence."[16] Where does this sense of commonality come from?

Earlier exponents of the international society tradition assumed that a degree of cultural unity among states was an important part of any meaningful conception of international society. They recognized that a common culture was one of the most important foundations for international societies of

14. See B. A. Roberson, ed., *International Society and the Development of International Relations Theory* (London: Pinter, 1998); and David R. Mapel and Terry Nardin, eds., *International Society: Diverse Ethical Perspectives* (Princeton, N.J.: Princeton University Press, 1998).

15. See Tim Dunne, *Inventing International Society: A History of the English School* (London: Macmillan, 1998); and Nicholas J. Wheeler and Tim Dunne, "Hedley Bull and the Idea of a Universal Moral Community: Fictional, Primordial or Imagined?" in Roberson, *International Society,* 43–57.

16. See Hedley Bull, *The Anarchical Society* (London: Macmillan, 1977), 42.

the past. The ancient regional state systems or international
societies (e.g., the Mediterranean, China, South Asia), and of
course European international society more recently, all arose
within a single dominant culture, even if in some instances
a political hegemony was responsible for the spread of the
common culture that formed the more enduring foundation
of international society.[17]

How did the elements of a common culture facilitate such
civilizations and the workings of international society? Bull
suggests this happened in two ways. First, a common culture
makes for better communications and understanding between
states, and thus facilitates the definition of common rules
and the evolution of common institutions. Second, a common
culture reinforces the common interests that impel states to
accept rules and institutions that reflect common values.[18]

Today, European international society has become a global
international society. This global international society, however, is expanding around the world without any overt general
conception of what the common culture is or in what the
civilization is grounded, unlike the earlier Christian-shaped
culture that allowed the international society of "European
civilization" to develop. Because of the importance of culture
to the foundations of international society, Bull speculated
on how "the prospects of international society [were] bound
up with the prospects of the cosmopolitan culture," what we
would call the culture of Western modernity, which underlies the working of contemporary global international society.
And the question, of course, is whether an entirely secular
understanding of that culture can sustain its best, guide its
ambiguous, and constrain its worst aspects.

Bull distinguished between a "common intellectual culture" — a common language and a common epistemological

---

17. See Adam Watson, introduction to *The Evolution of International Society*
(London: Routledge, 1991); M. Wight, "De systematibus civitatum," in *Systems of
States* (Leicester: Leicester University Press, 1977), 21–45; and Nicholas J. Rengger,
"Culture, Society, and Order in World Politics," in *Dilemmas of World Politics,* ed.
John Baylis and N. J. Rengger (Oxford: Oxford University Press, 1992), 85–103.
18. Bull, *Anarchical Society,* 16.

outlook that facilitated communications and dialogue between states — and "elements of a common culture" more generally. The intellectual culture he divided into an "international political culture," which determined attitudes toward the state system, and a "diplomatic culture," which included the ideas and values of officials involved in formal diplomacy. In addition to these, Bull considered a common religion or a common moral code to be the "elements of a common culture," and also considered these necessary for international society, because they reinforced "the sense of common interests that united the states by a sense of common obligations."[19] While he held that even in the 1970s there are elements of a common culture in international society, at least at the elite level as part of the diplomatic culture, Bull recognized that the elite culture of diplomacy was already being eroded by the democratization of diplomacy and the rise of new varieties of mass politics, which have spread globally since then.

A related element to which he pointed was the increasingly common intellectual culture among the "global elite," which Peter Berger has more recently identified as the professors, intellectuals, development workers, and policy makers from the West, and their counterparts, the so-called modernizing elites of the Third World.[20] Even then Bull acknowledged its "roots are shallow in many societies," and he doubted whether the international political culture, even at the diplomatic level, embraced a common morality or set of common values. Nevertheless, Bull suggested that the preservation and extension of a cosmopolitan culture could provide what he called world, or global, international society with the kind of cultural unity that underpinned the culturally more homogeneous international societies of the past.[21] He acknowledged that this cosmopolitan culture favored the West, now a

---

19. Ibid., 31.

20. See Peter Berger, ed., *The Desecularization of the World: Resurgent Religion and World Politics* (Grand Rapids, Mich.: Eerdmans, 1999).

21. On the distinctions between "international society," "global international so-

common enough criticism of critical and postmodern perspectives on international relations. But Bull also speculated this cosmopolitan culture would have to absorb non-Western elements to a much greater degree if it was to provide the basis for a global international society.[22] Still, apart from appeals for "sensitivity" and scattered efforts at "dialogue," Bull's challenge remains largely unheeded. We may need other options.

The trends Bull speculated on in the 1970s have become more powerful with the global resurgence of religion and the struggle for authenticity and development after the end of the Cold War, making the resolution of his challenge more difficult. The notion of a common intellectual culture, even if its roots were shallow among the modernizing elites of the Third World at the time of independence, is now even shallower among both elite and mass society in developing countries today. Even at the level of the professional diplomat, efforts to identify a common moral culture or set of common values have been undermined by the fact that foreign policy is increasingly seen as a matter of social policy (e.g., debates over human rights, women in society, health care, population, and corporate or labor policies) and not as the building of a stable structure and the formation of a committed, capable leadership for international negotiations and diplomatic bargaining within it.

Furthermore, postmodernism has undermined the idea of a common intellectual culture with a common epistemological outlook (deriving from the Enlightenment) among the global elite — both Western elites and the Western-educated elites from around the world, who could have helped underpin a global international society. At the same time, a growing debate is taking place about whether globalization has created, discovered, or imposed new values in a global civil society. Thus, the idea of a cosmopolitan culture, even

---

ciety," and "world society," see "Beyond International Society," *Millennium* 21, no. 3 (1992).
    22. Bull, *Anarchical Society,* 317.

to the limited extent that it may have existed in the past, has been undermined by postmodern perspectives that may eviscerate ethical imperatives of their moral power in international relations. From the cosmopolitan perspective, the global resurgence of religion can only be greeted with dismay as religion once again becomes a source of intolerance and conflict in international relations.

The Decline of the Social Bond in International Society

The international society tradition of scholarly and professional understanding has come closer to what political theorists call "neorealism" and "neoliberal institutionalism." Whatever their differences, they both have a decided emphasis on the objective aspect of any social bond that constitutes international society, and this bond is often examined in response to two events. First, it is widely perceived that the hegemonic power of the United States has declined since the 1970s, especially since Vietnam. No longer does rhetoric about the United States being "the leader of the free world," backed by overwhelming nuclear power, seem compelling. This fact has provoked a quest for a theoretical as well as practical basis for international cooperation without the dominance of a single power. Second, the global resurgence of religion is increasingly perceived as evidence of a genuinely multicultural global international society for the first time in human history. The idea that secularization would automatically be a part of progress, eliminating conflicts based on religious difference, is no longer compelling either. Both events have undermined the subjective aspect of the social bond that constitutes international society.[23]

---

23. Until recently, the debate about the decline in U.S. hegemony has received more attention in the literature. See Charles Kegley, ed., *Controversies in International Relations: Realism and the Neoliberal Challenge* (New York: St. Martin's Press, 1995); and Robert Keohane, ed., *International Institutions and State Power: Essays in International Relations Theory* (Boulder, Colo.: Westview Press, 1989).

It could be argued that the subjective aspect of the social bond that constitutes international society has been in decline since the Westphalian construction of international society. Indeed, the Westphalian presumption in international relations was formed in the aftermath of the wars of religion. Religious and cultural pluralism could not be accommodated even within the more limited confines of European international society but had to be privatized, marginalized, made subservient to state power, or even overcome if there was to be international order.

The global expansion of international society, the incorporation of non-Western cultures and societies into a global international society, and the more recent global resurgence of religion have brought into prominence the role of religion and culture in international relations. Both events, the decline in the hegemonic power of the United States and the global resurgence of religion, require a better theoretical understanding of international cooperation and the basis of international order if there is to be cooperation, the compliance with international norms and international laws, or adherence to principles of international ethics in a truly multicultural global international society.

Both neorealism and neoliberal institutionalism emphasize the objective aspect of the social bond that constitutes international society by holding to a functional understanding of international society. British scholars have tried to bring together neorealism and the international society tradition, using Ferdinand Tönnies's concepts of *Gemeinschaft* and *Gesellschaft*. A *gemeinschaftlich* understanding of international society grows organically from a shared culture, involving bonds of common sentiment, experience, and identity. Such could be found in the interlocked system of the ancient Greek *poloi* or the city-states of Renaissance Italy as well as federations of tribal communities. These can be distinguished from a *gesellschaftlich* understanding of international society as something that is mechanical, contractual, and constructed. A *gesellschaftlich* understanding sees the development of international society as a rational and functional response to the existence of an increasing density of contacts and interests that form a coalition of interactions among states in an international system. In this view, it makes little difference whether or not peoples or states share a common culture. At some point, the regularity, intensity, and scope of their interactions will force the development of a degree of recognition and accommodation between them, and they will pragmatically work out rules for avoiding conflicts and for facilitating exchanges desired by states. International society can evolve functionally from the logic of anarchy without preexisting cultural or moral bonds.[24]

Neoliberal institutionalists give a variety of explanations, quite apart from either hegemonic stability or "idealist" appeals to altruism, for why states may adhere to international norms, laws, or regimes, but they explain why international cooperation is still possible only within a functional conception of international society. First, they effectively concede one of the realist explanations for international cooperation. States do pursue their self-interests, and one of those interests, as Hans Morgenthau has explained, is the concern of states to put their relations on a stable basis by providing for predicable and enforceable procedural rules or laws of conduct between states.[25]

Second, they argue that states can gain in economic terms by reducing transaction costs of monitoring compliance, building confidence if not trust, and creating the possibili-

---

24. See Barry Buzan, "From International System to International Society: Realism and Regime Theory Meet the English School," *International Organisation* 47, no. 3 (Summer 1993): 327–52; Barry Buzan, Charles Jones, and Richard Little, *The Logic of Anarchy: Neorealist Structuralism to Structural Realism* (New York: Columbia University Press, 1993); Andrew Hurrell, "International Society and the Study of Regimes: A Reflective Approach," in *Regime Theory and International Relations,* ed. Volker R. Rittberger and P. Meyer (Oxford: Oxford University Press, 1993), 49–72; Tony Evans and Peter Wilson, "Regime Theory and the English School of International Relations," *Millennium* 21, no. 3 (1992): 329–51.

25. See Robert Keohane, "International Institutions: Two Approaches," in *International Theory: Critical Investigations,* ed. James Der Derian (London: Macmillan, 1995), 279–307.

ties of mutual gain, as a result of the rational calculations between self-interested states. States also can gain in political terms, stability, and peace, rather than in conflict and war, by setting up regimes that can change the expectations of states and change the pattern of their transaction costs. Even under conditions of international anarchy, regimes can help provide important information, through monitoring, and help to stabilize expectations among states.[26] They may also make decentralized enforcement possible by creating conditions in which degrees of reciprocity can operate.[27] Thus, regimes can facilitate international cooperation in ways that are in the long-term rational interests of states even though they may not be in the short-term rational interest of states unless international institutions can change the rules and expectations of states in the international system.[28]

Third, neoliberals argue that the reputation of states may be another reason for compliance among states in international society. States may comply with the norms or laws of international society or cooperate in international institutions because of what this means for their reputation among other states. In a functional understanding of international society common to both neorealist structuralism and neoliberal institutionalism, what is missing is a shared sense of identity, of belonging, and of obligation among states in international society. In fact, the absence of such ethical claims is considered to be a positive aspect of the theory of neoliberal institutionalism because it seemingly presents a way for interested states to pursue international cooperation without appeals to altruism or hegemonic stability. It presents a theory that seems to use realist assumptions for idealist ends.

Although there has been a sense of discomfort among some scholars with a concept of international society with-

---

26. See Robert Keohane, *After Hegemony* (Princeton, N.J.: Princeton University Press, 1984).
27. See Robert Keohane, "Reciprocity in International Relations," in *International Institutions and State Power* (Denver: Westview Press, 1989), 132–57.
28. See Keohane, "International Institutions."

out a sense of shared identity, this lack of common identity is considered to be an inevitable consequence of modernity. Scholars do not consider a *gemeinschaftlich* understanding of international society to be useful for building a theory of cooperation in a global multicultural international society. Therefore, many argue that a *gesellschaftlich* theory of international society must be generated to explain why cooperation under international anarchy has taken place in the past. Moreover, such a theory must be prescriptive for how international cooperation can take place on a whole host of global issues that confront a multicultural global international society.[29]

Some Critiques of Secular Modernity

The neorealist and neoliberal theories of international cooperation, on the basis of which most postwar interaction has taken place, may not be as detached from concerns of religion and culture as the theory suggests. The shift from earlier American isolationism to engagement with the world requires looking for changes inside the United States as well as those in the wider world. In other words, it requires looking at the role of domestic politics in the construction and breakdown of regimes, and this may require a closer study of the relationship between Protestantism and hegemonic stability. Reinhold Niebuhr and an influential coalition of "Christian realists" and "Christian liberals" became what Heather Warren has called "the theologians of a new world order." They, perhaps more than any other group, helped change America's political culture so that it was willing to accept the responsibilities of leadership during the war. Also, it was they who, immediately after the war, not only backed the Marshall Plan but also engaged in the construction of the Bretton Woods

---

29. Ole Waever, "Four Meanings of International Society," in Roberson, ed., *International Society,* 92.

system.[30] This relationship between a form of ecumenical, if also rather hegemonic, Protestantism and a guiding moral-practical quest for stability during the turbulent postwar era is all the more striking because of the relative absence of any substantive theology of world order supporting an active engagement of the United States in international relations today. One wing of Protestantism has become more evangelical and the other more liberationist; neither is widely regarded by political theorists or specialists in international relations, even among those sympathetic to the place of theology and religion in international public life.[31]

The relationship between that form of Protestantism and the relative stability it brought suggests a factor common to both theories of neorealist structuralism and neoliberal institutionalism, which until recently has not elicited much comment, since it is assumed by both rather than explained. This factor is the "rationality" of states as actors, which served as an explanation for state action in ways that detached policies, judgments, and presumed values from the larger world of religions, cultures, or even civilizations in which states are socially and historically embodied. This omission seemed even more acute as more and more evidence came to the fore that states are not entirely self-generating realities but are molded by the societies within which they are em-

---

30. See Heather A. Warren, *Theologians of a New World Order: Reinhold Niebuhr and the Christian Realists, 1920–1948* (Oxford: Oxford University Press, 1997).

31. Most evangelicals, who have more recently come to dominate American Protestantism and exert influence on American politics, have often infused political discourse with views of government and world order rooted in certain interpretations of biblical eschatology. They have thus reinforced those trends in society that support neoisolationism or unilateralism in U.S. foreign policy. See Harriet A. Harris, "Theological Reflections on Religious Resurgence and International Stability: A Look at Protestant Evangelicalism," in *Religion and International Relations*, ed. Ken R. Dark (London: Macmillan, 2000), 24–49. Most liberationists have become so focused on the ideological interpretation of the local contexts of the marginalized that they have contributed little to reconstructing larger visions of human life, society, and destiny, visions that could do more to aid the dispossessed than their petty efforts. See Max L. Stackhouse et al., *Christian Social Ethics in a Global Era* (Nashville: Abingdon Press, 1988).

bedded.[32] Because of the spread of modernization, of which secularization was often considered to be an inherent part, the importance of religion to the embodiment of national states was either denied or no longer considered to be relevant to political analysis (as states were thought to become truly internationally respectable by making the inevitable transition from traditional to modern society). The "Westphalian presumption" has come to pervade the leading understandings of the evolution of international relations in the modern world, and actual formative forces were ignored.

One much debated critique of this view is found in the work of Alasdair MacIntyre, who has sharply disputed the idea of a rationality detached from culture. Indeed, some of his admirers have understood his argument, or augmented it, to the effect that it is not necessarily detached from religion either. Further, some argue, as do several contributors to this set of volumes, that this is not because religion is based on irrationalities but because profound religion has, in the depths of its traditions, highly reasonable dimensions that are indispensable to society and that it is irrational to subordinate these dimensions to the less rational interests of the state. Such criticisms have become now part of a well-known critique of the Enlightenment project with all its ambiguities in regard to the secular forms of realism and liberal institutionalism, especially since both claim self-evident rational superiority to the religious and cultural traditions that shape civilizations.[33] Less well-known, however, is his proposal re-

---

32. As a balance to the "bringing the state back" model for the future, this book offers a "state in society" approach. See Joel S. Migdal, Atul Kohli, and Vivienne Shue, *State Power and Social Forces: Domination and Transformation in the Third World* (Cambridge: Cambridge University Press, 1994).

33. As to whether MacIntyre's emphasis on social tradition means that he is a "radical" or a "conservative" is, of course, much debated. See Kelvin Knight, introduction to *The MacIntyre Reader*, ed. Kelvin Knight (Cambridge: Polity Press, 1998), 20–24; "Revolutionary Aristotelianism," in *Contemporary Political Studies 1996*, vol. 2, ed. I. Hampshire-Monk and J. Stanyer (1996); and Alasdair MacIntyre, "Politics, Philosophy, and the Common Good," in Knight, ed., *MacIntyre Reader*, 235–52. On the other hand, see Edward T. Oakes, "The Achievement of Alasdair MacIntyre," *First Things* (August–September 1996): 22–26; and Gilbert Meilaender, "Still Waiting for Benedict," *First Things* (October 1999): 48–55.

garding ethical pluralism among different social traditions. This, however, not only may be directly relevant to a dialogue between cultures and societies, but may suggest possibilities that he did not recognize with regard to interactions between religions and civilizations in a multicultural, multireligious global international society.[34]

According to MacIntyre, the moral problem of modern societies is that the moral concepts and ethical conceptions used in ethical discourse, including debates about war and peace, are fragments of conceptual schemes that have been separated from the historical and social contexts that give them meaning and coherence in discussions about morality. MacIntyre argues that these values and ethical conceptions about the nature of the good, what is just, what is right, and notions of obligation, and the rationality on which they are based, are socially embodied in particular social traditions and communities. There is no rationality independent of tradition, no "view from nowhere," and no set of rules or principles that will commend itself to all independent of their conception of the good.[35] What makes it "rational" to act in one way and not in another way is the conception of the good embodied in a particular social tradition or community.[36]

---

34. As Kelvin Knight remarks, "The full significance of MacIntyre's demolition job [of modern philosophies and politics] in *After Virtue* is only comprehensible in the light of his construction, in subsequent essays, of the premises of an alternative." Knight, introduction to *MacIntyre Reader*, 1.

35. See Alasdair MacIntyre, *After Virtue: A Study in Moral Theory,* 2d ed. (London: Duckworth, 1985); and *Whose Justice? Which Rationality?* (London: Duckworth, 1988).

36. The concept of a social tradition as MacIntyre treats it is this: Practices and the virtues necessary are part of a wider social and historical context called a social tradition. A set of practices constitutes a tradition. Traditions can be religious or moral (Catholicism, Islam, or humanism), economic (a particular craft such as basket weaving on the Somerset Levels, a profession, trade union, or guild), aesthetic (types of literature or painting), or geographical (centered on the history or culture of a house, village, or region). The concept has been ideologically used to contrast tradition with reason, and it has been used to compare the backwardness and stability of traditional society with the conflict and social change necessary for the emergence of modern society. For MacIntyre, however, the most important social conflicts take place *within* traditions as well as *between* them. These conflicts are about the various incommensurable goods that members of a particular tradition pursue, and *a viable tradition is one that holds conflicting social, political, and metaphysical claims in a*

Therefore, the "rationality" associated with the construction of the national interest cannot be separated from the matters of religion and culture that shape, inform, and determine the conception of the good among particular social traditions and communities.[37]

Another aspect of both neorealist structuralism and neoliberal institutionalism that has also elicited little comment, at least until recently, is the investigation of what constitutes the unit of analysis, the national states, on which the theory is based. States are simply assumed to be both the dominant actors and to have self-explanatory interests (i.e., national interests) that can rationally be appealed to so they can maximize their gains and minimize their losses in the international system.

The appeal to a rationality detached from religion or culture accepts uncritically the assumptions of the Enlightenment

---

creative way. When traditions begin to break down, modern bureaucratic organizations arise. Traditional societies have always had formal organizations, and those in authority have always had to justify themselves by appeals to the authority of the tradition the organization serves. Traditions, however, cannot continue to exist unless they are embodied and re-embodied in organizations, and organizations create managers. At least in traditional societies it would seem managers can only control the organization and not the tradition. This is the familiar story of the conflict between royal and church law in the twelfth century (within a tradition of kingship) or debates between the old and new astronomy in the seventeenth century (the story of the role of women in Christianity or Islam today). MacIntyre, however, claims there is a much greater danger from ideology in modern formal organizations where traditions are endangered. This is why the recognition of social tradition is necessary to understanding the relationship between conflict, ideology, and organization in political life. See Alasdair MacIntyre, "Social Science Methodology as the Ideology of Bureaucratic Authority," in Knight, ed., *MacIntyre Reader,* 53–68.

37. MacIntyre's philosophical argument is given anthropological depth and historical support by Adda Bozeman's study of international law in different civilizations (the West, Islam [the Middle East], Africa, India, and China). She concludes that "differences between cultures and political systems are functions primarily of different modes of perceiving and evaluating reality." Her study also shows, as Hedley Bull has pointed out more generally, that religion has been the main basis for order in most times and cultures. She also states, "Whether viewed as a set of concepts, norms, or social institutions, law everywhere is linked, explicitly or implicitly, with [these] schemes of social and political organization." Adda Bozeman, *The Future of Law in a Multi-cultural World* (Princeton, N.J.: Princeton University Press, 1971), ix–xiii. Her general perspective that political systems are grounded in cultures and that present-day international relations are therefore by definition also intercultural relations is elaborated in her earlier (and now updated book), *Politics and Culture in International History* (New Brunswick, N.J.: Transaction Publishers, 1994).

project as well as it considers the notion of identity to be irrelevant to foreign policy analysis. This is the case unless concerns about identity are transformed into concerns about the national interest. The identity of states is considered to be unimportant to both realists and liberals in international relations. The difference between them is between short-term and long-term conceptions of the national interest, since realists believe states seek rationally to maximize their interests in the short-term while liberals believe states can rationally seek to forgo short-term gain in order to achieve long-term common interests. In both perspectives the identity of the state is a given part of the explanation of state action. Both presume an instrumental view of reason, as if the rational, reasonable, and logical in human affairs is entirely utilitarian. Questions of order and identity are simply considered to be unimportant. Human beings are considered to act according to "purposive" action; that is, their actions are explained only by reference to the "interests" of the person, social group, community, or even state that performs them. They act in order to gain utility or to minimize their loss — that is, they purposively act to relate means to ends in a way that maximizes their utility or interests, which is thought to be the end of policy.[38]

The neorealist form of this theory of rational action, however, fails if individuals, social groups, or even states act not only to gain tangible things (e.g., territory or access to resources) but to establish, protect, or defend a certain conception of who they are or what they believe God wants them to become. They act not only because there are things they want to have but also because there is a certain conception or understanding of the kind of persons, societies, communities, or even states they want to be in the world. If this is the case, then a form of action in defense of authenticity, identity, and faithfulness is more fundamental than a form of action in defense of interests. What is or is not an interest depends on

---

38. See Erik Ringmar, *Identity, Interest, and Action: A Cultural Explanation of Sweden's Intervention in the Thirty Years War* (Cambridge: Cambridge University Press, 1996).

some conception of individual or collective authenticity and being, as well as some conception of the good life for individuals, societies, or even states. Thus, actions undertaken in order to establish, protect, or defend this someone, this conception of being, are more basic, and cannot be "re-described" in terms of interests because calculations of interests only make sense when they can be attached to a particular person, social group, or community who has them.[39]

On this basis, Eric Ringmar tries to answer one of the conundrums of modern European history: Why did Sweden intervene in the Thirty Years' War when it was obviously not in its national interest to do so? His provocative answer is that Sweden acted to establish the country's national identity rather than to defend its national interests. Similarly, explanations can be given for why Iraq invaded Kuwait during the Gulf War, why Somalia invaded Ethiopia in the Ogaden War of the 1970s, or even why Ethiopia went to war with Eritrea in the 1990s. Those explanations fail that rely on "rationality" and "interests," for they omit the importance of religious authenticity or cultural identity as an explanation for state action. This cultural explanation for state action is missed even in a relatively new approach to foreign policy analysis such as prospect theory.[40] According to this theory, states rationally calculate their gains and losses differently, and states are more "risk-averse" to make gains and are more "risk-seeking" to protect what they have. The prediction of Ringmar's alternative cultural theory, that states act to establish or defend an identity rather than to defend an interest, may provide a better explanation for many ethnonationalist and irredentist conflicts in international relations, but it also may provide a better explanation for the growing difficulties in promoting international cooperation in a multicultural global international society.

To be sure, this line of argument could lead us to the

---

39. Ibid.

40. See Jack S. Levy, "Prospect Theory, Rational Choice, and International Relations," *International Studies Quarterly* 41, no. 1 (1997): 87–112.

much debated hypothesis of Samuel Huntington, already mentioned. While he is surely correct that religion makes a great deal of difference in the formation of civilizations, the reception of his ideas in political science, economic, and international relations circles has not been positive. All that needs to be said here is that most of the criticisms focus on the mixed evidence in international politics for the "culture clash" thesis, the mutability of institutions and cultures, and the preferences of states regardless of the civilization in which they are based. Furthermore, many remark on the untidiness of some of his categories. For example, some of his civilizations are based on religio-cultural religions, such as Hinduism, and some on a specific religion, such as Islam, while other categories, such as "sinic" or "Japanese" are less clearly religious than ethnic in a strict sense.[41] While Huntington's argument is welcome — that policy makers must recognize more than they have the significant role that religion plays in defining the character and thus the interests of peoples and states in a civilization — it is not necessary to argue that real differences in this area must lead inevitably to war, to the "clash of civilizations." It could be that common features of humanity and, indeed, of faith can be recognized by people from other backgrounds, and it could be that a deeper "logos" underlies the capacity of people to dialogue across the boundaries of these religio-civilizational divisions than he, or for that matter MacIntyre, admits. It is partly against the neorealist presumptions that differences in these areas of life must be incommensurable or lead to inevitable clash in a violent fashion that the neoliberal institutionalist revival was prompted, as is evident in the wide-ranging writings of David Held, Michael Ignatieff, Mary Kaldor, Michael Doyle, and Andrew Linklater.[42]

---

41. See, e.g., J. O'Hagan, "Civilisational Conflict? Looking for Cultural Enemies," *Third World Quarterly* 16, no. 1 (1995): 19–35; A. Smith, "Dangerous Conjecture," *Foreign Affairs* 76, no. 2 (1997): 163–64; and S. Qadir, "Civilisational Clashes: Surveying the Fault Lines," *Third World Quarterly* 19, no. 4 (1998).

42. See David Held, *Democracy and the Global Order: From the Modern State*

Nevertheless, neoliberal theory also fails. Why states adhere to or comply with practices, norms, and laws is a fundamental part of the neoliberal explanation for international cooperation, and MacIntyre's probing questions have exposed the frailties of this view. Where do the dispositions and habits and virtues that sustain cultural and religious practices come from? The question is compelling, but he may not have taken his own lines of inquiry deep enough. Indeed, we might ask, in ways that MacIntyre avoids, where do the principles that engender a sense of righteous order and sense of ultimate destiny come from? Why are they so deeply embedded in the social fabric of every living culture that they are taken for granted? And why do so many societies falter or turn to some fanatic ideology if they begin to break down? How are these practices, and the virtues, principles, and purposes they embody, legitimated and institutionalized even amidst the relative anarchy of international society and the more pronounced anomie of political philosophy?[43]

Whither from Here?

At the beginning of the modern age, the Westphalian presumption subordinated religion to reasons of state internal

---

to *Cosmopolitan Governance* (London: Polity Press, 1995); Michael Ignatieff, *The Warrior's Honor: Ethnic War and the Modern Conscience* (New York: Vintage, 1998); Mary Kaldor, *New and Old Wars: Organized Violence in a Global Age* (London: Polity Press, 1998); and Andrew Linklater, *The Transformation of Political Community* (London: Polity Press, 1998).

43. According to MacIntyre, Durkheim described in the late nineteenth century how the breakdown of traditional forms of social relationship increased the incidence of *anomie,* or normlessness. As Durkheim characterized it, anomie was a form of deprivation, a loss of membership in those social institutions in which norms, including the norms of tradition-constituted rationality, are embodied. Since the beginning of the twentieth century, MacIntyre says, such marginalized victims of anomie have become philosophers! Alasdair MacIntyre, "Practical Rationalities as Social Structures," in Knight, ed., *MacIntyre Reader,* 135. "What Durkheim did not foresee," MacIntyre explains elsewhere, "was a time when the same condition of *anomie* would be assigned the status of achievement by and a reward for a self, which had, by separating itself from the social relationships of traditions, succeeded, so it believed, in emancipating itself. . . . What Durkheim saw as social pathology is now presented wearing the masks of philosophical pretension." MacIntyre, *Whose Justice?* 368.

to the rising nation-states and marginalized religion in international public life. This seemed to provide a solution to the problem of international order. Clergy could care for the national spirit, while soldiers and diplomats would care for national interests. This solution was successful for a time because the medieval feudal order, with its comprehending, church-led Christendom, was breaking down, and the rising nations of Europe became units of dynamic activity in the growing political, military, and cultural hegemony of Western modernity. The theological energy of the Reformation and the Counter-Reformation relocated much of their social influence, not only into the principalities of the nation-states but also into the new authoritative fields of science, economics, medicine, law, and technology, as is argued in volume 2 of this set. However, as those states began to contend with each other and to use religion to justify their conflicts, the dogmatic-political directions that these very same religious movements sometimes took in the West also had to be contained. Thus, the West became divided against itself. It produced both the religious revolutions of England and the antireligious revolutions of France, with movements in the German, Dutch, American, and Iberian territories variously not only adopting Protestant or Catholic perspectives but also adapting to pro- or antireligious ideologies. These complex developments variously generated globalizing influences that are now shaking the world. As a result, Western modernity and the institutions of international society that derive from it are being challenged by the global resurgence of religion within and beyond the West and by demands for authenticity in international development. The large-scale religious change now underway could eventuate in a genuinely multicultural global international society for the very first time.

Because of this global shift, it is doubtful whether neorealism and neoliberal institutionalism will be able to provide a basis for international order within a functional understanding of international society. Agreement on a whole host of global issues will be increasingly difficult in spite of appeals to rationality and common interests among states because of the way rationality, as it is most frequently understood by the advocates of these political philosophies, differs from place to place and time to time. The rationalities that are employed may have some common features, but they are also embedded in different religious and cultural traditions. Since many global issues increasingly penetrate states and affect the character of their societies, states will increasingly bring different values and conceptions of the good life to international negotiations.

It is doubtful, therefore, that an ethic of cosmopolitanism, at least once developed within the discourse of Western modernity, is compatible with the global resurgence of religion and demands for cultural authenticity in international development. Nor is it clear that we can return to or even simply adopt the traditional modes of bridging conflict. One mode is based upon natural law in the Aristotelian sense and has been taken up by Thomas Aquinas and the Roman Catholic Church. MacIntyre and others identify this view with the notion of virtue and the prospect of a global common good. The second mode is rooted in Platonic thought as revived in modern times by John Locke, Immanuel Kant, and the Protestant establishment in the Anglo-American world. It was taken up in the United Nations Declaration of Human Rights and embraced by the leadership of most of the world's religions. On these bases, it is held, the forces of globalization are creating or acknowledging global values — tolerance, democracy, progress, and human rights — in global society.

This essay has suggested that it is unclear whether these approaches to international order can take seriously the global resurgence of religion and cultural pluralism in international relations in the way Bull indicated, by absorbing non-Western elements to a much greater degree than has heretofore been the case. It has questioned their ability to be cosmopolitan and at the same time to show greater sensitivity to religious and cultural differences without resorting to cultural relativism or imperialism. Thus, for supporters of the natural law tradition or cosmopolitan ethics, the global resurgence of religion may well come to be greeted with dismay (also by some religious leaders) as religion once again becomes a source of intolerance and conflict in international relations.

There are many desirable aspects to these approaches to international order, and they no doubt find expression in the activities of various secular and religious NGOs as well as the World Council of Churches and various Councils of Catholic Bishops. Many are involved in ecumenical affairs, interfaith relations, human rights advocacy, humanitarian relief, and international development. Consequently, they have contributed to the growing debate about the notion of a global civil society. Nongovernmental efforts to find the moral element common among the world religions as the basis for a "global ethic" have also been promoted as a part of interfaith dialogue by the theologian Hans Küng,[44] the World Conference on Religion and Peace (Amman, Jordan, 1999), and by the self-styled Parliament of the World's Religions.[45] In addition, organizations such as the International Committee of the Red Cross (ICRC) have also tried to demonstrate the universality of their humanitarian principles by showing the consistency of these principles with the social ethics of the main world religions.[46]

Less clear are the practical implications of this growing body of academic literature and nongovernmental international activity. If the ICRC has demonstrated how many of

44. See Stephen Chan, "Hans Küng and a Global Ethic," *Review of International Studies* 25, no. 3 (1999): 525–30.

45. See R. H. Roberts, "Globalized Religion? The Parliament of the World's Religions (Chicago, 1993) in Theoretical Perspective," *Journal of Contemporary Religion* 10, no. 2 (1995).

46. See M. K. Ereksoussi, "The Koran and the Humanitarian Conventions," *International Review of the Red Cross* [IRRC] (May 1969); Yadh Ben Ashoor, "Islam and International Humanitarian Law," *IRRC* (March–April 1980); L. R. Penna, "Written and Customary Provisions Relating to the Conduct of Hostilities and Treatment of Victims...in Ancient India," *IRRC* (July–August 1989); Yolande Diallo, "African Traditions and Humanitarian Law: Similarities and Differences" (Geneva, ICRC pamphlet, n.d.); Yolande Diallo, "African Traditions and Humanitarian Law" (Geneva, ICRC pamphlet, 1978); Mutoy Mubiala, "African States and the Promotion of Humanitarian Principles," *IRRC* (March–April 1989).

the basic principles of international humanitarian law can be supported using the social ethics of the main world religions, this suggests, more broadly, that support for the institutions of international society can be found within the non-Western religions and civilizations as well as in those of the West. If this is the case, then research needs to bring together those scholars and theologians with a background in both the social ethics of the main world religions and the theory of international society. It will be important not only to identify areas of ethical agreement but to examine specific problems of the international order by asking questions such as the following:

What is the impact of the global resurgence of religion on the institutions of international society?

Can a better understanding of the social ethics of the main world religions influence and support the institutions of international society?

Are there ways in which the ethics of the world religions already influence foreign policy outcomes and assist diplomacy, development, humanitarian intervention, and conflict resolution?[47]

What has changed since the international order proposals of the last modern century, which both the global resurgence of religion and the rise of postmodernism indicate, is the collapse of confidence in the way Western modernity has understood the world. There is a growing openness in international relations and in international law to what different religious perspectives may have to offer the world. It may be time to consider a new approach to international order that overcomes the Westphalian presumption and takes the global resurgence of religion and cultural pluralism seriously in international relations. This is likely to require the development of a theology of world order, one that will take the contributions and perspectives of the world religions seriously. Among some scholars, this theoretical and multidisciplinary task of identi-

---

47. See R. Scott Appleby, *The Ambivalence of the Sacred: Religion, Violence, and Reconciliation* (London: Rowman & Littlefield, 2000).

fying common core ethical principles and norms among the main world religions on war and peace, the just war, pacifism, human rights, and peace-building is already a growing area of research and investigation.[48] My hope is that this project as a whole, and this essay in particular, can also point toward the answering of these questions.

48. See Harfiyah Abdel Harleen et al., *The Crescent and the Cross: Muslim and Christian Approaches to War and Peace* (London: Macmillan, 1998); David R. Smock, ed., *Perspectives on Pacifism: Christian, Jewish, and Muslim Views on Non-violence and International Conflict* (Washington, D.C.: U.S. Institute of Peace, 1995); and Cynthia Sampson, "Religion and Peacebuilding," in *Peacemaking in International Conflict,* ed. I. W. Zartman and J. L. Rasmussen (Washington, D.C.: U.S. Institute of Peace, 1995), 273–318.

– *Chapter 3* –

"When the Bull Is in a Strange Country, It Does Not Bellow"

TRIBAL RELIGIONS AND GLOBALIZATION

John S. Mbiti

In the face of globalization, proportionally little attention has been paid to tribal or indigenous religions, apart from the discussion of issues that can be applied to all religions in a general way. Out of the vast literature on globalization that I consulted (over three hundred books and articles), I could not find one article or book that addresses itself to the question of what is variously called indigenous, tribal, or primal religions and globalization. I venture, therefore, to put some thoughts together, in search of the place of indigenous religions within the parameters of the globalization debate. Indigenous religions and cultures have been involved directly and indirectly in globalization from the very beginning. However, discussions about globalization have taken shape essentially in Christian and Western secular circles and not in those of tribal religions.

"When the bull is in a strange country, it does not bellow" is an African proverb that points to the uncertain, maybe precarious, position of tribal religions on the global scene. As long as they stand on their home ground, where they are, or have been, deeply rooted in the culture, history, and social institutions of the people, tribal religions have bellowed. They have loudly announced their presence and identity. But on the global scene, where is their voice? Is their bellowing not loud enough? Or does globalization muffle their voice and marginalize them? Are tribal peoples being globalized together with, or in spite of, or entirely without their religions? Globalization means a new world, a largely foreign world for tribal peoples. How can they continue to bellow in such a strange land as this global scene? I want to address a variety of issues, with some illustrations of concrete cases, in the search of a place for tribal religions in the religious global scene.

The American Indians, for example, claim to have their "Ten Commandments," which reflect their teachings and religions and "are still topical today." These run as follows:

1. Treat the Earth and all that dwell thereon with respect.

2. Remain close to the Great Spirit.

3. Show great respect for your fellow beings.

4. Work together for the benefit of all mankind.

5. Give assistance and kindness wherever needed.

6. Do what you know to be right.

7. Look after the well being of mind and body.

8. Dedicate a share of your efforts to the greater good.

9. Be truthful and honest at all times.

10. Take full responsibility for your actions.[1]

These "commandments" evolved in a tribal and traditional context and seem to have been widened to become global. The current formulation would seem to aim at embracing more than the tribal societies. Since the earth is a global reality, the first commandment becomes a common outreach toward globalization. The second commandment lends itself also to

---

1. This text is from the Internet and was most recently revised on March 8, 1996. (It is difficult to discern how much the current formulation of these ten has been shaped by the confluence of tribal, Christian, and "New Age" cultural influences, and how much they are an ancient, indigenous, functional analogue to the tribal tradition of the ancient Hebrews.)

global dimensions if we understand the "Great Spirit" to refer to God. In this case, the commandment is more than a
localized concept and has a clear outreach beyond the tribal
boundaries. The third commandment starts within the radius
of tribal society, and while it may limit itself to the locals, it
does not necessarily do so, even if it does not directly make a
global appeal. The fourth commandment is open-ended, embracing "all mankind," and thus outwardly and intentionally
global. The remaining six commandments appeal to individual life on a local level, without necessarily going global, even
if they are not contrary to a global application.

Similar sets of commandments can be found in many other
tribal societies. Some elements are common, even if they may
be expressed differently.[2] They are the indispensable regulations that govern relations of people toward one another,
nature, and spiritual realities or beings. The latter generally
include God, the Great Spirit mentioned above, and the spirits that were created as such, those that are personifications
of natural phenomena and objects, and remnants of human
persons after death.

The question is whether these and other commandments
have a place on the global scene today. Largely they are confined to the traditions and worldviews of the tribal peoples
in such a way that they cannot be readily freed from that
setting and be transposed to become global concerns. While
globalization clearly needs economic, communications, and
political regulations and rules, it is not so clear whether moral
and ethical commandments have a place in them. To whom

---

2. For example, some of the Hebrew commandments (Exod 20:1–17) have parallels among the Maasai of Kenya and Tanzania, such as honoring one's parents
and forbidding stealing, killing (of other persons), and adultery. See Doug Priest, Jr.,
Doing Theology with the Maasai (Pasadena, Calif.: William Carey Library, 1990),
125ff. Similar parallels are found among other African peoples. Some scholars claim
that Moses derived the Ten Commandments from African sources while he lived in
Egypt. In any case, he fled from the court of the pharaoh because he had flouted the
commandment against killing another person, and he must have been aware of this
and other laws of the land. See, e.g., Yosef Ben-Jochannan, "Moses: African Influence on Judaism," in *The African Origins of the Major World Religions,* ed. Amon
Saba Saakana (London: Black Classics Press, 1988), 1–32.

or to what would "global" peoples be responsible in keeping, or flouting, such ethical commandments? In a sense, globalization as a social, economic, and political process knows or acknowledges no God and is neutral toward spiritual and ethical matters. In this respect, globalization recognizes no religion, even if many religions endeavor to globalize their image and activities.

Religio-Cultural Cults with Global Dimensions

In Brazil it is reported that, on the part of the peoples of African and Indian descent, the process of "moving" from strictly tribal grounds (in the wider sense of worldview, culture, history, and geography) to national (and hence partly global) grounds has given birth to a spiritist movement. This manifests itself in various ways and proportions that combine "ideas which originate in West Africa, pre-Columbian South America, and Western Europe about the vital forces of the spirit world." The process has seen a "mutation of their rituals" and has contributed to a "civil religion." "Elements borrowed from the spiritism of Alain Kardec were mixed with the religious elements of Catholicism (itself already a global reality), African, and Native American rituals and beliefs, with the result that these combinations gave birth to a new Afro-Brazilian cult named *umbanda*."[3]

This example from Brazil, as Maria Isaura Pereira de Queiroz describes it, is a good illustration of the challenge to tribal religions when they are placed in a globalizing context. The challenge was initially posed by the geographical removal of African tribal peoples, their settlement in a new and globalizing environment, their encounter with other tribal religions, and their later exposure to forces of technology and globalism. This points to one direction that tribal religions have taken. They have been submerged in a "strange country." On

3. Soumen Shen, quoting Maria Isaura Pereira de Queiroz, "Afro-Brazilian Cults and Religious Change in Brazil," in *The Changing Face of Religion*, ed. James A. Beckford and Thomas Luckmann (London: Sage Publications, 1989), 88–108.

the one hand, they yielded some of their ground and gave in to innovations. On the other hand, they let some of their elements be transformed. Thereby they opened themselves to embrace a wider following, while at the same time retaining much of their religious identity.

Pereira de Queiroz concludes that

> Only *umbanda,* among all the Afro-Brazilian cults, could really be characterized as a religious creation: it contained a set of beliefs which were different from the old tribal ones that lay at their roots. It was also widely different from Catholicism, spiritism, and the Indian cults. It was not only its faith but also its rituals, which had characteristics that had not existed in the ancient religions. Even the features, which persisted from ancient times, were arranged in a different way. . . . From all points of view, *umbanda* was a new religious creation.[4]

This happened at the same time as the growth of a metropolitan population. If it is "a new religious creation," it is on a global level and no longer confined to tribal boundaries. A "globalness" is evidently added to the "tribalness" of this religion, without it losing altogether its tribal identity and without being exclusively global.

However, some cultic groups in Brazil remained more or less within tribal boundaries, such as the *candomblé,* which underwent no such radical transformation as the *umbanda.* Pereira de Queiroz explains that "*Candomblé* continues to be the symbol of a clearly identified ethnic group in the wider Brazilian society. *Umbanda* has become the symbol of modern Brazilian society's singularity among the nations." Thus, the bellowing could and can still be heard, perhaps faintly but surely, in a strange land at the level of the modern nation-state. It needs to be pointed out, however, as Roger Bastide has argued, that the process of social and cultural development in Brazil was a complex one. Among other things,

---

4. Ibid., 102–3, 105.

Bastide points out, "In rural Brazil the de-Africanization of the blacks went hand in hand with the Africanization of the whites, producing both mulatto children and a mixed culture."[5]

An almost total resistance to global forces seems to have taken place among the people of Haiti. Here, the development of the *Voodoo* cult came about without opening itself sufficiently to be globalized the way *umbanda* did. *Voodoo* is not an African Religion, nor is it a blend of African Religion and other faiths. To be sure, some Christians participate in *Voodoo* activities. *Voodoo* can be compared to a vine growing from its original stem. In Haiti there is, of course, a change of geography and an adoption of some measure of the nation-state and Western styles of life by the descendants of the original African slaves. But *Voodoo* remains like a miniature bull bellowing on its own adopted ground, where the challenge of global forces is less perceivable. African Religion lost some original elements in Haiti, while other elements were highlighted more than they are on their native soil across the Atlantic. Is *Voodoo* a form of religious life thriving somewhere between native land and a global scene, among a people who are not a tribal people? Perhaps some other tribal religions may go in the same direction, retreating into a "safe" corner in fear of globalization. A retreat of this kind may activate religious conservatism, not only among tribal, but also among world religions. Such conservatism helps to provide an identity to people who fear changes and influence from outside.

Of contrasting interest is the case of the *Seng Khasi* movement in northeastern India. Feeling and/or seeing that tribal integrity was being threatened by extratribal forces of missionaries and colonial rulers, "sixteen Khasi non-Christian

---

5. Roger Bastide, *The African Religions of Brazil: Toward a Sociology of the Interpenetration of Civilizations,* trans. H. Sebba (Baltimore: Johns Hopkins University Press, 1978), 72. This work gives an insightful and fuller treatment of the process of encounter and creativity among different religious and cultural groups in Brazil: African, European, Indian, and their biological descendants.

young men" launched in November 1899 "a socio-cultural association" as an "organization of all the Khasis who adhere to the traditional religion." They were deeply concerned "for the future of their race." In this case, educated adherents of a strictly tribal religion first consolidated traditional religious values, which, they felt, were being "mercilessly attacked, denigrated and maligned," especially by foreign missionaries. Later, they stretched out beyond tribal boundaries (both geographical and in terms of worldview) and consciously sought global recognition. The projected outcome was the protection and preservation of a tribal religion with manageable modifications that stretch toward a global stature. The association "has now assumed the character of a distinct faith.... The *Seng Khasi* leaders proceeded in a highly selective fashion, and the selections operated in the direction of both modernity and monotheism. This enterprise, which canonized some elements of the old religion and preserved others, was certainly creative and idealized." The association is now an associate member of the International Association of Religious Freedom.[6] Is this an isolated case, in which forces of a global nature threaten or challenge the integrity of a tribal religion that, in turn, revives, reforms, and recreates itself into a formal faith-based religion claiming global recognition though not open to global expansion?

On the African continent, there seems to be a measure of ambiguity about the "old" (African Religion) and the "new" (religion in colonial and independent Africa). Examining some of the more than ten thousand religious movements in Africa, Bennetta Jules Rosette comes to the conclusion that "African movements that draw upon customary religious and political symbolism have often been regarded with a mixture of alarm and suspicion by both colonial governments and new regimes." She views these movements in terms of secularization rather than globalization. "The combination of

6. Soumen Sen, "The Changing Face of Khasi Religion," in Beckford and Luckmann, eds., *Changing Face of Religion,* 163–70.

the sacred and the secular domains in many new African religious movements creates thorny problems when analyzing the process of secularization."[7] But we cannot dismiss religious restlessness in Africa lightly. Africa is deeply rooted in traditional religion and is at the same time feeling and responding to global forces that come upon it or that it chooses to assimilate.

Another scholar of history who for many years has been closely associated with Africa sees a kind of marriage between traditional religions and (global) Christianity. Andrew Walls considers African Christianity

> in two capacities; first as a new period in the history of African religion, continuing the story begun in the "primal" or "traditional" religions; and second, as a new period in the history of Christianity.... African Christianity is a new development of African religion, shaped by the parameters of pre-Christian African religion as the Christianity of the Jerusalem Church of the Acts of the Apostles was rooted in the religion of old Israel.[8]

Is this an overstatement, to make the point that tribal religions of Africa are not only alive but have been integrated into the history of Christianity? This apparent integration has yet to be theologically demonstrated or interpreted.

Walls goes on to argue that there is a reordering of the worldview and an introduction of new symbols and sources. He holds that the "God-component" of African tribal religions, which existed everywhere, has been "exalted," while the "divinities-component," which was found in some areas, may involve a process of "demonization." The "God and ancestors component" remains ambiguous. Two new elements

---

7. Bennetta Jules Rosette, ed., *The New Religions of Africa: Priests and Priestesses in Contemporary Cults and Churches* (Norwood, N.J.: Ablex, 1979), 154.

8. Andrew Walls, "African Christianity in the History of Religions," in *Christianity in Africa in the 1990s,* ed. Christopher Fyfe and Andrew Walls (Edinburgh: Center for African Studies, University of Edinburgh, 1996), 116.

have entered the religious scene, namely, the person of Jesus Christ and the translation of the Scriptures.

Reflecting in another essay, Walls states, "Primal religions underlie all the other faiths," here especially Christianity and Islam, and often exist in symbiosis with them. Where in Africa and in the Pacific, new nation-states require a religious commonality to establish identities, such an "identity can only be found by reference to the past; in some cases like Malaysia, there is pressure to use traditional elements in patriotic movements. The various changes, which have impinged upon tribal religions especially since the Second World War, pose threats to them. The changes are universal." Tribal religions respond in one or more ways, of which he sees eight: recension, absorption, restatement, reduction, invention, adjustment, revitalization, and appropriation.

> All eight types of response have been found in primal religions since 1945, and all can be identified today.... [This] model points also to the principal change in primal religions since the Second World War: the search for a universal, not a purely local or ethnic, field of reference, a new focus suited to a village all now know to be global.[9]

This is an incisive and comprehensive model. It allows for flexibility of interpretation. It draws our attention to the fact that tribal religions are not idle when they meet forces of globalization. Walls's precise dating of different points of reference in the model remains open to question, though. It does not seem that tribal religions the world over would have been suddenly "ripe" to make these responses all at once in 1945, at the end of the Second World War. After all, that war was started and fought by largely Christian tribes of Europe and America, plus Buddhist and Shintoist (also tribal) Japan, largely as a contest between the tribal and world religious (Christian and Buddhist) aspects of their own history

---

9. Andrew Walls, *The Missionary Movement in Christian History* (Maryknoll, N.Y.: Orbis Books, 1996), 119–39.

struggling to dominate the expanding nation-state system. It was not, in a direct sense, a religious world war. Its immediate impact on tribal religions seems remote and in many cases only indirect, except that tribal people standing in the way of the resurgent Germanic and Japanese tribalism (especially Jews, Gypsies, and Slavs in Europe, and Koreans, Chinese, and Filipinos in Asia) felt its brunt most directly. Yet the war, originally a regional conflict, shook the entire world and inflicted gaping physical and ethical wounds that tapped and drained religious sanity. But I do not think that tribal peoples outside Europe in 1945 were raising ethical questions about this "other people's" war. They did not plan the self-devastation of "Christian" or "Buddhist" nations, nor take part in the "unreligious" massacre of peoples that was inflamed and propelled by racism and bigotry. Thus, we cannot allow the history of tribal peoples outside Europe to be tarnished by the history of Europe and East Asia in the twentieth century. Major points of historical reference for most tribal societies must be sought elsewhere, such as the colonial conquest and subjugation, the arrival of Christianity and missionary activities, the introduction of "modern" education, and new means of communication.

Some Examples of Responses

Tribal religions respond to global events and forces, most of which originate from outside their own religious orbit. But these responses are complex, mixed, and perhaps not static. Furthermore, the tribal religions themselves are not frozen or unaware of change.

In various writings on globalization, Roland Robertson highlights, among other things, the ambiguous role of religion. This seems to apply more to the worldviews that divide life (sharply or conveniently, institutionally or constitutionally) into religious and secular compartments. It does not seem to apply so strongly to tribal religions that, in contrast, are more integrated into the whole of human life and nature. Religion in traditional and tribal life is anything but ambiguous. Nevertheless, the movement toward globalization certainly poses ambiguous, foreign, and even threatening dilemmas. Issues of modernization, which scourge the statistically major religions, need to be tested to determine if and where they have an impact upon tribal religions.[10]

Robertson summarizes globalization as the entire world becoming a "single place."[11] This concept, insofar as it may apply to tribal religions, has yet to be explored. What bricks, what pillars, what rooftiles, what furniture, go toward creating the single place? Is the macro "single place" a conglomeration of many micro single places? Where do the different religions situate themselves, or get situated, in this single place? Who is at the center and who sets the agenda for the single place? Have tribal religions had a share in the realization of the single place, and do they feel themselves at home there? These questions point to religion, global responsibility, and human rights on a global level.

Human Rights and the Rights of Creation

As a whole, the missionary movement did not take up human rights adequately, either during colonial or in postcolonial times. In some cases, missionaries became themselves little more than merchants of religion in propagating the cultures (and politics) of their home countries. Being human, they also flouted human rights or turned a blind eye when these were flouted among indigenous peoples. In many cases in the nineteenth and twentieth centuries, as was the case during the colonial conquest of Latin America, with parallels in Africa and the Pacific, missionaries collaborated with colonial powers to forcefully or cunningly subdue and subjugate indigenous peoples. Apart from individual cases, they did

---

10. See Roland Robertson, "Globalization, Modernization, Postmodernization: The Ambiguous Position of Religion," in *Religion and Global Order*, ed. Roland Robertson and William R. Garrett (New York: Paragon House, 1991).

11. Ibid., 283.

not raise any alarm against the exploitation of local peoples
by commercial undertakings, such as mining and large-scale
farming, that were exported from Europe and America. It
would be calamitous if globalization would repeat these mistakes, would miss the right moment to make room for human
rights. If some want to put up resistance against globalization, if some want to enter into globalization on their own
terms, who will safeguard these rights of self-determination
balanced by global demands? Globalization is not an institution with its own laws, authority, and executive powers. But
must it function semiautonomously and semianonymously?
How can it put on a human face, a human heart, a human
ethic, and a human conscience?

Human rights are embedded in the different religious traditions of the world, including tribal religions. They are
ingrained in the traditions' ethics, morals, values, spirituality,
and responses to threats that face the total fabric of human life
(institutions, cultural heritage, education, survival methods,
and environment). It is possible to argue that global human
rights are born out of local rights, that they are found first
and foremost in particular spots, among particular peoples,
and applied by particular communities. These human rights,
tried and tested on local levels, can be lifted to global heights
and shared among all peoples as far as that may apply without it being at the cost of other human rights. They can only
qualify to be global if they include human rights from tribal
religions as well.

But globalization should not confine rights only to humans.
In its manifold manifestations, nature has its own rights — the
rights of the oceans and the mountains, of the fishes and the
birds, of the forests and deserts, of the soil and the earth itself.
If we hurt nature, nature will hurt us. I plead for the rights
of nature, and globalization is the platform where these can
be formulated and put into action. Persons are not alone in
the world, and our rights hinge upon the rights of creation.
The creation has a right to be.

Significantly, the first of the American Indians' "Ten Commandments" addresses the earth: "Treat the Earth and all that dwell thereon with respect." This recalls the famous speech of Chief Seattle of the Suquamish (Duwamish) and other Indian tribes in the State of Washington in 1854. The speech was in response to a proposed treaty under which the Indians were persuaded to sell two million acres of land for $150,000. It was a response to what was later to be a process of globalization: "How can you buy or sell the sky, the warmth of the land? The idea is strange to us. If we do not own the freshness of the air and the sparkle of the water, how can you buy them?...Every part of this earth is sacred to my people.... The very dust upon which you now stand...is rich with the blood of our ancestors, and our bare feet are conscious of the sympathetic touch.... How can your God become our God and renew our prosperity?... One thing we know...our God is the same God.... The earth is precious to Him, and to harm the earth is to heap contempt on its Creator."[12]

This Indian tribal concern has not been tucked away in the archives. It is a living concern, as Stan McKay points out, speaking specifically about American Indians, whom he calls "Aboriginal peoples":

> It might be helpful to view Aboriginal peoples as an "Old Testament people...." We, like Moses, know about the sacredness of the earth and the promise of the land.... We can relate to the vision of Abraham and the laughter of Sarah.... We call ourselves "the people" to reflect our sense of being chosen.... Indigenous spirituality around the world is centered on the notion of relationship to the whole creation. We call the earth our mother and the animals our brothers and sisters. Those parts of creation which biologists describe as inanimate we call our

---

12. Although there is some controversy about the original words of this speech, the thrust of the speech remains substantially the same. See, among others, the essay by Rudolf Kaiser, "Chief Seattle's Speech(es): American Origins and European Reception," in *Recovering the Word: Essays on Native American Literature*, ed. Brian Swann and Arnold Krupat (Berkeley: University of California Press, 1987), 213–17.

relatives.... Our leaders have often described how non-sensical it is to lay claim to the air, the water or the land; because these are related to all life.... We have developed myths and rituals, which remind us of the centrality of the earth in our experience of the truth about the Creator. For us, the Great Spirit is in the daily earthly concerns about faithful living in a relationship with the created order. Each day we are given is for thanksgiving for the earth.[13]

McKay reminds us of a major biblical view: "The earth is the Lord's and all that is in it" (Ps 24:1). He goes on to explain that "many teachings of the aboriginal North American nations use the symbol of the circle. It is the symbol of the inclusive caring community, in which individuals are respected and interdependence is recognized."[14] This image of the circle is explained further by J. Donald Hughes: When the Indians "wanted to make a picture of the universe, they drew a great endless circle, perhaps adding lines of the four directions inside. To them, everything was connected, everything partook of the roundness, everything shared the same life."[15]

Another Indian theologian, George Timber, points out the profound spirituality that tribal peoples attach to nature and the earth:

Indigenous peoples experience their very personhood in terms of their relationship to the land.... Native American peoples resist categorization in terms of class structure. Instead, we insist on being recognized as "peoples," even nations, with a claim to national sovereignty based on ancient title to our land.... A native

13. Stan McKay, "An Aboriginal Perspective on the Integrity of Creation," in *Ecotheology: Voices from South and North,* ed. D. G. Hallman (Maryknoll, N.Y.: Orbis Books, 1994), 214ff.

14. Ibid.

15. J. Donald Hughes, "From American Indian Ecology," in *This Sacred Earth: Religion, Nature, Environment,* ed. Roger Gottlieb (New York: Routledge, 1996), 144.

American theology must argue out of spiritual experience and praxis that God reveals God's self in creation, in space or place, and not in time.... Native American spirituality and values, social and political structures, and even ethics are rooted not in some temporal notion of history but in spatiality.... Of course, Native Americans have a temporal awareness, but it is subordinate to our sense of place.... All of existence is spiritual for us. That is our universal starting point.... When the Lakota peoples of North America pray *Mitakuze ouyasin*, "for all my relatives," they understand relatives to include not just tribal members, but all of creation.... Today there can be no genuine American Indian theology that does not take our indigenous traditions seriously.[16]

Hughes gives his own summary view of the Indian relation to nature:

Indians saw themselves as at one with Nature. All their traditions agree on this, Nature is the larger whole of which mankind is only a part.... All living things are one, and people are joined with birds and trees, predators and prey, rocks and rain in a vast, powerful interrelationship.... "We are in one nest," was a Taos Pueblo saying concerning humans, animals and birds.... All the outward forms seen by Indians in the natural environment concealed personality and power, which might be invoked.... Animals and plants were seen as spirits, too. The eagle soared so high in the sky that he was identified with the sun. Like human beings, the other creatures were believed to worship the mysterious powers in which they shared. The leaves of cottonwood trees rustling in the wind were believed to be their voices praying to the Great Spirit who gave them the power to stand upright. All the outward forms seen

16. George Tinker, "The Full Circle of Liberation: An American Indian Theology of Place," in Hallman, ed. *Ecotheology*, 218–24.

by Indians in the natural environment concealed personality and power, which might be invoked. So they were constantly speaking to those manifested inner realities in words that, they trusted, were understood. A daily morning prayer was usually addressed to the sun, as in this Kwakiutl example: "Look at me Chief, that nothing evil may happen to me this day, made by you as you please, GreatWalkingToandFroAllOvertheWorld, Chief." As the careful man passed beside a steep mountain, he would speak to it, "Please make yourself firm." Migrating birds were asked to take sickness far away. A Clayoquot Indian sang to a rough sea: "Breakers, roll more easily / Don't break so high / Become quiet."[17]

The image of the circle with its strong spirituality relating to nature, as the Indians conceive of it, speaks clearly to the concept of globalization — the setting of the world into a circle, into a "one place." That sounds like a vision that indigenous peoples can share at a level beyond their tribal boundaries. Indians are not alone in this. Let us now take up other illustrations from Africa and Australia.

Ecology, Tribal Peoples, and Globalization

In this same spirit are the parallel sentiments of African Religion, which is strongly sensitive to the sacred dimensions of nature. Accordingly, people personify natural phenomena like earthquakes and eclipses, and major, or mysterious, objects like the sun, stars, forests, lakes, waterfalls, thunder, and attribute life-beingness to them. They can speak of these as though they were "persons." Nature is not a dead and impersonal reality. It is filled with "spirit persons" of personified phenomena and objects. People recognize God and relate to Him/Her at the highest level of their spiritual awareness. Nature speaks of and points to its Maker and Sustainer. Western scholars and missionaries have belittled and even dismissed

---

17. Hughes, "From American Indian Ecology," 138, 144.

these spiritual insights of indigenous peoples, calling them "animism," "nature worship," or "spirit worship." This is extremely unfortunate. It only scratches the surface and misses the spiritual insights that lie in traditional religions. Among other things it also shows how naïve such designations can be.

Here is an African prayer for the welfare of nature. It comes from the Didinga people of the Sudan. It is directed toward a local situation but it points toward a global goal:

> O Earth, wherever it be my people dig, be kindly to
> them.
> Be fertile when they give the little seeds to your keeping.
> Let your generous warmth nourish them
> and your abundant moisture germinate them....
> O trees of forest and glade, fall easily under the ax.
> Be gentle to my people.
> Let no harm come to them....
> Conspire together, O earth and rivers:
> conspire together O earth and rivers and forests.
> Be gentle and give us plenty from your teeming plenty.[18]

The following prayer of fishermen from the Ivory Coast reveals how mystical or spiritual they take the rivers and other fishing waters to be. While saying this prayer, the fishermen offer a chicken at a point frequented by hippopotamuses and crocodiles:

> O river, I beg leave to take fish from thee, as my
> ancestors did before me.
> O river, rise up, engulf your sharptoothed monsters,
> and permit our young men to enter the water
> and enjoy themselves with the fish without being
> harmed.
> If there is acceptance from you,
> then show it by accepting this baby chick.
> If not, if you cannot control the monsters,

---

18. John S. Mbiti, *The Prayers of African Religion* (Maryknoll, N.Y.: Orbis Books, 1975), 69–70.

if one of them should harm our sons,
    then show it by refusing to accept this baby chick.[19]

These and similar prayers reveal a caring and respectful attitude toward nature as partner in creation. It seeks harmony with and appreciation of nature. It is an expression of partnership between persons, nature, and the spiritual realities, including God. Tribal religions are very much aware of this dimension of reality. That can be a valuable contribution to global concerns if room is found for it.

Indeed, the environment is a burning global concern. A good example of indigenous contribution to ecological renewal comes from Zimbabwe. In 1988, M. L. Daneel founded the Zimbabwean Institute of Religious Research and Ecological Conservation and in 1991, the Association of African Earthkeeping Churches. The main and practical objectives address the environmental "nakedness" of the land that has resulted from deforestation, overgrazing, destruction of trees and shrubs, desertification, and soil erosion. The ultimate goals of these two bodies are afforestation, wildlife conservation, and protection of water resources. The initial launching area of the project was in Masingo province of Zimbabwe, but eventually it began to extend to other parts of the country. With the support and cooperation of both Christian churches and followers of African Religion, the local population is working toward the realization of these goals. Indeed, people have been convinced both by traditional religiosity and biblical exposition of the deep significance of "renewing the earth." So Daneel writes:

> Environmental objectives are seen as being undergirded by a divine mandate. Ecumenicity has taken shape as churches share concretely a newly identified common commitment to healing the earth. A new brotherhood and sisterhood beyond the traditional ecclesial constraints has started to evolve — that between the creator

---

19. Ibid., 75.

God, earthkeeping humanity and the trees, plants, and wildlife. A new myth, arising from the common, holistic subconscious of Africa and blended with Christian perceptions of a realized, observable salvation for all creation in the here and now, has started to emerge.[20]

The impact of traditional religion upon this project emerges clearly in a treeplanting liturgy that comes from one of the participating churches. After being planted in the soil, the seedlings are addressed one after the other:

> You, tree, my brother, my sister,
> today I plant you in this soil.
> I shall give water for your growth.
> Have good roots to keep the soil from eroding,
> Have many leaves and branches,
> So that we can breathe fresh air,
> sit in your shade, and find firewood.[21]

Here is a direct address to trees (seedlings), acknowledging them as spirit-filled beings. This kind of mystical language is well-known in tribal societies and lends itself to transfer onto the global level.

In his fuller description and interpretation of this ecological project in Zimbabwe, Daneel highlights the role of indigenous (African) religion, in conjunction with Christian churches. He tells that his study has been to "probe the cosmological roots and belief systems of the Shona [people] as a motivating force in the mobilization of inculturated earthkeeping. The insight it generates may be significant for the development of a relevant ecotheology or environmental ethic in the global village." He calls for "a radical rethink of the prevailing anthropocentric ethic in industrial consumer societies," and for replacing it "with an ethic of responsibility and respect for all

---

20. M. L. Daneel, "African Independent Churches Face the Challenge of Environmental Ethics," in Hallman, ed., *Ecotheology,* 251.

21. Ibid., 257–58. See Daneel's fuller account of this project in *African Earthkeepers,* vol. 1 (Pretoria: University of South Africa Press, 1998).

creation." Daneel singles out a number of items from other
theologians looking at indigenous religions that contribute to
this "radical rethink." One is "the religious values within the
lifeways (that is, the functional interaction of cosmology and
culture)." Another is the "close identification" of indigenous
peoples "with the environment [and] their rituals of bonding in interpersonal relations." Nevertheless, he hesitates "to
suggest universal application of locally contextualized values." Focusing on the Shona people, Daneel, who grew up in
Zimbabwe in a Dutch missionary family, mentions items that
feature prominently in traditional societies: "Sense of place,
sense of community, ancestors and their living descendants,
ancestors and earth community, [and] communion with the
Creator."[22] But while appreciating the religious view of nature among tribal peoples, we cannot ignore activities among
tribal peoples that may also be destructive and damaging to
nature, especially in the human struggle for survival.

This calls for the search for and articulation of human
rights and nature's rights in tribal religions. These religions
are entitled to have a say in this central area. The closeness to
nature in which they live has sensitized them to the ecosystems
that function in their environment and beyond. For them,
nature is not merely a physical reality; it is a "being" that
persons can directly get in touch with, address, communicate
with, protect, and cultivate relations with. Holding a different
attitude toward nature, adherents of other religions have contributed greatly to ecological destruction and pollution. Does
the global platform have room for such relations between
persons and nature? This is a sensitive area, but different traditions with their baggage seem to be slowly moving toward
convergence around it.[23]

There are many examples of tribal peoples having been

22. Daneel, "African Independent Churches," 238ff.
23. See Frank J. Lechner, "Religion, Law, and Global Order," in Robertson and
Garrett, eds., *Religion and Global Order,* 263–80. See also the diverse discussions
in Thomas Robbins, William C. Shepherd, and James McBride, eds., *Cults, Culture
and the Law* (Chico, Calif.: Scholars Press, 1985).

disadvantaged. At one time they were the historical and legal owners or occupants of their land. Then settlers from other countries arrived and legally or illegally came to possess tribal lands. For example, the discovery of oil and minerals in tribal lands in more recent years has led to clashes between governments, international mining or drilling companies, and indigenous peoples. This tussle is amply illustrated by a case study from Australia, that vast "tribal land" of the Aborigines for at least thirty thousand years before convicts from overseas were forced to settle there over two centuries ago. The land was already seeded with sacred sites. Economic considerations of the present state governments have brought the issue of land, sacred sites, and Aboriginal rights to the foreground.[24]

In this case, the drilling for oil by Amax Exploration Company on Aborigines' sacred sites in Noonkanbah, Western Australia, precipitated a confrontation between tribal sensitivities and international economic considerations. It was clearly evident that, for the Aborigines, mining or drilling would "destroy their ceremonial sites, scar the land with which they had deep emotional and spiritual ties, spoil their hunting, cut them off from their natural resources of fruits, roots and seeds, and disrupt their community life." Nevertheless, the bulldozers of the Amax Exploration Company "cut through burial and ceremonial grounds, and a tree that they believed was the home of the spirit of Friday Muller, a former elder of the tribe, was damaged." It is no wonder that trouble ensued. Fierce legal protests and battles were of no avail, and the sacred sites were blasted into dust. The company answered to the global economy, but at the same time, its insensitive exploitation desecrated the sites and devalued their attached spirituality. In many places around the world, in many areas of life, the technological, economic, political,

---

24. Alice Frazer Evans, Robert A. Evans, with David A. Roozen highlight this issue in their case study on Aborigines' sacred sites in their edited volume, *The Globalization of Theological Education* (Maryknoll, N.Y.: Orbis Books, 1993), 104–21.

and cultural bulldozers from other cultures seem to tribal peoples to be headed for their villages, their cultures, their holy sites.

Commenting on this case study, L. Shannon Jung points out, "From the Aboriginal perspectives what is being threatened is not a piece of land that is modular, interchangeable with any other. It is the source of tribal identity and cohesion." As one aboriginal says in the case, this particular piece of land "provides not only for our physical needs, but for our spiritual needs also. Just looking at our land keeps up our spiritual life the same way reading the Bible keeps up the spiritual life of Christians." Another Aborigine explains,

> The land is my mother. Like a human mother the land gives us protection, enjoyment, and provides for our needs. . . . When the land is taken from us or destroyed, we feel hurt because we belong to the land and we are part of it. . . . [T]he land contains our information about our traditional way of life. It's written there. . . . It's like a library for our people and children. It's very sad when mining wipes out our library. . . . Land is breathing place for my people.[25]

Similar views and sentiments can be found among many tribal peoples the world over. Land is the mystical basis of their existence, their identity, their past, and their future. For Aborigines, the land is the point of reference that binds them to their worldview, which they express in terms of "dreamtime." Their life orientation looks not into the mathematical future dimension of time as such but into the mythical past, the dreamtime. Somehow, we have to wrestle with finding accommodation for the dreamtime in our modern globalization. The call for "globalization as ecumenical/interfaith dialogue" is not out of place.[26]

---

25. Rev. Badaltja Djiniyini and Rrurrambu, *My Mother the Land,* ed. Ian R. Yule (Galiwin'ku: Galiwin'ku Literature Centre, 1980), 8, 33, as cited in Evans et al., eds., *Globalization of Theological Education,* 116.

26. Evans et al., eds., *Globalization of Theological Education,* 116.

Through the human rights movement, globalization forces hopefully can be made more aware of this area of tribal existence. On their part, tribal religions can contribute the mystic and the spiritual to human relations with nature, the land, the waters, and the animals. They challenge the "global village" to regard, handle, and treat the land as "our mother," as our source of existence. Can tribal religions still "bellow" when they arrive there, or is their capacity to bellow castrated beforehand by some blind forces of globalization? Certainly globalization needs a spiritual face, a sensitive face, a tender face.

Members of tribal religions are clearly embraced in the orbit of the human rights movement, even if they may not have conscious participation in the movement as such. It is necessary to let them contribute toward the concept of human rights and hence enable them to rally to their defense and propagation. It would be a mistake for human rights to be turned into a monopoly of a single religious tradition. Converging human rights may be more numerous than diverging ones. The "single place" cannot afford to flout the rights of anyone to be there.

Death, Dying, and Eschatology

One of the areas of nature's rights and human rights that has yet to be taken up by the international community is the issue of death and dying. The twentieth century deprived millions upon millions of people of the right to die "naturally." Every person surely has a right to die peacefully and naturally, as far as that may lie within human abilities. The same can be said about biologically living parts of nature. But this right has been denied millions of persons who, in the twentieth century, have been killed in gas chambers, through genocide, in civil and international wars, homicides, and terrorist attacks. Lives have been cut short through deliberate plans and execution by a relatively small number of the so-called leaders. Other lives have been eliminated through unethical ideolo-

gies and greed for power and wealth. In other cases it is those
who take advantage of weakness in one section of society
that destroy human lives. In still other cases it is terrorists,
who wreak havoc in the name of their religion. Tribal religions in particular have been paralyzed by the devastating
killings of the twentieth century and by the vastly powerful
means and methods of killing people hitherto unknown in
tribal traditions. Some of these weapons of destruction, including the gun, have found their way into the hands of tribal
people, and they too have used the weapons to kill or destroy among themselves and their neighbors. Tribal religions
do not seem to be equipped to cope with modern and global
means of killing people or to halt the wave of such killings.
Furthermore, tribal peoples are exposed to massive killings
that occur locally, regionally, or that could potentially occur
globally. They easily become victims. These are dangers that
threaten all peoples of the world. Tribal religions should also
be recruited to search for ways of halting this tide of unnatural and often premature deaths that flout the personal right
to die naturally.

The globalization of death has wide implications. New and
often brutal methods of dying are being demonstrated all
over the world. Often people are not culturally and spiritually
prepared for these kinds of "modern" deaths. For example,
Islamic terrorists blew up the American embassy in Nairobi,
Kenya, on August 7, 1998, killing some 250 people and injur-
ing over 5,200 others. This devastating act also invaded and
blasted the privacy and culture of dying in Kenya. Because
of the wide network of kinship relationship in African society, these deaths and injuries reached the whole country in a
deeply personal way. The dead and the injured persons were
"my" brother, sister, wife's cousin, maternal uncle's daughter
from his third wife who herself is the daughter of the former
teacher Tilo Kasau from the Leopard clan.

In the tribal context, there is no such thing as a terrorist
death and no bomb victims. When a person falls sick, family
members, relatives, friends, and neighbors all visit the sick,

give support and encouragement to the sick person and his or her immediate family. If death is about to occur, family members remain around the sick, to comfort, to encourage, to bid farewell, and even to hold the body of the dying. Ordinarily, the corpse will still look like "so and so" when it is buried. In great contrast, the victims of the embassy bomb blast were denied time to be with friends and relatives, to be sick and die "at home." Parts of their bodies were dislodged and may never have been found under the rubble. Some bodies were so disfigured that they were buried with missing limbs, and others were buried unidentified. The terrorist bomb told these victims in effect that they had no right to die, that is, to die "normally," to die "according to custom." The people were simply blasted into death by the bomb, without warning, without preparation whatsoever. Terrorists abruptly took away both their lives and the right to die. Relatives and friends did not know how to mourn such "foreign" deaths and to nurse the wounds inflicted upon the nation. This form of death is outside the familiar and traditional culture of death and dying. The whole country was stunned, bled together, and grieved together. Tribal religions cannot understand this form of globalized death; they cannot embrace it in the orbit of their spirituality. It is too brutal, too shattering, too foreign, and too sudden. Is globalization equipped to disarm, to tame these sudden and devastating deaths caused by deliberate acts of persons?

What shall we do to cleanse, were that possible, the twentieth century of the ugly deaths it has witnessed? We have already discussed the tribal view of the killing in the Second World War, but class and ethnic and ideological killing also show up in the "gulag years" of the Soviet Union, the killing fields of Pol Pot in Cambodia, the demonic system of apartheid in South Africa, the "ethnic cleansings" in Yugoslavia, and much, much more. Of course, we dare not forget the brutal tribal massacres in Rwanda and Burundi, or vicious tribal hostilities over the centuries. But during the twentieth century, death became commercialized, politicized, and globalized. Death has done big business in the twentieth century. Who will pronounce forgiveness for what this past century did, calm our wounded conscience, and free us from the scars of our wounded history? Can globalization retrieve humanity from the ravages of "unnatural" deaths in the coming years?[27] Of course, there were also many positive contributions to the betterment of human life in the twentieth century, contributions that add meaning to the prospects for globalization; but too many of those contributions also stand in a pool of blood.

Tribal religions have their insights concerning death and dying, and about what goes on before and after death. Some years back, at an international gathering in Geneva, Switzerland, I conducted meditation sessions. At one of them, I asked the participants to place themselves at the final moment of their life and to say short prayers, if they wanted, before dying. Several did so. Afterwards someone from Indonesia came to me and said, "I wanted to say my 'dying prayer,' but I could not 'die' in a foreign language." On the global scene, nobody should be denied dying in his or her native way, customary way, and natural way.

For those who can afford it, modern medicine is doing great wonders in resisting death, as the essay by Allen Verhey, "The Spirit of God and the Spirit of Medicine," in volume 2 of this series demonstrates. But there are many faces to it. Some of the issues that he brings out apply, with due modifications, as much in tribal settings as they do in industrialized societies. Death on the global scene is death for all peoples, and they have a right to contribute to the understanding of this global phenomenon whose chains link all peoples together more firmly than anything else does. Naturally, a consideration of human death opens questions about the termination of other things animate and inanimate, from microbes to dinosaurs, from forests to mountains, from stars to galaxies. Did their death originally come about with the so-called fall of man and

---

27. See the essay by Donald Shriver, "The Taming of Mars: Can Humans of the Twenty-First Century Contain Their Propensity for Violence?" in vol. 1 of this series.

woman, which has imbued so much of Western theology? Or did they die already before humans were even created and evolved? This brings us to what Paul writes in his letter to the Romans: "The creation itself will be set free from its bondage to decay.... We know that the whole creation has been groaning in travail together until now" (8:21–22). Do they die in hope, consciously or unconsciously? If so, what kind of hope? What is the eschatology of human and cosmic death?

In his contribution to this set of volumes, David Tracy takes us a step further in the exploration of eschatological hope.[28] An eschatological hope is one of the strong points of the major religions, including Judaism, Christianity, Islam, and Buddhism, even if each depicts that hope differently from the others. However, we do not find eschatological hope as strongly or clearly represented in tribal religions. Part of this absence depends on their concepts of time, which, at least on the African scene, concentrate more on the present and the past, with a brief future dimension. There are no calendars that reckon years from a given date toward an indefinite future. The myths that surround human life are all about the past, especially the origin of people and the world, but none exist about the unknown future and the end. Nevertheless, contact with Western Christian mission has ignited great interest in local variations of eschatological hope. Good examples of these are the cargo cults of Oceania, especially Melanesia, and the vivid materialistic expectation of the return of Jesus as held in African congregations.

As we entered the new millennium, some (but less than expected) eschatological fever flared up. It depicted hopes about the end of one millennium and the beginning of another. Doesn't Christianity need theological guidance as it sails from one millennium into another? After all, these millennia are exclusively the creation of Christianity and not of another religious tradition. Christian theology should give the

---

28. See David Tracy, "Fundamental Theology, Hope, and the Mass Media: Can the Muses Still Inspire?" in vol. 1 of this series.

parameters to guide our sailing from one to the other. There
is need for some articulation of the eschatology of globalization, taking into account both the traditional eschatologies of
larger religions and the rising eschatologies of tribal societies
under the Christian umbrella.

Literacy and Tribal Peoples

The introduction of literacy, largely through Christian missions, has had a strong impact on the worldview of tribal
societies. Literacy is taken so much for granted in Western
and much of Asian society that its impact upon traditionally
nonliterate societies is not clearly recognized or appreciated.
Traditionally, tribal societies have functioned on the basis of
oral cultures, in which symbols are essential ingredients. The
introduction of literacy sets in motion the transformation of
culture and people's way of life even if this transformation
takes place slowly at first.

In letting literacy find a footing in their cultures, tribal societies are opening themselves to globalization. In a study
of the process of transition from spoken to written texts,
in connection with African religion, John M. Janzen makes
several observations that seem applicable to many tribal societies. He made the study on the coastal peoples of Angola,
Congo (Kinshasa), and Congo (Brazzaville). He argues that
literacy unleashes transformation upon the entire culture. He
points out that oral tradition has not vanished. It continues
to function and thus supplement the channels of written communication. "It is apparent that the acquisition of literacy in
African Religion has not, ipso facto, led to the end of oral uses
of language in religious experience and expression" (such as
riddles, proverbs, songs, stories, epics, and dreams).

Many African religious traditions [including indigenous,
Christian, and Islamic] are involved in one or another
stage in this transition to literacy. The consequences of
such a transition are far reaching. Literacy as such, per-

mits a greater degree of uniformity in a religious order. It permits the existence of such an order on a larger social scale; it permits the renewal of cultural and spiritual traditions to occur with reference to the past-in-the-present; it permits a greater participation in the central ideas of a religious order.[29]

Is literacy a move toward globalization, and is it as such a unifying factor? Literacy is a powerful tool of globalization. Perhaps it is also indispensable. Although there is a strong move toward literacy in many African countries, this amounts to partial literacy. In many cases, the process is more or less reversed when children and young people leave school and college. In many other cases, there is virtually no reading material outside of schoolbooks, the Bible in some cases, and occasional newspapers. Reading material is not easily available or is simply too expensive for many who have attended school in their earlier years. Thus, many enter into a slow process of deliteracy, and function or live almost the way pre-literate persons function. At the global level, more needs to be done to increase literacy abilities and skills, in order to make literacy a positive contribution towards globalization.

Theological Education

We all realize that theological education is very central to our profession, and many of our contributions address themselves to this issue.[30] Christianity shares this task with other religious traditions. Christian theological education increasingly has enlarged its scope to include the teaching of other world religions. But tribal religions are not yet included. Perhaps

---

29. John M. Janzen, "The Consequences of Literacy in African Religion," in *The Theoretical Explorations in African Religion,* ed. Wim van Binsbergen and Matthew Schoffeleers (London: KPI, 1985), 225–52.

30. See the general introduction by Max L. Stackhouse in vol. 1 of this series, and "The Teaching Ministry in a Multicultural World," by Richard Osmer in vol. 2. See also "Observation and Revelation: A Global Dialogue with Buddhism," by Kosuke Koyama, and "Christian Contributions to the Globalization of Confucianism (Beyond Maoism)," by Sze-kar Wan in this volume.

in a few cases they are politely relegated to the "optional" if not "exotic" courses. Clearly, however, the tribal religious heritage has not yet been given a meaningful or clear place in theological education in the West.

Statistics indicate clearly that the church in Oceania and Africa, and in some pockets in Asia, is made up of Christians who largely come out of the tribal religious setting. Communities holding tribal religions become Christian more readily than those who adhere to Hinduism, Buddhism, Islam, or Confucianism do. However, tribal Christians do not enter the church with empty heads or hands. They bring with them the memories and gifts of the tribal religious heritages into the Christian orbit. The Bible is translated into their languages. Immediately they identify themselves with the Bible, and as one African said, "We do not just read the Bible. It is the Bible that reads us!" A vast world of theological reflection opens up through, initially, the preaching of the gospel, conversion, and reading and hearing the Bible. Out of the 2,261 full or partial translations of the Bible at the end of 2000, 632 were in African languages, 565 Asian, 397 Oceanian, 200 European and Middle Eastern, 391 Latin American, 73 North American, and 3 artificial languages.[31] These Bible translations indicate that over 70 percent are into languages of the "southern" regions, i.e., Africa, Asia, Oceania, and Latin America.

The implications of this are enormous. The Bible has become the book of the southern regions, and theology, as far as it may be based on the Bible, has become increasingly conceptualized in the largely tribal languages of the South. Does theological education in the West try even remotely to keep up with this shifting of statistics? Theological education in the West owes it to itself to open its task to what is happening theologically elsewhere in the world, especially in

---

31. United Bible Societies, *World Report* (Reading, England: UBS, 2000). For confusing administrative purposes, the languages of northern Africa are counted under "Europe." This gives in reality an increase of African and decrease of European figures.

tribal settings. The North maintains a monopoly of theology, but the Bible is now stationed linguistically in the South, in tribal languages. In the globalization of the Bible, tribal languages may have to set the agenda or play the tune. There is even a call from Asia for the "recycling of Christianity." So Kwok Puilan writes, "Some of our traditional Christian beliefs need to go through a recycling process so that they can be re-appropriated for the contemporary world."[32] This could mean that on the global scene, Christian theology has to offer a portrait that is more in keeping with wider intercultural and intertheological characteristics.

At one time, out of fourteen master of arts theses written by students at the United Theological College, Suva, Fiji, twelve dealt directly with biblical themes in relation to traditional, tribal concepts and practices.[33] This small sample is indicative of the impact of the Bible on Christian life and thought not only in the Pacific but also in Africa and Asia. What do people see and hear when they read the Bible in their own languages? How do they look afresh at theological themes and doctrines with which the church in the North is so familiar? Do the northern churches, perhaps, need fresh blood? And not only new blood but also ecumenical relations that involve sharing not only money but resources, personnel, and theology? Yet I wonder whether theological education in the West has room for anybody else's voice. Unless theological horizons are extended, theological institutions would be paying only lip service to globalization. Any radical change of theological education must take into serious consideration the arrival of tribal worldviews on the global scene. This may be painful to established theological institutions.

The fact is that in the tribal areas where the church is thriving, much of Western theology has become increasingly redundant and irrelevant. How much of it becomes redundant

---

32. Kwok Puilan, "Ecology and the Recycling of Christianity," in Hallman, ed., *Ecotheology.*
33. See Kerry Prendeville, "Pacific Regional Seminary Theses and Syntheses," *Pacific Journal of Theology* (Suva, Fiji) 2, no. 3 (1990): 98–100.

also on the global level? This was the discovery that Kosuke
Koyama from Japan made when he worked as a missionary
in Thailand. Going to preach to a village congregation one
Sunday, he realized that he could not preach the gospel to the
people through the *Summa Theologiae* of Thomas Aquinas
or the *Church Dogmatics* of Karl Barth. He needed to heed
Paul's words in 1 Corinthians: "For though I am free from
all persons, I have made myself a slave to all....I have become all things to all persons...for the sake of the gospel"
(9:19–23). Koyama's theological education was changed. He
not only read it in library volumes but also heard it in the
fields where people were plowing with their water buffaloes
or thatching their leaking roofs. His first major theological
work was born.[34]

Theological activity on the tribal scene is asking questions
that cannot be answered only from traditional library research. Will theological education in the West ever get out
into the streets without an umbrella, get wet and hear the
birds singing? When will theological education bring into the
classroom the woman whom the crowd wanted to stone, and
for whom Jesus improvised a shield to save her? It is significant that this is the only time we hear twice that "Jesus bent
down and wrote with his finger on the ground" (John 8:1,
11). He "won" that soul quietly, while writing in the sand.
Much theological activity is taking place on the ground and
in the streets, in the fields where people are, where the church
is. The church is the author of Christian theology: oral, written, symbolic, and liturgical theology. The church is more on
the streets than in the library. While I was a visiting professor
at Princeton Theological Seminary, I was tempted to go out
and look for the Samaritan woman in the streets, to bring
her into the lecture room and with my students listen to her
theological views. But I did not have the courage to yield to
this temptation. Nevertheless, I am convinced that the million voices of the Samaritan woman are as valid a source for

34. See Kosuke Koyama, *Water Buffalo Theology* (London: SCM Press, 1974).

doing theology as are the thousands of books and journals in our libraries.

Indigenous peoples are becoming conscious of their own contribution to Christian life. The World Christian Gathering of Indigenous Peoples (WCGIP) held its first assembly in New Zealand, hosted by the Maori people of Aoteroa. The second assembly in Dakota in 1998 was attended by more than eighty native groups from eighteen countries, representing a wide spectrum of church traditions. "For some of the delegates, it was the first time they had used their tribal dances and songs for worship and it had a 'liberating effect,' " said cochairperson Richard Twiss. "Native people who have been Christians for many years experienced affirmation from the Lord.... There was a lot of rejoicing, a lot of weeping, a lot of people breaking free from 'bad theology,' " he said. It is further reported about the Dakota assembly that

> The North American hosts...claimed their heritage for Christ in their own true, traditional style. With war whoops punctuating the soft throb of First Nation drums, 100 native Americans, adorned in eagle feathers and rawhide tassels, wound through the hall. The soft rustle of wampum bead and rattles whispered in time to the rhythmic padding of moccasined feet. Brilliant reds, yellows, and white flashed from their ceremonial regalia as the Indians danced the traditional strut-stepped choreography reminiscent of a bygone era on the Great Plains. The shrill spine-chilling whoops declared that they were ready to engage in spiritual battle for Christ.[35]

Is this a foretaste of theological things to come from the native, indigenous, or tribal peoples, who have now begun to feel freer on the globalized platform to claim their cultures under the Christian umbrella? But more still needs to be done than simply wearing the outward regalia.

---

35. United Bible Societies, *World Report* (1999), 13–14.

The joint book *Apologia: Contextualization, Globalization, and Mission in Theological Education* is a stimulating challenge for theological education. As Donald W. Shriver says about it in the foreword: "It is a book that begins in dialogue and ends with same. It is not afraid to ask Christians to converse with partners as old as Abraham and Sarah [what about Hagar?], as remote as Hindus.... It encourages me to pursue my own profession as a theologian with many new partners around the world."[36] Indeed, there are many "old" partners in doing theology, but "new" ones are few and maybe suspect in some theological quarters. Theological education everywhere should lead us all toward the goal of having both new and old partners. Perhaps only that way will we be able to learn and practice the globalization of theology. Theological education has to take risks and broadly function on a truly multicultural and even multireligious basis.[37]

If we are to globalize theological education, this must not be allowed simply to become the universalization of one theological tradition, however rich and historically rooted. We have to avoid the danger of theological education in one part of the world becoming globalized at the expense of other areas. Only if there are no bulldozers on the global scene can the bull step on the platform and, feeling at home, bellow with the full strength of its lungs.

---

36. Donald W. Shriver, foreword to Max L. Stackhouse et al., *Apologia: Contextualization, Globalization, and Mission in Theological Education* (Grand Rapids, Mich.: Eerdmans, 1988), xvi. See also Evans et al., eds., *Globalization of Theological Education.* Contributors discuss crosscultural dialogue, globalization as justice, and mutuality in global education in the form of case studies. This team has also been promoting global theological education for many years.

37. The essay by Richard Osmer in vol. 2, "The Teaching Ministry in a Multicultural World," has useful insights about the teaching ministry of the church as catechesis, edification, and discernment, to which I would add celebration.

– Chapter 4 –

CHRISTIAN CONTRIBUTIONS TO THE GLOBALIZATION OF CONFUCIANISM (BEYOND MAOISM)

Sze-kar Wan

First awakened by the velvet revolution of 1989 and further buoyed by the explosion of information technology of the last decade, expectations run high that a global civil society is poised to emerge in which citizens of different nationalities and ethnicities enter into association with each other under the democratic conditions of pluralism, tolerance, understanding, and respect. Globalization, it is said, is fast erasing all traditional boundaries and weakening power cliques based thereon, even if, in its economic form, it is also creating new elites. The wider process, however, has already created, and will continue to create, transnational organizations such as Amnesty International, the United Nations, and the Helsinki Watch. These organizations are capable of transporting across geographical barriers and natural borders civil values such as human rights, self-determination, and freedom to countries that have traditionally been hostile to them. This new cosmopolitanism, freshly energized by the Internet and broadband telecommunication lines, will empower individuals and unleash in them new levels of autonomy, rebellion, impediment, intervention, and other similar values that exist in symbiosis with a popular culture that is itself being universalized. This new age is supposed to be able to challenge regional potentates and insular autocrats to change their old, tired ways of conducting business, if only we can recognize the global public sphere that is being invisibly formed and shape it so that it can fulfill the promise for all to have equal access.[1]

Such exuberant optimism, however, evident mostly in Europe and the United States,[2] must be balanced by the sobering reality that is China. Year after year, reports on human rights list China as one of the most flagrant offenders. The Religious Right of North America consistently harps on religious persecutions by the communist state. Even corporations whose first considerations rarely have anything to do with public morals complain about the Chinese government's pattern of capricious disdain for contractual obligations. Is China the massive exception to the inexorability of globalization? How is it possible to herald the advent of globalization when China, intransigent with its tradition-laden histories and massive population, appears to have successfully resisted integration into this supposed universal path? Posed in another way, can and will China develop a civil society in step with the rest of the world? China's entry into the WTO may require it.

While it would be a stretch to claim that religion in general

---

1. Special thanks go to my colleague William Everett, who read successive drafts of this essay and helped me with his usual informed, probing comments.

See, e.g., Michael Walzer, "The Idea of Civil Society," *Dissent* (Spring 1991): 293–304; Michael Walzer, ed., *Toward a Global Civil Society* (Oxford: Berg Hahn Books, 1995), 2–4; John Keane, *Civil Society: Old Images, New Visions* (Stanford, Calif.: Stanford University Press, 1998), 109–13.

2. John Keane suggests that we are witnessing "an emerging European civil society comprising a *macédoine* of personal contacts, networks, conferences, political parties, social initiatives, trade unions, small businesses and large firms, friendships, and local and regional forums" (*Civil Society,* 111). There are grounds for doubts, however, as Keane himself points out: Genocidal wars are being waged still, and the swelling population of refugees remains as intractable a problem today as it was in the immediate aftermath of the communist collapse (112). In the case of the United States, critics such as Robert Bellah have charged that, despite its long tradition of formally free associations, it has become in recent decades less an effective democracy than an oligarchy controlled by corporate interests; see the introductory essay in Robert Bellah et al., *Habits of the Heart: Individualism and Commitment in American Life,* rev. ed. (Berkeley: University of California Press, 1996); and Richard Madsen, *China's Catholics: Tragedy and Hope in an Emerging Civil Society,* Comparative Studies in Religion and Society (Berkeley: University of California Press, 1998), 14.

and Christianity in particular could provide full answers to these complex sociopolitical questions, it would equally be a mistake to ignore how a global religion like Christianity continues to make an impact on the world today, even to thrive in a communist state like China. It is unclear whether the much heralded "Christianity fever" in China is an overstatement. Those who rely mainly on the churches registered with the government offer a moderate view of the growth of Protestants and Catholics in China,[3] while observers who focus on unregistered house churches have a much more enthusiastic assessment.[4] But there is no denying that Protestants, and to a lesser extent Catholics, have been, by Western standards, wildly successful in attracting adherents to their churches. What was a Protestant population of merely 700,000 in 1950 when foreign missionaries were ushered out of China has swelled to perhaps twenty million. The growth of the Catholic Church is less spectacular, from some three million to ten, roughly the same as the population growth, but is nonetheless still respectable.[5]

Samuel Huntington's celebrated paradigm of world civilizations clashing with one another across cultural and religious fault lines, of course, pits the Christian West against, among others, Confucian China.[6] Such an open invitation for confrontation is obviously out of step with an international civil society shaped not by violent collision but by dialogue and cooperation. But more than that, Huntington is simply mistaken in making Christianity the proprietary essence of the

3. Alan Hunter and Kim-Kwong Chan, *Protestantism in Contemporary China*, Cambridge Studies in Ideology and Religion (Cambridge: Cambridge University Press, 1993), 199.

4. See Tony Lambert, *The Resurrection of the Chinese Church* (London: Hodder & Stoughton, 1991), 139–54, esp. 146–53. Lambert's sources are often anecdotal, however.

5. Madsen, *China's Catholics*, 39, 137. It must be admitted, however, that statistics on Christians are notoriously unreliable, since ideological factors often come into play and unregistered Christians are by definition not included in the count. See Hunter and Chan, *Protestantism in Contemporary China*, 171–75, for reasons accounting for the Protestant success in China since 1979.

6. Samuel P. Huntington, *The Clash of Civilizations and the Remaking of World Order* (New York: Simon & Schuster, 1996).

West. In light of the statistical reality that the vast majority of self-professed Christians live not in the West but outside it — in Africa, Asia, and Latin America — Huntington's exclusive claim for Christianity appears hopelessly outdated. His view of Christianity is premised on a superficial understanding of the church, which always claims globalism as its birthright and universality as its end. What Huntington fails to recognize is that lived religions, Christianity included, often surprise academics by crossing cultural borders and conceptual boundaries. They take root in and resculpture societies in which they did not originate, and they are thereby transformed into hotbeds of intercultural as well as intracultural conversations.[7]

Not only is Huntington's model based on flawed assumptions, it is also an unproductive starting point for understanding China. It completely ignores the progressive Chinese intellectuals' severe critique of traditional Confucianism in favor of Westernization. The iconoclastic television series *River Elegy,* for example, which helped fuel the failed prodemocracy movement of 1989, rejects all forms of authoritarianism, with a not-so-veiled reference to Confucianism and communism. China today, according to its authors, must leave behind the murky past of the muddy Yellow River for the clear, blue ocean of the modern West. If anything, they advocate an assimilation to Western values to replace Confucianism, a proposal that can hardly be called confrontation. To view through Huntington's dark lenses is to become blind to the multihued debates and thoroughgoing self-criticism taking place in China today.

Still, even if Christianity continues to be a visible presence in the Chinese scene, as we have every reason to expect it to be, what kind of role is it ready to play in China's shifting political culture? And if it has a role, how will it contribute

---

7. On this regard, see the penetrating analysis of Christianity's crosscultural potentials in Lamin Sanneh, *Translating the Message: The Missionary Impact on Culture,* American Society of Missiology Series 13 (Maryknoll, N.Y.: Orbis Books, 1989).

to the ongoing conversation on self-definition, reformation, and revitalization in China today? These are questions this essay intends to articulate further.

Between State and Citizens: The Elusive Chinese Civil Society

What kind of civil society China has and ought to develop has long been raised by reform-minded Chinese intellectuals. Answers to that question revolve around the complex relationship between the state and its citizenry. In the liberal days of the 1980s, a move was afoot to locate the civil rights of the citizenry not in the individual but in the citizens' obligations to the state as well as in the state's structural promise of stability and equality.[8] Shen Yue, one of the earliest theorists, based the concept of "townspeople's rights" (*shimin quanli*) on Marx's idea of *bürgerliche Gesellschaft,* with the latter roundly mistranslated then as "bourgeois society" in Chinese (*zichanjieji shehui*). But the advent of a market economy, according to Shen, has recovered the meaning of the root word *Burg* ("a fortified place, such as a castle or walled city"), the proper context for a *bürgerliche Gesellschaft,* into *chengshi* ("town"), understood rightly as comprised of *cheng* ("a fortified place") and *shi* ("market"). The townspeople's rights are therefore guaranteed, even required, by the protected exchange of commodities in the market, available to both the proletariat and bourgeoisie.[9]

---

8. On the following Chinese views, I have depended on the thorough research of Ma Shu-Yun, "The Chinese Discourse on Civil Society," *China Quarterly* 137 (1994): 180–93.

9. Shen Yue, "Zichanjieji quanli ying yi wei shimin quanli" ('Bourgeois right' should be 'townspeople's right'), *Tianjin shehui kexue* (*Tianjin Social Sciences*) 4 (1986); "'Shimin shehui' bianxi" (An investigation of 'townspeople's society'), *Zhexue janjiu* (*Studies of Philosophy*) 1 (1990): 44–51; cf. Ma, "The Chinese Discourse," 183–84. Shen's work was recognized even by the government; the first of his articles was abstracted in the official *People's Daily* (November 24, 1986), according to Ma (183 n. 34). Shen later came under attack for having misrepresented Marx's notion of *Bürger;* see Xi Zhaoyong, "'Shimin shehui bianxi' de bianxi" (An investigation of 'investigation of townspeople's society'), *Zhexue janjiu* (*Research on Philosophy*) 5 (1990): 31–36; cf. Ma, "Chinese Discourse," 184. But Shen's point

This attempt to advance the rights of the people by transcending class distinction was furthered by Huang Dao, who
argued that there is a mutuality between state and citizenry
as crystallized in the notion of "civic awareness." While the
citizens are an integral component of the state, they must
reciprocate by demonstrating their duties toward the state.
While the state must safeguard the civil rights of its people,
responsible citizens must demonstrate their loyalty by abid-
ing by the laws and ordinances of the state and defending
the stability of social order.[10] Huang did make a distinction
between "bourgeois individualistic consciousness," which he
rejected, and "social collectivism," which he considered the
proper basis for civil society in China. But he nevertheless
succeeded in conceptualizing "civic awareness" as a category
independent of class and as the focal point of the citizens'
private and public interests. The groundwork was thus laid
for reformulating the categories of Chinese citizenry.[11]

From this we can see that the initial Chinese discussion was
pursued with the tacit, therefore unquestioned, assumption
that the state must play an inextricably leading role in the formation of civil society. Even those who located civil rights in
Western-styled individualism were irresistibly drawn back to
an evaluation of the state's irreducible presence. Li Zhiguang
and Wang Suli, for example, appealed to individualism as the
legitimate basis for civic awareness, but they did so by query-
ing the condition under which individual awareness could be

---

has to do with how the concept has changed over time in the context of the bur-
geoning market economy. After all, Jürgen Habermas uses *bürgerliche Gesellschaft*
(as "bourgeois society" by his translators) to refer not to the bourgeoisie but to the
public sphere (*Öffentlichkeit*), which is the convergence of different associations; see
Jürgen Habermas, *The Structural Transformation of the Public Sphere: An Inquiry
into a Category of Bourgeois Society* (Cambridge, Mass.: MIT Press, 1989).

10. Huang Dao, "Lue lun shehuizhuyi gongmin yishi de shidai tezhi" (A brief
discussion of the contemporary characteristics of socialism's civic awareness), *Lilun
yuekan* (*Theoretical Monthly*) 1 (1988); cf. Ma, "Chinese Discourse," 184.

11. The emphasis on the citizens' civic obligation as the basis of a civil society
can also be found in Ju Mingzhou, "Wenhua shi gongmin shehui xingwei de zhidu
tixi" (Culture is the system of behaviors in a civil society), *Liaoning daxue xuebao*
(*Liaoning University Journal*) 5 (1989): 28–32; cf. Ma, "Chinese Discourse," 185.

developed.[12] "Mass," as in the term "mass society," connotes in Chinese subordination (*qun*) to personal rulers, whereas "citizen" is associated with individual rights and equality in the West. In retaining the concept of "mass society," both in traditional and contemporary Chinese social thoughts, therefore, China has preserved a dependence on personal rulership (*ren zhi*). Only when this is replaced by governance-by-law (*fa zhi*), many argue, could China hope to lay a favorable foundation for democracy and turn the masses into citizens. In short, most Chinese, and especially the intellectuals, concurred that the state must maintain a posture of benevolent guardianship over the transformation of society prior to 1989. So concludes Ma Shu-Yun:

> In its initial phase, the focus of the Chinese domestic discussion of civil society was on the creation of a modern citizenry through inspiration of "civic awareness" by the state among the people.... While advocating individual rights and freedom, the Chinese domestic discussants of civil society recognized the inevitable existence of the state. The civil society in their mind is one that will maintain a harmonious relation with the state, rather than a hostile rejection of it.[13]

Two events in 1989, however, drove the Chinese to rethink the relationship between citizens and state. In the days following the bloody June Fourth crackdown at Tiananmen Square, the hoped-for groundswell of support from the people for the fallen demonstrators never materialized. Once the leaders went underground, their supporters dispersed and dissolved into the masses. Even though the oppressive regime was supposed to have lost its "mandate," the world continued its silent acquiescence. By contrast, the Eastern European revolution succeeded in large part not by violence or political

---

12. Liu Zhiguang and Wang Suli, "Cong qunzhong shehui zouxiang gongmin shehui" (From mass society to civil society), *Zhengzhixue yanjiu (Research on Political Science)* 5 (1988); cf. Ma, "Chinese Discourse," 184.

13. Ma, "Chinese Discourse," 185.

coup but as a result of broad-based support garnered from intellectuals, trade unions, and the churches, especially the Catholic Church. "Communism was not defeated by military force," recounts Vaclav Havel, "but by life, by the human spirit, by conscience."[14] The Chinese intellectuals witnessed in vivid fashion not only the transformation of a political order but the heart of that transformation. What gave power to the powerless was a civil society distinct from and, in times of need, in opposition to an authoritarian regime. The exiled Chinese journalist Liu Binyan praised the courage of his Eastern European counterparts to confront the communist state and party and called for China to develop a civil society strengthened by "a flowering of all kinds of independent organizations, especially free trade unions."[15]

As a result of these events, Chinese intellectuals, now mostly writing in exile, utterly lost confidence in the Chinese state's capacity to undergird the development of a civil society. Chen Kuide (under the pseudonym of Hua Yifu), whom Ma credits for being the first to reopen the post–June Fourth civil society discourse, accused the Chinese government, in collusion with the Communist Party, of attempting "to strangle civil society in the cradle."[16] The solution, he later amplified, could only be a reconstruction of a civil society that is structurally detached from the state.[17] Relying

14. Vaclav Havel, "The Power of the Powerless," in *Open Letters: Selected Writings 1965–1990 by Vaclav Havel*, ed. P. Wilson (New York: Knopf, 1991), 125–214.

15. Liu Binyan, "China and the Lessons of Eastern Europe," *Journal of Democracy* 2, no. 2 (1991): 3–11; cf. Ma, "The Chinese Discourse," 188. See also Su Shaozhi et al., "Zhongguo de gongmin shehui de fazhan qushi" (The development of Chinese civil society), in *Dangdai zhongguo de guojia yu shehui guanxi* (The relationship between state and society in modern China), ed. Zhou Xueguang (Taibei: Guiguan, 1992), 91–102.

16. Chen Kuide, "Cong zhengzhi wenhua de jiaodu kan 'liu si' yizhounian" (Reflections on the first anniversary of June Fourth from the perspective of political culture), *Jiushi niandai* (*The Nineties*) (June 1990): 54–55; cf. Ma, "Chinese Discourse," 187.

17. Chen Kuide, "Lun zuqun shehui de wudao he gongmin shehui de chongjian" (On the nonsense of collective society and the reconstruction of civil society), *Zhishifenzi* (*The Intellectuals*) (Summer 1991): 23–30; cf. Ma, "Chinese Discourse," 187–88.

on Jürgen Habermas, Chen suggested that the Chinese civil society ought to be situated between the state and its citizens but separate from ideology so that it could constitute a public sphere. For this reason, he preferred to translate "civil society" as *minjian shehui* ("people-based society").[18] On the basis of his survey of post-1989 Chinese writers on the question of civil society in China, Ma concludes, "Among exiled Chinese intellectuals civil society has become fashionable. The common emphasis has been on independence from the state."[19]

But is it possible to extricate the civil society from the state? Post–June Fourth writers rather facilely assumed that once nongovernment organizations and similar free associations have gathered enough independence from the state, a civil society would naturally spring up. In fact, state and society form a paradoxical relationship. According to Edward Shils, a healthy civil society embodies two complementary characteristics. While a civil society has to be independent from the state, it nevertheless must also maintain some form of effective ties with the state.[20] Although Shils is surely right in noting that "the virtue of civil society is the readiness to moderate particular, individual or parochial interests and to give precedence to the common good,"[21] it is the state's function to provide the right conditions for the pursuit of the "common good" in passing and enforcing reasonable laws and guaranteeing freedoms that form the bases for a healthy civil society.

What is true in general is even more true in traditional

---

18. Chen Kuide, "Chongjian gongmin shehui" (Reconstructing civil society), in Zhou, ed., *Dangdai zhongguo*, 60–61, but see also 61–77. See also Xie Wen, "Zhongguo gongmin shehui de yunyu he fazhan" (The birth and development of civil society in China), in Zhou, ed., *Dangdai zhongguo*, 107–21; Su et al., "Zhongguo de gongmin," 79–105; Ma, "Chinese Discourse," 188–91 (a survey of post-1989 Chinese writers).

19. Ma, "Chinese Discourse," 191.

20. Shils adds that a civil society must also be characterized by the presence of civility. Edward Shils, "The Virtue of Civil Society," *Government and Opposition* 26, no. 1 (1991): 3–20.

21. Ibid., 16.

Chinese society, in which there seems to be no discernible distinction between state and society. William Rowe, Mary Rankin, and most recently Timothy Brook, Michael Frolic, Roger des Forges, as well as other prominent scholars of Chinese social history, have all tried to document the existence of autonomous organizations in Chinese history. In two richly textured studies of autonomous organizations in Hankou, William Rowe directly challenges Max Weber's assertion that China failed to develop Western-style capitalism in part because of an absence of urban political autonomy and a predominance of family-based social structure. Instead, Rowe claims to have found corporate groups and free associations in late Qing and early Republican China.[22]

This thesis receives confirmation from Mary Rankin, who suggests that central power after the Taiping Rebellion had already in the mid-nineteenth century shifted from the state to the local urban elites. The result was the maintenance of local education, social welfare, and so on falling into the realm of society rather than state. Also the rapid rise of the merchant class, especially in treaty ports but also in the hinterlands, played midwife to the establishment of a public sphere.[23]

---

22. William T. Rowe, *Hankow: Commerce and Society in a Chinese City, 1796–1889* (Stanford, Calif.: Stanford University Press, 1984), 4–5 and passim; see also William T. Rowe, *Hankow: Conflict and Community in a Chinese City, 1796–1895* (Stanford, Calif.: Stanford University Press, 1989).

23. Mary Backus Rankin, *Elite Activism and Political Transformation in China: Zhejing Province, 1865–1911* (Stanford, Calif.: Stanford University Press, 1986). This "public sphere" (*gong*), according to Rankin, "refers more specifically to the institutionalized, extra-bureaucratic management of matters considered important by both the community and the state. Public management by elites thus contrasted with official administration (*guan*), and private (*si*) activities of individuals, families, religions, businesses, and organizations that were not identified with the whole community" (15). See also Mary Backus Rankin, "The Origins of a Chinese Public Sphere: Local Elites and Community Affairs in the Late Imperial Period," *Etudes Chinoises* 9, no. 2 (1990): 13–60. Joining both Rankin and Rowe is David Strand, who cites the establishment of newspapers in the 1920s in Beijing, the discussion of city management in parks, brothels, teahouses, and same-village guilds, pavilions, and temples as examples of a public sphere (in Habermas's sense) in early republican China. See David Strand, *Rickshaw Beijing: City People and Politics in the 1920s* (Berkeley: University of California Press, 1989); and David Strand, "Protest in Beijing: Civil Society and Public Sphere in China," *Problems of Communism* 39, no. 3 (1990).

These claims of having discovered an independent public sphere in Chinese society are premature, however. Frederic Wakeman rightly observes that few of these formal and informal institutions were truly independent from the state and therefore did not constitute a separate sphere as such.[24] Furthermore, to what extent these social groups had the kind of social and nomistic cohesion necessary for the formation of associations is open to question. And whether these institutions took on a socioreligious legitimacy that shaped an entire ethos, as Weber would have wondered, remains a debatable issue. All this research points out not so much a civil society independent of the state as its very opposite — namely, the inextricable role the state plays in all areas of social life, even in organizations normally thought to be autonomous in the West. Similar searches for cohesive social groups, but now groups not so much independent of but in cooperation with the state, have been recently conducted,[25] and this has led to the conclusion that

> Opposing or excluding the state is what gives civil society its critical force. But it also narrows the concept down from the original breadth of its historical meaning. We have found that to speak of civil society as a real social possibility, it is necessary to bring the state back into the discussion. . . . In the Chinese context, we have found it necessary to view the state as an active factor, both in the contemporary Leninist setting and in the imperial period, when . . . the state was a "far more

---

24. Frederic Wakeman, "The Civil Society and Public Sphere Debate: Western Reflections on Chinese Political Culture," *Modern China* 19, no. 2 (1993): 108–38. Wakeman's article is a lengthy critique of the works of Rowe, Rankin, and Strand, on which I have depended much for this discussion. Rowe's and Rankin's articles in the same issue of *Modern China* are in many ways responses to Wakeman: William T. Rowe, "The Problem of 'Civil Society' in Late Imperial China"; and Mary Backus Rankin, "Some Observations on a Chinese Public Sphere," both in *Modern China* 19, no. 2 (1993): 139–57 and 158–82, respectively.

25. See, e.g., Timothy Brook, "Auto-Organization in Chinese Society"; B. Michael Frolic, "State-Led Civil Society"; and Roger V. des Forges, "States, Societies, and Civil Societies in Chinese History," all in Timothy Brook and B. Michael Frolic, eds., *Civil Society in China* (Armonk, N.Y.: M. E. Sharpe, 1997).

conspicuous element in constructions of the moral world than in the West." Chinese states may have been demonstrably authoritarian, but they also contributed much of "the moral terrain on which to stand."[26]

In this view, Western-style civil society has never been realized in the history of China; nor is there reason to believe that a society fully independent of the state is ever realizable, even desirable. As the iconoclastic May Fourth has amply shown, and as the early Chinese Communist efforts at disarming oppressive societal customs and rituals in the 1950s have reinforced, a society can become so ill that only draconian measures — initiated, maintained, and executed by the state — could heal. A society given to its own device might more naturally exhibit competition, selfishness, parochialism, and runaway solipsism, as in the case of a corrupt, stagnant Confucianism clutching societal life in its death grips. Echoing the bitterness of the May Fourth writer Lu Xun, the authors of the controversial *River Elegy* charged, "What Confucian culture has given us over the past several thousand years is not a national spirit of enterprise, a system of laws, or a mechanism of cultural renewal, but a fearsome self-killing machine that, as it degenerated, constantly devoured its best and its brightest, its own vital elements."[27] Whether they were aware of it or not, it was the leadership of the Communist regime, a state empowered by popular acclamation in its early years, that overreached into societal, communal, and even personal spheres and finally disabled the "fearsome self-killing machine" that the authors claimed was Confucianism.

It was up to the exiled sociologist Wang Shaoguang to criticize the blind faith placed on a form of civil society that does

---

26. Timothy Brook and B. Michael Frolic, "The Ambiguous Challenge of Civil Society," in Brook and Frolic, eds., *Civil Society in China,* 10; citations in the quote are from Brook, "Auto-Organization in Chinese Society."

27. Quoted in Tu Wei-ming, "Cultural China: The Periphery as the Center," in *The Living Tree: The Changing Meaning of Being Chinese Today,* ed. Tu Wei-ming (Stanford, Calif.: Stanford University Press, 1994), 31. Along the same line could also be cited films by Zhang Yimou, many of which are banned in China.

not involve the state. The results are not necessarily equality and democracy. Economic disparity among citizens might become more severe without the regulation of the state, and the tyranny of an authoritarian state might be replaced by the tyranny of greedy capitalists. A Chinese civil society actually requires the state to intervene, "to limit the rights of private property, to moderate the regulation mechanism of the market, to minimize economic and social disparity." The issue, therefore, is not that the state in a democracy must not intervene, but "on behalf of whom to intervene, for what to intervene, and how to intervene." Democracy does not mean that the state plays no role in social and economic spheres but "that state and society must democratize simultaneously" and "the state should democratically intervene in economic and social functions."[28]

In the Chinese case, therefore, we must look for a civil society that not only maintains a degree of autonomy from the state but *simultaneously* cultivates ties to it and presses it toward a more genuinely democratic order. This complex relationship of independence and connection between society and state that characterizes a civil society is well expressed by Shils:

> Although autonomy vis-à-vis the state is one of the features of a civil society, the autonomy is far from complete. Civil society operates within the framework set by laws. The laws of such a society are, among other things, intended to hold conflict in check by compelling adherence to agreements, and by inflicting sanctions on actions which criminally damage other persons. Laws require that rights within the civil society be respected and that duties be performed.[29]

A civil society ought to stand in distinction from but at the same time in tension with both the state and society.[30] Draw-

---

28. Wang Shaoguang, "Pochu dui *Civil Society* de misi" (Breaking the fixation on civil society), in Zhou, ed., *Dangdai zhongguo,* 22.

29. Shils, "Virtue of Civil Society," 16.

30. This is the conclusion of Keane, *Civil Society,* chap. 2. Keane hopes to see

ing on John Keane's discussion of Hegel and Paine, Heath
Chamberlain distinguishes between society and *civil* society,
and concludes that *"both* state *and* society [are] essential
components of a healthy civil society."[31] The relationship
between state and society in the case of China is a complex one: "A viable civil society depends ... on its separation
from the state," but at the same time, "the state can be a
powerful ally and instrument in the process [of sustaining
a viable civil society]."[32] In different terms but in the same
vein, Peter Huang calls for the recognition of a "third realm"
that, like Habermas's "bourgeois public sphere" *(bürgerliche
Öffentlichkeit)*, is distinct from state and society. But unlike
Habermas's loaded term, this "third realm" simply describes
the space between state and society, with perhaps an implied
relationship to both.

Church as an Association of Civility

The conclusions reached by the Sinologists coincide remark-
ably with what Peter Berger and Richard Neuhaus have called
the "mediating structures" between the individual and the
state.[33] These structures have usually been understood to refer
to voluntary associations, of which churches as well as other
religious organizations are an integral part,[34] that are fundamental to the vitality of civil society in the Anglo-American

---

civil society as a mediating notion situated midway between the Hobbesian "security
state" and Paine's total absence of state control. Keane's nuanced understanding of
civil society is discussed by Heath B. Chamberlain, "On the Search for Civil Society
in China," *Modern China* 19, no. 2 (1993): 205–9; and Huang Philip, " 'Public
Sphere'/'Civil Society' in China? The Third Realm between State and Society," 216–
26, in the same issue. See the similar conclusion more recently by Brook and Frolic,
"Ambiguous Challenge," 8–16.

31. Heath B. Chamberlain, "On the Search for Civil Society," 205; his emphasis.
See Keane, *Civil Society,* chap. 2.

32. Chamberlain, "On the Search," 209.

33. Peter Berger and Richard Neuhaus, *To Empower People: The Role of Mediating Structures in Public Policy* (Washington, D.C.: American Enterprise Institute,
1977).

34. Robert Wuthnow, *Christianity and Civil Society: The Contemporary Debate*
(Valley Forge, Pa.: Trinity Press International, 1996), 1–8, esp. 8.

context. Basic to an associational civil society is the principle of separation of power, which, according to James Luther Adams, is the means by which individuals participate in the process of making social decisions.[35] Herein lie both allure and danger with voluntary associations. While voluntary associations provide the necessary social space for individuals to exercise self-government, the same, if left unregulated by law and detached from the state, could become parochial and inward-looking, neglecting their public obligations and forfeiting their place in an enlightened public discourse.[36] In fact, the insularity of a closed group can produce bigotry and all forms of self-aggrandized chauvinism.[37] Indeed, should triads and other seditious secret societies in China be considered alongside ancestral clubs and churches as associations constructive toward a civil society? The mere existence of voluntary associations is no guarantee in itself against tyranny and abuse. As Wang Shaoguang pointed out, in spite of a vibrant tapestry of associational life comprising trade unions, writers' guilds, the Catholic Church, and so forth, which contributed mightily to overthrowing the Communist regime, Eastern Europe has yet to produce an unadulterated democracy.[38] In light of the ensuing Balkan conflicts, which resulted in genocides and other horrific atrocities, his 1991 premonitions have turned out to be prophetic.

If that is the case, one would have to examine thoroughly

---

35. James Luther Adams, *On Being Human Religiously,* ed. with an introduction by Max L. Stackhouse (Boston: Beacon Press, 1976), 58–59.

36. Ibid., 76–82.

37. A parallel case can be drawn from social anthropology. Etienne Balibar has argued that Lévi-Strauss's concern to regard all cultures as equally valid and above criticism by others has unwittingly led to the ultrarightists' xenophobic rhetoric in his home country of France. If all cultural groupings have an equal right to insular existence, so goes the argument, immigrants and minorities must not be allowed to participate in the mainstream either. Thus, an originally anti-imperialistic strategy to protect minority rights by sealing them off from intercultural and crosscultural exchanges gave rise to political chauvinism. See Etienne Balibar, "Is There a 'Neo-Racism'?" in *Race, Nation, Class: Ambiguous Identities,* ed. Etienne Balibar and Immanuel Wallerstein (London: Verso, 1991), 17–28; see also Homi Bhabha, *The Location of Culture* (London and New York: Routledge, 1994), 37–67.

38. Wang, "Pochu dui," 22–26.

life in associations in general, in the church specifically, and
the qualities they manifest. Without attempting to work out
the relationship between citizens and state, it is possible to
focus on civility as the quality that characterizes a healthy
association. Richard Madsen has applied this to his study of
the Catholic Church in China with productive results: "To
be part of the 'conditions of liberty' [Ernest Gellner's term]
not only does a group have to be civilian — at least partially
independent and self-governing — it also has to have civility — it needs to embody and sustain certain kinds of moral
relationships."[39] Central to Madsen's proposal are Robert
Putnam's four characteristics of civility.[40] First, members of
an association must display "civic engagement" and be "alive
to the interests of others." Second, the association must be
characterized by "horizontal relationships of reciprocity and
cooperation" over "vertical relationships of authority and
dependence." Third, there must be highly developed expectations and practices of solidarity, trust, and tolerance. Finally,
an association that evidences civility is open to interaction
and involvement with other overlapping associations, so that
group loyalties and interests can be modulated, expanded,
even attenuated.[41]

In theological terms, the construction of a healthy association depends on an allegiance pledged by its members to
a transcendent principle higher than itself. While an association has its own rules and principles for self-governance
within its boundaries, it also must avoid absolutizing itself
above all else, in order to safeguard itself against the destructive tendencies that come with a self-enclosed organization.
In short, I argue that Chinese intellectuals should pay much
greater attention than they have to the central symbol of governance in Judaism and Christianity, namely, the concept of

---

39. Madsen, *China's Catholics,* 14. For his conclusion on how the Chinese
Catholic Church displays a manifest lack of civility, see 15 and 134–38.

40. Robert Putnam, *Making Democracy Work: Civic Traditions in Modern Italy*
(Princeton, N.J.: Princeton University Press, 1993). Putnam bases his conclusions in
this book on a study of democratic development in northern Italy.

41. Ibid., 87–90; cf. Madsen, *China's Catholics,* 14, 134–35.

covenant, which stands at the root of Western democracy.[42] They need to come to terms with the historical and symbolic resources that inform, give rise to, and nourish social and political thoughts in the West.

Robert Bellah and the other authors of *Habits of the Heart* have subtly called this kind of excavation into the depths of one's cultural and historical deposits a recovery of one's "community of memory":

> Communities ... have a history — in an important sense they are constituted by their past — and for this reason we can speak of a real community as a "community of memory," one that does not forget its past. In order not to forget that past, a community is involved in retelling its story, its constitutive narrative, and in so doing, it offers examples of the men and women who have embodied and exemplified the meaning of the community. These stories of collective history and exemplary individuals are an important part of the tradition that is so central to a community of memory.[43]

The heretofore excision of religious and cultural values from the discussion of modern Chinese political thought has been unfortunate, for politics and morality are inextricably bound up together in Chinese culture, and history is replete with examples of such cooperation. Only an inclusion of religious values could allow Christianity and deep-seated Chinese

---

42. In suggesting that a covenantal view of democracy lies at the base of Christianity, I am not denying the diverse ways in which Christianity has interacted with democracy. As Wuthnow points out, "The North American form of civil society derived its strength from dissident religious groups who constructed a pluralistic society for the sake of freedom. In European nations in which Christianity has been acting as cultural and civic guardianship, however, Christian militancy had to be suppressed before a pluralistic democracy could gain ascendancy." Wuthnow, *Christianity and Civil Society* 6–7, but see also 45.

43. Robert Bellah et al., *Habits of the Heart: Individualism and Commitment in American Life* (New York: Harper & Row, 1985), 153. See also Richard Madsen, "The Public Sphere, Civil Society, and Moral Community: A Research Agenda for Contemporary China Studies," *Modern China* 19, no. 2 (1993): 190–94. Madsen uses the concept of "community of memory" as a central methodological symbol for a renewed search for moral community in Chinese history.

religiosity to come into conversation with each other. Such a concern has been raised by the exiled playwright Su Wei, who suggests that while Eastern European civil society might hold some attraction, Chinese intellectuals might look for "new ideological resources" from within China's own cultural and spiritual heritage.[44] But a Christian encounter with Confucian China might ironically help unearth and legitimate more promising covenantal hints buried deep in the long-forgotten memory sediments of Chinese civilization. A recovery of covenantal thoughts could rekindle near-extinguished embers that smolder still in the collective Chinese hearth.[45] While a project of this sort cannot predict the future, this recovery of memory could take place in two parallel developments: in the strengthening of the Chinese Christian church as a self-sufficient covenantal community based on New Testament principles, and in the holding up of Christian thoughts as a mirror reflecting back to Chinese intellectuals their own deepest, long-obscured, historical and moral mission, which is an integral part of China's cultural legacy.

In China's modern search for democracy, therefore, Chinese intellectuals cannot forget their past but must seek to recover it in all its nuanced richness. But given the general repudiation of a calcified and stagnating Confucian tradition since the early part of the twentieth century, the way back to a dialogical rendezvous with their past must take a detour through the West. This means recovering root values that have informed Western democracy; chief among these is Christian covenantal thought. I will suggest in this essay that one of the ways in which this alliance of the intervention and recovery can be accomplished is by, on the Christian side, an examination of covenantal thoughts in the New Testament, in particular the writings of Paul, and on the Chinese side, a

---

44. Su Wei, "Man tan Beijing de wenhua quanzi" (Some thoughts on the cultural circles in Beijing), *Zhuguo zhichun* (*China Spring*) (January 1992): 61–65; cf. Ma, "Chinese Discourse," 188.

45. I owe this felicitous imagery to Lamin Sanneh, *Translating the Message: The Missionary Impact on Culture* (Maryknoll, N.Y.: Orbis Books, 1989).

combing through Confucianism for covenantal clues, both in theoretical forms and realized patterns.

Christian Covenantal Thoughts: The Pauline Paradigm

Social ethicists in the West have recently reopened the question of covenantal thought and its relation to politics (Daniel J. Elazar), governance (William Everett), and public theology (Max Stackhouse). For scriptural support, however, most have depended exclusively on the Old Testament and have ignored the witnesses to first-century covenantal development in the New Testament, especially Paul.[46] Causes for this imbalance are easy to understand: Ever since the nineteenth century, the notion of covenant has often been conceived as a private relationship between God and the individual, so much so that its corporate, social, and political dimensions are visible only in the explicit formulations found in the Old Testament. Elazar, for example, thinks that the early Christians subverted the old biblical covenantal polity into an individualistic one because Jesus has become the sole mediator of the Christian covenant, the New Testament idea of grace, and that they turned a corporate covenant into personal empowerment.[47] Elazar

---

46. Some appeal to Hebrews, due to the many uses of the term by its author. But according to the book's Middle-Platonic views, the "earthly covenant" has been superseded by a "heavenly covenant" in the death of Jesus, so that anyone who holds on to a covenant that is applicable to earthly matters belongs to the old covenant that is outdated and invalid. The covenantal structure of Hebrews is finally so otherworldly that it must be deemed antisocial and antipolitical, except in the sense that some of the key terms for covenant were translated into the Latin Vulgate as *sacramentum,* and sacramental thought had a vast impact on later social life.

47. Notice Elazar's quoting of Delbert R. Hillers, *Covenant: The History of a Biblical Idea* (Baltimore: Johns Hopkins University Press, 1969), cited in Daniel Elazar, *Covenant and Polity in Biblical Israel: Biblical Foundations and Jewish Expressions,* The Covenant Traditions in Politics I (New Brunswick, N.J.: Transaction Books, 1995), 26: "Christianity embraced the covenant idea as one of the foundations, reinterpreting the old biblical covenant establishing a people as a polity to a covenant of grace between God and individual humans granted or mediated by Jesus." William J. Everett, *God's Federal Republic: Reconstructing Our Governing Symbol* (New York: Paulist, 1988), 106–7, earlier echoed this evaluation of the early Christians and particularly Paul: "Christians seized on the Davidic covenant, therefore, to understand Jesus as God's promise to us for all the ages. The monarchical principle

sees covenant as a hierarchical rather than a democratic enterprise.[48] New Testament scholars, for their part, reinforce this impression by their insistence that covenantal thought does not lie at the center of Paul's thinking. Consequently, ethicists could perhaps be excused for appealing to Reformation history and premodern thoughts such as Puritanism for support. Indeed, on this point, certain of the Protestant Reformers anticipated what current scholarship is now revealing about covenantal thought, as we shall see.

In the historical encounter between Christianity and China, however, there is no such recourse. Nineteenth- and early-twentieth-century Chinese saw Christianity not so much as a political philosophy as a religion based on a book, and thus the Bible has become the only unambiguous symbol (in Tillich's sense) for Christianity. In spite of gunboats, military incursions, and other trappings of imperialism, and in spite of persistent patterns of missionaries collaborating with imperialistic ambitions, Christianity made its inroad into Chinese culture through the biblical text.[49] How to read philosophical and political theories out of it constituted — and still does — a central problem for Chinese Christians.[50] Whether and, if so, to what extent the biblical material, especially the New Testament, corroborates covenantal thought is therefore of paramount importance to the possibility of covenantal

---

of the Davidic covenant triumphed over the confederal form of the Mosaic covenant. The distaste for law and the preference for paternalism in St. Paul further distanced Christians from the confederal heritage, replacing it with God's special covenant with Christ, the redeemer who will come again." Also p. 114: "Christians had augmented [the ancient covenant] in the classical period by distinguishing between the corporate covenants of the people and the covenant of individuals with God through Christ."

48. Elazar, *Covenant and Polity*, 43: "Christianity emphasizes the unilateral character of God's action as a form of grace."

49. Catholic missions, of course, started much earlier than those of the Protestants, and the former did not place much emphasis on the Bible in their evangelization. Such missions, however, were mainly limited to isolated pockets in cities and the hinterland. An argument could be made that the first time Christianity made an impact on Chinese culture was when the translated Bible became widely read as literature. See essays in Irene Eber et al., eds., *The Bible in Modern China: The Literary and Intellectual Impact* (Sankt Augustin, Germany: Monumenta Serica, 1998).

50. The analogous situation is to define Confucianism by the *Five Classics* and *Four Books*.

thought playing a role in Chinese Christianity and suggesting a public theology in the Chinese context.

The New Covenant and the New People of God: Galatians

Recent New Testament scholarship has uncovered exegetical and sociological clues in Paul's writings that would place covenant in the forefront, if not the center, of Paul's thinking. Whether or not Paul could be called a "covenantal theologian" I will not resolve here; it is enough to show that Paul's ecclesiology and eschatology were greatly indebted to covenantal thinking bequeathed to him by his Jewish heritage.

Contrary to many impressions, ancient or modern, Paul never spoke ill of the Jewish covenant. In Romans 9:4, in a passionately autobiographical confession of his close identification with his Jewish heritage, Paul proudly proclaims the Israelites' possession of the covenants. In 2 Corinthians 3:6, Paul counts himself empowered by God to be appointed as minister of a "new covenant — not of letter but of the Spirit." The context of 2 Corinthians 3 is polemical: Paul trains his rhetorical arsenals on what he sarcastically calls "superlative apostles" (2 Cor 11:5) or simply "false brothers" (2 Cor 11:13). But the structure of 2 Corinthians 3:6 makes it abundantly clear that the issue before Paul and his opponents was not a dispute between the old and new covenants; rather, it was over what sort of new covenant it ought to be: While the covenant of the Spirit leads to life, the covenant of the letter leads to death.

This controversy brings to light several important aspects of first-century covenantal thought. First of all, the notion of new covenant, initially expounded by Jeremiah (31:31) and kept alive by Ezekiel, was clearly current among not just Pauline Christianity but first-century Judaism in general, as, for example, it was with the covenanters of Qumran. It was most likely current among Paul's opponents as well, since this was why Paul had to argue about the true nature of this new covenant. It stands to reason, therefore, that the new covenant language was popular also among Law-abiding missionaries.[51] Secondly, even though Paul railed against the Law throughout his career and especially in Galatians, there is no indication from his extant letters that he ever abandoned the covenantal language. No doubt this is because he did not want to cede to opponents the exclusive use of covenantal concepts. It was of utter importance to Paul how the new covenant was to be understood and defined.

Accordingly, we should read his letter to the Galatians as a concerted effort at redefining the covenant. It is common knowledge that Paul in Galatians rejects the centrality of the Law; Paul's negative statements toward the Law can be amply documented throughout the letter (2:16, 19; 3:2–5, 21–24; 4:21–5:1, and so on). But he does so in order to set one covenant over against another. The original Abrahamic covenant is chronologically prior to the Mosaic covenant established on Mount Sinai; the earlier is superior to the latter, and the original cannot be replaced by what comes later (Gal 3:15–20). Such an exegetical move — an original one in the history of Jewish exegesis — allows Paul not only to decentralize the Law and relativize any salvific significance that might be attached to it; it also shifts Paul's focus from casuistry associated with the Law and the Mosaic covenant to the promise associated with God's election of Abraham.[52] Paul

---

51. The possibility for the existence of such a group is raised by J. Louis Martyn, "A Law-Observant Mission to Gentiles: The Background of Galatians," *Scottish Journal of Theology* 38 (1985).

52. Let us leave aside the historical question whether Paul might have misinterpreted or misrepresented the Judaism of his time. There is good evidence that the straw man of casuistry that Paul sets up for himself and his Galatian audience never had any counterpart in first-century Judaism. As E. P. Sanders's classic work has amply demonstrated, the kind of legalism that Paul attacks in Galatians was at best a distortion of the profound interpretation of the law in first-century Judaism. See E. P. Sanders, *Paul and Palestinian Judaism: A Comparison of Patterns of Religions* (Philadelphia: Fortress Press, 1977), 419–28, 543–56. But regardless of whether or not Paul was accurate or whether his rhetorical barbs were trained at specific groups (both perennial problems in the annals of Galatians studies), it does not lessen the intention of his argument, which is a renewed understanding of the Abrahamic covenant of promise.

argues that once the Galatians received the Spirit at their conversion (3:1–5; 4:1–7), that is proof that the divine promise to Abraham is now fulfilled among them (3:14).[53] The new covenant, in other words, is characterized by the Spirit's active participation in the community of Jesus Christ.

The intent of this new covenant, far from fracturing the covenantal people into a disjointed collection of unrelated individuals, as modern scholars often allege, in fact reconstitutes believers as a new people of God. The boundaries distinguishing them from outsiders are no longer drawn through the criterion of ethnicity, or for that matter through class or gender: "For there is no Jew or Greek, slave or free, male and female, for all of you are one in Christ Jesus" (3:28). Paul's major concern in Galatians is to define the covenantal people by means of new criteria that do not include circumcision or any other ethnic markers, hence his animus toward the Law. Instead, the new covenantal people are marked by promise and its correlative volitional reception of that promise. The upshot is a new universalism that throws open Abraham's original covenant to all who are willing to receive the eschatological Spirit and be bound by the law of love. As a result, Gentile believers, on the basis of their reception of the Spirit, can now be called the "seed" (*sperma*) of Abraham.[54]

---

53. I have elsewhere provided detailed exegetical arguments to show that Paul thinks the reception of the Spirit which the Galatians experienced at their conversion is proof that the Abrahamic covenant is now fulfilled among the Galatians. The original promise of heir and land, therefore, is now fulfilled in Christ and the giving and reception of the Spirit (3:1–5; 4:1–7). See Sze-kar Wan, "Abraham and the Promise of the Spirit: Galatians and the Hellenistic-Jewish Mysticism of Philo," *Society of Biblical Literature 1995 Seminar Papers* 34 (1995): 6–22.

54. That Paul has in view not individuals but the *whole* people is clear from the fact that earlier Paul called Jesus Christ the singular *sperma* of Abraham (3:16). Rabbinic interpretation takes the singular *zera* as a collective singular to refer to the whole people of Israel, a move Paul was clearly familiar with, for he retains this sense when he says that the believers put on Christ at baptism (3:27) and mystically become a whole people (3:29). This again confirms that Paul is working within the Jewish covenantal tradition.

This corporate reading of Galatians can be corroborated by two recent studies. Since the work of E. P. Sanders, New Testament scholars have accepted "covenantal nomism" as a defining characteristic within first-century Judaism. See Sanders, *Paul and Palestinian Judaism;* and James D. G. Dunn, "The Theology of Galatians: The Issue of Covenantal Nomism," in *Pauline Theology, vol. I: Thessalonians, Philippi-*

If the foregoing is correct, Galatians should be seen as a covenantal document describing the pedigree of the believers (continuity with the Abrahamic covenant), the formation of the covenantal community (the presence of the eschatological Spirit in the midst of the Galatians), and the fundamental character of the community (love). The ethical section of Galatians, accordingly, is not an afterthought to its theology but should be seen as ethical stipulations that are a standard part of any covenantal document.[55]

The Love of Christ and the Law of Christ

The glue that holds the Pauline covenant together is love. Later letters of Paul (especially 1 and 2 Corinthians) and the even later Deutero-Pauline letters (Colossians, Ephesians, and the Pastorals) still have to develop the internal structure of this covenant further, but the basic contours stay the same. There is a mutuality between members of the new covenantal community, so that the rights of each member are supported through love (Gal 5:6; 1 Corinthians 13). This love is defined by Christ's giving of himself (Phil 2:6–11), so that love between members must also be characterized by the cross, the symbol of God's love to us through Christ, the foundational event of the new covenantal people. Using himself as a model

---

ans, Galatians, Philemon, ed. J. Bassler (Minneapolis: Fortress Press, 1991), 125–46. Paul was evidently no exception; he like his Jewish contemporaries was committed to the Jewish covenant, and Galatians was his conscious attempt to place the Gentile Galatian Christians in continuity with the Abrahamic covenant. A second line of research that supports a corporate reading of Galatians is the ethnographic interpretation of Paul by Philip F. Esler, "Group Boundaries and Intergroup Conflict in Galatians: A New Reading of Gal. 5:13–6:10," in *Ethnicity and the Bible,* ed. M. G. Brett (Leiden: Brill, 1996), 215–40. Asking questions of group boundaries and the distinction between insiders and outsiders, Esler suggests that Paul is in fact creating a new ethnic group. On this, see also Daniel Boyarin, "Was Paul an 'Anti-Semite'? A Reading of Galatians 3–4," *Union Seminary Quarterly Review* 47, nos. 1–2 (1993): 57–80.

55. See John M. G. Barclay, *Obeying the Truth: A Study of Paul's Ethics in Galatians* (Edinburgh: T. & T. Clark, 1988); and Charles H. Cosgrove, *The Cross and the Spirit: A Study in the Argument and Theology of Galatians* (Macon, Ga.: Mercer University Press, 1988). These works consciously foreground the ethical sections as central to the reading of Galatians.

recipient of God's love through Christ, Paul says in Galatians 2:19–20, "That which now I live in the flesh I live in faith of the son of God, who loves me and gave himself up for me." Since the Galatians' own conversion experience (3:1–5) is supposed to be modeled after this, one can draw the inference that the new covenantal people is bound by love to each other: "For in Christ Jesus, neither circumcision nor uncircumcision counts for anything, only faith working through love" (5:6). To make this character explicit, Paul bids the Galatians to turn to Leviticus 19:18: "Love your neighbor as yourself." Even though the Law is supposed to have lost currency in the new covenant, the new life is stipulated by the love for each other.[56] Instead of being governed by a law that binds the community members to predefined roles, the new life is characterized by a freedom that relies on the members' love for each other. The former is marked by strictures that serve to limit damages, the latter is characterized by promise; the former absolutizes a static pattern, the latter highlights the importance of dynamic negotiation between members.

In Biblical Hebrew, the covenantal *hesed* ("steadfast love" or "bonding fidelity") is the basis on which God established a relationship with Israel. The concept connotes mutuality, so much so that the reciprocity of the *hesed* obligation is the content of *berit* ("covenant" or "pledged sacred association"; 1 Sam 20:8). *Hesed* connotes mercy and covenantal faithfulness, but it also implies the recognition of ethical principles of responsibility, stated in legal form, that govern both ruler and people. Thus, as the *hesed* of the ruler protects his dominion, so *hesed* is what gives security to the subjects in their mutual dealings. But since the concept denotes kindness and grace

---

56. Scholars have debated whether the second half of Galatians (5:2–6:10) is integral to the letter as a whole. But the question pales in importance when seen in light of the book as a covenantal document. The so-called ethical section of Galatians is neither an afterthought nor an inconsistent addition to the theology of Galatians; it should rather be seen as part of the stipulations that are part and parcel of a covenant. For controversy and recent solutions to the problem, see Richard B. Hays, "Christology and Ethics in Galatians: The Law of Christ," *Catholic Biblical Quarterly* 49 (1987): 268–90; Barclay, *Obeying the Truth*; and Cosgrove, *Cross and the Spirit*, 5–38.

on the part of a superior, it is also connected to "salvation," "peace," "love," and "righteousness."[57]

Thus reclaiming the Old Testament *hesed*-structure and its ethical-legal stipulations while renewing the understanding of promise in light of the sacrificial love of Christ, Paul is able to collect these concepts under the paradoxical term "the law of Christ" (Gal 6:2). It is paradoxical because Paul has just given up the Jewish law, and the formulation conveys the impression at first glance that Paul is merely replacing one set of casuistries for another. But this cannot be further from the truth. The foundation upon which the law of Christ is built consists of the original promise of God to Abraham as well as covenantal love. The actual ethical injunctions in Galatians 5:19–23 are no different from moral codes of Paul's day. Indeed, they cannot be if the new covenantal community is to exist in society as a functioning constituency; the community must, in many respects, be bound by the same laws and the same ethical expectations as other communities in society. After all, God has "written on the hearts [of all peoples], to which their own conscience also bears witness," certain key ethical insights (Rom 2:13–16). But these old injunctions and morals are now used in the pursuit of building the covenantal community of promise. Far from a legalistic use of law for the purpose of prevention, which stands in judgment of the guilty, the law of Christ is seen as an active agent that promotes relationship between members of the community. So the opposite of misusing freedom for fleshly intentions ("[Do not use] freedom as an opportunity for the flesh"; Gal 5:13) is not a negative prohibition ("Do not do X") but rather a positive exhortation to build one another up ("But through love become slaves to each other"; v. 13b). Likewise, after a standard moral discussion on flesh and spirit (Gal 5:16–26), the true sign of fulfilling the law of Christ turns out to be "bearing one another's burden" (6:2a).

---

57. Rudolf Bultmann, "*eleos,* etc.," *Theological Dictionary of the New Testament,* vol. 2 (1964), 479; see also Hans Conzelmann and Walter Zimmerli, "*chairo,* etc.," *Theological Dictionary of the New Testament,* vol. 9 (1974), 381–87.

The Self-Emptying Cross
and Relationship to Outsiders

Recalling Robert Putnam's notion of civility, we can see that a covenantal community along the Pauline model easily fulfills the first three of his characteristics. A community of love eschews self-interest while inculcating a "civic engagement" among members. One is even asked to sacrifice personal freedom by becoming a slave to each other for the sake of building up others. Such a community self-evidently views authority as based not on any "vertical relationships" but on "horizontal relationships of reciprocity and cooperation." As a community formed out of being "one in Christ Jesus," it derives its own sense of solidarity, trust, and tolerance from a mystical union of the divine.

The only question is whether such a community is in danger of closing itself off from outsiders and other "overlapping associations." It is possible to attend to this issue by appealing to Paul's theology of the cross. In his contention for the loyalty of Corinthians, Paul stresses the centrality of weakness and suffering in authentic Christian life. The Christian story is inaugurated by the paradigmatic sufferings of the crucified Jesus, a point already emphasized in 1 Corinthians. Paul advances beyond that argument in 2 Corinthians, asserting that hardships endured paradoxically demonstrate the energy of God's grace in an authentic covenantal community. As Christ's humiliation and death unleash the power of resurrection, weaknesses also occasion a ministry of glory. Paul sees a homology between the sufferings that a community experiences and those of Jesus — substantial evidence of a community's union with Christ, a union enriched by but not limited to mystical and ecstatic encounters. What has been experienced by Paul is also available to all members of the covenantal community. Their present possession of the eschatological Spirit guarantees that they, with unveiled faces, can enter into union with Christ directly, without intermediaries. A true community thus denudes its native strengths and empties its own claims.

Another tool Paul uses to combat sectarian tendencies is the notion of "new creation." An apocalyptic and cosmic concept, it is used as an architectonic symbol for the church. The Pauline church is not a ghettoized secret society after the fashion of mystery religions. Rather, it actively promotes reconciliation between warring members within the community (Gal 6:15; cf. 5:6) and foreshadows God's reconciliation of the world to himself (2 Cor 5:16–21).[58]

Nevertheless, it is still a real question whether Paul has successfully dealt with the sectarian tendencies endemic to his views of covenantal community. The cross in a communal context is admittedly a powerful deterrent to self-aggrandizement. But it is not a constructive concept, and it cannot be used to inform institutions of their relationships and obligations to the public beyond the community. This sectarian tendency was to manifest itself in full forms in second- and third-generation Pauline churches, as well as in the Johannine community. The apocalyptic notion of new creation holds greater promise in this regard, since it encompasses the whole cosmic order that is being restored and holds the covenantal community accountable to a set of demands outside the community. But the concept was never developed fully in Paul's theology or integrated into his covenantal thinking. In the only two places where Paul appeals to the concept (Gal 6:15; 2 Cor 5:17), it is used, ironically, to settle differences *within* the Christian community. In Galatians 6:15, the new creation is the basis for reconciliation between circumcised and uncircumcised members of the church; in 2 Corinthians 5:17, Paul appeals to it as reason for reconciliation between himself and those in the Corinthian community opposed to his apostleship. In neither case does he seem interested in building bridges between the community and the world at large or launching what we might call a public theology. The "world" to his apocalyptic mind is

---

58. Paul S. Minear, *Christians and the New Creation: Genesis Motifs in the New Testament* (Louisville, Ky.: Westminster/John Knox Press, 1994), 111–12.

evidently so corrupt as to discourage all constructive efforts. Consequently, "new creation" remained a tantalizing hint of a public theology whose potential was never fully realized in the early church.

In sum, a covenant is based on promise rather than contractual obligation. In contrast to a nomistic understanding of covenant, which defines the law as a preventive measure and as a boundary marker, Paul recovers the dimension of ethical principle and promise lying at the heart of the covenantal memory, a memory anticipated in the Abrahamic narrative. It is the incarnation, the death of Christ, and the collective, communal experience of the eschatological Spirit that help redirect our attention to the original promise. In this regard, the new covenant, at least as formulated by Paul, is no different from the old; the post-Easter covenant highlights and makes real the promise that made the original covenant possible to begin with.

Furthermore, the Pauline renewal of covenantal thought does not do away with the law but places it in service of the communal good. Love characterizes the covenantal community, and the "law of Christ" is its concrete manifestation. The law of Christ is no different from the common morality of many cultures in many respects. Thus, members of the covenantal community stand under the same moral judgment as any nonmembers. But covenantal members are energized and enlivened by love for each other, a love that finds its source in Christ's death and in God's promise to Abraham. Members of the community are bound to each other by a love-centered ethic, and each is ready to give himself or herself up for the larger good of the community. But such allegiance is not oppressive, because the whole community stands under the cross. While the covenantal community is a visible sign of the emerging new creation, it is not strictly equated to it. Perfection will be realized only in the ultimate future, the *eschaton,* before which time it dare not absolutize itself.

Covenantal Clues in Confucian
Sociopolitical Culture

It has been observed, rightly, that Chinese political thought, which underlies much of Confucian ideology and culture, does not distinguish between politics and morals. Nowhere is this total integration of the political and moral spheres more clearly expressed than in the etymology of the term *zheng,* the central concept in Chinese government, which is capable of meaning both "governance" and "moral rectitude." The ideal statesman is therefore also the embodiment of ethical responsibilities, so much so that a political thinker must needs be a moral philosopher as well. This state of perfection is reflected in the celebrated phrase, "inner sageliness and outer kingliness" *(nei sheng wai wang).*[59]

A perfect combination of these two qualities, the moral and the political, was rare. After the unification of China in the third century B.C.E., emperors — that supreme symbol of power and authority in rulership and governance — seldom exhibited sageliness. Empires were founded, with few exceptions, on military conquests, and the subsequent maintenance of the empire was invariably left either to the whims of prime ministers or in the hands of minor bureaucrats. The learned Confucian officials — moral symbols of culture and society — for their part have never been in any position of directly commanding an empire. They either were in the employ of less-than-ideal rulers who governed on the basis of naked ambition or, when the inevitable compromise became impossible, chose the life of a hermit. The result was an ongoing tension between the rulers and the intellectuals.

But given their mediating position between the ruling class, on the one hand, and the people, on the other, the Chinese intellectuals might represent the best hope of creating a "social

---

59. Found in the *Tianxia* chapter of *Zhuangzi.* The Confucian philosopher Tu Wei-ming takes the saying to mean "that sageliness *takes precedence over* kingliness and that only a sage is qualified to be a king." Tu Wei-ming, *The Way, Learning and Politics: Essays on the Confucian Intellectual* (Singapore: Institute of East Asian Philosophies, 1989), 19.

space" within Chinese culture and of maintaining "a differentiation in the community, a separation of powers."[60] In practice, though, that was never the case. In spite of independent academies and the Confucian involvement in education, no enduring institutions ever arose independent of the governing powers. On the contrary, because of the statewide examination system that served as an effective means of recruiting talents for government, Confucian scholars early on were co-opted into the political system. Once the Confucian classics became the official canon, the whole project of learning was incorporated further into the social rubric of Chinese society. The end result was a Confucianism thoroughly politicized, with its ethics never making any impact on the inner life of emperors and its being manipulated by the ruling class for idcological control.[61]

What made the intellectuals uniquely qualified to provide a power balance to the ruling elite, at least in theory, and, by the same token, what makes them prone to being manipulated for social control, is that they claim to speak for the people. They claim to identify with the *hoi polloi,* because all have the same access to the common *dao.*[62] The Chinese intellectuals are therefore situated between the government and the people.

As part of identifying with the people, the Chinese intellectuals have unbounded optimism in their ability to know heaven. This is so because "Heaven sees as the people see; heaven hears as the people hear" (*Mencius* 5A5).[63] Heaven represents the transcendent order, with which the Confucian scholar maintains an intimate relationship. Confucius could claim he had an intimate relationship with heaven, and

---

60. For the function of "social space," see Adams, *On Being Human Religiously,* 57–59.

61. Tu, *Way, Learning and Politics,* 25–26.

62. At least according to the Mencian-*Zhongyong* metaphysical line of interpretation. See Xu Fuguan, "The Tragic Fate of Chinese Intellectuals in an Extraordinary Time," in *Intellectuals and China,* ed. Zhou Yangshan (Taipei: Shibao wenhua chuban, 1980), 74–75.

63. Cf. Tu, *The Way, Learning and Politics,* 19.

heaven might even occasionally endow him with revelation.[64] He understood himself to have established a mutual pact with heaven, the transcendent principle that nourishes all life and guarantees the moral nature of law and society (*Analects*). This pact was never as overtly revelational as in Judaism, Christianity, or Islam, for heaven can be inscrutable and may even fall silent. But the Confucian scholar could detect its will and its mandate and communicate it to the people.

Is the Chinese case closer to natural law than to covenant? Yes and no. What is manifested in nature can be static and hierarchical — at least this was how natural law was originally conceived in Stoicism — and Chinese intellectuals have been known to support such a structure. But because they also believe in an ontological linkage between heaven and human nature, each individual has the potential within himself or herself to judge the prevailing social order. Heaven can be capricious, and one must exercise reverence as well as diligence to discern the will of heaven. The mandate of heaven can also be manifested through the actions of the masses, so one must be a keen observer of society. The gap between what things are (being) and what things might be (becoming) is not eternally etched in some calcified law of nature but is localized in the autonomous self who must negotiate with heaven to realize what that should be. This was especially clear during the Song-Ming Period (tenth to sixteenth centuries), when internal examination was used as a form of social critique.[65]

---

64. Ibid., 9–10.
65. Two distinctive ways of thinking were developed during the Song-Ming Period, what Chang Hao has called "cosmological morality" and "ontological morality." Chang Hao, "Neo-Confucian Moral Thought and Its Modern Legacy," *Journal of Asian Studies* 39, no. 2 (1980): 267–68. Cosmological morality linked the social order, with its Confucian doctrine of "three bonds" and "five constants," to the cosmic order, thus rendering the state order absolute. In this regard, the Chinese order most resembles the medieval European order based on natural law. Ontological morality, on the other hand, posited an inner unity between the human mind, the true self, and heaven. This gives the human mind a transcendent power independent of the external order. See also Thomas A. Metzger, *Escape from Predicament: Neo-Confucianism and China's Evolving Political Culture,* Studies of the East Asian Institute (New York: Columbia University Press, 1977), 158–61; and Hoyt Cleveland Tillman, *Utilitarian Confucianism: Ch'en Liang's Challenge to Chu His,* Harvard

Hence the development of *liangxin* ("conscience"). On the other hand, this negotiation is carried out only within the autonomous self. While the possibility for intersubjective linkage always exists in the Confucian schema — thereby necessitating social pacts — it was seldom realized in Chinese history. Somehow, the only viable "mediating structure" between the individual and government was the family.[66]

Chinese Individualism and Human Relatedness

The celebrated totalism[67] in Chinese cosmo-ethical thinking begins with the cultivated self and expands outward to include family, community, nation, and finally the cosmos. This is the famous eight steps in *Daxue (The Great Learning)*. In conjunction with covenantal thought, therefore, the question must then be asked, to what extent does this ethical realm extend beyond the level of personal cultivation to the social and political? The answer will involve trekking through terrains of the age-old debate between those who advocated ethics of pure motive and integrity and those who advocated ethics of results, or the so-called metaphysical wings of Confucianism and their utilitarian counterparts. What we look for are covenantal notions of equality and social pluralism in federated thought.

Like Pauline theology, Confucianism has similarly gone through an individualistic interpretation, but for different reasons. The classics have long described a totalistic vision of moral transformation that emanates from the self in ever expanding circles that encompass one's self, family, country, and cosmos. The purist school in Confucianism notices the transcendent ground of morality based both in heaven and in human nature. Likewise, principles (*li*) reside both external

East Asian Monographs 101 (Cambridge, Mass.: Harvard University Press, 1982), 206–8.
    66. Whether this was because historical circumstances (e.g., the imperial system) forbade it or the moral epistemology did not allow for it is a question this essay will not be able to answer.
    67. The term is that of Metzger, *Escape from Predicament* 61.

to the moral subject as well as internal to him or her. Accordingly, moral transformation of the cosmos thus begins with the moral and spiritual cultivation of the self.

To portray principles as both internal and external, however, is to posit a dualistic schema of understanding all phenomena and a tacit admission that human nature does not possess all necessary and sufficient grounds for total transformation. If some principles are external to human nature, it follows that one would have to observe outside phenomena for the completion of what ought to be the self-sufficient ground for moral transformation. The problem was at the center of neo-Confucian thought since the Song Dynasty. Steadfast dualists like Zhu Xi and the Cheng Brothers before him maintained the importance of observing nature (*kewu*) in addition to cultivation. Consistent monists like Lu Xiangshan and Wang Yangming argued that *kewu* should mean not the "investigation of things" external to oneself but rather the "rectification of things" by the use of one's mind. If the mind is fully equipped with all necessary principles and is ontologically one with heaven, observation of nature could not possibly add anything to an already full complement; it is but an occasion for the mind to judge the relative merits and demerits of any thing or affair.

What this debate makes manifestly evident, as Metzger has convincingly shown, is the breach in the linkage between the internal and the external in neo-Confucianism.[68] Without the tradition of compartmentalizing the inner from the outer, *vita activa* from *vita contemplativa,* human nature from heavenly nature, as is common in Western tradition, neo-Confucians and their descendants strive to overcome this breach with inevitable failure, thus occasioning a "sense of predicament."[69] With the failure of reforms, the loss of the northern heartland of the Northern Song Dynasty, and eventually the disempowerment of the scholar-official ideal in

---

68. Ibid., 70–77.
69. The term is Metzger's.

the Qing Dynasty, Confucianism lost its social and political components and turned inward, becoming at the end codes of conduct aiming at private spirituality rather than cosmic transformation.

Another reason for this privatization of Confucianism is its elitist assumption. As Song scholars struggled to reform the government, their common assumption was that only an educated person could exercise control over the reform and shepherd the society through its transformation. With the loss of political power and the gradual waning of their influence in court, however, their sphere of influence became increasingly restricted. The classical ideal of transforming the cosmos shrank to maintaining order and managing the affairs in the family, where and only where one could extend one's moral power to its fullest. Furthermore, unlike the primitive society in which central control was nonexistent, China's imperial court made sure that these prominent families never developed into independent spheres of influence or entered into alliances that could rival the central government. The sort of balance of power and voluntary associations — conditions that were chiefly responsible for the rise of federalism, the political basis for the development of alliances and federated unions in medieval Europe — that developed in Europe never took shape in China. Confucianism was increasingly marginalized into a family ethics until its formal demise in 1911.

In spite of these rich "covenantal" clues, Chinese intellectuals never developed anything in Chinese history that resembled covenantal thoughts or, by extension, the free associations of the West. Why? Chinese intellectuals never attained an independent status. While they performed a priestly function on behalf of the people, they did so as part of the ruling class. The Chinese intellectuals' totalistic vision (which embodies total transformation of all things under heaven) further reinforced the ruling monolith and discouraged separation of powers in Chinese society. Subsequently, Chinese intellectuals never self-consciously developed any ecclesiology or created any social space for themselves. This is why autonomous associations in Chinese history are distinct from the free associations of the West.

It is in this context that we can ask: Does Christianity have something to offer to the emerging civil society in China? To the end of answering that question, or better yet articulating the question in a clearer fashion, I have surveyed three major areas of research that bear on the question: the search for civil society in contemporary Chinese social thought; Pauline theology, formed as Paul's own religious and cultural tradition, modified by Jesus Christ, faced a new cosmopolitan situation and thus reconstructed covenantal thinking for peoples beyond ancient Israel; and Confucian sociopolitical culture with its own profound but seldom fulfilled ethical potential. Behind these disparate areas of inquiry stand four sets of dialogical partners: Western political theorists, Chinese intellectuals (and their respective cultural and religious heritages), Jewish and Christian covenantal thoughts, and Confucian sociopolitical traditions. The two most readily identifiable sets of partners are obviously the modern social and political theorists and Chinese intellectuals in search for civil society. They both share a common language and an identical set of common concerns, and the conversation is correspondingly most direct. Results from that conversation, however, have yielded a dissatisfaction with a strictly Western understanding of civil society. While in the West a civil society is possible only when there is a clear distinction between state and society, or, as Adams suggested, when there is a sharp "differentiation in the community, a separation of powers,"[70] the search for comparable models of civil society in China based on such a separation of spheres has proved disappointing. Even in cases where autonomous organizations successfully carry out administrative and managerial functions in local areas they serve, we invariably find also the long reach of the state. As is often the case, most of these functions are initiated and in-

---

70. Adams, *On Being Human Religiously*, 58.

stalled by the state. This unique phenomenon has caused some writers to use the phrase "state-led civil society"[71] to describe the Chinese case, a description that gives Western social theorists pause. As a result of this comparison, some scholars have called for a total reevaluation of the notion of civil society that might integrate more fully the Chinese paradigm into the global discussion of civil society.[72]

However, an alternative view may be more compelling in the long run. At least, I have struck out on a different path to reconciling these two different views of society, and in the process I have introduced the other two sets of contributors to the discussion. Taking seriously the historical dimension in the formation of any moral community, I have delved into the symbolic universes standing behind the sociopolitical thoughts both in the West and in China and have examined the cultural and religious values that inform them. In the West, covenantal thoughts in the Jewish-Christian tradition gave rise to the modern notions of democracy and civil society (although many secular thinkers do not know whence their best insights derive). I have traced some of the decisive roots of such thinking to the New Testament, in particular the Pauline writings, recognizing that some highly questionable interpretations of those traditions have historically led some in the West in antidemocratic directions. In China, on the other hand, it was a metaphysical Confucianism that for years determined the patterns of sociopolitical involvement. Even though Confucianism no longer explicitly dictates the political agenda of today, it nevertheless still shapes the terms and language in which people think about political issues, and it continues to influence the contours of thought behind East Asian sociopolitical thinking. We ignore these background facts — as Marx wrote of other matters — to our own peril.

But what is the value in this dialogue between historical pasts? Have Paul and Confucius anything meaningful to say

---

71. So the title of Brook and Frolic's aforementioned essay, "The Ambiguous Challenge of Civil Society."
72. Brook and Frolic, "Ambiguous Challenge," 14–16.

to each other in a sociopolitical discourse? At first glance
the two have very little in common: Paul's vision rarely goes
beyond the construction of the community, and Confucianism discloses a totalism that ranges from personal virtues to
cosmic restoration. Nevertheless, both Pauline theology and
Confucianism are concerned with the formation of communities that are characterized not by utilitarian goals or mere
contractual agreements but by morality. Both accede and
subscribe to principles and purposes that transcend the immediate community: *lex Christi* undergirded by love in the
case of Paul and the inscrutable *dao* in the case of Confucius.
And both understand a moral community so formed as the
necessary condition under which ultimacy is to be realized: in
Paul's case an eschatological community waiting for the final
consumption, and in the case of Confucianism the expansion
of such a moral community to encompass the whole cosmos.

From these common grounds are also issued challenges to
both camps. From the perspective of Pauline theology, the
lack of boundary between those inside a Confucian community and those outside is troubling. In fact, the concept of a
community limited to like-minded members organized under
the umbrella of a common vision, except in isolated cases,
has never taken root in Confucianism, and whenever associations were formed they never enjoyed the kind of broad-based
support that was necessary to challenge state rulers or at
least provide an alternative to them. If it is true that "humanity is essentially associational and human history is the
history of associations," as Adams has claimed,[73] then what
we have in Chinese history is a collapse of association into
family, an assimilation of the two, so that association is replaced by bloodline, intentional ethical construction by family
morality, covenant by kinship.[74] Chinese history shows that
Confucianism has never been able to break through the cap-

---

73. Adams, *On Being Human Religiously*, 67.
74. Deutero-Pauline communities also went through a similar metamorphosis
when the primary symbol of covenant was displaced by that of house or family
(*oikos*).

tivity in which kinship holds the associational life of Chinese civilization.

On the other hand, from the perspective of Confucianism, the Pauline community is probably too sectarian in its orientation. There is little indication from within the confines of a Pauline covenantal community, at least in its classical formation, that it could take part in the larger, broader political discourse and social construction. While it is self-contained, cohesive, and institutionally vibrant, it is unclear how it could initiate a conversation with the outside world, except in an indirect way of being a member of a mature, stable civil society that is already formed. But if a civil society is wanting in the first place, a Pauline community, with all its sectarian tendencies, might find it difficult to call for, even initiate, its formation.

In spite of the sectarian danger, however, the conclusion seems inescapable that the very contribution Christianity could make is precisely in strengthening the Confucian sociopolitical culture in the area of community building. A love-centered community in which members give themselves for each other and in which all pledge an allegiance to transcendent principles and purposes higher than themselves is what Confucian China has been unable to produce. The Christian community is therefore a new alternative social structure heretofore unknown in Chinese culture.

The Chinese Protestant churches today have inherited these issues as they attempt to negotiate a course of self-determination free of outside — foreign or domestic — influences, all the while trying and earnestly intending to participate in the social and political life of the nation. They are confronted by two related problems. On the one hand, a Confucian familism in the form of imperial traditions of authority relentlessly inserts itself into the life and structure of the churches. Among state-recognized churches, official policies of the government are often indistinguishable from the official ones of the church. Among unregistered churches organized outside state-sanctioned patterns and orbits, the government, with the help of official churches, pursues policies that range from harassment to persecution. The solution to this problem, however, cannot be the standard separation of church and state in the liberal, secular West, for the second of the problems the Chinese Protestant churches face — sectarianism inherited from Pauline Christianity — presents an ever menacing threat of restricting the ethical and political participation of the church in the sociopolitical and economic life of the nation. In this connection, Confucian familism reinvents itself in the church as a parochial sect closed off from active conversation with state and society and often dominated by patriarchy. Neither option is particularly attractive, but the solution must be found in the context of a renewed self-definition of the church as a covenantal community, that is to say, a community founded on covenantal motifs that can be harvested from both the Confucian and Christian heritages.

– Chapter 5 –

HINDUISM AND GLOBALIZATION

A CHRISTIAN THEOLOGICAL APPROACH

M. Thomas Thangaraj

The process of globalization has come to affect every aspect of life in today's world, and religions of the world are not exempt. The process of globalization challenges Hinduism, one of the ancient and living religions of the world, as well. In this essay, I offer a Christian theological assessment of what is happening within Hinduism and among Hindus in the face of globalization today. I am aware that I am examining the situation and making proposals as a Christian theologian who, although raised in and nourished by a Hindu-shaped culture, is an outsider to the Hindu religious community. But I do attempt as much as I can to arrive at an empathetic understanding of what is going on in the face of globalization's challenge to Hinduism.

This essay is organized under three sections. In the first section, I offer an overview of the history and central teachings of Hinduism. This overview is offered with the help of two terms, namely, "geo-piety" and "bio-piety." It is followed by an explanation of the impact of the process of globalization on such a portrait of Hinduism today. The third section explicates a Christian theological approach to what Hinduism offers to the present setting of globalization.

Hinduism: Defining the Term

There are two initial difficulties that one has to overcome before one attempts to understand the history and central themes of Hinduism. The first of these is the use of the term "religion" itself. As William Everett has pointed out:

> The concept of religion as a discrete set of ideas, organizations, rituals, and behaviors is a modern creation resulting from the differentiation of society into spheres of governance, family, economy, education and the like. Religion is one of those social "functions." This is a peculiarly unhelpful way to try to understand the peoples of the [Indian] subcontinent. The notion of "religion" tends to separate aspects of life that for most Indian people are fused together.[1]

Though the term "religion" does not really do justice to defining and understanding Hinduism, it has been used by modern scholars of religion, historians of India, and anthropologists to describe the vast cluster of philosophies, ritual practices, beliefs, traditions, and loyalties that are named Hinduism. The Hindus themselves over the centuries have come to accept it as a term for describing their own tradition. We need to take note of this aspect when we attempt to understand Hinduism. We cannot assume that Hinduism has the same kind of ideational framework, organizational or associational structure, and/or discrete and well-defined creedal positions that one associates with religions such as Christianity and Islam or even Buddhism. While I take note of this difficulty, I use the term "religion" to designate Hinduism in this essay for want of any other better term.

---

1. William J. Everett, *Religion, Federalism, and the Struggle for Public Life: Cases from Germany, India, and America* (New York: Oxford University Press, 1997), 64. See also the essay in this volume by Diane Obenchain. [That Hindu society is profoundly "organic" in its structure compared to modern Western pluralist ones, as Everett argues, is surely correct, but questions can be posed in regard to Everett's view in that it appears to others that classic Hindu theories of ritual, ethics, and law, and, indeed, similar theories from other ancient peoples in complex civilizations, were fully alert to the differences between political events and institutions, such as joining an army and going to war, familial ones, such as weddings or the birth of a child, economic ones, such as the establishment of a market or having a harvest, or religious ones, such as offering a sacrifice or joining a festival. See vols. 1 and 4 in this set. — Ed.]

The second difficulty is with the term "Hinduism" itself. "Hinduism" is not the name that the Hindus gave to their religion. It was given by the Muslim and European Christian invaders to designate the religion that they encountered in India. As Klaus Klostermaier writes:

> It is impossible to give a precise definition of Hinduism or to point out the exact place and time of its origin. The very name *Hinduism* owes its origin to chance; foreigners in the West extending the name of the Province of Sindh to the whole country lying across the Indus River and simply calling all the inhabitants *Hindus* and their religion *Hinduism.*[2]

However imprecise the term, it does indirectly confirm the idea of a generalized "geo-piety," and the Hindus themselves have appropriated that name for their religion and use it even today.

Quite often the terms "Indian" and "Hindu" are confused and used as synonyms. This is mainly because "Hindu" signified more the cultural-geographical landscape than the religious tradition. It did not describe the doctrines and practices of the religion of India. As it is often said, Hinduism represents a federation of religious traditions rather than a single unified religion.

The early inhabitants of the land we now call India, Pakistan, and Bangladesh operated with the overall name of *dharma* to designate their religion. *Dharma* means order, justice, conduct, and/or religion. At times, religion was referred to as the *sanatana dharma* (eternal order). While foreigners and visitors to India used the overarching term "Hinduism," and while the local inhabitants at times used *sanatana dharma,* by and large the religious practices and beliefs held among the people of the subcontinent of India were and continue to be known by their local names and

---

2. Klaus Klostermaier, *A Survey of Hinduism,* 2d ed. (Albany: SUNY Press, 1994), 30–31.

by their varied forms. These practices and beliefs are tied to land, sacred rivers, holy mountains, and local shrines. For example, the Saivites of Tamilnadu (those who name Ultimate Reality/God as Siva) called their religion *saivam,* while the Vaishnavites (those who name Ultimate Reality/God as Vishnu) called theirs *vainavam.* Quite often, religions were known as devotion to particular gods and goddesses. For example, the worshipers of Murugan in Tamilnadu may refer to their faith more often as *murugabhakti* (devotion to Murugan, who is the son of Siva) than as Hinduism. This was and is true not only of temple worshipers in the cities or at pilgrimage sites but of most of the popular and village Hindus as well.

Hinduism as "Geo-piety"

"Geo-piety" means that Hinduism came primarily to be defined by its geography rather than by a founder, a book, a set of doctrines or creed, or a paradigmatic event. It is basically defined by its location. It is a piety based on geography. Geo-piety is, thus, not only a name given to the religion of India by outsiders; on the contrary, the very local expressions of Hinduism confirm this. Indeed, the local traditions are largely influenced by what is called *sthalapuranas,* that is, the mythologies of the geographical location that tell the mighty acts of a particular form of God in that locality. Each temple in India, for example, will have a *sthalapurana* that describes how God (named differently in different locations) took a particular form and acted out God's plan for the well-being of that village. Piety at this point is clearly tied to the particular region. Thus, the sacred *dharma,* with its narratives, rights, duties, and distinctive practices, is that order which exists in a given geographical locale. The geo-piety, indeed, leads to a "geo-logistic" conception of the right order of things.

One may challenge this characterization of Hinduism philosophically on the grounds that the naming of Ultimate Reality as "Brahman" (the nondualistic Reality) does not require any

geographical location for a Hindu believer. The highly cultivated intellectual "Vedanta" tradition within Hinduism is a
paramount illustration of this form of Hinduism. Thus, for a
philosophical Hindu, the nondualistic view of Ultimate Reality together with the perception of "world" as *maya* (illusion)
would imply a relativization of the local. While this is true in
theory, most Hindus, including many philosophically inclined
ones, do operate with a devotional attachment to geographical locations in their observance of religious practices and
rituals.

The geo-logistic character of Hinduism has seriously affected the way Hindus have dealt with the modern idea
of nation-state. While Western-educated Indian leaders such
as Mahatma Gandhi, Jawaharlal Nehru, and Babasaheb
Ambedkar viewed the nation-state of India with a Western
democratic lens, others today have come to a different way
of understanding the same. The idea of "Hindutva," as pro-
pounded first by V. D. Savarkar, is a direct consequence of
the geo-logistic character of Hinduism. Savarkar wrote, "A
Hindu means a person who regards the land of Bharat Varsha,
from Indus to the Seas, as his Fatherland as well his Holy-land
that is a cradle of his religion."[3] Such a perception puts those
who are non-Hindus (especially Christians and Muslims)
in a very precarious position. The Indianness of Christians
and Muslims is under scrutiny and doubt. For example, the
religio-nationalistic activities of RSS (Rashtriya Suyamsevak
Sangh), the more militant, activist wing of the Hindutva
movement and one that often challenges non-Hindu beliefs,
practices, and organizations at the grass roots, are motivated
by a geo-logistic view of religion.

The rise of Hindutva, however, is not so new even as a
political movement. For example, a generation ago, the influence of this religious orientation was evident. The legislative
assemblies of the states of Orissa and Madhya Pradesh in

---

3. As quoted in Peter van der Veer, *Religious Nationalism* (Berkeley: University
of California Press, 1994), 31.

the late 1960s attempted to pass laws that would control and curtail Hindus' conversion to either Christianity or Islam.[4] Although the Constitution of India provides room for citizens to profess, practice, and propagate any religion they choose, the geo-logistic view of religion would not, in fact, allow that possibility at the local levels. Furthermore, a religion that is built on "voluntary association," the joining of a religious association according to individual choice, irrespective of the geographical locale of the religious group into which one is born, would promote conversion and change, whereas a geo-logistic view of Hinduism continues to see conversion as a denial of one's national and spiritual identity as an Indian or a resident of the land of India. Before that, in 1956, a central government commission, the Niyogi Committee, inquired into the activities of the Christian missionaries to delineate any instances of coercion or compulsion. That report, as well, operates with this geo-pietistic/geo-logistic view of Hinduism.[5]

Another illustration, perhaps a much more dramatic one, is the host of events that led to the attack and demolition of the mosque at Ayodhya on December 6, 1992.[6] Babari Masjid, the mosque at Ayodhya, was built during the early part of the sixteenth century when Babar, the first Mogul emperor, was reigning over most of northern India. The local *purana* (story, legend, mythology) claims that this particular mosque replaced a Hindu temple that stood on that spot celebrating the birthplace of Rama, one of the incarnations of the god Vishnu. Therefore, there have been attempts all along, more so during the last fifty years, to reclaim that sacred space for Lord Rama. One can see how a geo-logistic view of religion is operative here.

---

4. M. K. Kuriakose, ed., *History of Christianity in India: Source Materials* (Madras: SCM Press, 1982), 426.

5. Ibid., 390.

6. See van der Veer, *Religious Nationalism*, 152–62. I have depended heavily on this monograph in understanding this event.

Hinduism as "Bio-piety"

The Hindu *dharma* is not only determined by geography, it is also determined by biology. *Dharma* can be translated as "duty" in two dimensions, namely, that of the individual and that of the social group. The social dimension is known as *varna dharma* and the individual, *ashrama dharma*. We need to look carefully at both of these to uncover the meaning of religion they convey. *Varna dharma* is what is known as the caste system. The word *varna* means "color," and the early stratification of society in India had been based on color. But in normal usage, *varna* stands for the caste system, which stratifies society into four major groups of subcastes, namely, Brahmin (priest), Kshatriya (warrior), Vaishya (merchant), and Sudra (laborer). Each group is assigned specific jobs, tasks, and modes of behavior. Each group is also given detailed laws and regulations concerning their tasks and behaviors. The *Laws of Manu,* one of the earliest scriptural texts (ca. 200 B.C.E. to 200 C.E.), contains detailed discussions on the arrangement of caste hierarchy.[7] The defining marks of caste are birth, assigned profession, endogamy, commensality, hierarchy, and ideas of pollution.

The four groups mentioned earlier are only large groupings; each caste (*varna*) is divided into hundreds of subcastes (*jati*). There is also a fifth group, *panchamas,* who are the "untouchables" or the "outcastes." During the days of the independence struggle, the fifth group was referred to as *harijan* (people of God) and later were designated as "scheduled castes" by the Indian constitution. They have become known widely as "Dalits" (the oppressed or crushed people) in recent years, a name they have claimed for themselves.

While this is a pan-Indian stratification of society, there are several nuances and modifications to this stratification peculiar to each regional and linguistic area within India. This system of hierarchical classification was legitimized by mytho-

---

7. See Max Müller, ed., *Sacred Texts of the East,* vol. 25 (London: Clarendon Press, 1888).

logical, scriptural, and theological warrants.[8] Being a Hindu is closely linked to one's place or status within this system. Each person's religious and social duty is defined by that person's place within this system. One can see how religious life is intimately related and tied to one's biological position. One striking example of this bio-pietistic character of Hinduism is the practice of endogamy. Members of a particular caste or subcaste are permitted to marry only those within their own caste. In this sense, one may call the practice of Hinduism "bio-piety."

The second dimension of *dharma* is known as *ashrama dharma,* which stratifies the individual's life into various stages. These stages are *brahmacharya* (student), *grahasta* (householder), *vanaprasta* (forest-dweller), and *sanyasa* (wandering ascetic). In the stage of *brahmacharya,* one is expected to study diligently as a student and obey his or her elders and gurus. Then comes the stage in which one is married and begins to run a household. Such a stage has its own demands on the individual. As one matures in parenthood, one is required in the third stage to have periods of solitude and meditation and thus to prepare for the last stage, in which one wanders from temple to temple, from one holy place to another, and thus matures in the path of final liberation. In this, the bio-piety also leads to a sense of the right ordering of life, the bio-logistic character of Hindu religion. One of the effects of such an understanding of the individual journey of *dharma* is the manner in which the question of age is addressed. One's age is seen as an indicator of one's wisdom and growth in spiritual life, and thus the young are required to obey the older folks precisely on the basis of such an understanding. The *dharma* of a person is tied to one's biological clock.

The "biological" characteristic of Hindu piety is indicated

---

8. For example, the origin of the castes is defined as Brahmins emerging from the head of God, Kshatriya from the chest, Vaishya from the thighs, and Sudras from the feet. The Bhagavad Gita claims that God created this system: "The system of four castes was created by Me, according to the distribution of the qualities and their acts." *Bhagavad Gita,* trans. Winthrop Sargeant (Albany: SUNY Press, 1993), 69.

further by the place of women in the Hindu understanding of *dharma*. The patriarchal character of Hindu society is strengthened by the way women are excluded in the classification of both *varna* and *ashrama*. The *Laws of Manu* clearly place women in a subservient and submissive role in the religious and social order of things.

Such a description of Hinduism as "geo-piety" and "bio-piety" should not lead us to think of Hindu faith in static terms. Hinduism has had a very dynamic history in which it has gone through several changes, and it has accommodated itself to several impacts, trends, and influences from both within and without. But one thing is clear: In the midst of all these, Hinduism has retained its strong links to geography and biology. New holy sites have developed over the last several years in India. For example, the Adi Parasakti tradition in Tamilnadu came into being in the latter part of the twentieth century and is flourishing with its own shrine, holy man, teachings, and practices. The way that movement has tapped into the caste system for its organization and political participation by appealing largely to particular caste groups within Tamilnadu is interesting and intriguing. One can see that the connection to geo-piety and bio-piety continues to be the framework within which the new traditions define themselves and flourish.

Globalization and Hinduism

Our portrayal of Hinduism as "geo-piety" and "bio-piety" helps us to see certain implications for the way in which Hinduism may face the question of globalization. Let me use Robert Schreiter's description of globalization as the working definition for this discussion. He explains the idea of globalization with two terms — extension and compression. Schreiter is, in certain respects, dependent on the work of Roland Robertson, yet he places the interpretation of the processes of globalization in the context of theological motifs in a way that Robertson does not seek to do. Thus, he is able to expound the concept of globalization as it impinges more directly on the work of Christian theologians. On globalization as extension, he writes: "Globalization is therefore first of all about extension. It extends the effects of modernity throughout the world via the communication technologies that create a network for information flow. Computers, modems, faxes, and the Internet make possible this swift transfer."[9] The second element in globalization is compression: "[T]echnological innovations compress both our sense of time and our sense of space.... The rapidity of movement ... disparages attaching any significance to the past and makes the future even more short."[10] In a way, our sense of space has been altered in highly significant ways. What do these phenomena of extension and compression mean for Hinduism?

The process of extension that began with modernity has significantly changed the face of Hinduism. It has transformed it into a *world* religion. It is no longer tied so tightly to the soil of India either geographically or intellectually. It is available as an option to all those who are "shopping" for a religious tradition. This new face of Hinduism had its dramatic moment when Swami Vivekananda, a nineteenth-century reformer-saint, addressed the World Parliament of Religions at Chicago in 1893. He placed the Vedanta version of Hinduism as an option for the people of the globe. Moreover, the availability of and the accessibility to the scriptural writings of Hinduism have also made Hinduism into a world religion. Not only migration but print media, radio, TV, and the Internet have put Hindu faith on the religious map of humanity and not simply within India or Southeast Asia. The long tradition of academic study of Hinduism in the West has also contributed to the extension of Hinduism to all parts of the globe. The Hindu gurus who travel widely all over the world attract disciples from all communities irrespective of religion, race, or gender. A cursory look at the religious land-

9. Robert Schreiter, *The New Catholicity: Theology between the Global and the Local* (Maryknoll, N.Y.: Orbis Books, 1997), 9.
10. Ibid. 11.

scape of the United States will tell us how the Hindu tradition is a live option for Americans with its temples, gurus, meditation centers, study groups, Hindu organizations, and so on in almost every major city.

Such an extension into different parts of the globe is not totally novel. Hinduism had traveled long ago to Indonesia, Sri Lanka, Nepal, and other countries in South Asia. What is novel is the extent and the manner of this extension. It is an extension that is accompanied by compression. The compression factor of globalization will not allow for an easy compartmentalization of Hinduism according to its geographical locality. A Hindu in Norway and a Hindu in India are brought together on the Internet and cannot avoid questions of who and what they are in the "globalized" world. Both geo-piety and bio-piety come under stress by the combination of extension and compression.

The Impact of Globalization on Geo-piety

Hindu ties to geography come under pressure from the compression factor of globalization. National and regional boundaries do not make sense any more. Within India itself, the particular regional traditions are no longer dominated by their geographical location. The advancement in transportation has made regional traditions into pan-Indian or national traditions. For example, Vivekananda's teachings and tradition are no longer tied to West Bengal in northern India. The Vivekananda Rock in the Indian Ocean at Kanyakumari, at the very tip of southern India, attracts Hindu pilgrims from all over India and tourists from around the world. The observer can notice how the distinctions between Saiva and Vaishnava traditions, and the distinctions between Indian and "foreign" Hindus, are blurred in the piety of the tourist-pilgrim.

This is much more clearly noticed in the religiosity of Hindus who live in the West, especially in the United States. While building Hindu temples in the United States, Hindus are conscious of this blurring of boundaries and include a host of images within a single temple. In reporting the installation of a new Hindu temple in Malibu, California, the *Los Angeles Times* quoted the president of the Federation of Hindu Associations as saying, "In India, temples may be just devoted to Vishnu or just to Shiva, but in this country the trend is to combine deities in each place."[11] It also quoted an accountant who lives in Brentwood: "Our philosophy and approach is to satisfy all Hindus as well as other Americans."[12] This is true of almost all the temples in the United States. The Hindu temple of Atlanta, Georgia, which is basically a Vaisnavite temple with Sri Venkateswara as the presiding deity, has within its sanctuary the images of Siva and Durga. Another temple in Atlanta has the image of Mahavir, the founder of Jainism, among the images of gods and goddesses. These various temples in the United States are all "compressed" into a listing on one website: www.hindutemples.com.

New geographical locations for practicing the Hindu faith bring with them new ways of being a Hindu. The traditional family-centered character of Hindu religious education, in which a guru would be invited into the home, is no longer adequate to nurture the young in religious beliefs and practices. The pace of life in India has become faster; the joint-family system has broken down, and the religious education of Hindu children is finding new means. New methods are now being used for educating the future generations of Hindus in India. Comic books with Hindu mythology are one of the major sources of educating a young Hindu today. The proliferation of Hindu shrines in the cities in India is also indicative of this anxiety. New temples and shrines pop up in many major cities in India every day. The philosophy departments in various universities in India are becoming places of Hindu religious education. The introduction of the academic study of religion in India is yet another example of addressing the need for religious education of young people.

---

11. *Los Angeles Times,* June 6, 1998, 4.
12. Ibid.

The need to educate the Hindu in his or her tradition is all the more important for Hindus living outside of India. The introduction of Sunday classes in the Hindu temples in the United States is one such response to the need. Regular series of lectures are arranged by Hindu organizations and temples in which "preachers" from India are invited to address the young and the old. Vishwa Hindu Parishad (VHP) has branches in several cities in the United States and the Hindu Students Council sponsored by VHP holds conferences to educate and motivate Hindu youth into a living Hindu tradition. VHP has also initiated the formation of university groups in the United States and Canada. The 1996 conference of the Hindu Students Council had the following theme: "Hindu Youth: Linking Ancient India to Modern America." The very theme suggests the pressure that is put on the geo-piety of Hinduism. The 2000 conference chose "One World, One Future: Hindu Identities in the New Millennium." Here again one detects a pressure on geo-piety.

How does Hinduism deal with this compression? One way is to get unduly worried about the apparent loss of Hindu identity and follow a fundamentalist path to address the issue at hand. The Ayodhya incident is an example of this, as is the rise of the Hindutva movement. Being a Hindu religiously and being an Indian both culturally and politically are conflated into one, and the rhetoric of Hindu nationalism comes into prominence. Though such a narrowly defined Hindu nationalism was present even during the time of the independence struggle (though in a dormant form), it became a vital force in the life of the Hindus in the last decade of the twentieth century. The success of the Bharatiya Janata Party (BJP) in the 1997 elections and their ability to form a stable government at the national level is indicative of this trend. Of course, the government formed by the BJP collapsed in 1998, but after a brief interlude, the people of India again elected the BJP to form the national government in October 1999. One should also notice that the recent nuclear test conducted by the BJP-led government is another expression of the kind of nationalism I am referring to here. As one editorial mentions, the nuclear test is seen as the sign of a strong government and a desire to be a significant power in world politics:

> The West and its media is treating India in a very partial manner and with no respect and reciprocity.... Now for the first time, it seems that the BJP government will try to correct these distortions in the international field. It seems that for the first time in 50 years, there is a government which can bring pride and status to the country which is long overdue.[13]

The nuclear test was viewed widely as a clear case of India's desperate political attempt to find its rightful place in the international family of nations. It was also seen as a way of restoring pride to the country in the international context. Furthermore, it helped to satisfy the demands of the Hindu nationalists who desire to proclaim the power of a "Hindu" nation in the midst of its Muslim, Buddhist, and Communist neighbors.

Another way of dealing with compression is to move in the direction of discovering new forms of inculturation. The path of inculturation will assist in the emergence of new identities among Hindus. Emigration has forced Hinduism to face this. The sacred rivers, mountains, and sites are no longer available to the Hindu diaspora. The American (or East Asian or African) Hindu cannot depend much on geo-piety because he or she must learn to "sing the Lord's song in a foreign land." Therefore, there are attempts to find geo-pietistic accommodations. For example, the Hindu Temple of Atlanta is built on a hill by Highway 85 on the south side of the city, and the presiding deity in that temple is Lord Venkateswara, who resides on a hill at the famous temple at Tirupathi in South India. Here is an attempt to "recreate" the geography to enable

---

13. "Welcome Vajpayee! A Strong Government Was Long Overdue," *News-India Times* 28, no. 13 (March 7, 1998): 55.

geo-piety. Lord Venkateswara's presence is now relocatable, and in that sense globalized.

The process of inculturation in this displacement is interesting and informative. The Hindu temples in the United States have to follow local county ordinances with regard to safety, zoning, and other matters. Such requirements give the temples an ethos that any Hindu who enters such a temple can become aware of right away. To cite one example, temples in India are not carpeted from wall to wall; in the United States, they are. It does feel different to enter a Hindu temple in Atlanta in comparison to those in India.

The Impact of Globalization on Bio-piety

The process of globalization has a significant influence on the bio-piety of Hinduism as well. This influence comes to Hinduism in at least two ways. First, though the concept of nation-state precedes the present process of globalization, one can recognize that the very idea of a nation-state is an affront to the bio-pietistic character of Hinduism. The idea of "nation-state" has developed in the West along with the basic notions of democracy, ethnic transcendence, perceptions of citizenship, and equality before law. Since the time the nation-state was introduced in India, one can notice how that process has questioned the monarchical, patriarchal, and caste-oriented structures of India. The constitution of India clearly affirms the equality of all before the law, irrespective of their bio- and geo-connections. It purports to transcend barriers of caste, creed, and language. Men and women are technically placed on equal status before the law. Thus, the whole notion of "nation-state" is an affront to the bio- and geo-pietistic roots of Hindu tradition.

Second, globalization has introduced new hierarchies within Indian society, based on political strength and economic power. The dismantling of the traditional caste hierarchy had begun right from the days of the British. New jobs had been introduced into the social fabric of India, and those jobs upset to some extent the arrangement of professions in the caste system. For example, railway engineer, college professor, and officer of the Indian Administrative Service (IAS) were all new jobs that upset the equilibrium of the caste hierarchy. Though in the beginning the upper castes were quick to exploit the new jobs for their own advancement within the British Empire, soon and especially after political independence, the new jobs affected the framework of the caste hierarchy. With globalization and the liberalization of the economy in recent years, the creation of a new elite, new power holders, and new technicians has exerted its pressure on the caste arrangement. The new hierarchy that has emerged disrupts the operational viability of Hindu bio-pietistism.

In addition to the new hierarchy, information technology and the media are introducing young people in India to a new form of egalitarianism. There is a cultural inflow into India from the West that compels people in subtle ways to question their traditional hierarchical arrangements. Most thinkers in the West and in India are worried about the influence of MTV and other such TV channels on the young people of India. This fare is often seen as bad for India, which has its own culture spanning thousands of years. While that is true, one is also aware that, for example, the portrayal of men and women in MTV is definitely a challenge to the bio-pietistic arrangement of Hindu community. More and more young men and women adopt the Western dress and imitate the men and women who appear on MTV. Anyone who has watched MTV would know that MTV is thoroughly iconoclastic when it comes to any form of hierarchy and discrimination based on age or gender.

Third, when the Hindu religious community becomes international in character, it has to face the problem of redefining its ties to *varna dharma*. Let me mention two specific areas of concern. There is a growing number of non-Indians, such as Europeans and North Americans, who are embracing Hinduism in its different forms. These persons may belong to either a sect headed by a guru, the International Society for Krishna-Consciousness, or local Hindu communities in the West. How does one fit these persons within the *varna dharma*? An attempt to define such persons' *varna dharma* would involve revising the caste arrangement simply as a system of division of labor, and purging it of its connection to birth, endogamy, and concepts of pollution. Hindus are under significant pressure to think along these lines. Such a rethinking will question and affect the bio-pietistic framework of Hinduism.

This is one of the reasons why the Vedanta form of Hinduism is more attractive to non-Indians than other forms. There are American followers of Vedanta who would not call themselves Hindus because such a naming of themselves would entitle them to a connection with the land of India and the social arrangement of India. I know a swami in Atlanta who is a monk of the Ramakrishna Order. He is a white American who walks around with slacks and shirts (at times a saffron shirt). He is always quick to tell me that he is not a Hindu but a Vedantin. When I asked why he calls himself so, he told me that if he were a Hindu he would have to dress like a Hindu, go to India often, and be part of the caste system, and that he was not defined by any of those. How Hinduism is going to consider the people of other nations within its bio-pietistic framework will be a big challenge for Hinduism in the globalized world of today.

Hindus who marry across racial, ethnic, and cultural boundaries bring pressure on the bio-piety of Hinduism as well. Interreligious and interracial families do bring a significant challenge to Hindu bio-piety. Children born in these families would find it difficult to negotiate their place within the caste arrangement. Most of them, invariably, would and do choose to function without any reference to the caste system at all.

A Christian Theological Approach

How does Christian theology approach this phenomenon? How does a Christian theologian address the struggles of

Hindu brothers and sisters in the newly emerging global community? What are the issues that invite Christian theologians to enter into conversation with Hindus both in India and abroad? Let me highlight four of the issues that I consider pertinent to the encounter between Hinduism and globalization.

New Catholicity

Robert Schreiter has described one of the effects of globalization on Christian theology in this manner:

> Theology must be able to interact with globalization theory out of its own internal history and resources and not be simply reactive to it. It seems to me that the concept of *catholicity* may be the theological concept most suited to developing a theological view of theology between the global and the local in a world church.[14]

Schreiter goes on to define this new catholicity as wholeness, fullness, and exchange and communication. I find that the views expressed by Schreiter with regard to Christian theology are directly relevant to the concerns of Hindus in the context of globalization. What is required of Hindus today is to work toward a *new* catholicity that frees them from the constraints of both geo-piety and bio-piety. This catholicity demands that Hindus ask themselves this question: What would it mean to say that Hinduism is a universal faith, taking into account the historical particularities of our situation and the particularities of our faith expressions?

In this area of concern a conversation between Hindus in India and those abroad has already begun. Nonresident Indians (NRIs) bring to the forefront the question of catholicity. According to the NRIs, a new form of inculturation is required of Hindus today. One of the Hindu thinkers describes it as a way of forging a new identity and complex cultures of solidarity:

---

14. Schreiter, *New Catholicity*, 188–219.

Rather than fall prey to the culturalist notion that all "races" must take their place on the American spectrum of high cultures, we must fight to forge complex cultures of solidarity. Rather than turn to "India" for the pure tradition, we must be able to turn to the complexity of "India" in order to take elements of the tradition which are meaningful solutions to our own local questions. Rather than graft on cultural components which make no sense in our New World, it would be far better to take those things Indian which we can place on our heads in order for us to raise hell globally.[15]

This is not only true of NRIs; it is applicable to Hindus in India as well. The effects of globalization on the younger generations demand that Hindu youth in India need to be confronted with a much more "catholic" view of Hinduism than one that is controlled by geo-piety. Especially in the context of the new emerging consumerist culture in India, Hinduism has to find ways to express its faith in catholic terms. While bemoaning the ethnic tensions in India and the accompanying fundamentalist movements, Sarita Sarvate has this to say:

Where will we go from here? Will we reunite and recreate the exciting multi-cultures of our youth? Or will the ethnic tensions in India climax to fracture the country further, into individual states, divided along religious and language barriers? I think not. I think the religious fervor in India will die, and its place will be taken by something more insidious; the internationalization of India. The signs of it are there already. McDonalds and cable TV and minivans and microchips are fast changing India's diverse landscape to create a homogeneous

---

15. Vijay Prashad, "Forging a New Identity: We Must Forge Complex Cultures of Solidarity," *Little India* 7, no. 4 (April 30, 1997): 56. This essay contains excerpts from his *Contours of the Heart: South Asians Map North America* (New York: Asian American Writer's Workshop, 1996).

consumer culture, a big brown America. And that will be the ultimate tragedy.[16]

Another part of the puzzle is the way in which Hindus in India and the NRIs differ in defining Hindu faith and the clashes that it generates. In commenting on the controversy over M. F. Husain's paintings of the Hindu goddesses, the newspaper *The Hindu* criticizes the overzealous NRI Hindus:

> It is amusing to read in the newspapers letters written by the NRIs on the controversy about M. F. Husain's paintings of the Hindu Goddesses. While criticizing Husain, these people often also take the liberty to preach Hinduism to the Indians here. When the non-resident Indians speak of their version of Hinduism, to the so-called "ignorant and pitiable" Hindus who live here in India, one becomes a little uneasy.... They leave their motherland with the sole objective of fulfilling their material ambition, which itself is the antithesis of the true practice of Hinduism.[17]

The editor goes on criticize the NRIs for their guilt complex and their "ostentatious places of worship to visit either during week-ends or at the time of distress." He states further that one should be an insider to understand the nuances of the Hindu faith, because perceiving Hinduism as a "single solid monolithic block, at times, hides its rich pluralistic dimensions." As one can see, the path to new catholicity is fraught with many complex issues and questions. This is an area where Christians and Hindus need to be in dialogue with one another.

Catholicity as Universality and Orthodoxy

One could argue that Hinduism has always been catholic from its ancient beginnings. Is not its accommodative spirit as

---

16. "Whither to, the Indian Melting Pot? Is India Destined to Become a Big Brown Version of America?" *India Currents* 11, no. 5 (August 31, 1997): 64.

17. Editorial in *The Hindu*, July 14, 1998.

expressed in the Vedas indicative of its catholic character? For example, the oft-quoted verse from Rig Veda states, "Truth is One: and the sages call it by different names." Is not this an expression of catholicity? Based on this long-standing tradition, Hindus during the modern period have adopted slogans such as "All religions are essentially the same," "All paths lead to the same destination," and "One God, many ways!" The Hindu reform movements in the nineteenth and twentieth centuries have operated with these slogans. The Vedanta version of Hinduism as promoted by Ramakrishna Paramahamsa and Swami Vivekananda has asserted that Hinduism is the most universalist of all religions. Such universalistic statements have served as powerful political tools to deal with the impact of Islam and Christianity on Indian religion and culture. They may continue to be used as tools to meet the challenges of globalization. But it is becoming clear to many that one needs a new form of "universal," which we name as "catholicity" in the new situation.

The catholicity that we are referring to here is different from Hindu universalism. It invokes both universality and orthodoxy. Schreiter's discussion is again relevant here. He describes catholicity (within Christian history) as that which defines the characteristics of the church, known as the "marks" of the church.[18] He writes, "One approach to exploring catholicity or the catholic meaning of the Church is to examine how the Church understands itself in a world in which it lives."[19] Hinduism, in a similar fashion, is facing the issue of self-understanding in the new and globalized world. It has to enter into a conversation with all its constituents on the essentials of Hindu faith in the postmodern world. What is the "mark" of a Hindu community in India or abroad? In other words, what distinguishes a Hindu in the absence of any clear links to geo-piety and bio-piety? Here waits an intense theological discussion for Hindus through-

---

18. Schreiter, *New Catholicity,* 119ff.
19. Ibid., 122.

out the world. Christian theologians who are aware of their own religion's struggle with catholicity over the centuries can be valuable conversation partners to Hindu thinkers and theologians today. Here the diaspora Hindus have a specific contribution to make. Living within contexts dominated primarily by a Christian religious ethos, they are compelled to define their Hindu identity more in terms of "theological" viewpoints than through appealing to bio- and geo-piety. I have often met young Hindu men and women in the United States who find themselves totally dissatisfied with Hindu self-definitions that depend on land, culture, and temples. They are looking for a "catholic" Hindu faith that can maintain its Hinduness through its beliefs and practices rather than simply on familial, ethnic, national, and cultural ties.

Institutional and Associational Ecclesiology

We are dealing with two very different categories when we speak of "catholicity" and "universalism." The Christian view of catholicity and the Hindu idea of universalism are quite different from one another. The idea of catholicity in Christianity is constructed around a well-developed (over a period of several centuries) and well-defined (though in multiple ways) category called *ecclesia*. The concept of *ecclesia* can be understood in three distinct forms, as Everett has outlined.[20] The three forms are communal, institutional, and associational. In the communal form, one notices a weaving together of rituals, beliefs, and customs in the network of family, land, economy, and so on. In Hinduism, one recognizes this kind of ecclesiological form expressed as "an amalgam of bio- and geo-piety."[21]

In the present context of globalization, Hinduism experiences pressure on its communal ecclesiology. It finds itself lacking in institutional form. It had operated with the caste

20. Everett, *Religion, Federalism, and the Struggle*, 151–52.
21. Ibid., 151–53.

structure (and, within that, several monarchical political frameworks) of the larger society as its way of organizing itself. But given the parliamentary democracy in India and the compression experienced through globalization, Hinduism may need to find new institutions to sustain the religious life of Hindus. The Hindutva movement tries to bypass this issue by reinterpreting the constitution of India in theocratic terms. It has tried to exploit the present constitutional framework to appeal, in a sense, for a "Hinducratic" state. It is attempting to bring an alliance between the bio- and geo-piety of Hinduism and the democratic republican structures of Indian political life. The constitution, with its federalist structure, simply cannot accommodate such a "Hinducratic" state.

While the Hindutva movement has obvious constitutional hurdles to the promotion of a Hindu state, the diaspora Hindus are experimenting with other forms of institutionalizing their Hindu faith. The way in which the Hindu temples in the United States function is one model of organizing Hinduism on the institutional level. The governing bodies of these temples act as central administrative mechanisms within which the various programs of the temple — such as Sunday classes, language classes for second-generation Hindus, events promoting Indian art and culture, and occasional religious discourses — gain an "ecclesial" character.

There is a lack of associational form as well. Associations operate by "organizing the purposes of individuals who covenant to form or join"[22] an association. But the Hindu community by its caste structure has blocked the formation of such religious associations, which depend on individual and voluntary membership. Its close ties to land and geography have also stood in the way of forming associations. The proliferation of Hindu associations since independence — such as RSS, Vishwa Hindu Parishad, Sangh Parivar, and others — is indicative of both the Hindus' recognition of the need for an associational ecclesiology and their attempt to remedy the

---

22. Ibid., 152.

situation. Here again, as one can readily recognize, bio-piety and geo-piety do not lend themselves easily to associational form. In the meantime, more and more caste-based political associations have come into being since the independence of India, mostly as lobbying groups within the democratic political structure of India (which means that some politicians must, or at least do, cater to caste loyalties).

The problem that I have presented here is primarily due to the fact that while a Christian view of *ecclesia* is informed by two major categories, "covenant" and "publicity," Hindu universalism has been largely defined by a mystico-theological view of the Ultimate as being one with many names. The most recent disturbances in India with missionaries' attempts to convert Dalits to Christianity signal both the absence of institutional and associational ecclesiology within Hinduism, and the need for the concept of "covenantal publicity," to use Everett's term. This means, then, that Christians and Hindus need to be more in dialogue with one another with regard to one another's ecclesiologies. This is also an area where the NRIs may offer leadership, because they are the ones who face the need for institutional and associational ecclesiology in an acute manner.

Hinduism and the Eschatological Community

The final issue that needs to be faced deals with the future of Hinduism and the future of humanity as a whole. In other words, how does Hinduism view its future in the globalized world, and what is the vision that Hinduism offers of the future of humanity? With regard to the future of Hinduism, there have been grand visions by both Hindus and others. L. K. Advani, a past president of the BJP, has said this: "This century [the twentieth] belonged to Europe while the 21st will belong to Asia, and it should be a Hindu century."[23] Klaus Klostermaier, a historian of religions, expresses a similar sentiment: "Hinduism is organizing itself; it is articulating its

---

23. Interview by Rajiv Malik in *Hinduism Today,* October 31, 1997, 31.

own essentials; it is modernizing; and it is carried by a great many people with strong faith. It would not be surprising to find Hinduism the dominant religion of the twenty-first century."[24] A fundamentalist Hindu and a non-Hindu historian of religions are making very similar predictions about the future of Hinduism. It is difficult to assess these predictions given the very nature of prediction itself. Only future generations can truly evaluate such a vision of the future of Hinduism.

How does Hinduism view the future of humanity, or in Christian theological terms, the eschatological community? How does that vision match with the future of Hinduism? Klostermaier himself offers us a picture of that community to come:

> [Hinduism] would be a religion that doctrinally is less clear-cut than mainstream Christianity, politically less determined than Islam, ethically less heroic than Buddhism, but it would offer something to everybody, it would delight by its richness and depth, it would address people at a depth that has not been reached for a long time by other religions or by the prevailing ideologies. It will appear idealistic to those who look for idealism, pragmatic to the pragmatists, spiritual to the seekers, sensual to the here-and-now generation.[25]

As a Christian theologian, I see here a vision of the eschatological community that is governed by tolerance and diversity. The Rig Vedic proclamation, "Truth is One: the sages call it by different names," will become the cornerstone of this eschatological community. It will be reinforced by the political-theological assertion that all religions, though different, are equally valid paths to human flourishing. Such a vision is very attractive to the postmodern, globalized persons of today.

---

24. Klostermaier, *Survey of Hinduism*, 475.
25. Ibid.

At the same time, one is compelled to ask the following questions: What is the theological core that can challenge some of the negative consequences and demonic powers that seem to accompany the processes of globalization? What is the kind of politics that might deliver justice and peace to humanity in light of the extremities of globalization? What are the ethical values that are nonnegotiable when it comes to judging the effects of globalization? Are there such nonnegotiable ethical values at all? There are not clear-cut answers to these questions, and it is not at all clear that Klostermaier's characterization of what Hinduism might offer can be of much help. However, here again we have an arena where Christians, Hindus, and others can be invited to dialogue and conversation. Thanks to globalization, it is possible for all to engage in this conversation at any time and in any place because time and space have been compressed.

– Chapter 6 –

OBSERVATION AND REVELATION

A GLOBAL DIALOGUE WITH BUDDHISM

Kosuke Koyama

Religion can be said to be an awareness of the inner word. Its message invites people to think, and its public rituals inspire people to act and to live in community. Religion is always true religion for the devotees of any particular religion; however, any religion has both positive and negative elements. It may support human rights, yet fail to stand strongly against injustice. While it admonishes against human greed, its temples exist in symbiosis with business and the commodification of spiritual values.[1] Religions engage, sometimes with fanatic zeal, in the game of worldly power, posing to human conscience a tormenting puzzle of the cohabitation of humility and arrogance. There is no human being upon the earth free from religion's ambiguous influence.

In the acceleration of globalization that we are experiencing today, I see a contradiction. On the one hand, it represents a reprehensible system of global economic exploitation and cultural imperialism; on the other, it invites us to the vision of one world prospering in human meaning. The former invokes the image of King Ahab coveting Naboth's vineyard. The latter directs our attention to Jeremiah's vision of *shalom* which says, "Seek the welfare of the city [one global world]... for in its welfare you will find your welfare" (Jer 29:7). With

---

1. See the discussion on commodification in William Schweiker, "Responsibility in the World of Mammon," in vol. 1 in this series.

this striking contradiction, globalization challenges human destiny. Religions are displaying their wisdom and vitality in negotiating with the force of globalization. The jury is still out.[2]

With Christianity and Islam, Buddhism is known as a universal religion, and it aspires to inform the whole of humanity. It is in principle and intention free of what John Mbiti treats as "tribal" traditions, what Thomas Thangaraj calls "geo-piety" and "bio-piety," and what Sze-kar Wan sees as "imperialism" and "familism."[3] Its adherents today number some 325 million people. In shaping civilizations stamped with its own noble words and symbols, it is one of the eminent historic traditions of spiritual persuasion. To explore the Buddhist wisdom vis-à-vis the forces of globalization, we can perhaps best focus on the global dialogue between observation and revelation. This is a decisive issue, especially from a Christian point of view, for a profound theological insight in that tradition is that "reason is not destroyed by revelation, just as revelation is not emptied by reason."[4] In fact, an engaging dialogue between human observation and divine revelation may well be beneficial, even necessary, to the health of human civilization.

Human Observation, Divine Revelation

What is human observation? An ancient Japanese ruler observed, "Decisions on important matters should not be made

2. "Globalization connotes different meanings according to geographical/linguistic contexts. We speak of globalization as an ambiguous process operative in today's world, holding together both positive and negative elements. Positively, globalization works against sectarianism. Negatively, it threatens, and even destroys, often in subtle ways, local values, cultures, economies and political structures all around the world.... Globalization is a strategy of international capital to create more markets for itself and to restructure the relationships of production." Mission Studies, *Journal of the International Association for Mission Studies* 13 (1996): 88. A similar view is found in the contribution by John Mbiti in this volume.
3. See their essays in this volume.
4. Paul Tillich, *Systematic Theology*, vol. 1 (Chicago: University of Chicago Press, 1952), 131.

by one person alone. They should be discussed with many."[5] Galileo Galilei's observation of the heliocentric solar system and Charles Darwin's *The Origin of Species* prominently illustrate scientific observation engaged by outstanding human minds. A boy observes, "Daddy, why do white people treat colored people so mean?" as Martin Luther King, Jr., recounted in his famous "Letter from the Birmingham Jail" of 1963. A Christian ethicist observes, "There is no deeper pathos in the spiritual life of man than the cruelty of righteous people."[6]

What is divine revelation? Revelation is that kind of knowledge or event the source of which is beyond human origin. Concretely speaking, Judaism, Christianity, and Islam are religions of divine revelation. "Thus says the Lord" is decisive to them. The awesomeness of the divine freedom and sovereignty is stated: "For as the heavens are higher than the earth, so are my ways higher than your ways and my thoughts than your thoughts" (Isa 55:9).

Revelation is the totally unexpected word of God. "God called to him out of the bush, 'Moses, Moses!'" (Exod 3:1–6). "Before I formed you in the womb I knew you, and before you were born I consecrated you" (Jer 1:4–10). "Saul, Saul, why do you persecute me?" (Acts 9:1–19). The apostle Paul introduces himself as "sent neither by human commission nor from human authority, but through Jesus Christ and God the Father, who raised him from the dead" (Gal 1:1). "You did not choose me but I chose you" (John 15:16).

Jewish scholar Emil L. Fackenheim has said:

The God of Israel is no mythological deity which mingles freely with men in history. He is beyond man — so infinitely beyond human reach that an opening of the heavens themselves is required if He is to become humanly accessible. Few are the men to whom such an

---

5. "The Seventeen-Article Constitution of Prince Shotoku," *Sources of Japanese Tradition*, vol. 1 (New York: Columbia University Press, 1958), 51.
6. Reinhold Niebuhr, *An Interpretation of Christian Ethics* (New York: Seabury Press, 1935), 138.

opening was ever granted, and the reports of these few are so obscure as to be unintelligible to nearly all others. So infinitely is the Divine above the human! Nevertheless, the Midrash insists that not messengers, not angels, not intermediaries, but God Himself acts in human history — and He was unmistakably present to a whole people at least once.[7]

Basic to the idea of revelation is the faith that the transcendent God "acts in human history." Judaism, according to Fackenheim, is rooted in the concrete salvation of God that Israelites experienced at the Red Sea. There God "was unmistakably present to a whole people." Fackenheim continues: "[T]he maidservants at the Red Sea saw what even Ezekiel did not see."[8] As Reinhold Niebuhr wrote, "The most important characteristic of a religion of revelation is this twofold emphasis upon the transcendence of God and upon His intimate relation to the world."[9]

Niebuhr's "twofold emphasis" is not, however, "unmistakably present" to everyone. The Israelites saw it. The Egyptians did not. At Caesarea Philippi, Jesus says to Peter, "Blessed are you, Simon son of Jonah! For flesh and blood has not revealed this to you, but my Father in heaven." Not to everyone but to Peter the mystery was revealed. But he then "sternly ordered the disciples not to tell anyone that he was the Messiah." Jesus talks about his suffering. Peter stumbles (Matt 16:13–26). "God's presence in history" is enigmatic ("My ways [are] higher than your ways").

Religion is a poem awakening the human soul to the theme of ultimate importance. The language that relates the mystery of the "twofold emphasis," the language of the Bible and of the Qur'an,[10] cannot be confined in the pale of rational dis-

---

7. E. L. Fackenheim, *God's Presence in History* (New York: Harper Torchbooks, 1970), 4.

8. Ibid., 9.

9. Reinhold Niebuhr, *The Nature and Destiny of Man,* vol. 1 (New York: Charles Scribner's Sons, 1941), 126.

10. "God, there is none but He, the alive, the ever real. Slumber takes Him not,

course. The "twofold emphasis" is not a subject of scientific discourse. Science seeks demonstrable, objective descriptions of reality. Can the inspiring words "you shall love the alien as yourself" (Lev 19:34) be expressed in the language of scientific observation of the *kosmos* (as known by cosmology) and the *bios* (as known by biology)? The future happiness of global civilization depends on the quality and character of dialogue between these two universal minds, the scientific and the religious.

The religious message has vitality if it is localized and contemporized, that is, if it is ethically engaged in the "here and now." The transcendence intimated in the Near Eastern monotheistic traditions is, in a radical fashion, ethically engaged. In the Buddhist East, the *nirvanic* salvation is contemporized in one's monastic endeavor to overcome greed.[11] Ethical engagement here and now is authentically present in both Christian and Buddhist traditions, although Buddhism presents its global ethical ideals without referencing God.[12] The words of Jesus uttered in the famous parable of the Good Samaritan, "Go and do likewise" (Luke 10:29–37), also globalize ethical engagement. This truth of nonimperialistic localization/ contemporization is a positive

---

nor sleep. Everything in the heavens and in the earth is His, and who — His leave apart — shall intercede with Him? He knows everything that mankind have presently in hand and everything about them that is yet to be. Of a knowledge like His they are entirely uncomprehending — unless He gives them leave to know. In the vastness of the heavens and the earth His Throne is established. Tirelessly He preserves them. So great is His majesty" (The Qur'an 2:255).

11. "Greed," in Pali, *tanha*, "the attachment to illusion likened to a throat parched and burning with thirst." Takeuchi Yoshinori, *The Heart of Buddhism* (New York: Crossroad, 1991), 162. The Buddha accepted the moderate and reasonable desires of everyday life. He condemned intense "thirsting desire." He maintained the view that "extremes" are destructive, as the introductory part of the Four Noble Truths discourse confirms. One can perceive a subtle connection between *tanha* and "boosting": "Idolatry is the elevation of a preliminary concern to ultimacy. Something essentially conditioned is taken as unconditional, something essentially partial is boosted into universality, and something essentially finite is given infinite significance" (Tillich, *Systematic Theology* 16).

12. The "maldistribution of wealth is intrinsically evil because it destroys the rich through over-consumption and the poor through malnutrition" writes Lily De Silva, head of the Department of Pali and Buddhism in the Peradeniya University in Sri Lanka in *Dialogue* (Columbo: Ecumenical Institute, 1989), 41.

spiritual force that can globalize religious salvation. If the ethical proposal is positive, globalization is creative; if negative, it is destructive.

In these two traditions, the nonimperialistic localization/ contemporization becomes concrete in the "Awakened One" and the "Anointed One." The very concepts of "awakened" and "anointed" come from different religious and cultural soils. One meditated under a tree while the other was crucified upon a tree. The contrast in the form of salvation suggested by these two images defies any easy scheme of comparison. In the religious sphere, radical contrast is possible. Contrast should be welcomed as an element that educates and expands the relationship between human observation and divine revelation.

Each concrete tradition has created a civilization based on its respective symbolism of universality: Christianity commends the universal truth of radical *attachment,* as in "God so loved the world . . ." (John 3:16). Buddhism proclaims as universal the principle of *detachment.* The monks, having renounced home, know that "Love cometh from companionship; In wake of love upsurges ill; Seeing the bane that comes of love, Fare lonely as rhinoceros."[13] What does this contrast say to global ethics?

Little is known of the historical Jesus or of the historical Gotama. They are known only through the traditions of their respective faith communities, one through the New Testament and the other through the Mahayana hagiographical literature such as the famed *Buddhacarita kavya sutra* ("Poetic Discourse on the Acts of the Buddha") by Asvaghosa of the second century. These documents are message-oriented (*kerygmatic*). Must religious messages be historical? What do we mean by "history"?

Both traditions demonstrate complex interpretations and appropriations of the faith over time. There is neither a simple Buddhism nor a simple Christianity. There are "many Bud-

---

13. E. Conze, ed., *Buddhist Scriptures* (New York: Penguin, 1959), 79.

dhisms" within Buddhism as there are "many Christianities" within Christianity. Which Christianity and which Buddhism is more meaningful and functional in a world that recognizes the plurality of truth? Humanity is weary of easy transcendental solutions for confusing temporal human problems. Much damage has been done by the misuse of transcendence.

The Buddhist *Dharma*[14] and the Christian *Ruah*[15]

Scholars usually begin Buddhist study with the doctrine of *paticcasamuppada,* the Conditional Arising or Dependent Origination (Pali: *paticca,* "due to," "dependent on," and *samuppada,* "arising," "becoming"). The fundamental form of the doctrine is: "This being, that becomes; by the arising of this, that arises." This is the principle by which the basic law of human existence is observed, described, and explained:

conditioned by ignorance, activities;
conditioned by activities, consciousness;
conditioned by consciousness, mind-and-body;
conditioned by mind-and-body, six sense-spheres;
conditioned by six sense-spheres, contact;
conditioned by contact, feeling;
conditioned by feeling, craving;
conditioned by craving, grasping;
conditioned by grasping, becoming;
conditioned by becoming, birth;

---

14. Derived from the Sanskrit root *dhr,* "sustain, support, uphold." It denotes the positive ideas: universal truth, right doctrine, foundation, the cosmic principle, duty, moral obligation, virtuous and meritorious deeds, good government, and so forth. The Greek word *logos* is translated as *dharma* in the Thai translation of the Gospel according to John. The Chinese word *dao* corresponds closely to it.

15. The Hebrew *ruah* and the Greek *pneuma,* "breath, wind," makes a person physically alive and spiritually meaningful and bonds that person into a community of faith and action. It is God "who gives breath to the people" (Isa 42:5). "I will cause breath to enter you, and you shall live" (Ezek 37:5). Death comes when breath is taken away, as in the case of the flood (Gen 7:22). Idols are lifeless and meaningless since "there is no breath" in them (Jer 10:14). Loving relationships are based in it: The tragic Job laments, "My breath is repulsive to my wife" (19:17). The *ruah* is the seat of the emotions, intellect, and will.

conditioned by birth, old age and death, grief, lamen-
tation, suffering, sorrow and despair come into
being.
Thus is the arising of this mass of ill.[16]

Obviously, this formulation must be a later elaboration of
a simpler formulation. It is possible, though with some difficulty, to follow the chain of thought developed here. Scholars
have suggested that ignorance (*avijja*), craving (*tanha*) and
suffering (*dukkha*) are the three prominent points of the Conditional Arising. From ignorance comes craving and from
craving comes suffering. This is the diagnosis. How then can
this "mass of ill" be eliminated? Eliminate ignorance, then
craving will disappear. When craving disappears, suffering
will disappear. This is the therapy.[17]

The Four Noble Truths (*aryasatya*) is understood to be
Buddha's reformulation of the truth of Conditional Arising for popular understanding. The first truth is *suffering*
(*dukkhasatya*), followed by the *cause of suffering* (*samu-
dayasatya*). After this diagnosis, the therapy section begins.
The third truth is the *cessation of suffering* (*nirodhasatya*),
followed by the *path* that leads to the cessation of suffering (*margasatya*). The contents of the Conditional Arising
and the Four Noble Truths obviously coincide. Prominent in
these formulations are three distinctive words linked to one
another: *avijja, tanha* and *dukkha*. These doctrines are cen-

---

16. Conze, *Buddhist Scriptures,* 187.

17. Takeuchi defines *avijja* as "the fundamental unknowing at the root of our existence" (Takeuchi, *Heart of Buddhism,* 159). It refers to ignorance of the *dharma*.
Dukkha means" suffering," "unsatisfactoriness," or "imperfection." It is one of the
three characteristics of human existence with *anicca* (nonpermanence) and *anatta*
(no-self or no-soul). "Suffering is essentially the emotional result or living manifestation of the qualities of impermanence and insubstantiality of all beings. It is a
Buddhist axiom that that which changes cannot produce lasting satisfaction." Winston L. King, *A Thousand Lives Away* (Oxford: Bruno Cassiver, 1964), 19. In his
essay in this volume, John Mbiti writes, "The twentieth century deprived millions
upon millions of people of the right to die 'naturally.'" The Conditional Arising
concludes with the words, "Thus is the arising of this mass of ill." It must be an
affirmation of Mbiti's observation.

tral for the Buddhist faith communities throughout the world. They constitute an honest *observation* on human life.[18]

In one of the most ancient Buddhist texts we read, "If all attachment (by means of wisdom) is destroyed, (no further) suffering grows up."[19] This, for the Buddhist, is the meaning of salvation. To know this is the awakening that will lead a person to *nirvana,* "a state of everlasting radiant smiles with nobody smiling" (according to Buddhadasa Indapanno, a Thai monk). Knowledge of the human predicament gained by this observation is the heart of the Buddhist tradition. Attachment is the undesirable "hot" condition of the soul. Here is a remarkable piece of dialogue between the Buddha and his followers: "Monks, when one's turban or head is ablaze, what is to be done?" "Lord, when one's turban or head is ablaze, for the extinguishing thereof one must put forth extra desire, effort, endeavour, exertion, impulse, mindfulness and attention."[20]

This is the spirit of monastic ethical Buddhism. Monastic Buddhism moves toward this goal and, to that extent, is "hopeful." Buddhism accepts the Hindu doctrine of the *karma* (action and reaction). The *karma* works objectively. "If you do good, good will come to you, if you do evil, evil will come to you," as Thai monks and their people on the street say. The *karma* has positive and negative implications. If you extinguish the fire, good will come to you; if you fail to do so, evil will come to you.

Mahayana Buddhism, which appeared in northwestern India about the second century c.e. and spread into China, Korea, and Japan later on, seeks to save those who are incapable on their own of mustering the "extra desire, effort, endeavor..." to extinguish the burning turban. In Mahayana, Buddha the monk is transformed into Buddha the

---

18. See Hajime Nakamura, "The Basic Teachings of Buddhism," in Dumoulin et al., eds., *Buddhism in the Modern World,* 3–31.

19. *Udana: Solemn Utterances of the Buddha,* trans. Bhadragaka (Bangkok: Mahamakuta-Raja-Vidyalaya, 1954), 23.

20. *The Book of the Kindred Sayings,* part 5 (London: Pali Text Society, 1930), 372.

savior of infinite mercy who will gather all lay people, including those who are not *nirvana* specialists, into the Great Vehicle (*mahayana*) to take them to the zone of the "Wisdom Beyond" (*prajnaparamita*). This new compassionate figure of the Buddha inspired extensive metaphysical and cosmological speculation about the person of the Buddha. For the original monastic Buddhism, the Buddha is essentially an accomplished ascetic monk who lived and died. Mahayana speculation originates from the observation that not all of us are *nirvana* specialists.

The words "extra desire, effort, endeavor ... " suggest the presence of a moral self. This self is, however, only a constantly changing aggregate (*skandha*) of five elements: body (*rupa*), feeling (*vedana*), recognition (*sanna*), imagination (*samkhara*), and discrimination (*vinnana*). The self is impermanent (*anicca*) and is in a constant state of change. There is a moral self but not a substantive self (*anatta*). This anthropology of no-self is expressed as emptiness (*sunyata*) in the Mahayana tradition. According to the great Mahayana philosopher Nagarjuna (ca. 150–ca. 250), emptiness is not the opposite of fullness. Emptiness "transcends and embraces both emptiness and fullness.... True Emptiness is wondrous Being."[21] The source of human freedom is located in this wondrous emptiness. Mahayana thought may be distinct from, but is not unrelated to, the original monastic tradition, of which a Thai monk says:

When objects make contact with the eye, observe and identify them, and know what action has to be taken with whatever is seen. But don't permit like or dislike to arise. If you permit the arising of like, you will desire; if you permit the arising of dislike, you will want to destroy. Thus it is that there are likers and haters. This

---

21. Masao Abe, *Zen and Western Thought* (New York: Macmillan, 1985), 126–27.

is what is called "the self." To go the way of the self is suffering and deception.[22]

Either through the monastic development of insight or through Mahayana emptiness one may extinguish the fire of craving. The Buddhist *dharma* is an observation of human life. One of the royal children of King Mongkut of Thailand, who later became Prince Vajirananavarorasa, *sangharaja,* described his physical existence with these words:

> Conditions (of mind and body) are unstable,
> Conditions (of mind and body) are *dukkha,*
> Conditions (of mind and body) are ownerless.[23]

This is what the tradition seems to say about the liberative core of Buddhism. Buddhism observes, gives diagnosis, and prescribes therapy for human ills. It is not a revelation religion. "Religion is *a system of observation and practice,*" says Buddhadasa Indapanno.[24] Such Buddhist observation is broadly persuasive.

However, it must be acknowledged that the hearing of the canonical word does not mean that the hearers will practice the word. How to deal with the split between hearing and practicing? If the original word is often not practiced, what is the use of studying it? Why study the Conditional Arising?

First, we must recognize critically this split within ourselves and in our faith communities. Sincere religious life begins with such recognition. Second, though the sacred word may not be practiced, it is necessary for us to hear it. The ancient saying, "One does not live by bread alone, but by every word that comes from the mouth of the Lord" (Deut 8:3), is undeniably true. Third, we are aware of the bliss that accom-

---

22. Buddhadasa Indapanno, *Buddha Dhamma for Students,* trans. Ariyananda Bhikkhu (Bangkok: Thammasat University, 1966), 7.

23. Prince Vajirananavarorasa, *Vinayamukha* (Bangkok: Buddhist University of Thailand, n.d.), viii.

24. Buddhadasa Indapanno, *Christianity and Buddhism,* Sinclaire Thompson Memorial Lecture (Bangkok: Thailand Theological Seminary, 1967), p. d in introduction.

panies a morally upright life. The sacred word encourages our moral endeavor. Fourth, such acknowledgment will put all of us on an equal footing. This may effect a slowdown of our powerful drive toward self-righteousness. "As a flower that is lovely and beautiful, but is scentless, even so fruitless is the well-spoken word of one who does not practice it," says the *Dhammapada* (no. 51).

The *ruah*, by contrast, intimates the mystery of human freedom in emotions, intellect, will, and community. It is concomitant with the biblical idea of humans made in the image of God. Since both "breath" and "image" come from God, they cannot be separated. The universal *ruah* bestows the grace of transcendence in human life and hence makes the spiritual quest possible. The globalization of religious and ethical values and scientific engagements are possible because of the universal *ruah*. It is the *ruah* that examines the quality of human civilization. The *ruah* can appreciate both divine revelation and human observation. It is through *ruah* that we are able to hear, wherever we are and whenever we live, the sharp prophetic critique: "Its rulers give judgment for a bribe, its priests teach for a price, its prophets give oracles for money" (Mic 3:11).

Our spiritual quest is concomitant with our observation of life. The truthfulness of the quest corresponds with that of observation. Gotama Siddharta became the Awakened One in his observation of human life. On the basis of the materials available to us today on Buddhism, and the way this tradition portrays Gotama, it seems fairly safe to say that the overcoming of human greed is at the center of the Buddhist message. The Gotama of Buddhism says that greed is the number one human problem. The biblical *ruah-pneuma* appreciates that Buddhist insight.[25]

---

25. The Buddhist scripture consists of three "baskets" (*pitaka*): the life and sermons of the Buddha (*sutta pitaka*), the monastic discipline (*vinaya pitaka*), and the systematics (*abhidhamma pitaka*). The first, often compared with the Christian Gospels, is the one from which we draw the knowledge of the life and preaching of the Buddha.

Buddha's central message may be grasped differently. One may say that the "impermanence of all things" (*anicca*) or the view that human existence is "suffering" (*dukkha*) is the core message of Buddhism. Or one may recite "The Three Gems" (*tri-ratna*) of the *Buddha,* the *Dharma,* and the *Sangha,* in which one may find refuge (*Buddham saranam gacchami, Dhammam saranam gacchami, Sangham saranam gacchami* [*Pali*]), as the essence of the Buddhist tradition. How about the remarkable Mahayana idea of emptiness (*sunyata*)? Or the profound religious emotion expressed by thirteenth-century monk Shinran of Japanese Pure Land Buddhism, which became something of a common bit of folk wisdom: "Even a good man will be received in Buddha's Land, how much more a bad man!" There are many inspiring foci in this great spiritual tradition, each of which has invoked impressive religious experience and philosophical speculation. In view of such an abundant possibility, on what basis can I suggest that overcoming greed is so central to the Buddhist message?

The problem of greed is a key, effective focus of Buddhist truth. I call it a "focus" through which other truths can be appreciated properly in the way the Buddhist tradition suggests us to do. Greed is highly subjective, but it is also a global reality, though it is manifested differently in different communities or cultures. This focus is meaningful as I think about global ethics. The theme of human greed speaks to me persuasively and, I believe, to many others also.[26]

When I say with the Buddhist that greed is the universal human problem, I am thinking of it as the root energy that manifests itself in the various areas of human life: greed after

---

26. My understanding of Christianity is subjective also. During the Pacific War (1941–45), Christianity meant to me, a fifteen-year-old Christian boy in bomb-devastated Tokyo, a critique of the Japanese imperial cult, a national frenzy in divinization of a human person, all because of the greed for status, power, and national pride. The Christian idea that a human being cannot be God was my focus. Ever since then I have judged the quality of civilization by this *ruah*-based focus. Focusing implies simplification. I accept the risk of simplification. In the theological life guided by the *ruah,* however, simplification is not absolutization.

time, space, power, prestige, honor, wealth, longevity, mobility, religion, sexual gratification, racial and gender superiority, and so on. These manifestations have serious social impacts. I am also aware of the entanglement between human greed and civilization. Is civilization possible apart from human greed? The historical phenomenology of greed is complex. I agree with Walter Rauschenbusch: "The great sin of men is to resist the reformation of predatory society."[27] And I follow the Buddha in rejecting "thirsting greed," which, in biblical theology, is self-idolatry.[28]

Ecce Dharma and Ecce Homo

To say that according to the Buddha, human greed is destructive is redundant, because the truth that human greed is destructive can stand by itself. The universal *dharma* transcends concern for "who said so." The Buddha left no successors; his gift to posterity was the *Dhamma* itself, as many have observed. The historical Buddha is dispensable. The focus is on the *dharma*. Buddhism teaches "detachable truth," as do the Hindu Vedic and the Chinese Confucian and Daoist traditions. The *dharma* gains and retains its *dharma* quality by demonstrating universal validity in and by itself. For the Buddhist, *ecce homo* (John 19:5) is unnecessary. Instead, *ecce dharma!* There is no profit in pursuing a "quest for the historical Gotama" in the way that many have engaged in a quest for the historical Jesus. The *dharma* once discovered can stand by itself, even as the scientific equation $E=mc^2$ is effective independent of the person called Einstein.

The *dharma* of the Conditional Arising, through the logic of cause and effect, warns against human greed. I find this

---

27. Walter Rauschenbusch, *A Theology for the Social Gospel* (New York: Macmillan, 1917), 184.

28. Is the desire to clone through genetic technology an acceptably "healthy" greed that will enhance the quality of civilization? Can we apply the concept of greed here? When might such enterprise become "sickly" greed? See Ronald Cole-Turner, "Science, Technology, and the Mission of Theology in a New Century," in vol. 2.

way of thinking intelligent. The Conditional Arising is not scientific in the strict sense, but it coincides with the form of scientific thinking: "this being, that becomes." One mode of the scientific attitude of "this being, that becomes" is demonstrated in *Guns, Germs, and Steel* by Jared Diamond. Diamond's subtitle, *The Fates of Human Societies,* does not imply a misfortune to the human spirit imprisoned by an immutable oracle. Rather, it refers to a process of reasoned historical "conditional arising." "Why were Europeans the ones to colonize sub-Saharan Africa?" asks Diamond. He competently answers this question by explaining the "accidents of geography and biogeography."[29] In the spirit of "this being, that becomes," the whole book tells us why we are what we are, and why we are where we are today.

Consilience by Edward O. Wilson also demonstrates "this being, that becoming." Wilson proposes "The Unity of Knowledge" on the basis of biology. "What we call *meaning* is the linkage among the neural networks created by the spreading excitation that enlarges imagery and engages emotion."[30] This fits nicely with the Buddhist anthropology of the ever flowing five aggregates that make a person a person. Wilson, observing the human being in the light of evolutionary biology, declares his opposition to those he calls "transcendentalists."[31]

In both works one can detect a friendly relationship between one form of the scientific mind and the Buddhist doctrine of Conditional Arising. Buddhist observation belongs to the empiricist camp, to use a category employed by Wilson. Buddhism has no "gap God" who tries to linger in the ever diminishing space of mystery. "This being, that becomes" is more central than the person of the Buddha. *Ecce dharma.*

Buddhism agrees with the Jewish rejection of mythological deity, but it also distances itself from a God who is infinitely

---

29. Jared Diamond, *Guns, Germs, and Steel: The Fates of Human Societies* (New York: Norton, 1998), 397, 400–401.
30. Edward O. Wilson, *Consilience* (New York: Knopf, 1998), 115.
31. Ibid., chap. 11.

beyond the human. It finds no benefit in accepting such a transcendent God who might engage in supernatural intervention. Thus, a Buddhist with *ecce dharma* insight, in response to the paragraph of Fackenheim quoted earlier, might respond that while God's presence in history is crucial for Judaism, Christianity, and Islam, it is a subject of no significance for Buddhism. It is the *dharma* that matters.

The Christian concept of truth is *attached* to the person of Jesus Christ. For Christianity, the quest for the historical Jesus is inevitable. *Ecce homo* is essential. Christianity confesses that Jesus *is* the Anointed One. Jesus is the truth-person who lived, was crucified, died, rose from the dead, and is exalted at the right hand of God. Christianity maintains that this life story *is* the truth. Buddhism, in contrast, confessing that Gotama is the Awakened One, invites us to the *dharma* of awakening, not to the person of Gotama.

Christian theology proclaims that Jesus Christ affected human history at its base. Hence, "who said what, where, and when" becomes important. All words are reconstructed in accordance with the impact of the *ecce homo*. Christian truth cannot be timeless and "detached." This is "scandalous" (1 Cor 1:23). As the crossing of the Red Sea is decisive for the Jewish people (according to Fackenheim),[32] so the event of Jesus Christ is decisive for Christians. The word that was in the beginning (John 1:1) is not free from history. As the ancient creed puts it, he "suffered under Pontius Pilate." In his moment of death, the martyr Stephen saw Jesus *standing* at the right hand of God (Acts 7:56). Indeed, the urgency of Christ's impact upon history is symbolized by the risen Christ who is standing.

In Buddhism, the truth of defeating greed is detachable from the person of Gotama, hence *ecce dharma*. In Christianity, the truth of human life is essentially attached to Jesus, hence *ecce homo*. The Buddhist truth is packageable, while Christian truth is not.

---

32. Fackenheim, *God's Presence in History*, 8–14.

"Fare Lonely as Rhinoceros" and "God's Foolishness"

The contrast between the religions of the *ecce dharma* and the *ecce homo* is reflected in the understanding of the nature of community in the *Sangha* and the church. Reading *sutta pitaka,* one notices the sustained tone of the admonition to "fare lonely as rhinoceros." In the *Dhammapada* we read: "By oneself, indeed, is evil done; by oneself is one defiled; by oneself is evil left undone; by oneself, indeed, is one purified. Purity and impurity depend on oneself. No one purifies another" (no. 165). "Better it is to live alone. There is no fellowship with a fool; let one live alone doing no evil, being care-free, like an elephant in the elephant forest" (no. 330). Indeed, the last words of the Buddha are reported to have been:

> Therefore, O Ananda, be ye lamps unto yourselves. Be ye a refuge to yourselves. Betake yourselves to no external refuge. Hold fast to the Truth as a lamp. Hold fast as a refuge to the Truth. Look not for refuge to any one besides yourselves.... Decay is inherent in all component things! Work out your salvation with diligence![33]

Those who seek the ultimate salvation of the *nirvana* must understand the value of the admonition to "fare lonely as rhinoceros." For the general populace, it points to the ideal lifestyle, though they are not required to live it. They should see the connection between this admonition and "Do not cling to that which is passing!" Hence, "fare lonely as rhinoceros" or as "an elephant in the elephant forest" does not immediately signify the promotion of an antisocial ethic. It rather paints the picture of freedom from clinging.

The Buddha observes the concrete human condition. Thus, his teaching is said to be that which is empirically seen (*samditthiko*), free from time confinement (*akaliko*), and the

---

33. *Maha parinibbana suttanta,* in *Dialogues of the Buddha,* part 2 (Bangkok: Pali Text Society, 1966) 108, 173.

kind of which one can confidently say, "Come and see" (*ehi-passiko*). His *dharma* is always open to "come and see" and "try it yourself." Can we deny that "purity and impurity depend on oneself"? Then we are prepared to read an inspiring missionary call in *mahapadana suttanta* (the Sublime Story): "Fare ye forth, brethren, on the mission that is for the good of the many, for the happiness of the many, to take compassion on the world, to work profit and good and happiness to gods and men."[34]

The *mahapadana suttanta* narrates extensively how the Buddha "because of his pitifulness towards all beings, looked down over the world with a Buddha's Eye" and decided to preach the "Truth, deep, hard to perceive, hard to understand, calm, sublime, no mere dialectic, subtle, intelligible only to the wise." The "private Buddha" (*pacceka Buddha*) becomes now the preaching Buddha. Buddha's decision comes from his sympathy (*anukampa*) to the suffering world. It seems to me the truth of "ignorance-craving-suffering" is not hard to perceive. Many would understand and many would be profited. It will surely cause "happiness to gods and men."

Mahayana's mythological *bodhisattva* figure expands the compassion expressed in the Buddha's missionary call. His compassion is symbolized by the provision of the Great Vehicle to carry religious illiterates to the zone yonder where salvation is. The *bodhisattva* refuses to enter the bliss of the *nirvana* until everyone has reached there. The compassion of the *bodhisattva* is indiscriminate. It is not prejudiced by religious merit or demerit. Even those who have little understanding of "ignorance-craving-suffering" will be saved.[35]

---

34. *Mahapadana suttanta*, in *Dialogues of the Buddha*, 36.
35. Allen Verhey, in his essay in vol. 2, "The Spirit of God and the Spirit of Medicine," writes, "The contemporary Samaritan will never be good with *only* compassion, but a *just* compassion is indeed required. The virtue of justice is essential to those who would be (even) Fair Samaritans." With the *bodhisattva,* the intensity of compassion erases the question of justice. It is this element that generates an enduring religious fascination about this mythological figure. This symbol seems to say that compassion to be genuine must finally become indiscriminate. See Rom 11:32.

This unconditional compassion is taught notably by Japanese Pure Land (*Jodo*) Mahayana Buddhism.

The religion of monastic discipline may become self-serving. The "fare lonely as rhinoceros" is inevitably elitist. Sooner or later, a monastic religion must be joined by a religion of indiscriminate compassion in order to meet the needs of the people on the street. This explains the spiritual necessity for the rise of Mahayana Buddhism. The appearance of the preaching Buddha implies a subtle critique of "fare lonely as rhinoceros." No religion can become a universal faith only by way of "fare lonely as rhinoceros" (although a famous Western philosophical definition of religion says, "Religion is what the individual does with his own solitariness").[36]

The "fare lonely as rhinoceros" concept is essentially foreign to Christianity and Islam, though an interpretation of it as "Do not cling!" has relevance to the teachings of both religions. Christianity and Islam are, in many ways, compassion-centered Mahayana-type religions. All 114 *suras* of the Qur'an, except one, begin with the declaration: "In the name of God, the Merciful, the Compassionate." The book of Exodus expresses the fundamental biblical theology of compassion: "The Lord, the Lord, a God merciful and gracious, slow to anger, and abounding in steadfast love and faithfulness" (34:6). God is sovereign in God's compassion (*hesed, rachum, agape*). Hence, "good" Christians in every generation have been confronted by the difficult saying of Jesus: "Truly I tell you, the tax collectors and the prostitutes are going into the kingdom of God ahead of you" (Matt 21:31).

Christianity recognizes that *ecce homo* carries the risk of characterizing God as foolish. The Christ crucified is a "stumbling block to Jews and foolishness to Gentiles." At the foundation of the Christian faith is this disturbing reversal: "God's foolishness is wiser than human wisdom." The power of God is hidden in this scandalous Christ (1 Cor 1:18–25).

---

36. A. N. Whitehead, *Religion in the Making* (New York: Macmillan, 1926),16.

The teaching of the *ecce dharma,* on the contrary, is spared from such a perplexing dilemma.

The Christ crucified is understood by the first Christian community not just as a public spectacle but as the demonstration of solidarity of God with people. That "he humbled himself and became obedient to the point of death — even death on a cross" is none other than the intense moment that opens the way for a new community based on love (Phil 2:8; 1 John 4:19–21). The "power of God" expressed itself in this incomprehensible way (Rom 11:33). Instead of the monastic "fare lonely as rhinoceros," the biblical tradition is "do justice, love kindness, and walk humbly with your God" (Mic 6:8). These three emphases of Micah are embodied in the life of Jesus. The people of faith make up the body of Christ. The body of Christ is not a solitary but a community reality. And it is a community of the "reversal."

With regard to the crucified Christ, Fackenheim's remark that "the reports of these few [revelatory events] are so obscure as to be unintelligible to nearly all others" deserves to be considered carefully. In revelation, our concern is not with "God-in-general, history-in-general, providence-in-general and their acceptability to modern-man-in general."[37] There is a scandal of particularity. In contrast to cultured and well-cogitated observation, revelation is raw. It is abrupt. It is uncontrolled and uncontrollable. It is "foolish." Yet the "barefoot Moses" — the Moses who is touched by the reversal, by "God's foolishness is wiser than human wisdom" — engages in dialogue with God. The theme of Moses' dialogue is emancipation. The people are to walk out from the bondage of Egypt *en masse!*

The scandal of the *ecce homo* pervades the New Testament. In the Gospel we read, "Is there anyone among you who, if your child asks for a fish, will give a snake instead of a fish? [observation]. . . . How much more will the heavenly Father give the Holy Spirit to those who ask him! [reve-

---

37. Fackenheimer, *God's Presence in History,* 8.

lation]" (Luke 11:11, 13). Here, *this* truth points to *that* truth. Jesus' response to the payment of tax to the emperor (Matt 22:15–22; Mark 12:13–17; Luke 20:20–26) presents a similar structure. The New Testament boldly pronounces pan-sacramentalism: "In him all things hang together" (Col 1:17). At the center of this sacramental theology is the scandal of the Christ crucified (1 Cor 2:2). The revelation cannot be emptied by reason. The mystery of God's foolishness remains.

Calvin's *Institutes* or the *Documents of Vatican II* would not be possible apart from observations made on human life. The sower of Jesus' parable would find the Buddhist warning (observation) of "the cares of the world and the lure of wealth" appropriate (Matt 13:22). In the Qur'an, which rejects any hint of the dual nature of divine/human, observation tends to be overwhelmed by revelation. Yet one notices the awesome eschatological seriousness of Allah (revelation) "when the infant girl, buried alive, will be asked for what sin she was murdered" (observation; 81:8, 9).

A religion of revelation is ever confronted by a question: "Have we understood revelation correctly?" The human mind, always tempted to self-righteousness, distorts the understanding of revelation. In fact, both observation and revelation are open to distortion, but while the authority of observation is continuous with human reasoning, that of revelation is discontinuous. The latter can claim the aura of absolute authority. Absolute authority is, however, in the hands of the one who names this or that as absolute. The damage inflicted by the misuse of revelation is greater than that of observation since revelation contains the element of transcendence. Humanity yearns for a transcendence that is free from fanaticism, that truly reveals "the Lord, the Merciful and the Compassionate."

How can we know that a certain interpretation of revelation is correct or mistaken? The value of both observation and revelation is located in the power to create wholesomeness (*shalom*) in human community. If human observation, in conflict with revelation, speaks more inspiringly and persuasively to humanity and brings more healing to human community, then eventually revelation will be discredited. That which creates genuine wholesomeness in the human community must be accepted as truth. But the truth may be scandalous: "Do not think that I have come to bring peace to the earth; I have not come to bring peace, but a sword" (Matt 10:34). And is it observation or is it scandal to say that "the tree is known by its fruit" (Matt 12:34)?

Buddhist observation does not involve the "reversal" dialectic, though there is a hint of it in Japanese Pure Land Buddhism ("Even a good man will be received in Buddha's Land, how much more a bad man!"), as I have mentioned earlier. But Shinran contradicts the spirit of monastic discipline and its sense of moral achievement leading to *nirvana*, the *summum bonum*. The idea of "God's foolishness is wiser than human wisdom" is irrelevant to the Buddhist message.

Nontheistic and No-Self Orientation

Often the contrast between the two faiths is noted in terms of theism: theistic Christianity and nontheistic Buddhism. According to Buddhist teaching, as in Confucian teaching, "God-talk" is unprofitable and even a hindrance to the sincere pursuit of human fulfillment. The psalmist may have written, "Fools say in their hearts, 'There is no God'" (Ps 14:1), but the Buddha and Confucius are not fools. The word "God" does not carry the same meaning to Semitic and Asian worlds. The characterization of Buddhism as "nontheistic" is for Jewish, Christian, and Islamic consumption only. It has no meaning for Buddhists. The giraffe must not blame the zebra for not having a long neck.

Christianity is theistic philosophically, but it is free from theistic confinement theologically. That is to say, Christianity uses theistic words and thought-forms, but the biblical God is not identical with the theistically described God. "God is a Spirit, infinite, eternal, and unchangeable, in his being, wisdom, power, holiness, justice, goodness and truth" answers the Westminster Shorter Catechism (Q. 4. "What is God?").

This theistic answer reduces God to "dry bones," to abstract concepts. Theistic language is vulnerable to the danger of fossilization. The biblical God cannot be contained by theism or nontheism. "Is not my word like fire, says the Lord, and like a hammer that breaks a rock in pieces?" (Jer 23:29). Instruction on theistic language and *preparatio evangelica* should not be taken as identical. We are less alarmed by the nontheism of Buddhism when we know that the biblical God is not identical with the theistic God. For Buddhism, the thought of tension between the philosophical and the theological is irrelevant. Buddhism distances itself from theological God-talk. It speaks for the diagnosis and therapy of human ills.

The biblical God is invisible and beyond human comprehension. Orthodox theologian Gregory Palamas of the fourteenth century said, "For God is not only beyond knowledge, but also beyond unknowing." The invisible God is mysterious and unpredictable, while the visible *dharma* is rational and predictable. While the former suggests surprise and danger, the latter offers calmness and safety. The contrast is between an invisible *person* ("Thus says the Lord") and a visible *dharma* of "come and see" (diagnosis and therapy). This nontheistic diagnosis-therapy religion can avoid questions that Christianity struggles with.

With an invisible God, idolatry becomes a possibility. The human soul is tempted to make the invisible God visible. This is the perennial fascination of idolatry. The knowable *dharma* of diagnosis and therapy does not incite idolatry. There is no need to make visible that which is already visible. The human spirit does not live in an ambiguous relationship with the visible *dharma*. It is in the sphere of the invisible God that the agonizing question "Why does the way of the guilty prosper?" (Jer 12:1) arises.

For Buddhism, the question "What is God?" is irrelevant. The question "Which God is the true God?" is also irrelevant. All theistic questions disappear. Humanity is now faced by the one simple system of Buddhist diagnosis and therapy for the human condition.

Conditional Arising and the Four Noble Truths (diagnosis
and therapy) hold humans responsible for the *continuity* of
cause and effect. This creates a sense of personal moral responsibility. On the other hand, a God that is not bound by
Conditional Arising creates the possibility of *discontinuity* in
ethical thought.[38]

Theistic or nontheistic, the truth speaks, according to Buddhism, at the point of human effort to overcome one's own
greed. Conditional Arising is neither theistic nor nontheistic.
It is a chart that shows the location of malignant greed. Notes
of condemnation or accusation or punishment are absent in
Conditional Arising or in the Four Noble Truths. They do not
say "God" is displeased with the failure of the human moral
performance. They do not mention the idea of "original sin."
They simply tell us where we are in the chain reaction of
ignorance-craving-suffering.

Both lay people and monks are to abstain (1) from taking
life, (2) from taking what is not given, (3) from sensuous mis-
conduct, (4) from false speech, and (5) from intoxicants as
tending to cloud the mind. These are the Five Precepts. Viola-
tion of these precepts constitutes "evil." In the *Dhammapada*
we read, "Make haste in doing good; check your mind from
evil [*papa*]" (no. 116). "Not to do any evil, to cultivate good,
to purify one's mind — this is the teaching of the Buddhas"
(no. 183). The Buddhist view is that it is within human possibility to eradicate evil by "purifying one's mind." *Papa* is that
which defiles one's mind. The question of why there is evil in
a world governed by a just God is irrelevant to Buddhism.

In the teaching of the Five Precepts, Buddhism and Christianity can meet meaningfully without laboring over the
complexity of theistic and nontheistic language, an issue that

---

38. See Søren Kierkegaard's treatment of the question, "Is there such a thing as a
teleological suspension of the ethical?" in his *Fear and Trembling* (Princeton, N.J.:
Princeton University Press, 1954), 10. Also, discontinuity is suggested in the stories
of the divine protection of Cain the murderer (Gen 4:15) and Jesus' resolute rejection
of Peter's advice (Matt 16:23). The all-active and all-powerful Allah of Islam brings
discontinuity to human history as well: "The only words We say to a thing, when
We desire it, is that We say to it 'Be,' and it is" (Qur'an 16:40).

is largely not applicable to Buddhism. The Five Precepts come from the observation of human life. Buddhism is essentially the Five-Precept-religion. It is humanistic in that it encourages moral endeavor.[39] In its core teaching, it distances itself from theistic or metaphysical speculation.[40]

Not only is the Buddhist tradition nontheistic, in striking contrast to Christianity, Buddhism, as has been pointed out, teaches no self (*anatta,* translated in some Thai Buddhist literature as "ownerlessness") as the true identity of persons.[41] One must be freed from the illusion (*maya,* "fabrication") of a substantive self. Buddhadasa Indapanno writes:

> Anything in this world is perpetually flowing, forever breaking up, that is, it is impermanent. So we have to equip ourselves well with heedfulness. Don't go playing with those things! They will bite you. They will slap your face. They will bind and hold you fast. You will be made to sit and weep, or perhaps even to commit suicide. . . . Nothing whatsoever should be grasped at or clung to.[42]

All in this world is perpetually flowing. It is the illusion of "I" and "my" that produces greed. Buddhadasa continues:

> Now it is usually proclaimed eloquently, also mistakenly and misleadingly, that birth, aging, and death are suffering. But birth is *not* suffering, aging is *not* suffering, death is *not* suffering in a case where there is no grasping

39. The Five Precepts, especially the first and the fourth precepts, are compatible with the nurture of human rights. See John Witte, Jr., "The Spirit of the Laws, the Laws of the Spirit: Religion and Human Rights in a New Global Era," in vol. 2.

40. Buddha's refusal to respond to metaphysical questions is illustrated by his "parable of the arrow." See, e.g., Mircea Eliade, *From Primitives to Zen* (New York: Harper & Row, 1967), 570–72; and Raimundo Panikkar, *The Silence of God* (Maryknoll, N.Y.: Orbis Books, 1989), 3–36. The Buddha's silence with regard to metaphysical problems is called *avyakrta.* One further note: Walter Rauschenbusch regrets that "theology has made the divinity of Christ a question of nature rather than character" (*Theology of the Social Gospel,* 150). Christian theology could have had a more fruitful contact with the religion of the Five Precepts had Christ's character, not nature (such as in the "two-nature doctrine"), been accented.

41. See *Vinayamukha.*

42. Buddhadasa Ludapanno, *Buddha Dhamma for Students,* 5.

at "my" birth, "my" aging, "my" death. At the moment, we are grasping, regarding birth, aging, pain, and death as "mine." If we don't grasp, they are not suffering; they are only bodily changes. . . . A mind is *empty* (unencumbered, or disengaged, or free) when it is free of craving, aversion, and delusion.[43]

Bhikkhu Khemo of Bangkok lists the Five Fetters to be "belief in a personal self, doubt, faith in the efficacy of religious ceremonies and rituals, sensual desire, and ill will."[44] Note that "belief in a personal self" comes first. This radical suggestion is rooted in the idea that everything in the world is in a state of constant change. The universal ethical message of this is "Do not grasp!"

The everyday meaning of the *anatta* teaching is "Do not grasp." If one does not grasp, one is well positioned to keep the Five Precepts. *Sunyata* or "emptiness" (Japanese: *mu*) is a state of "complete non-grasping." Therefore it creates within the human mind a profound sense of freedom.

The concept of the illusion of "I" or "my" as "grasping" can be appreciated by Christians. Niebuhr's "twofold emphasis" inspires us to meditate on the idea that the transcendent God is not "self-grasping." The act of creation — to create the free being outside the divine self — signifies self-denial on the part of the Creator. Paul shares with us the ancient hymn of the self-emptying of Christ: "Make your own the mind of Christ Jesus who, being in the form of God, did not count equality with God something to be grasped" (Phil 2:5–11).[45]

43. Ibid., 51, 60.
44. Bhikkhu Khemo, *What Is Buddhism? 341 Questions and Answers* (Bangkok: Nahamakularajavidyalaya, 1935), 91.
45. Masao Abe, the Japanese Zen scholar, in his *Zen and Western Thought,* says that "emptiness must empty itself" (8 and 129.) One must not cling to emptiness. I interpret Abe's insight to mean that one must be unaware of the emptiness with regard to emptiness. This must be the moment of the Zen enlightenment, or *satori.* On the human condition of "grasping," Niebuhr writes, "The real evil in the human situation, according to the prophetic interpretation, lies in man's unwillingness to recognize and acknowledge the weakness, finiteness and dependence of his position, in his inclination to grasp after a power and security which transcend the possibilities

Both Buddhist *dharma* and Christian theology oppose the inflation of self. The *dharma* holds that the very concept of "I" constitutes a fetter, while Christian theology understands that the "I" is real and sacred, embodying the image of God, and that this "I" can deny itself for the sake of public good and practice what is commanded by Christ: "Go and do likewise." I hold that the Buddhist concept of the "I" as a fetter is not necessarily in conflict with the Christian call. If one is not fettered, one is free to "go and do likewise."

The *Sangha* Ethic and a Royal Polity

The English word "monk" or "monastery" etymologically implies being alone. The Buddhist word *sangha* refers to a community of *bhikkhus* (monks), comprised at minimum of three or four individuals. A *bhikkhu* is one who has placed himself under the code of precepts (*patimokkha*) of the *sangha*. The *patimokkha* of Thai Buddhism numbers 227 precepts. Each *bhikkhu* though living in the community of the *sangha* is individually a "lone rhinoceros." *Patimokkha* is about the principal training in the pure life (*adibrahmacarikasikkha*).

The first four of the 227 precepts of Thai Buddhism are called the "Defeat Group." They prohibit (1) sexual intercourse, (2) taking anything worth more than five masok (about one baht) without the owner's consent, (3) intentional murder, and (4) falsely claiming the possession of the highest truth of humankind. The monk who violates any one of these four is "defeated." After the Defeat Group comes the "Formal Meeting Group," of which precept 12 forbids "in revengeful anger falsely accusing another monk of an offence against any of the first four precepts." The Formal Meeting Group moves down through less serious offenses to the last group, called the "Training Rules Group," which covers precepts 146 through 227, including number 152 ("A monk should keep

---

of human existence, and in his effort to pretend a virtue and knowledge which are beyond the limits of mere creatures" (*Nature and Destiny*, 1:137).

his eyes lowered when going through a village") and number
173 ("A monk should keep his gaze fixed on his alms bowl
while receiving alms").

What are the social and political roles of the *sangha* ethic?
Does this ethic promote the abolition of war, just distribution
of wealth, and eradication of racism and ethnic conflict? Such
a direct question cannot be avoided. It is not surprising that
the *nirvana*-oriented *sangha* of "fare lonely as rhinoceros" has
done little to involve itself in these social issues. However, the
spiritual impact of the orange-robed monks on the streets of
Thailand, Sri Lanka, and Myanmar upon the general public is
quite notable. Leading the life according to the *patimokkha,*
they impress people of the futility of greedy acquisitiveness.
They, and any public action taken by them, bear significant
living social symbolism.[46] If "fare lonely as rhinoceros" is
individualistic, the Five Precepts clearly indicate the social-
ethical dimension. Early in the tradition of Buddhism, the
virtue of mercy is taught.[47]

The dialogue between the two traditions, the monastic
and the Mahayana, will strengthen Buddhist social ethics.
This dialogue will continue so long as all Buddhists recognize the problem of human greed as primary. With this
basic recognition, their ethics will move in the direction
of the "eradication of poverty and creating employment
opportunities, improving living standards, expanding education facilities, providing better health facilities, promotion of
human rights, disarmament."[48]

---

46. The Buddhist monk Thich Quang Duc burned himself alive in Saigon on
May 11, 1963, in protest against an alleged suppression of the Buddhist religion.
The self-immolation was undeniably politically motivated. Elsewhere, the Japanese
Nichiren Buddhist School, the Soka Gakkai, has its own political party, Komeito,
active since 1964, though it pronounced its separation from the Soka Gakkai in
1970.

47. The primitive Buddhist words to denote "love" are four: *kama, tanha, piya,
pema.* The first two cause *dukkha* and therefore must be negated. The last two
recognize the possibility of love of others without self-love. The Mahayana scriptures
teach the all-comprehending sympathy (*metta, karuna, mahakaruna*) of the Buddha.

48. Lily De Silva, "Insights from the Teachings of the Buddha for Promoting
Justice and Peace in the Modern World," *Dialogue* (January–December 1989): 53.

One of the Hindu ideologies that has had a far-reaching impact on Hindu civilization is the idea of incarnation (*avatar,* "descent"). The Hindu suggestion is that the historical Buddha is an *avatar* of the eternal *dharma.* The idea of *devarajah* ("god-king") has been supported by the *avatar* ideology. Elaborate Hindu ceremonies and symbolisms surround the religious and social cult of *devarajah.*

In Thailand, the *devarajah* ideology developed from the time of the Sukothai kingdom of the thirteenth century. The king is understood to be an embodiment of the Buddhist *dharma* and the protector of the community of monks, the *sangha.* He is the link between the human and divine worlds. Cosmology and hierarchy find a felicitous harmony in the person of the king. The modernization of Thai politics was achieved when this time-honored religio-political metaphysics showed the flexibility to accept the form of a constitutional monarchy in 1932. Here the historical was united with the cosmological. In this unity is the secret of the enormous popularity enjoyed by the present Buddhist king, Phumipol. Stanley J. Tambiah writes, "Thus it comes as no surprise that in the 1973 insurrection students marched down Bangkok's Rajadamnern Avenue carrying, right in front, the National Flag, the Buddhist Flag and portraits of the King and Queen."[49] The Thai popular attachment to the *devarajah* ideology has not disappeared even in the busy westernized life of modern Bangkok.

The Conditional Arising is rational. The *devarajah* doctrine is mythological. Human community needs a balanced presence of both rational and mythological. When the latter overwhelms the former, as in the case of the Japanese imperial cult during World War II, the people suffer. In the case of Buddhism, fanaticism is recognized as such when it ignores the kind of rationality demonstrated in the Conditional Arising. This occurred when the Thai monk Kittivuddho said that

49. Stanley J. Tambiah, "Sangha and Polity in Modern Thailand: An Overview," in *Religion and Legitimation of Power in Thailand, Laos, and Burma,* ed. Bardwell L. Smith (Chambersburg, Pa.: Anima Books, 1978), 123.

"killing communists is not demeritorious; it is just like when we kill a fish to make a stew to place in the alms bowl for a monk. There is certainly demerit in killing the fish, but we place it in the alms bowl of a monk and gain much greater merit."[50]

The idea of the divine right of the king, which for too long undergirded the power of monarchs in Western civilization, did not have the blessing of the biblical prophetic tradition. For the prophets, the king did not occupy the cosmological center or the hierarchical peak, since cosmology is subordinated to theology ("God is the creator of the cosmos"). The invisible God, not the king, is the supreme authority. Hence, the person of the king is essentially downsized and demythologized. The prophet Nathan who confronted king David expressed this radical principle (2 Samuel 12).

The Nathan episode reminds us of the critical issue that perpetually faces humanity — the elevation of the conditional to the unconditional (Paul Tillich), from which all kinds of violence emanates. The logic and content of the Conditional Arising and the Four Noble Truths prevent such boosting. At this critical point, Christian theology meets the Buddhist *dharma*. The Buddhist observation of human existence and its Five Precepts cool the passion that tends to foster absolutization.

The image of the *devarajah,* symbolizing both transcendental and temporal values through rich rituals, creates a sense of incongruity with the *nirvana* ideal. Yet this has not become a serious problem, since the Hindu/Buddhist cosmology is more relaxed than the Christian cosmology, which is subordinated to the higher principle. The Buddhist mystery stays inside of the cosmos, while the Christian mystery steps out of the cosmos. The contrast is between cosmological mysticism and eschatological mysticism.

Hebrew prophetism warns of the lure of cosmological

---

50. Cited in the essay by Charles F. Keyes, "Political Crisis and Militant Buddhism in Contemporary Thailand," in *Religion and Legitimation of Power,* 153.

charms (Jer 7:18). The New Testament warns of the pull of the "elemental spirit of the cosmos" (*stoicheia tou kosmou;* Gal 4:9). The primacy of *theos* over *kosmos* is foundational in biblical teaching. The essential Buddhism of the Conditional Arising warns against the charms of the cosmos. Here Buddhism comes nearer to Christianity than Hinduism, which thrives with the symbolism of cosmic charms. Buddhism is less charmed than Hinduism by the cosmos. The essential character of Buddhist universalist ethics is expressed in the statement: "No brahman is such by birth. No outcaste is such by birth. An outcaste is such by his deeds. A brahman is such by his deeds."[51]

Civilization is a system of power distribution. It is unavoidably vulnerable to the germs of human greed. Having lived through most of the twentieth century, I cannot say that "rulers are not a terror to good conduct, but to bad" and that "authority does not bear the sword in vain" (Rom 13:1–7). The Buddha would resonate with Jeremiah: "Woe to him who builds his house by unrighteousness, and his upper rooms by injustice; who makes his neighbors work for nothing, and does not give them their wages" (Jer 22:13). The great American creed, "We hold these truths to be self-evident, that all men are created equal," is also tarnished by human greed. In the historical reality, "these truths" have not been "self-evident" in the empirical sense. The Buddhist observation thus makes a critical comment on the foundational philosophy of American existence. It does support, by implication, the political system of the independence of the three branches of government as a device to check the power of greed. Greed is a universally relevant subject. Human reason or moral sense must be alert to the invasion of greed into community. The true religion challenges false dominion. It dedicates itself to

---

51. Quoted by J. A. Hutchison, *Paths of Faith* (New York: McGraw-Hill, 1969), 131. In his "The Taming of Mars: Containing Violence in the Coming Century," in vol. 1, Donald Shriver writes, "The principle that Christians must try to follow here is empathy without ethnic preference." This is the principle indeed that divides between true and false religions. The true religion must inspire "empathy without ethnic preference."

the establishment of true dominion. The Buddhist critique of human *greed* and the Christian practice of the *reversal* anticipate righteous *dominion.*

Conclusion

The religions of the Anointed One and of the Awakened One cannot be easily compared. Each shows its own spiritual integrity and coherence. Once again, a giraffe cannot blame a zebra for not having a long neck. Also, it must again be acknowledged that faithful adherents of both teachings often fail to practice what their founders taught.

The Buddhist observation has not been in conflict with other great spiritual traditions of Asia, such as those of Confucius and Lao Tze. It has remained nonconflictive with Christianity and Islam. It, in turn, is not threatened by other possible observations on human life, including those of Galileo or Darwin. Marx's critique of capitalist greed may illustrate greed critique presented in the Conditional Arising. Against a crisis or conflictual picture of the world, I value the simple and forceful Buddhist critique of human greed. Simple it is. Yet it deserves global attention.

I have placed the Conditional Arising at the center of my interpretation of the Buddhist message. The Conditional Arising is rationally constructed. In the thought of Niebuhr, however, "History is not rational. At least it does not conform to the systems of rational coherence which men construct periodically to comprehend its meaning."[52] Likewise, I see human greed, in its source, and even in its manifestations, as irrational; it is self-destructive. Buddhism, however, understands greed as a rational reality.

Buddhism is, in its core, the Five-Precept religion. In the Five Precepts the practical truth of this religion is located. The *dharma* invites us by saying, "Come and see." There have been rich discussions on the human propensity toward evil,

---

52. Niebuhr, *Nature and Destiny,* 1:289.

on the social desirability of love, on sympathy, and on human community in the extensive spiritual and intellectual life of the Buddhist *oikumene*. What can Christian theology contribute to the Buddhist life? The doctrine of love? Of evil? Of sin? Of salvation? I think the presentation of these subjects *can* and *do* make a contribution to Buddhism. Such endeavors must be appreciated. There must be open, honest, and mutual traffic on the matter of faith understanding between the two traditions.

Yet, finally, there is only one contribution that Christian faith can make to the Buddhist world. It has to do, inevitably, with the scandalous name of Jesus Christ. *Ecce homo!* What does Christian piety perceive in the moment of the *ecce homo*? There it sees God who is full of *pathos* (Abraham Heschel). "My mind is turning over inside me. My emotions are agitated all together" (Hos 11:8, *Anchor Bible Commentary*). The God of pathos gives the distinctive mark to the biblical faith. What kind of pathos? It is a pathos overflowing with love and justice directed toward our history as embodied in Jesus Christ. But how are we to share this overflowing pathos with the Buddhist world?

Obviously, the simple Buddhist focus on the *tanha* cannot bring the global king Ahab to repentance. But confirming the saying of Jesus, "You cannot serve God and *mammon*" (Matt 6:24), the *sangha*, by its members wearing the orange robes and observing the Five Precepts with the people, demonstrates the movement of truth in the midst of human community. Thirsting greed undermines *shalom* on a global scale in today's world. The thirsting greed must be rejected.

– Chapter 7 –

MUHAMMAD IN MUSLIM TRADITION AND PRACTICE

THE CRUCIBLE OF FAITH AND THE SPHERES OF DOMINION

Lamin Sanneh

The Role of Muhammad in Islam

Muhammad's authority was stamped on Islam in a decisive way, and it left Islam as a religion of profound personal agency. Though later Muslim authorities spoke of the religion as *din al-fitr* ("natural religion"), meaning that it is inscribed into humanity's natural constitution as psychological inevitability, the fact remains that the Prophet's personal example confirmed Islam as something fit for personal decision and choice. Later developments added numerous layers of structure and interpretation to Islam's personal challenge, yet there still subsisted throughout the centuries of development, expansion, and setback this decisive call to the individual, a call that originated with the Prophet himself and is repeated in the regular multiple daily call of the muezzin. The real globalization of Islam by means of the effective institution of the caliphate and by virtue of the lively intellectual streams that flowed from the Muslim encounter with Greek science and philosophy, the lucrative trading networks that knit together Fez and Marrakech in the Maghrib with Sarmakand and Sinkiang in the East, the great art and architectural monuments that ring the world of Islam, from Agra and Timbuktu to Istanbul and Isfahan — all this evidence of global historical success and cultural sophistication remained subordinate to the ethical imperatives of personal commitment. The Qur'an relates that commitment to the central, nonnegotiable concept of *'ibadah,* of servanthood under God, of delegated moral stewardship. In the final analysis, Muhammad's personal example was decisive, so that Islam remained a matter of universal theological obligation, whatever the admirable worldly trophies the believers acquired and accumulated. It was his example that showed converts and cradle Muslims alike, as well as all of creation, to be involved in the drama of truth and obedience.

Consequently, although Muhammad lived a long time ago, he remains a living presence. If Muhammad is remote, it is remoteness of historical uniqueness, not of metaphysical difference from us. He is exalted in his humanity, not in spite of it. As Ernest Renan said of Islam's roots in space and time, the religion was born in the full glare of global history: "Its roots are at surface level, the life of its founder is as well known to us as those of the Reformers of the sixteenth century."

Muhammad's person also became the subject of rich religious feeling, the channel that received and refined the immense outpouring of praise and tribute. A little-known Swahili poet takes up the theme of Muhammad as tribute for all humanity:

The very existence of this universe, its cause was our Hashemite.

Muhammad is the lord of two worlds, the earth and the heavens and the animated beings, spirits and men of every sort, from the Arabs for the foreigners. It is our prophet who rules, ordering good things and denying bad ones, he is the one who defeats people and kills them by saying: "No" or: "So be it." He is the beloved of his Lord, we may hope for his intercession, he is the right guide of his Community, in the midst of terror and turmoil. He has called people towards the

true religion, and whoever follows him and believes in
him, has an important reason for his trust: God will
save him at the resurrection. He surpasses all the other
prophets in appearance, character, and nature, they do
not even approach him in appearance, nor in his knowledge, nor in his capacity to work miracles. All the other
prophets have their rank assigned to them in relation to
the prophet; they possess one handful of water from the
ocean of his knowledge, or one sip, and that is all, where
there is the great and beneficial rainfall. They are all just
standing near their lord, each one like a single dot in
the great volume of all knowledge, in the celestial tablet.
They are just like one vowel mark in the great book of
wisdom.

He is the confessor, the form and meaning which have
been completed; finally the Omniscient placed him apart
to be the beloved of the Generous. In his goodness he has
no rival, either among the prophets or the angels, God
cleansed him so [he] became pure, His jewel, His dear
beloved. Leave off speaking, I forbid you, the word of
praise of the Christians for the prophet Jesus. You may
render complete homage to the prophet, praise in any
form you like his good qualities. Any form you like for
his essence, do not fear, attribute his nobility to his descent, attribute it also to his rank, any form you like
for rendering him homage. Because his virtues are very
many, their number has no conceivable limit; any form
of praise a person can mention, they will never be completed no matter how long that person speaks. If his rank
and the miracles he performed would be duly praised, a
person, if so able, would have died and even rotted, being called by his name still while still persisting. He did
not come to bring us fear; his whole religion contains
God's riches, and we merely have to listen to him and to
obey, we do not have to feel doubt nor suspicion. The
intelligence of the people is being pressed down, they do
not know the reality of the prophet, far away and near

by he is the same, the human eye does not accept to look
at him.... He is like the sun because of his virtues, and
they are like the stars, this we know, in order for their
light to shine, it is necessary that the sun has not yet
come out, that there is darkness. Noble in his mien is
the prophet, his character is well disposed. He has gathered goodness, he is exceedingly kind, always appearing
cheerful and smiling. His mildness is like a lovely flower,
and his nobleness like the full moon, his generosity is
like an ocean, his solicitude is like time. The prophet, if
you would see him in his full splendour, would be quite
unique, like a king, surrounded by many warriors. Like
a pearl in its oyster shell, when he begins to speak it
emerges, and its place, my brothers, is when he speaks
and smiles. There is no perfume that matches the sand
on which he lay down, a tree in Paradise it is, for him
who may enjoy the smell, it is his bliss.[1]

In his influential biography of the Prophet, Tor Andrae
echoes the Muslim attitude by observing that poetic hyper-
bole is natural to religious memory and reminiscence and
constitutes a common bond among religions. For that reason, Andrae argues, religious history must take the kernel of
simple facts along with the elaborate elements of pious imagination to understand not only what might then just be a relic
but also how the faithful might obtain succor from it. His
apologia finds more than an echo in the particular example
of the Prophet of Islam:

Our earliest Gospel [Mark] begins with the baptism of
Jesus at the Jordan, and his consecration to the office of
the Messiah. The authentic history of Muhammad begins in like fashion with his appearance as a prophet
in Mecca. What is related of his earlier experiences is
mainly legendary. If I do not here completely ignore
these pious legends, which otherwise belong more prop-

---

1. Cited in Jan Knappert, *Swahili Islamic Poetry* (London: Heinemann, 1971).

erly to the history of the beliefs of his followers than to the biography of the Prophet, my reason is that it is important, merely from the historical point of view, to become acquainted with the great personalities of the world religions dressed in those garments in which the pious faith of their followers have clothed them. The manger of Bethlehem and the song of the angels belong to the portrait of Jesus, and the fourfold contact with suffering and renunciation of the pleasures of the palace to the portrait of Buddha. Something of the magic of their personalities, which we might not understand in any other way, speaks to us through the poetry of faith.[2]

The poetry of faith can illuminate interfaith understanding, as when an Egyptian writer, inspired by the homage the Qur'an pays to Jesus, writes a Christmas carol in honor of Jesus in accordance with Muslim sensibility. The theme of power, so true to Muhammad's own career, runs through the carol, but with irony and hesitation, in view of Jesus' life and work:

Kindness, chivalry, guidance and humility were born
The day Jesus was born. His coming brightened the
        world,
His light illuminated it.
Like the light of dawn flowing through the universe,
So did the sign of Jesus flow.
He filled the world with light,
Making the earth shine with its brightness.
No threat, no tyranny, no revenge, no sword, no raids,
No bloodshed did he use in his call to the new faith.
A king he lived on earth,
But wearying of his state,
He substituted heaven for it.
To his faith wise men were attracted,

---

2. Tor Andrae, *Muhammad: The Man and His Faith*, trans. T. Menzel (New York: Harper Torchbooks, 1960), 31.

Humble, submissive and weak before him.
Their submission was followed by the submission
Of kings, common folk and sages.
His faith found roots on every land
And anchors on every shore.[3]

Muhammad's birth also has the element of the marvelous and even of overweening power suffusing it. A typical account speaks of how the thrones of royalty were overturned, the idols of heathendom crashed to the ground, and the wild animals of East and West as well as creatures of the sea prophesied good tidings when the happy news of his birth was announced. His mother was told in a dream to call his name "Muhammad" because his final reward will be "praised" (*ahmad*).

He was born pure, circumcised; his umbilical cord was cut by the hand of Divine Power. He was born fragrant and endued with pomade, his eyes coloured with kohl of divine care.... [T]he glowing stars became more brilliant and with their light the depth and height of the sacred and of forbidden things became illuminated. With him light came forth which shone for him over the castles of imperial Syria. And whoever had the valley of Mecca for his home, could see it and its significance. The palaces in the cities of the Persian kings began to crack, those palaces for which Anushirwan had raised the roofs and made them symmetric. And fourteen of the highest pinnacles came crashing down. The Persian empire was broken because of the terror of what would befall it and despoil it. The adored sacred fires in all the realms of the Persians were extinguished. All this happened

---

3. The carol is by Ahmad Shawqí from his *Great Events in the Nile Valley.* See Kenneth Cragg, *Jesus and the Muslim: An Exploration* (London: Allen & Unwin, 1985), 41; and A. J. Arberry, *Aspects of Islamic Civilization* (London: Allen & Unwin, 1964), 367.

when the full moon rose brightly and Muhammad's face appeared.[4]

Barriers to Understanding

In her intimate exposition of the life of the Prophet, Annemarie Schimmel has documented with a wealth of detail this same theme of the unrivaled esteem the Prophet enjoys across the entire spectrum of believers. Given the role religious psychology has enjoyed in Western culture, beginning with Augustine and coming right down to Thomas Merton and C. S. Lewis, it would be fair to say that it is not so much subjective feelings that stump us as the accumulation of historical detail, so that, whether with Augustine or with Lewis, we are inclined to spiritualize or metaphorize the simple facts of life. Consequently, religious and "historical" scholarship is steeped in moral sentiments, no less so than when we reduce description to questions of personal taste and individual feeling. The procedure that allows us to read ourselves into historical events and personages is of a piece with our own projects of self-realization rather than being a genuine giving over of ourselves to the infinite and transcendent, the trusting of ourselves to a power beyond ourselves. For that reason, Muslims' attitude to the Prophet as the "other" to whom they turn for aid and succor is in conflict with the Western approach of measuring the Prophet by our rules of relevance, taste, and feeling. In the modern West, our sensibilities are conditioned for consumption, for self-gratification, and, accordingly, religious figures are accessed as "role models," as people "like us." The universe of the modern West, inhabited by look-alikes, is filled with models of our own image. In that universe, prophets are heroic individuals; they typify reward for personal striving and effort rather than being

---

4. Cited in Jan Knappert and Andrew Rippin, eds., *Textual Sources for the Study of Islam* (Manchester: Manchester University Press; Chicago: University of Chicago Press, 1986), 67–68.

channels of grace and power. Nothing has caused greater misunderstanding with Muslims than the Western unwillingness
to let the mountain of heroic individualism (of "heroization")
come to Muhammad. Instead, Muhammad must come to our
mountain.

The Muslim contrast with the Christian West may be instructive here. For all its boasting of the historical-critical
method, the West persists in seeing myths as role models, so
that in the work of historical reconstruction, say, on the life
of Jesus, the West remains skeptical, even if the evidence is
sound by critical standards. Thus, if an account is supported
by reliable evidence, or if scholars assume it is reliable because it seems hostile, as with the so-called Satanic Verses
of the Qur'an or the cleansing of the temple in Mark's Gospel, it is used to justify a rejection of the principle of the
canon. Accordingly, the modern West feels that the Jesus of
history who is reconstructed from hard historical evidence
comes down to nothing more than a tribal Jewish Jesus bound
by his context, an antiquarian curiosity who is as such of
little utility for our times. Alternatively, a Hellenized Christ
of the Gospels, thickly embedded in the imaginative inventive-
ness of his Greek Gentile followers who insinuated themselves
into the story, remains a figment of the imagination. So if we
could establish the historical Jesus we would have no current
use for him, and if the matter resides with the Greek construction of a cosmic Christ that would have no standing in
reality either. The two approaches have an identical outcome,
perhaps because both proceed from a premise of skepticism.

Thus, the value the West places on critical detachment renders it deaf to the overtones of stories whose historicity the
original accounts would have had no intention of suggesting.
So the West takes stories as evidence of historical imperfection, as evidence only of the penchant for invention and as
proof that religious actors lack a sense of critical historical
distance, whereas we ought to see such stories as boundary
markers that allow religious actors not only to make history,
not only to indwell events with habits of the heart, but to

record and interpret them. In the illusory pursuit of the distinction between history and myth, between critical historical detachment and subjective personal bias, the West seems incapable of appreciating the profound power of poetry and metaphor, the persuasive nature of narrative in the religious life, especially narrative that describes the experience of moral resistance as it breaks down from being exhausted in its own defiance. Instead, the West sees such narrative as proof of failure of the historical sense in religious people, as evidence of sublimation. The poetic imagination is thus dissected with our tools of historical deconstruction, with the awkward result of otherwise compelling historical figures like Clio and Cleopatra stumbling credulously into the realm of myth, or else rising as role models.

On Religious Biography

When Muslims look to Muhammad as the clue to the special character of faith history, they challenge us to see in biography the true locus of global historical purpose. Ever since Thucydides, Western scholars have tended to treat biography as lacking in global significance. Biography is kin to subjective personal illusion. As a genre in the modern West, it straddles the twilight zone between retirement from active life and archival acquisition. For example, in his classic study of leading Victorian personalities, Lytton Strachey (1880–1932) began with an ironic observation that historians are disinclined to write about subjects about which they know too much. Rather, he insists, for the historian, ignorance is the first requisite, the ignorance that simplifies and clarifies, that selects and omits with placid perfection. It would explain why the religious subject, even without biography, is a stumbling block for the historian — because it contains at its core the claim to true and final knowledge. So Strachey chose a different path in proposing to write a biography of Victorians. Over the vast ocean of historical knowledge he would lower down into it here and there a little bucket so that he could scoop up, not the entire content, but a rare specimen that is characteristic of the whole. The scholar of biography, Strachey affirmed, should expose, expound, and illustrate, not explain and object and repudiate. The biographer has no business to be complimentary, but to lay bare the facts of the case as he or she understands them, dispassionately, impartially, and without ulterior intentions:

> Human beings are too important to be treated as mere symptoms of the past. They have a value which is independent of any temporal processes — which is eternal, and must be felt for its own sake. The art of biography seems to have fallen on evil times in England. We have had, it is true, a few masterpieces, but we have never had, like the French, a great biographical tradition; we have had no Fontenelles and Condorcets, with their incomparable *éloges,* compressing into a few shining pages the manifold existences of men. With us, the most delicate and humane of all branches of the art of writing has been relegated to the journeymen of letters; we do not reflect that it is perhaps as difficult to write a good life as to live one.[5]

As it is, both the Qur'an and the Bible in their different ways brim with personalities as bearers of world-shaking truth, those on whom the universe itself turns. Our modesty in these matters does not serve us well when it comes to God's rule of having divine agency mediated by many channels, not the least of which is human agency. We evade the issue if we claim that human weakness precludes such a role. When it comes to it, we are not similarly inclined when it concerns our claim of rational agency, our claim, that is, of the power to distinguish between true and false, right and wrong, or good and bad. Yet we cannot attack human agency in the domain of moral laws without threatening it also in the do-

---

5. Lytton Strachey, *Eminent Victorians* (New York: Harcourt, Brace & Co., 1918), viii.

main of reason, so that a tilt in the direction of discounting confidence in religion would force a balancing move in the direction of discounting confidence in reason. Both religion and reason involve normative human agency, whether that agency be in fact-finding as regards empirical evidence or in formulating judgment on the basis of faith in truth and justice. In the matter of religion, furthermore, human agency is both the subject of moral injunctions, a vital constituent of moral claims, and the object of those claims. Religion is rule and sacrament, the sphere of objective social practice and ethical conduct, of acts, customs, and their ordered, public configuration and expression, and, too, the domain of subjective moral dispositions, of inclinations of the will, of inner motives and intentions and their safeguard.

Such a view of religion as comprehensive truth does not sit well with the Western practice of "schematizing" reality through a mesh of analytic rules, now with an appeal to global validity. In that analytic tradition, religion is excluded, or else it is reduced to an isolated soft option as "myth," without any claim to the hard prerogatives of truth and objectivity to which real history is entitled. The attitude still persists that myths and legends demand deconstruction rather than being "indwelled." But that approach, with its prickly view of history, has hindered us from engaging in meaningful global encounter, since other cultures do not necessarily have the same understanding of religion or myth. It leaves us with the attitude that unless other cultures can think in our categories, they are excluded from sharing in the rewards and privileges of our achievement, an attitude that is a setback for a broadened international outlook. It is for that reason that the Muslim tradition and its solid sense of Muhammad's historical significance continue to slip to the shadow side of the West's self-understanding. Even in the irenic hands of Thomas Carlyle, for example, Muhammad is emphasized as hero in the aesthetic, imaginative sense, a prophet of sensibility rather than the Prophet and intermediary of God, though he may be that too. Muhammad as an aesthetic value becomes a module in the project of heroic personal construction, a strand of the heroic saga, and shares that status with countless others, including Byron, Coleridge, and even Cromwell — wherever common patches of creative impulse exist among them.

It is necessary for the West first to overcome its impoverished understanding of biography as such in order to see Muhammad as Muslims see him. Muslims are less inhibited. There is in Islamic literature rich evidence of Muhammad's biographical preeminence in the hearts and minds of Muslims. Carlyle was right in this sense to fix on his human distinction:

> They called him Prophet, you say? Why, he stood there face to face with them; bare, not enshrined in any mystery; visibly clouting his own cloak, cobbling his own shoes; fighting, counseling, ordering in the midst of them: they must have seen what kind of man he *was,* let him be *called* what you like! No emperor with his tiaras was obeyed as this man in a cloak of his own clouting.[6]

The very things that the West finds tedious and monotonous in the repetitive details of Muhammad's life are the things in which Muslims find reason for confidence. Muhammad for them is not the thinker who produces abstract systems of thought, proving his case by logical demonstration. Rather, Muhammad is rooted in the very substance of time and space. His voice vibrates throughout the range of Muslim life, action, and feeling, his outward manner and demeanor the demonstration of inward *barakah*. It is this externality of Muhammad, this embodied presence of his, that demonstrates to Muslims the validity of the truth he proclaimed. Muhammad's historical concreteness is thus the close-knit fabric with which Muslims clothe the divine injunctions. Thus, otherwise mundane acts like washing, cutting one's nails and hair, eating, marrying and raising a family, greeting people, selling and buying, and so forth, carry unique

---

6. Thomas Carlyle, *On Heroes, Hero-worship and the Heroic in History,* ed. Carl Niemeyer (Lincoln: University of Nebraska Press, 1966), 71.

merit in the particular setting of the Prophet's life. He made
barakah live.

Consequently, Muslims have a rich source of biographical
detail on the Prophet's life, the source we know as *hadith*.
Through its formal, stylized channel, Muhammad's historical concreteness is configured and conveyed in the steady
flow of metaphor, anecdote, episode, and reminiscence. Often
the chains of transmission are so thick with names of witnesses and raconteurs that the substance of what is reported
is disproportionately slight, causing us to wonder why a lone
fly might be worth all the day-long elaborate industry of
the spider's web. Yet it would be wrong to judge the *hadith* solely by the rules of critical abundance. The *hadith*
presents Muhammad not just as one who spoke but as one
who was also spoken for by others. We have in the *hadith*
not just one biography but innumerable biographies, or else
biographical vignettes and cues, what the science of *hadith*
calls *'ilm al-rijal*. *Hadith* became an exemplary channel, a
vessel that drips with what is contained in it, as al-Ghazali
said elsewhere.[7] Men and women who would otherwise be
inconsequential by the rules of historical grandeur arrived in
our company as witnesses, or witnesses of the witnesses of
Muhammad, and, riding on the Prophet's coattails, they became themselves models of moral excellence. The track of
biography proceeded, then, on the repeatability of biographical example, so that an idea or practice was attached to a
tone, to a face, and to a gesture. The soundness of the chain
of transmission turned on the trustworthiness of the links
of witnesses, with the slight danger of distortion occurring,
either because an otherwise worthy-sounding account failed
by its weak link or a spurious tradition slipped through by
being predicated of a recognized name. While clearly depending on the memory of real persons, biographical reminiscence
might, therefore, complicate the historical record, requiring

---

7. Cited in Duncan Black Macdonald, *The Religious Attitude and Life in Islam*
(London: Darf Publishers, 1909), 222–23.

us to check the links of the chain of transmission for evidence of motivated intervention. It is to this critical task that scholars like Wensinck, Goldziher, and Schacht have called our attention.

Al-Shafi'i (d. 820), the great Muslim jurist of Cairo, carried this critical task to its triumphant conclusion by establishing the principle of *hadith* ("tradition") as the structure of Muslim authority. As such, al-Shafi'i created the Muslim canon singlehandedly. For him, the idea and ideal of community were central to the value and use of tradition. Community for al-Shafi'i had the specific meaning of a group of recognized leaders and experts who use their knowledge to agree on something affecting public order and personal life. Al-Shafi'i believed that agreement under those circumstances gave the weight of truth to what was thus agreed upon, for in his view it was impossible for the community to agree in error. Error, he said, arose from separation and not from collective decision making. In reality, al-Shafi'i insisted, there could be no total or enduring error when it came to the true meaning of the warrants vested in the community, such as Scripture, the *sunnah*, and common-law judgments. For al-Shafi'i, then, a living community was responsible for maintaining sound tradition.

However, al-Shafi'i was not just interested in tradition simply for the sake of protecting community interests. Rather, he defended the community because he saw it as necessary to preserving the tradition of the Prophet Muhammad. For him, theory and practice, warrant and sanction, belonged together. He came pretty close to breaching the rule of the divine-human incompatibility of official theology. That *sunnah* ("custom") of the Prophet is the superstructure of Muslim law, religion, ethics, education, worship, and devotion, and al-Shafi'i could claim credit for making it the foundational structure of mainstream Islam. His book on the subject, called the *Risalah*, brings together the skill of a legal systematizer with the energy of a collector of tradition to effect a major global reform by streamlining local and regional deviations in the interpretation of scripture and law. Al-Shafi'i simply soars in his steady drive to secure the authority of tradition for a Muslim community in serious danger of breaking up. For that task, he set up clear rules to uphold the authority of the *sunnah,* rules that we may summarize as follows:

> The Prophet enjoys a special status (*wahy*) as God's approved messenger.
>
> The Prophet's *sunnah,* therefore, has lying upon it the seal of divine approval.
>
> The *sunnah* of the Prophet and the Qur'an as revelation are *ex hypothesi* always in agreement.
>
> Therefore, conflict between the *sunnah* and the Qur'an cannot happen, a case of united we stand, divided we fall.
>
> The *sunnah* may therefore replace the Qur'an if the Qur'an has nothing to say
> on any subject. But even if the Qur'an has something to say, the *sunnah* can still
> add to it by giving explanations and illustrations.

By these steps, al-Shafi'i established the rule that no one was allowed to ignore tradition in Islam. He gave encouragement and a sense of unity to Muslims who were scattered in many different places, were experiencing many different political events, and were observing many different customs. With his work, everyone could agree on what Muslims should do and why.

Yet by making tradition that important, al-Shafi'i opened the door for people to fabricate stories about the Prophet, stories that even the most careful of scholars could not control entirely. Thus, one *hadith* reputedly originating from the Prophet has him saying, "Whatever is said and found to be beautiful, it can be attributed to me," the sort of catchall that is welcomed by the scrupulous and unscrupulous alike. What happened, then, was that Muslim experts tried to sift and organize the stories so that they could be included in official handbooks and collections and maintained as canonical. However, such collections, called *ahadith,* were not just ornaments for people to decorate an idea they liked but were put to great use to allow Muslims to overcome differences among themselves and achieve a sense of communal unity. It was for the sake of that sense of unity that many of the handbooks even allowed sound or holy stories about the Prophet to exist alongside weak or even doubtful stories. So these handbooks became an important resource for preserving Muslim unity across centuries and cultures. The sense of Muslim identity was thus strengthened, especially as Islam spread into new societies.

Al-Shafi'i's success in establishing the authority of prophetic tradition strengthened Islam's global position and enabled Muslims to practice their religion and make changes they saw as fitting without losing touch with the past. In effect, al-Shafi'i created the idea of a living tradition that allowed Islam as Islam to enter new cultures and societies outside the Arab heartland. That was how Islam came to Africa, where Muslims followed the advice of al-Shafi'i and that of another Muslim scholar, Imam Malik (d. 796) of Medina.

Both al-Shafi'i and Imam Malik emphasized the importance of traditions of the Prophet. However, Imam Malik was more interested in the practices and customs of the apostolic community in Medina on the assumption that the Prophet's Companions (*ashab*) and Successors (*tabi'un*) were in the best position to receive and interpret the Prophet's actions and intentions, while al-Shafi'i narrowed the issue more precisely to the Prophet's own acts and teachings which, once ascertained, would be binding on Muslims everywhere, not just on those in Medina. It was the systematic globalization of faith and obedience. Al-Shafi'i maintained a rigorous uniform rule by insisting that everything should come within the jurisdiction of the Prophet's *sunnah,* either explicitly by reference to his teaching and conduct or implicitly by analogy and precedent. Whereas Imam Malik began his account by saying something like, "This is the agreed-on way of doing things among us," or "according to the way things are done among us," often showing that much of the community's decision making was based on the customs (*athar,* to be distinguished from *sun-*

nah) of the Companions and the Successors, al-Shafi'i, on the other hand, pressed for consistency by arguing that it was wrong to set aside the Prophet's *sunnah* by a recourse to those lesser than him, as were the Companions and Successors. Furthermore, even analogy (*qiyas*), an otherwise valid legal mechanism, must nevertheless be set aside in deciding cases where a relevant *hadith* exists.

Accordingly, al-Shafi'i surveyed the world of Muslim legal practice and decisions to find anomalies and contradictions in the miscellany of local custom and practice. He proceeded to formulate clear and simple rules to explain why the *sunnah* of the Prophet should have primacy over those of his apostolic successors. He made clear that his aim was to streamline local practice by securing the foundations of the Prophet's heritage before it was covered over by contradiction, by confusion, by defective knowledge, and by breaks in the chains of *hadith* transmission. If the Prophet's *sunnah* was allowed to suffer decline, he reasoned, then the Qur'an itself would be at risk, for both were God's word — what was left over from the Qur'an was gathered in the *hadith* so believers would have a faithful, complete record. In spite of that fact, al-Shafi'i worried that local usage threatened to override the canon. His work was made for him.

Al-Shafi'i was the great systematizer of Islam. With an allergic reaction to arbitrary lawmaking in the community, he offered as remedy a scrupulous requirement of unqualified compliance with prophetic norm and conduct. Still, in spite of their different emphases, al-Shafi'i and Imam Malik complemented each other by stressing the central importance of the Prophet's *sunnah* on the premise that the divine lawgiver created and upheld the apostolic office, and that the apostolic office in turn rested on divine authority.

Truth and Ordinariness

Al-Shafi'i's great intellectual revolution had a profound, enduring effect on the evolution of Islamic institutions. It all stemmed from a very simple fact: the overwhelming figure of the Prophet himself. Muhammad so dominated his age that he became its rule, symbol, and ideal. He was presented in such tireless detail, depicted with such unforgettable repetition, and his name was so highly revered in the devotional cycle that concern with his biography stirred the global landscape of religious and historical understanding. On every detail of routine and personal style, alike on circumstances and persons, Muhammad alighted as precept and principle. His range was moral, not geographical.

If the pious disciples embellished Muhammad's biography, however, they did not do so completely at the expense of the commonplace. That commonplace concerns the ordinary and natural character of his birth and upbringing, a character still preserved in the oldest records we possess, and one that, furthermore, survives in all cycles of learned as well as devotional reflection (*dhikr*) on his *sunnah*.

Virtually all Muslim authors on the subject stick more or less to the following outline. Muhammad was born in about 570 C.E., the exact date of his birth not being certain. His parents were Aminah and 'Abdallah. 'Abdallah died before Muhammad was born, as did his mother when the child was six. Muhammad was raised by a wet nurse, Halimah, and was placed under the care of his grandfather, 'Abdul Muttalib, who died when Muhammad was eight. Then he was handed over to Abu Talib, his uncle and the father of 'Ali, the future fourth caliph. Thus, as sura 93 points out, God found Muhammad an "orphan [*yatim*] and succored him . . . and guided him." Pious tradition added a colorful flourish to the detail by regarding him as the *yatimah*, the pearl of priceless worth, as Annemarie Schimmel has pointed out.

As a young boy, Muhammad engaged in trade, accompanying his uncle in the Syrian caravan trade. On one such trip he encountered the monk Bahira, who recognized the seal of prophethood between the child's shoulders. Muslim accounts speak of Bahira testifying to Muhammad's future stature as the prophet foretold in John's Gospel, the reference being to the "Comforter" that Jesus promised his own disciples (John 14:16–17, 26). That has become a source of much interest among Muslims and controversy with Christians. Muhammad was then twelve years old. At age 25, Muhammad married Khadijah at her instigation, the woman who had employed him in her caravan trade. The marriage was a reward for Muhammad's honesty, though she was fifteen years his senior. She bore him four daughters, as well as a son or two, who died in infancy. Khadijah was a tower of strength to Muhammad, putting the weight of wealth, social clout, and experience behind him. Thus, when Muhammad was going through a dark night of the soul, with great doubts gnawing at his resolve, it was Khadijah who acted to steady his will and to calm his nerve. He used to retire to the hills surrounding Mecca to meditate privately. That was the setting in which he received the call to prophethood.

Much ambiguity surrounds the actual details of the call. Two versions are combined in the standard account of Ibn Ishaq (d. 768). In one strand of the account, Muhammad receives a vision at night in an unlit cave, and is summoned to recite the words of the revelation, those being the opening words of sura 96. This strand contains what some scholars believe to be a case of special pleading by those with an exegetical ax to grind, namely, the wish to promote sura 96 to the first place of the Qur'an because the inaugural word of the sura, in the imperative mood *iqra* ("recite"), is a cognate of the verbal noun *qur'an* ("recital"). In the other strand, a vision comes to the Prophet in daylight, or at least when the "clear horizon" (81:19) is glanced by the light of the rising sun as he stands on the open hills. This incident is described in sura 53, which also contains the famous Satanic Verses. Among other things, the sura speaks of a divine or a celestial being who stood in the highest part of the horizon and approached to a distance of "two bows, or even closer" before revealing the matter to the Prophet.

Whether in the strand with the unlit cave or in that of the clear horizon, the accounts represent Muhammad as having a frightful time of it. "Sometimes the Revelation comes like the sound of a bell," he testified. "That is the most painful way. When it ceases I have remembered what was said. Sometimes it is an angel who talks to me like a human, and I remember what he says."

As closely examined by W. Montgomery Watt in his two-volume biography of the Prophet,[8] the early preaching of Muhammad was taken up with the themes of resurrection and judgment, of a fierce eschatological eruption that would leave no one unanswerable, though faithful Muslims would abide its terror and receive the divine reward. There is a strong eschatological seriousness about the Meccan phase of Muhammad's preaching. In later revelations, especially those occurring at Medina, the tone shifts, not always all at once, to administrative questions and individual and collective guidelines, as happens when religious protest has acquired the power to impose its will.

At any rate, at Mecca Muhammad came into conflict with the leading citizens, who perceived him as a threat and a social upstart. For about a decade, from 610 to 619, Muhammad continued to receive revelations until he was able to gather a fairly sizable number of followers. In 619 he lost Khadijah through death, and in a similar fashion his uncle, Abu Talib. They were indispensable pillars of his movement as well as being a source of personal strength and inspiration. Their deaths affected him deeply and exposed him even more to his Meccan antagonists. In 621 Muhammad was approached by a party of sympathizers from Yathrib, an agricultural settlement to the north, lying on the sensitive artery that carried the caravan trade with Syria. These sympathizers appealed to him to come to Yathrib to help mediate in their internal quarrels, in effect, asking him to take over leadership of their community. With the circle of hostility narrowing around him in Mecca, Muhammad responded eagerly, if cautiously, to the Yathriban

---

8. Montgomery Watt, *Muhammad at Mecca* (Oxford: Clarendon Press, 1953); and *Muhammad at Medina* (Oxford: Clarendon Press, 1956).

overture; he did not want a premature leak of his plans lest he arouse Meccan hostility. He sent some of his Meccan followers ahead of him while he made secret preparations to leave with Abu Bakr, an early convert and one destined to succeed the Prophet as caliph. Yathrib was to be renamed "the city of the Prophet," *madinatu-n-nabi,* shortened to *Madina* or *Medina.*

The historical circumstance of the transfer to Medina being so propitious in retrospect has afforded lavish incentive for pious legend. One such legend recounts how after Muhammad and Abu Bakr had taken refuge in a cave en route to Medina, a spider spun its web and pigeons built their nests over it to shield the pair from the pursuing Meccans, a pursuit referred to in the Qur'an (9:40). Muhammad reached Medina in September 622. The Muslim party he had sent out had preceded him in the city, arriving there in June of the same year. The Islamic calendar observes June 622 as year one of the *hijrah,* the emigration from Mecca, for although the Prophet was later in leaving Mecca, the decision to do so had been made.

Soon after arriving in Medina, Muhammad promulgated a constitution in an effort to govern the place. In the constitution he offered protection and security to the warring tribes living there, including a sizable Jewish community.

The Muslims introduced a new element of social stratification, one based not on blood and kinship solidarity but on religion and obedience to the Prophet. At the top of the social order was the Prophet himself, followed by his companions (*ashab*), the ranks of emigrants (*muhajirun*), the Medinan helpers (*ansar*), the tributary populations, captives taken in razzias and similar sources, and those waiting to be subdued. Such were the delineations of the new Pax Islamica, so that at Medina, Muhammad became both his own Paul and Constantine, a double role that left Islam a religion and a state.

Mecca continued to resist Muhammad, and he for his part could not rest till he annexed it to his purpose. In 624, in a famous battle that took place at Badr near Medina, the Muslim forces, surprised and outnumbered, overcame enormous odds to break up the Meccan lines and to put the enemy to flight. Badr was celebrated as a miraculous victory, and the Qur'an refers to it as the time when God acted by the hands of the faithful Muslims to assure success. "Not you cast when you cast," it affirms, "but God cast" (8:17). Badr joined the military instrument to the office of prophecy and set it up as the confirmation of God's election of the Muslims.

Perhaps success had gone to the heads of the victors, for the next year saw them in another battle with the Meccans. That was at Mount Uhud, where that time the Muslims suffered serious losses. Some of the Prophet's best soldiers were lost in action, though he himself escaped with his life. He lost two teeth and sustained an injury on his left foot.

In 627 the Meccans tried again to storm Medina but were repulsed. The following year the Prophet decided to perform the *hajj* ("pilgrimage") to the Ka'ba which, since about 623 or 624, had replaced Jerusalem as the *qiblah,* the direction for the prescribed prayers of *salat.* Though he did not that year perform the *hajj,* he concluded a treaty with the now pacified Meccans, who recognized his right of access to the Ka'ba. It was a matter of time before he took Mecca itself, which he did without contest in 630. He proceeded to clean out the Ka'ba of all its idols and sacred images and to reconsecrate it to Muslim service. He then returned to Medina.

After Khadijah died Muhammad married several women, including 'A'isha, a young virgin and a favorite wife of his, widows of soldiers who had died in battle, and Zaynab, the ex-wife of his adopted son, Zayd. A Coptic slave girl who was given to the Prophet bore him a son who died before he was two. His wives were respectfully called "the mothers of the faithful" (33:6). After his death they were allowed to remarry (33:53).

In 632 Muhammad again made the *hajj* to Mecca from Medina. It turned out to be his farewell pilgrimage. According to standard exegesis, he received confirmation of his mission on that occasion when God assured him, "I have perfected for you Islam your religion" (5:5). On June 8, 632, Muhammad died in 'A'isha's apartments. 'A'isha was then eighteen. His burial site was called the *Rawdah* ("the green"), the mausoleum in Medina that pilgrims visit, praying, "I bear witness that thou art the Apostle of God. Thou hast conveyed the message. Thou hast fulfilled the trust. Thou hast counselled the community and enlightened the gloom, and shed glory on the darkness, and uttered words of wisdom."

Abu Bakr's assurance to the grief-stricken Muslims, that although Muhammad was dead yet God lives, has served the cause more than he intended, for it is precisely in the assurance that God lives that Muhammad has found room to proliferate in the devotions and allegiance of Muslims the world over. Thus, in the great monotheistic witness of the faithful, the name of the Prophet is joined to that of God, and Muhammad becomes the gateway to monotheistic fidelity. Muslims might forgive anyone for taking the name of God lightly, but not so the name of Muhammad. We evade the Muslim sense of religious loyalty if we avoid the figure of the Prophet in the mistaken belief that it is God alone who commands obedience. God has in Muhammad everything God must have in earthly or heavenly company, so any attempt to separate God from the charge of the Prophet is to presume on God's prerogative. For Muslims, Muhammad is God's own preference. To say he is not God, as Muslims insist, is not the same as saying he is God's in the crucial sense of the inalienable possessive. Muslims feel that insofar as we are concerned as human beings, Muhammad is necessary and essential to participation in the divine scheme for human life. The Prophet is the indispensable guarantor of Islam's particularity, for it is he who prevents Islam's being ground into an inoffensive, general, religious blend.

This particularity has several possible directions in the age of globalization and multi-culturalism, and it is not certain what will happen to the structures and identity of Islam in the face of changes in society, consciousness, and values supported by technology and economic innovation. One possible direction is what is widely regarded as inevitable and characteristic of Islam, by outsiders, at the beginning of the twenty-first century — a militantly patriarchal fundamentalism that threatens not only its neighbors but the less devoted and the minorities and women within its boundaries. This is not the internal view of Muslims, although Isma'il al-Faruqi once defended Islam's right to having earned the enmity of the world because Islam, he boasted, fought the world as a sphere of unbelief. He wrote that Islam

> is the only religion that contended and fought with most of the world religions on their own battleground, whether in the field of ideas or on the battlefields of history. . . . Moreover, . . . Islam is the only religion that in its interreligious and international conflict with Judaism, Christianity, Hinduism, and Buddhism, succeeded significantly and in major scale in all the fights it undertook. . . . No wonder, then, that it is the religion with the greatest number of enemies, and, hence, the religion most misunderstood.[9]

Al-Faruqi's provocative remark about Islam being a misunderstood religion not only in the West but indeed in the whole world gives uncompromising meaning to the discourse of global consciousness, for, not being a perspectivalist, he seemed to be arguing for a special merit accruing to Islam from its principled intolerance of difference. In his flint-edged view of religion, conflict and misunderstanding are an honorable safeguard against tolerance and peaceful coexistence.

However, al-Faruqi's exclusive view of Islam's preeminence skirts an important theological question, often affirmed elsewhere among Muslims, about humanity having meaning and worth from the fact of God having created them rather than

---

9. Isma'il R. al-Faruqi, "Islam," in *The Great Asian Religions*, ed. Wing-tsit Chan (London: Macmillan, 1969), 307.

from their subduing others. In a real world of interdependence, religious truth-claims require not just a prickly loyalty that feeds on a persecution complex but a caring neighborliness animated by a sense of God's justice and mercy. It is hard to believe that the challenge of such interdependence can be evaded entirely by the instinct of self-preservation, for Muslims as well as for Christians and others.

The real test for people of faith is affirming the theocentric basis of human dignity without rescinding the warrants of community-based faith traditions. In the Islamic case, the tradition of combining monotheistic witness to God's sovereign mercy with upholding the authority of the Prophet, by the use of political and military power where appropriate and necessary, offers an answer to the question of relating ideals to lived experience. Accordingly, we should at this point return to a reflection on the parallel meaning of the Prophet for the global Muslim community marked by faith and personal devotion.

The Spiritual Heritage

Muhammad was called *uswa hasana* (33:21), "the beautiful model," "the felicitous exemplar." His followers believed that God had sent him "as a mercy for the worlds" and that God and His angels pronounce blessings on him (33:56). The words of the Qur'an might be those of Muhammad himself: "Lo, as for me, my Lord has guided me unto a straight path, a right religion, the community of Abraham, the upright, who was no idolater. Say: Lo, my worship and my sacrifice and my living and my dying are for God, Lord of the worlds" (6:162).

In the *shahadah* ("witness"), Muhammad's name is invoked to give Islam its distinctive monotheistic flavor. As Wilfred C. Smith has rightly observed, the reference to Muhammad in the *shahadah* is not so much a reference about him as an individual as about his role as the bearer of the revelation, so that Muhammad becomes in effect "an aspect of

God's activity," a channel and guide for seeking and apply-
ing the truth in life and devotion. It is an idea that runs like
a silver thread in all Muslim life and conduct down through
the ages.

A modern commentator has written, "For Muslims the
moral and spiritual worth of the Prophet is not an abstraction or a supposition; it is a lived reality, and it is precisely
this which proves its authenticity retrospectively." As we saw
earlier, al-Shafi'i as the architect of Islamic jurisprudence pi-
oneered a revolutionary legal methodology by establishing
the *sunnah* of the Prophet as a canonical source. He built
the immense structure of Islamic classical law on that single
foundation, an achievement that has continued to affect all
subsequent development of the law. At a less technical level,
the words of al-Ghazali (1058–1111) illustrate what practical
lessons might be derived from what is judged authentic in the
biography of Muhammad. He wrote in his magnum opus, the
al-Ihya 'Ulum Din (chapter 20), thus:

> Know that the key to happiness is to follow the *sunna*
> and to imitate the Messenger of God in all his coming
> and going, his movements and rest, in his way of eating,
> his attitude, his sleep and his talk. I do not mean this
> in regard to religious observance, for there is no reason
> to neglect the traditions which were concerned with this
> aspect. I rather mean all the problems of custom and us-
> age, for only by following them is unrestricted succession
> possible. God has said: "Say: if you love God, follow me,
> and God will love you" [*súrah* 3:29], and He has said:
> "What the messenger has brought — accept it, and what
> he has prohibited — refrain from it!" [*súrah* 59:7]. That
> means, you have to sit while putting on trousers, and
> to stand when winding a turban, and to begin with the
> right foot when putting on shoes.[10]

---

10. Cited in Kenneth Cragg, *The Call of the Minaret,* rev. ed. (Maryknoll, N.Y.:
Orbis Books, 1985), 92.

Islamic theological thought is profoundly marked by this idea of obedience — the word *islam* itself means "submission," hence "muslim," "the submitted one." Allied to the thought is the notion of necessary "disobedience" to the dominions and powers, as expressed in the popular devotional cry, "There is no power or strength in any but God." The concepts of service and servanthood are related to that doctrinaire defiance of idolatry, of the world's false absolutes, of history or modernization or development or globalization as a self-sufficient autonomous process. The true dominion is that of God, and it is not permitting of rivals. The world is God's, and only God has legitimate worldwide claims. So the worldwide appeal of secular globalization represents an unacceptable challenge for Muslims. Thus, the theological understanding of obedience brings us to a particular form of global responsibility — the subduing of the world by the rules of service and servanthood, by the rules of what the Qur'an calls ethical answerability (45:40ff.). Global awakening is not just global opportunity but an occasion for the imperative of ethical awakening.

A feature of Muslim thought is that religion is not only what is commanded but what is forbidden, not only what is but what should not be. Accordingly, the *shahadah* both proclaims God's sovereign transcendence and proclaims the repudiation of false absolutes. Islam is truth with a witness. As the Swahili poet expresses it, the Prophet rules by ordering the good and forbidding the bad. Islam displays its monotheistic faith by also standing up for the high calling of its disbeliefs. Globalization must not be allowed to become a moral subterfuge or substitute, a new engine for ambition and greed, for what the Qur'an calls "the insolence of man" (96:6ff.), with specific reference to the haughty commercial oligarchy the Prophet stared down in first-century Mecca. Globalization should be a call for a moral *jihad,* for a moral struggle against the dominions and powers and in solidarity with God's design for human life.

Responses from a Christian Perspective

It would be both unrealistic and facile to call for a dupli-
cation within historic Christianity of the *sunnah* theme of
Islam, though Butler's *Lives of the Saints* evokes the feeling.
Yet a close consideration of the Muslim attitude to biography
and society should challenge any lingering suspicion that lived
reality can only be a subversion of the truth and a distraction
from history. We should be imaginative enough to appreciate
what Muhammad has meant to Muslims rather than persisting with the attitude that if we remain adamant long enough
in our repudiation, especially when supported with historical-
critical claims, Muslim confidence will crumble. Whatever
such an attitude might imply about the dubious status we give
to Muslim claims, stubbornness is not a single-edged weapon
of religious combat. Both sides know well enough the coarse
marks the crusaders cut in each other's collective memory, for
every time we hear the rattle of name-calling or the stampede
of exclusivism, we open wounds with the crude clamps of
that earlier age. It does not require any generosity of spirit to
meet each other under that weight.

At this advanced, restive stage of the West's triumphant
secular development, we would do well to learn from Muslims how religion and politics, church and state, private and
public, have much to do with each other. The fact that
Muhammad combined in his own person the functions of
Paul and Constantine has given Muslims an important basis
for religious participation in the world, for a religious stake at
the heart of the globalization process. Islam is not a parochial
retreat from the world but a summons to consecrate it to
God. Beyond that, Muslims understand better than many contemporary Christians the significance of religion not just as
something we *think* about, not just as an intellectual game,
though Muslims are among the most rigorous in matters of
the mind, but as something we *act on* and *act out,* especially
in being true to our servant role in the world.

In the light of such Muslim scruples, we in the West must

question the assumptions of the laissez-faire liberalism by virtue of which the public domain has been sequestered and religion driven from it, or else by virtue of which religion has been "residualized," in the language of the social and economic sciences. With those assumptions we eventually made the fateful shift from ethics to economics, from liberty as an inalienable right of the child of God to property as individual and personal interest, and from equality before God and under the law to equality of opportunity, with its outrageous inequalities of status, race, education, and wealth. According to Clinton Rossiter, the old liberalism and the new conservatism are indistinguishable on this point, for both exchanged the hierarchy of property and patronage for that of wealth and power, and freedom for success. Accordingly, it could be said that an elite culture of free enterprise is not any less impervious to the rule of God in human affairs than one of pedigree and privilege.[11]

If this interpretation of our contemporary situation is accurate, then religion as global defiance is a proper and timely outgrowth of religion as faithful obedience to God. As Rabbi Naamah Kelman put it, the Jewish people were "globalized" when Joseph was sold into slavery in Egypt by his brothers. Yet Joseph never forgot his Israelite roots, and seized the opportunity to return to his family and reconcile with his brothers.[12] In a similar way, Muslims are unwilling to accept that we should be free to love our neighbor as ourselves provided it is the neighbor in our "neighborhood" of race or class, rather than the neighborhood as defined by God's injunction without the presumption of wealth, power, pedigree, or privilege. Needless to say, there are immense problems in making religion of politics, or politics of religion. Thus does the Qur'an recall the salutary lesson of the Queen of Sheba

---

11. See Clinton Rossiter, *Conservatism in America: The Thankless Persuasion,* 2d ed. (New York: Vintage Books, 1962), esp. chap. 5, "American Conservatism, 1865–1945, or The Great Train Robbery of American Intellectual History."

12. Naamah Kelman, "Globalization and Religion," *Current Dialogue,* no. 33 (July 1999): 36–37.

who, possessed of a mighty dominion, saw fit to push God out of the way and to lead her people to sin by worshiping idols (27:20–34), just as Manasseh made all Israel to sin (2 Kgs 21:1–18). In her error and before she was suitably dispossessed, the Queen of Sheba had the disconsolation of apprehending her fate, and so she observed, "Kings, when they enter a city, disorder it, and make the mighty ones of its inhabitants abased" (27:34). It is, she learned, a false dominion that does not submit to the rule of the true God. The Qur'an places God right at the center of responsible stewardship of power, right at the center of global power, for the true dominion, the true sovereignty, is God's alone. It is impossible in this conception to speak of the sovereignty of politics, or of economics, or of culture, or of family, or, indeed, of nature. Only God is sovereign, however necessary human mediation may be at the same time. In any case, the "sovereignty" of secular discourse does not have the same weight in Muslim thought that it has, or is claimed to have, in the West.

Thus, in bringing the discussion into line with Christian reflections, we in the West can appreciate the moral significance of the challenge of globalization as we consider how for Muslims Muhammad's life and example constitute the source and legitimation of reform: Islam was born in the Prophet's *hijrah* even though Muslims also believe it was conceived in heaven. For its part, the church was born at Pentecost whence it became a thoroughgoing Gentile movement. After Pentecost, Christianity became a religious movement on the peripheries of Bethlehem and Jerusalem, on the margins of the synagogue and in the sunset of the empire, as Christian communities sprang up in Antioch, Ephesus, Philippi, Corinth, Thessalonika, Athens, Rome, Alexandria, and beyond. If the *hijrah* confirmed and preserved the Arabicness of Islam, and, within that, the universal authority of Mecca and Medina, Pentecost, by contrast, allowed the church to dispense altogether with the original Aramaic and Hebrew of Jesus' preaching and, with that, Jerusalem, as exclusive for orthodoxy, and to embrace languages and cultures hitherto considered alien to the law and the prophets. The *hijrah* ensconced Islam in the birthplace of Muhammad, and even Shi'ite separatism has not challenged that. By contrast, Pentecost uprooted Christianity from Jesus' birthplace and transplanted it across the world beyond. Muslims have drawn on the *hijrah* concept to justify purges of local practice and to institute reforms in accordance with the Prophet's *sunnah*. Pentecost, on the other hand, has been seized on by charismatic and holiness movements to take Christianity to the fringes of official practice, or at any rate to a stage well beyond the gospel or *sunnah* of Jesus. There was no Pentecost in Bethlehem.

Mutual instruction is still possible between Muslims and Christians, in terms, say, of their contrasting strengths and weaknesses. The Arabicity of Islam that is enshrined in the rule of the nontranslatable Qur'an enables the religion to enter local cultures and give them a Meccan orientation. That Islam has more or less succeeded in this orientation where it has succeeded at all amounts to a considerable achievement. That has been its strength. By contrast, the fact that at least in its modern expansion, Christianity through vernacular translations of the Scriptures has consecrated the indigenous medium attests to its strength in linking its spread to vernacular creativity. And therein lie also their respective weaknesses. By establishing vernacular translation into a principle of religious conversion, Christians unleashed all the consequences of local rivalry and schism, whereas by adhering to the rule of nontranslatability Muslims disenfranchised the vernacular as a canonical medium, suppressing thereby a unique and precious source of indigenous vitality.

By the same token, Christians could reaffirm with as much confidence as is consistent with the West's global hegemony the essentially Gentile character of the church, a character stamped upon it by the Spirit itself. The Pentecostal insight continues to have revolutionary implications for interreligious as well as crosscultural understanding. The disciples had no doubt that Gentile Antioch had no less an exalted place in God's scheme than Jerusalem, that all hitherto taboo cultures and peoples stood fully and unconditionally admitted into the fellowship cleansed of their stigma, and that the native idioms were sanctioned to bear the full and authentic message of God's love and mercy.

This revolutionary conception of religious truth was made possible by the birth, suffering, death, and resurrection of Jesus Christ, the One who redeems persons and their cultures from the stigma of exclusion and untouchability. Our difference with Muslims on this point cannot be overlooked. The nontranslatability of the Qur'an does not deny the significance of language and culture, only that it assigns to the untranslated Arabic Scripture a jealous priority that may not be surrendered or compromised in canonical worship, whereas Christian translatability concedes an identical significance for language and culture by the radically different procedure of linguistic interchange.

Yet our divergence on details of practice and understanding should not minimize our unity on the broader theme of the theocentric character of faith and worship. John Paul II expresses it thus:

> I believe that we, Christians and Muslims, must recognize with joy the religious values that we have in common, and give thanks to God for them. Both of us believe in one God, who is all justice and all mercy; we believe in the importance of prayer, of fasting, of almsgiving, of repentance and of pardon; we believe that God will be a merciful judge to us at the end of time, and we hope that after the resurrection he will be satisfied with us and we know that we will be satisfied with him.[13]

This theme of shared religious values, and particularly the pope's insistent appeal to the dignity of human personhood,

---

13. Address to the young Muslims of Casablanca, Morocco, August 19, 1985, in Byron L. Sherwin and Harold Kasimov, eds., *John Paul II and Interreligious Dialogue* (Maryknoll, N.Y.: Orbis Books, 1999), 63. The phrase "being satisfied with God" is echoed in the Qur'anic verse, "The Lord shall give thee, and thou shalt be satisfied" (93:5). The reference is to Muhammad's straightened circumstances as an orphan.

finds a parallel in a remarkable passage in a thirteenth-century
Sufi text. The text offers a symbolic commentary on the words
of Jesus about being born again in order to enter the true
dominion:

> Jesus said, "None will enter the dominion of the heav-
> ens unless he is born twice. . . . " [T]he most marvelous,
> wonderful, mighty, and perfect divine act is the human
> being, who is compounded of all the worlds. Everything
> that is scattered throughout the two engendered worlds
> [of the higher and lower dominions] is brought together
> within him. He is the viceregent of God, the shadow
> of the divinity, and the epitome and quintessence of the
> engendered things. Everything was created to perfect his
> level. When he attains completion and returns to his own
> world, the heavens will be rolled up. On that day the
> bodies will be lost within the spirits, just as today the
> spirits are lost within the bodies. *On the day We shall
> roll up heaven as a scroll is rolled up for the writings.
> As we originated the first creation, so We shall bring it
> back again — a promise binding on Us; so We shall do*
> [21:104].[14]

Still, this theocentric stress in Islam, what Hendrik Kraemer once called Islam's "super-heated conception of revelation and of God as white-hot majesty, white-hot omnipo-
tence, white-hot uniqueness,"[15] is relieved by Muhammad's
"chosenness," by the nearness of his spiritual kinship, by his
unique and personal mediation, as exemplified in his title of
Mustafa, the "chosen one." The combining of that theocentric
faith with Muhammad's prophetic mission has helped to give
practical expression to Islamic norms and teachings across
the vistas of space and time, something that the notion of
role model does not adequately express. The concept of *dar*

---

14. Cited in William C. Chittick, ed. and trans., *Faith and Practice of Islam: Three
Thirteenth Century Sufi Texts* (Albany: SUNY Press, 1992), 44ff.

15. Hendrik Kraemer, *The Christian Message in a Non-Christian World* (London:
Edinburgh House Press, 1938), 221.

al-islam, the sphere of faith, thus expresses both this timeless aspiration concerning God's rule in human life and a timely commitment to the practical means for bringing that about, with the Prophet's personal mediation to help bring it about. The Sufis, such as Shaykh al-'Alawi (1869–1934) of northern Africa,[16] would claim further that *dar al-islam* should first be an inner spiritual disposition (*hal*) and only secondarily a territorial unit (*balad*), a view with possibilities for political inclusiveness and multicultural tolerance. It is a harbinger of how in an age of restive globalization the Muslim heritage stands poised to meet new challenges, and in the process to be renewed without being weakened.

A Summary with Questions for the Future

This essay describes the themes that have given canonical form to the Muslim community, themes in which the Prophet is norm and model, the rule of conduct, and the channel of grace. The main findings are these:

1. In spite of Islamic theological scruples denying the divinity of Muhammad, and in spite of the modern West's perception of him as a "role model," Muslims nevertheless have perceived him as a fount of blessing. Muhammad shares the kind of divine intimacy no other human being shares with God. But this has not resulted in the downgrading of the human details of his birth, life, and work. These two facts of Muhammad's exalted status and the interest in the human side of his life have shaped and defined Islam's canonical identity and its historic mission.

2. Muslim authorities moved very early on to put in place formal arrangements and the necessary structures to promote Muhammad's unique status as divine envoy and moral exemplar, as paragon of obedience to God and commander of

16. See Martin Lings, *A Moslem Saint of the Twentieth Century: Shaikh Ahmad al-'Alawi* (London: Allen & Unwin, 1961). Al-'Alawi said he learned early in his spiritual training that a far greater challenge faced him as a Muslim than snake charming or any other arcane feat, and that challenge was mastering his own soul (52).

the faithful. Accordingly, the reception of the Qur'an as the revealed word of God was accompanied by devoted attention to the Prophet's biography, two branches of study that formed a staple of classical Islamic scholarship. The book of the Prophet upholds the book of God, and so you cannot depend on the book of God without depending on the book of the Prophet also.

3. The scholar responsible for canonizing the Prophet's *sunnah,* his customs and precepts, was the ninth-century Egyptian jurist, al-Shafi'i. He rallied the Muslim community to the view that the same lawgiver who gave the Qur'an was the one who chose Muhammad as the seal of the prophets. Muhammad was the gatekeeper of the meaning and intention of what God revealed in the Qur'an, and as such is vital for tradition, thought, and practice. So naturally Muhammad's precepts and practices carried decisive authority for what God said and intended.

4. Al-Shafi'i's accomplishment gave coherence and legitimacy to the development of Muslim tradition and institutions. Accordingly, traditions of the Prophet were tracked down, vetted, collected, catalogued, and compiled, providing the Islamic world with uniform rules and norms and a towering sense of the centrality of the Prophet. The *hadith* movement inspired into being global structures for the formal development of Islamic thought, institutions, and practices. Directives on the spheres of state, economic, family, and personal conduct were issued and standardized. Religious ideals, ethical prescriptions, and ritual organization all felt the impact of what al-Shafi'i accomplished with the primacy of Muhammad's *sunnah.* It was a comprehensive achievement. No sphere of Muslim life was unaffected.

The crucial issue for the early Muslims was the role of state authority in religious life, because, having decided that personal life and public conduct together belonged under the normative jurisdiction of religion, the believers created structures and institutions to rule over both spheres. It was a move that avoided two extremes, either religion as mere abstraction, as norm without content, or religion as cultural reinforcement, as content without norm. Both extremes led to an identical abdication of responsibility. We may describe the process this way:

a. Muslims were entrusted with the safekeeping of the faith and were given the means to maintain and defend it against the infidels and backsliders. The responsibility of Muslims was first and last to the faith and for custody of the space to which by God's order the faith was entitled. Thus, the sphere of faith, *dar al-islam,* constituted the limits of tolerance vis-à-vis its opposite of *dar al-harb* ("the sphere of unbelief, of enmity"). Religion was not only about what God commanded, but about what God forbade, and so, on the one hand, *dar al-islam* comprised what was approved and commended as much as, on the other hand, it excluded what was forbidden and reprehensible. Islam's normative injunctions stress what Muslims believe as much as what they disbelieve. Islam is truth with a witness, and for that reason Muslims assumed the state instrument for remedy and correction as well as for reward and incentive.

b. But, we may ask, and ask in different ways, is the state instrument so reliable and so upright that we can entrust religion to it? Are the vicissitudes of politics a dependable basis for effecting God's purpose for human life? Is our status as children of God interchangeable with the ups and downs of state power? Can the political sphere function as the ultimate moral sphere? Can the political edict, even if anointed as a *fatwa,* substitute for God's will? Is political success determinative of salvation? Can the state compel our obedience to God? Can it grant or suspend our dignity as human beings? Is political necessity sufficient for moral commitment? Are transcendence and savoir faire identical? Can means replace ends? Is religion only political usefulness? All these questions have in common Muslim confidence in the state as a necessary ally of religion, as a required partner in the work of God. Is that confidence misplaced or is it justified? Can we make religion instrumental, and the instrument religious, without corruption?

c. Whatever the final answer, one response, meanwhile, is to say that God's sovereignty is not coequal with state jurisdiction, however necessary and desirable the state may be. Government by habit prefers the useful to the moral, and a strong government will require the moral to be useful. The integration of personal life and public conduct should not require the false absolutization of the state, nor its corollary of the false relativization of religion. The teaching of the Qur'an about obedience as a branch of human servanthood and of human stewardship of creation is anchored in divine transcendence, not in divine abdication to human beings. In the Qur'anic view, any form or degree of state moralization would only incubate human insolence and violate the divine sovereignty. Religion is not just the straw in otherwise politically useful bricks.

d. The next contemporary step of upholding a theocentric stake in the public realm on the basis of *'ibadah* (servanthood under God) can be supported from the Qur'an, though the precedent of the Prophet's *Pax Islamica* in Medina affirms a public role for religion, affirms, that is, a case for an ordered public realm as a prerequisite of religion. In any case, globalization could provide timely incentive for recasting the concept of *dar al-islam* from a territorial rule to the ethical rule of truth and obedience, guided by what John Paul II called our shared spiritual values and our common moral stewardship of the spheres of life.

BIBLIOGRAPHY

Abe, Masao. *Zen and Western Thought.* New York: Macmillan, 1985.

Adams, James Luther. *On Being Human Religiously.* Ed. with an introduction by Max L. Stackhouse. Boston: Beacon, 1976.

Andrae, Tor. *Muhammad: The Man and His Faith.* Trans. T. Menzel. New York: Harper Torchbooks, 1960.

Appleby, R. Scott. *The Ambivalence of the Sacred: Religion, Violence, and Reconciliation.* London: Rowman & Littlefield, 2000.

Arberry, A. J. *Aspects of Islamic Civilization.* London: Allen & Unwin, 1964.

Ashoor, Yadh Ben. "Islam and International Humanitarian Law." *IRRC* (March–April 1980).

Athyal, Jesudas M. *Relevant Patterns of Christian Witness in India.* Thiruvalla, India: CSS Publisher, 2000.

Balibar, Etienne. "Is There a 'Neo-Racism'?" In *Race, Nation, Class: Ambiguous Identities,* ed. Etienne Balibar and Immanuel Wallerstein. London: Verso, 1991.

Barclay, John M. G. *Obeying the Truth: A Study of Paul's Ethics in Galatians.* Edinburgh: T. & T. Clark, 1988.

Bastide, Roger. *The African Religions of Brazil: Toward a Sociology of the Interpenetration of Civilizations.* Trans. H. Sebba. Baltimore: Johns Hopkins University Press, 1978.

Bellah, Robert. "Religion and the Shape of National Culture." *America* 181, no. 3 (July 1999).

———. *Tokugawa Religion.* Glencoe, Ill.: Free Press, 1962.

Bellah, Robert, et al. *Habits of the Heart: Individualism and Commitment in American Life.* Rev. ed. Berkeley: University of California Press, 1996.

Berger, Peter, and Richard Neuhaus. *To Empower People: The Role of Mediating Structures in Public Policy.* Washington, D.C.: American Enterprise Institute, 1977.

Berger, Peter, ed. *The Desecularization of the World: Resurgent Religion and World Politics.* Grand Rapids, Mich.: Eerdmans, 1999.

Bhabha, Homi. *The Location of Culture.* London and New York: Routledge, 1994.

Bhagavad Gita. Trans. Winthrop Sargeant. Albany: SUNY Press, 1993.

Bhikkhu Khemo. *What Is Buddhism? 341 Questions and Answers.* Bangkok: Nahamakularajavidyalaya, 1935.

The Book of the Kindred Sayings. Part 5. London: Pali Text Society, 1930.

Boyarin, Daniel. "Was Paul an 'Anti-Semite'? A Reading of Galatians 3–4." *Union Seminary Quarterly Review* 47, nos. 1–2 (1993).

Bozeman, Adda. *The Future of Law in a Multi-cultural World.* Princeton, N.J.: Princeton University Press, 1971.

———. *Politics and Culture in International History.* New Brunswick, N.J.: Transaction Publishers, 1994.

Brook, Timothy. "Auto-Organization in Chinese Society." In *Civil Society in China,* ed. Timothy Brook and B. Michael Frolic. Armonk, N.Y.: M. E. Sharpe, 1997.

Brook, Timothy, and B. Michael Frolic. "The Ambiguous Challenge of Civil Society." In *Civil Society in China,* ed. Timothy Brook and B. Michael Frolic. Armonk, N.Y.: M. E. Sharpe, 1997.

Brown, Chris, Peter Sutch, and David Morrice. "Communitarianism and Its Critics." *Review of International Studies* 26, no. 2 (April 2000).

Browning, Don S., gen. ed. *Family, Religion, and Culture Series.* 10 vols. Louisville, Ky.: Westminster John Knox Press, 1997–99.

Buber, Martin. *I and Thou.* Trans. Ronald Gregor Smith. New York: Charles Scribner's Sons, 1958.

Bull, Hedley. *The Anarchical Society.* London: Macmillan, 1977.

———. "Beyond International Society." *Millennium* 21, no. 3 (1992).

———. "The Revolt against the West." In *The Expansion of International Society,* ed. Hedley Bull and Adam Watson. Oxford: Clarendon Press, 1984.

Bultmann, Rudolf. "*eleos,* etc." In *Theological Dictionary of the New Testament.* Vol. 2. 1964.

Buzan, Barry. "From International System to International Society: Realism and Regime Theory Meet the English School." *International Organisation* 47, no. 3 (Summer 1993).

Buzan, Barry, Charles Jones, and Richard Little. *The Logic of Anarchy: Neorealist Structuralism to Structural Realism.* New York: Columbia University Press, 1993.

Capps, Walter. *Religious Studies: The Making of a Discipline.* Minneapolis: Fortress Press, 1995.

Carlyle, Thomas. *On Heroes, Hero-Worship, and the Heroic in History.* Ed. Carl Niemeyer. Lincoln: University of Nebraska Press, 1966.

Carman, John B. "W. Brede Kristensen." In *The Encyclopedia of Religion.* Vol. 8. Ed. Mircea Eliade. New York: Simon & Schuster Macmillan, 1995.

Chamberlain, Heath B. "On the Search for Civil Society in China." *Modern China* 19, no. 2 (1993).

Chan, Stephen. "Hans Küng and a Global Ethic." *Review of International Studies* 25, no. 3 (1999).

Chang Hao. "Neo-Confucian Moral Thought and Its Modern Legacy." *Journal of Asian Studies* 39, no. 2 (1980).

Chen Kuide. "Chongjian gongmin shehui" (Reconstructing civil society). In *Dangdai zhongguo de guojia yu shehui guanxi* (The relationship between state and society in modern China), ed. Zhou Xueguang. Taipei: Guiguan, 1992.

———. "Cong zhengzhi wenhua de jiaodu kan 'liu si' yizhounian" (Reflections on the first anniversary of June Fourth from the perspective of political culture). *Jiushi niandai* (The nineties) (June 1990).

———. "Lun zuqun shehui de wudao he gongmin shehui de chongjian" (On the nonsense of collective society and the reconstruction of civil society). *Zhishifenzi* (The intellectuals) (Summer 1991).

Chittick, William C., ed. and trans. *Faith and Practice of Islam: Three Thirteenth-Century Sufi Texts.* Albany: SUNY Press, 1992.

Clements, Keith, ed. *Friedrich Schleiermacher: Pioneer of Modern Theology.* Minneapolis: Fortress Press, 1991.

Cobb, John. *Talking about God in the Context of Modern Pluralism.* Ed. David Tracy. New York: Seabury Press, 1993.

Cole-Turner, Ronald. "Science, Technology, and the Mission of Theology in a New Century." In *God and Globalization.* Vol. 2: *The Spirit and the Modern Authorities,* ed. Max L. Stackhouse with Don S. Browning. Harrisburg, Pa.: Trinity Press International, 2001.

Conze, E., ed. *Buddhist Scriptures.* New York: Penguin, 1959.

Conzelmann, Hans, and Walter Zimmerli. "*chairo,* etc." In *Theological Dictionary of the New Testament.* Vol. 9. 1974.

Cosgrove, Charles H. *The Cross and the Spirit: A Study in the Argument and Theology of Galatians.* Macon, Ga.: Mercer University Press, 1988.

Cragg, Kenneth. *The Call of the Minaret.* Rev. ed. Maryknoll, N.Y.: Orbis Books, 1985.

———. *Jesus and the Muslim: An Exploration.* London: Allen & Unwin, 1985.

Daneel, M. L. *African Earthkeepers.* Vol. 1. Pretoria: University of South Africa Press, 1998.

————. "African Independent Churches Face the Challenge of Environmental Ethics." In *Ecotheology: Voices from South and North,* ed. D. G. Hallman. Maryknoll, N.Y.: Orbis Books, 1994.

Dark, Ken R., ed. *Religion and International Relations.* London: Macmillan, 2000.

des Forges, Roger V. "States, Societies, and Civil Societies in Chinese History." In *Civil Society in China,* ed. Timothy Brook and B. Michael Frolic. Armonk, N.Y.: M. E. Sharpe, 1997.

De Silva, Lily. *Dialogue.* Columbo, Sri Lanka: Ecumenical Institute, 1989.

————. "Insights from the Teachings of the Buddha for Promoting Justice and Peace in the Modern World." *Dialogue* (January–December 1989).

Despland, Michel. *La Religion en Occident: Evolution des ideés et du vecu.* Montreal: Fides; Paris: Cerf, 1979.

Despland, Michel, and Gerard Vallee. *Religion in History: The Word, the Idea, the Reality.* Waterloo, Ont.: Wilfrid Laurier University Press, 1992.

Diallo, Yolande. *African Traditions and Humanitarian Law.* Geneva: ICRC pamphlet, 1978.

Diamond, Jared. *Guns, Germs, and Steel: The Fates of Human Societies.* New York: Norton, 1998.

Djiniyini, Rev. Badaltja, and Rrurrambu. *My Mother the Land.* Ed. Ian R. Yule. Galiwin'ku: Galiwin'ku Literature Centre, 1980.

Doyle, Michael. *Ways of War and Peace.* New York: Norton, 1997.

Dumont, Luis. *Homo Hierarchicus: The Caste System and Its Implications.* Chicago: University of Chicago Press, 1970.

Dunn, James D. G. "The Theology of Galatians: The Issue of Covenantal Nomism." In *Pauline Theology.* Vol. 1: *Thessalonians, Philippians, Galatians, Philemon,* ed. J. Bassler. Minneapolis: Fortress Press, 1991.

Dunne, Tim. *Inventing International Society: A History of the English School.* London: Macmillan, 1998.

Eber, Irene, et al., eds. *The Bible in Modern China: The Literary and Intellectual Impact.* Sankt Augustin, Germany: Monumenta Serica, 1998.

Eck, Diana L. *Encountering God.* Boston: Beacon, 1993.

Eickelman, Dale, and James Piscatori. *Muslim Politics.* Princeton, N.J.: Princeton University Press, 1996.

Elazar, Daniel. *Covenant and Polity in Biblical Israel: Biblical Foundations and Jewish Expressions.* The Covenant Traditions in Politics 1. New Brunswick, N.J.: Transaction Books, 1995.

Eliade, Mircea. *Cosmos and History: The Myth of the Eternal Return.* New York: Harper & Row, 1954.

―――. *From Primitives to Zen.* New York: Harper & Row, 1967.

―――. "History of Religions and a New Humanism." *History of Religions* 1 (Summer 1961).

―――. *Myths, Dreams, and Mysteries.* New York: Harper & Row, 1960.

―――. *Patterns in Comparative Religion.* New York: Sheed & Ward, 1958.

―――. *The Sacred and the Profane.* New York: Harcourt, Brace & World, 1959.

Ereksoussi, M. K. "The Koran and the Humanitarian Conventions." *International Review of the Red Cross* (May 1969).

Esler, Philip F. "Group Boundaries and Intergroup Conflict in Galatians: A New Reading of Gal. 5:13–6:10." In *Ethnicity and the Bible,* ed. M. G. Brett. Leiden: Brill, 1996.

Evans, Alice Frazer, Robert A. Evans, with David A. Roozen. *The Globalization of Theological Education.* Maryknoll, N.Y.: Orbis Books, 1993.

Evans, Tony, and Peter Wilson. "Regime Theory and the English School of International Relations." *Millennium* 21, no. 3 (1992).

Everett, William J. *God's Federal Republic: Reconstructing Our Governing Symbol.* New York: Paulist, 1988.

―――. *Religion, Federalism, and the Struggle for Public Life: Cases from Germany, India, and America.* New York: Oxford University Press, 1997.

Fackenheim, E. L. *God's Presence in History.* New York: Harper Torchbooks, 1970.

Fackre, Gabriel, Ronald Nash, and John Sanders. *What of Those Who Have Never Heard?* Downers Grove, Ill.: InterVarsity Press, 1995.

Faruqi, Isma'il R. al-. *Al Tawhid: Its Implications for Thought and Life.* London: International Institute of Islamic Thought, 1992.

―――. "Islam." In *The Great Asian Religions,* ed. Wing-tsit Chan. London: Macmillan, 1969.

Feil, Ernst. *Die Geschichte eines neuzeitlichen Grundbegriffs zwischen Reformation und Rationalismus (ca. 1540–1620).* Göttingen: Vandenhoeck & Ruprecht, 1997.

―――. *Religion: Die Geschichte eines neuzeitlichen Grundbegriffs von Frühchristentum bis zum Reformation.* Göttingen: Vandenhoeck & Ruprecht, 1986.

Finn, John. "Human Rights in Vienna." *First Things* (November 1993).

Fiorenza, Francis Schüssler. "Religion: A Contested Site in Theology and the Study of Religion." *Harvard Theological Review* 93, no. 1 (January 2000).

Fogel, Robert William. *The Fourth Great Awakening and the Future of Egalitarianism.* Chicago: University of Chicago Press, 2000.

Fregosi, Paul. *Jihad.* New York: Prometheus Books, 1998.

Frolic, B. Michael. "State-Led Civil Society." In *Civil Society in China,* ed. Timothy Brook and B. Michael Frolic. Armonk, N.Y.: M. E. Sharpe, 1997.

Gellner, Ernest. *Postmodernism, Reason, and Religion.* London: Routledge, 1992.

Gilkey, Langdon. "Plurality and Its Theological Implications." In *The Myth of Christian Uniqueness,* ed. John Hick and Paul Knitter. Maryknoll, N.Y.: Orbis Books, 1995.

Glendon, Mary Ann. *Rights Talk: The Impoverishment of Political Discourse.* New York: Free Press, 1991.

———. "What Happened in Beijing." *First Things* (January 1996).

Goudge, Thomas A. "Evolutionism." In *Dictionary of the History of Ideas.* Vol. 2. New York: Charles Scribner's Sons, 1973.

Green, Ronald M. *Religion and Moral Reason: A New Method for Comparative Study.* New York: Oxford University Press, 1988.

———. *Religious Reason: The Rational and Moral Basis of Religious Belief.* New York: Oxford University Press, 1978.

Greene, Theodore M. "Introduction: The Historical Context and Religious Significance of Kant's *Religion within the Limits of Reason Alone.*" In Immanuel Kant, *Religion within the Limits of Reason Alone.* New York: Harper & Row, 1960.

Habermas, Jürgen. *The Structural Transformation of the Public Sphere: An Inquiry into a Category of Bourgeois Society.* Cambridge, Mass.: MIT Press, 1989.

Hajime Nakamura. "The Basic Teachings of Buddhism." In *Buddhism in the Modern World,* ed. H. Dumoulin et al. New York: Macmillan, 1976.

Harleen, Harfiyah Abdel, et al. *The Crescent and the Cross: Muslim and Christian Approaches to War and Peace.* London: Macmillan, 1998.

Harris, Harriet A. "Theological Reflections on Religious Resurgence and International Stability: A Look at Protestant Evangelicalism." In *Religion and International Relations,* ed. Ken R. Dark. London: Macmillan, 2000.

Havel, Vaclav. "The Power of the Powerless." In *Open Letters: Selected Writings 1965–1990 by Vaclav Havel,* ed. P. Wilson. New York: Knopf, 1991.

Haynes, Jeff. *Religion in Third World Politics.* London: Open University Press, 1994.

Haynes, Jeff, ed. *Religion, Globalization, and Political Culture in the Third World.* London: Macmillan, 1999.

Hays, Richard B. "Christology and Ethics in Galatians: The Law of Christ." *Catholic Biblical Quarterly* 49 (1987).

Heim, S. Mark. *Salvations: Truth and Difference in Religion.* Maryknoll, N.Y.: Orbis Books, 1999.

Held, David. *Democracy and the Global Order: From the Modern State to Cosmopolitan Governance.* London: Polity Press, 1995.

Held, David, et al. *Global Transformations: Politics, Economics, and Culture.* Stanford, Calif.: Stanford University Press, 1999.

Hick, John. *A Christian Theology of Religions.* Louisville: Westminster John Knox Press, 1995.

———. "The Non-absoluteness of Christianity." In *The Myth of Christian Uniqueness,* ed. John Hick and Paul F. Knitter. Maryknoll, N.Y.: Orbis Books, 1995.

———. "A Religious Understanding of Religion: A Model of the Relationship between Traditions." In *Inter-religious Models and Criteria,* ed. J. Kellenberger. New York: St. Martin's Press, 1993.

Hick, John, and Paul Knitter, eds. *The Myth of Christian Uniqueness.* Maryknoll, N.Y.: Orbis Books, 1995.

Hillers, Delbert R. *Covenant: The History of a Biblical Idea.* Baltimore: Johns Hopkins University Press, 1969.

Huang Dao. "Lue lun shehuizhuyi gongmin yishi de shidai tezhi" (A brief discussion of the contemporary characteristics of socialism's civic awareness). *Lilun yuekan* (Theoretical monthly) 1 (1988).

Huang Philip. " 'Public Sphere'/'Civil Society' in China? The Third Realm between State and Society." *Modern China* 19, no. 2 (1993).

Hughes, J. Donald. "From American Indian Ecology." In *This Sacred Earth: Religion, Nature, Environment,* ed. Roger Gottlieb. New York: Routledge, 1996.

Hunter, Alan, and Kim-Kwong Chan. *Protestantism in Contemporary China.* Cambridge Studies in Ideology and Religion. Cambridge: Cambridge University Press, 1993.

Huntington, Samuel P. *The Clash of Civilizations and the Remaking of World Order.* New York: Simon & Schuster, 1996.

————. *Political Order and Changing Societies.* Cambridge, Mass.: Harvard University Press, 1968.

Huntington, Samuel P., and Lawrence Harrison. *Culture Matters: How Values Shape Human Progress.* New York: Basic Books, 2000.

Hurrell, Andrew. "International Society and the Study of Regimes: A Reflective Approach." In *Regime Theory and International Relations,* ed. Volker R. Rittberger and P. Meyer. Oxford: Oxford University Press, 1993.

Hutchison, J. A. *Paths of Faith.* New York: McGraw-Hill, 1969.

Ignatieff, Michael. *The Warrior's Honor: Ethnic War and the Modern Conscience.* New York: Vintage, 1998.

Immanuel Kant. *Religion within the Limits of Reason Alone.* New York: Harper & Row, 1960.

Indapanno, Buddhadasa. *Buddha Dhamma for Students.* Trans. Ariyananda Bhikkhu. Bangkok: Thammasat University, 1966.

————. *Christianity and Buddhism.* Sinclaire Thompson Memorial Lecture. Bangkok: Thailand Theological Seminary, 1967.

James, William. *Varieties of Religious Experience.* New York: New American Library.

Janzen, John M. "The Consequences of Literacy in African Religion." In *The Theoretical Explorations in African Religion,* ed. Wim van Binsbergen and Matthew Schoffeleers. London: KPI, 1985.

Jensen, Lionel M. *Manufacturing Confucianism: Chinese Traditions and Universal Civilization.* Durham, N.C.: Duke University Press, 1997.

Jochannan, Yosef Ben-. "Moses: African Influence on Judaism." In *The African Origins of the Major World Religions,* ed. Amon Saba Saakana. London: Black Classics Press, 1988.

Joshi, Satyakam. "Tribals, Missionaries, and Sadhus." *Economic and Political Weekly* (Mumbai) 34, no. 37.

Juergensmeyer, Mark. *The New Cold War? Religious Nationalism Confronts the Secular State.* Berkeley: University of California Press, 1993.

Ju Mingzhou. "Wenhua shi gongmin shehui xingwei de zhidu tixi" (Culture is the system of behaviors in a civil society). *Liaoning daxue xuebao* (Liaoning University journal) 5 (1989).

Jung, Moses, Swami Nikhilananda, and Herbert W. Schneider, eds. *Relations among Religions Today.* Leiden: Brill, 1963.

Kaiser, Rudolf. "Chief Seattle's Speech(es): American Origins and European Reception." In *Recovering the Word: Essays on Native American Literature,* ed. Brian Swann and Arnold Krupat. Berkeley: University of California Press, 1987.

Kaldor, Mary. *New and Old Wars: Organized Violence in a Global Age.* London: Polity Press, 1998.

Keane, John. *Civil Society: Old Images, New Visions.* Stanford, Calif.: Stanford University Press, 1998.

Kegley, Charles, ed. *Controversies in International Relations: Realism and the Neoliberal Challenge.* New York: St. Martin's Press, 1995.

Kelman, Naamah. "Globalization and Religion." *Current Dialogue* 33 (July 1999).

Keohane, Robert. *After Hegemony.* Princeton, N.J.: Princeton University Press, 1984.

———. "International Institutions: Two Approaches." In *International Theory: Critical Investigations,* ed. James Der Derian. London: Macmillan, 1995.

———. "Reciprocity in International Relations." In *International Institutions and State Power,* ed. Robert Keohane. Boulder, Colo.: Westview Press, 1989.

Keohane, Robert, ed. *International Institutions and State Power.* Boulder, Colo.: Westview Press, 1989.

Keyes, Charles F. "Political Crisis and Militant Buddhism in Contemporary Thailand." In *Religion and Legitimation of Power in Thailand, Laos, and Burma,* ed. Bardwell L. Smith. Chambersburg, Pa.: Anima Books, 1978.

Kierkegaard, Søren. *Fear and Trembling.* Princeton, N.J.: Princeton University Press, 1954.

Kim Kyong-Dong. "Confucianism, Economic Growth, and Democracy." *Asian Perspective* 21, no. 2 (Fall 1997).

———. "Confucianism and Capitalist Development in East Asia." In *Capitalism and Development,* ed. L. Sklair. London: Routledge, 1994.

———. "The Distinctive Features of South Korea's Development." In *In Search of an East Asian Development Model,* ed. P. Berger and H. Hsiao. New Brunswick, N.J.: Transaction Books, 1988.

King, Winston L. *A Thousand Lives Away.* Oxford: Bruno Cassiver, 1964.

Kitagawa, Joseph M. "Joachim Wach," In *The Encyclopedia of Religion.* Vol. 15. Ed. Mircea Eliade. New York: Simon & Schuster Macmillan, 1995.

Klos, Frank W., C. Lynn Nakamura, and Daniel F. Martensen, eds. *Lutherans and the Challenge of Religious Pluralism.* Minneapolis: Augsburg Fortress, 1990.

Klostermaier, Klaus. *A Survey of Hinduism.* 2d ed. Albany: SUNY Press, 1994.

Knappert, Jan. *Swahili Islamic Poetry.* London: Heinemann, 1971.

Knappert, Jan, and Andrew Rippin, eds. *Textual Sources for the Study of Islam.* Manchester: Manchester University Press; Chicago: University of Chicago Press, 1986.

Knight, Kelvin. "Revolutionary Aristotelianism." In *Contemporary Political Studies 1996.* Vol. 2. Ed. I. Hampshire-Monk and J. Stanyer. 1996.

Knight, Kelvin, ed. *The MacIntyre Reader.* Cambridge: Polity Press, 1998.

Knitter, Paul. "Inter-religious Dialogue: What? Why? How?" In *Death or Dialogue?* ed. Leonard Swidler et al. London: SCM Press, 1990.

———. *Jesus and Other Names: Christian Mission and Global Responsibility.* Maryknoll, N.Y.: Orbis Books, 1996.

———. *No Other Name? A Critical Survey of Christian Attitudes toward the World Religions.* Maryknoll, N.Y.: Orbis Books, 1985.

———. *One Earth, Many Religions: Multifaith Dialogue and Global Responsibility.* Maryknoll, N.Y.: Orbis Books, 1995.

———. "Toward a Liberation Theology of Religion." In *The Myth of Christian Uniqueness,* ed. John Hick and Paul Knitter. Maryknoll, N.Y.: Orbis Books, 1995.

Koyama, Kosuke. *Water Buffalo Theology.* London: SCM Press, 1974.

Kraemer, Hendrik. *The Christian Message in a Non-Christian World.* London: Edinburgh House Press, 1938.

Krieger, David J. *The New Universalism: Foundations for a Global Theology.* Maryknoll, N.Y.: Orbis Books, 1991.

Kristensen, W. Brede. *The Meaning of Religion: Lectures in the Phenomenology of Religion.* 2d ed. The Hague, 1960.

Küng, Hans. *A Global Ethic for Global Politics and Economics.* New York: Oxford University Press, 1997.

———. *Global Responsibility: In Search of a New World Ethic.* New York: Crossroad, 1991.

Küng, Hans, ed. "Parliament of World Religions' Global Ethic." *National Catholic Reporter.* September 24, 1993.

Küng, Hans, with Josef van Ess et al. *Christianity and the World Religions: Paths to Dialogue with Islam, Hinduism, and Buddhism.* New York: Doubleday, 1986.

Küng, Hans, with Julia Ching. *Christianity and Chinese Religions.* New York: Doubleday, 1989.

Kuriakose, M. K., ed. *History of Christianity in India: Source Materials.* Madras: SCM Press, 1982.

Kwok Puilan. "Ecology and the Recycling of Christianity." In *Ecotheology: Voices from South and North,* ed. D. G. Hallman. Maryknoll, N.Y.: Orbis Books, 1994.

Lambert, Tony. *The Resurrection of the Chinese Church*. London: Hodder & Stoughton, 1991.

Lauer, Quentin. "Hegel, G. W. F." In *The Encyclopedia of Religion*. Vol. 6. Ed. Mircea Eliade. New York: Simon & Schuster Macmillan, 1995.

Lechner, Frank J. "Religion, Law, and Global Order." In *Religion and Global Order*, ed. Roland Robertson and William R. Garrett. New York: Paragon House, 1991.

Lee, Robert. *Overcoming Tradition and Modernity: The Search for Islamic Authenticity*. Boulder, Colo.: Westview Press, 1997.

Levy, Jack S. "Prospect Theory, Rational Choice, and International Relations." *International Studies Quarterly* 41, no. 1 (1997).

Levy-Bruhl, Lucien. *Primitive Mentality*. Trans. Lilian A. Clare. New York: Macmillan, 1923.

Lings, Martin. *A Moslem Saint of the Twentieth Century: Shaikh Ahmad al-'Alawí*. London: Allen & Unwin, 1961.

Linklater, Andrew. *The Transformation of Political Community*. London: Polity Press, 1998.

Little, David, and Sumner B. Twiss. *Comparative Religious Ethics: A New Method*. New York: Harper & Row, 1978.

Liu Binyan. "China and the Lessons of Eastern Europe." *Journal of Democracy* 2, no. 2 (1991).

Liu Zhiguang and Wang Suli. "Cong qunzhong shehui zouxiang gongmin shehui" (From mass society to civil society). *Zhengzhixue yanjiu* (Research on political science) 5 (1988).

Macdonald, Duncan Black. *The Religious Attitude and Life in Islam*. London: Darf Publishers, 1909.

MacIntyre, Alasdair. *After Virtue: A Study in Moral Theory*. 2d ed. London: Duckworth, 1985.

———. "Politics, Philosophy, and the Common Good." In *The MacIntyre Reader*. Ed. Kelvin Knight. Cambridge: Polity Press, 1998.

———. *Whose Justice? Which Rationality?* London: Duckworth, 1988.

Madsen, Richard. *China's Catholics: Tragedy and Hope in an Emerging Civil Society*. Comparative Studies in Religion and Society. Berkeley: University of California Press, 1998.

———. "The Public Sphere, Civil Society, and Moral Community: A Research Agenda for Contemporary China Studies." *Modern China* 19, no. 2 (1993).

Maha parinibbana suttanta. In *Dialogues of the Buddha*. Part 2. Bangkok: Pali Text Society, 1966.

Malik, Rajiv. Interview in *Hinduism Today*. October 31, 1997.

Mapel, David R., and Terry Nardin, eds. *International Society: Diverse Ethical Perspectives.* Princeton, N.J.: Princeton University Press, 1998.

Martyn, J. Louis. "A Law-Observant Mission to Gentiles: The Background of Galatians." *Scottish Journal of Theology* 38 (1985).

Ma Shu-Yun. "The Chinese Discourse on Civil Society." *China Quarterly* 137 (1994).

Mayall, James. "International Society and International Theory." In *The Reason of States,* ed. Michael Donelan. London: Allen & Unwin, 1978.

Mbiti, John S. *The Prayers of African Religion.* Maryknoll, N.Y.: Orbis Books, 1975.

McDermott, Gerald R. *Jonathan Edwards Confronts the Gods: Christian Theology, Enlightenment Religion, and Non-Christian Faiths.* New York: Oxford University Press, 2000.

McKay, Stan. "An Aboriginal Perspective on the Integrity of Creation." In *Ecotheology: Voices from South and North,* ed. D. G. Hallman. Maryknoll, N.Y.: Orbis Books, 1994.

Mead, Sidney E. *The Nation with the Soul of a Church.* New York: Harper & Row, 1975.

Meilaender, Gilbert. "Still Waiting for Benedict." *First Things* (October 1999).

Metzger, Thomas A. *Escape from Predicament: Neo-Confucianism and China's Evolving Political Culture.* Studies of the East Asian Institute. New York: Columbia University Press, 1977.

Migdal, Joel S., Atul Kohli, and Vivienne Shue. *State Power and Social Forces: Domination and Transformation in the Third World.* Cambridge: Cambridge University Press, 1994.

Minear, Paul S. *Christians and the New Creation: Genesis Motifs in the New Testament.* Louisville, Ky.: Westminster John Knox Press, 1994.

Mubiala, Mutoy. "African States and the Promotion of Humanitarian Principles." *IRRC* (March–April 1989).

Müller, Max. *Essays on the Science of Religion.* Vol. 1: *Chips from a German Workshop.* London: Longmans, Green & Co., 1867.

———. *Introduction to the Science of Religion.* London: Longmans, Green & Co., 1873.

Müller, Max, ed. *Sacred Texts of the East.* London: Clarendon Press, 1888.

Na'im, Abdullahi Ahmed An-. *Toward an Islamic Reformation.* Syracuse, N.Y.: Syracuse University Press, 1990.

Nelson, Robert H. *Economics as Religion.* University Park: Pennsylvania State University Press, 2001.

Ng Kam Weng. *Perfect Revelation.* Jalan, Malaysia: Pustaka Sufes, 1995.

Niebuhr, Reinhold. *An Interpretation of Christian Ethics.* New York: Seabury Press, 1935.

———. *The Nature and Destiny of Man.* Vol. 1. New York: Charles Scribner's Sons, 1941.

Oakes, Edward T. "The Achievement of Alasdair MacIntyre." *First Things* (August–September 1996).

Obenchain, Diane B. "Revelations of the Dragon: Observations on Christianity and 'Ru' (Confucianism) in China Today." *Princeton Seminary Bulletin* 21, no. 2, n.s. (2000).

O'Hagan, J. "Civilisational Conflict? Looking for Cultural Enemies." *Third World Quarterly* 16, no. 1 (1995).

Osmer, Richard. "The Teaching Ministry in a Multicultural World." In *God and Globalization.* Vol. 2: *The Spirit and the Modern Authorities,* ed. Max L. Stackhouse with Don S. Browning. Harrisburg, Pa.: Trinity Press International, 2001.

Otto, Rudolf. *The Idea of the Holy.* Trans. John W. Harvey. Oxford: Oxford University Press, 1923.

Outka, Gene, and John P. Reeder, Jr., eds. *Religion and Morality.* New York: Anchor Books, 1973.

Panikkar, Raimon. *The Intra-religious Dialogue.* New York: Paulist, 1999.

———. *The Silence of God.* Maryknoll, N.Y.: Orbis Books, 1989.

Penna, L. R. "Written and Customary Provisions relating to the Conduct of Hostilities and Treatment of Victims in Ancient India." *IRRC* (July–August 1989).

Prashad, Vijay. *Contours of the Heart: South Asians Map North America.* New York: Asian American Writer's Workshop, 1996.

———. "Forging a New Identity: We Must Forge Complex Cultures of Solidarity." *Little India* 7, no. 4 (April 30, 1997).

Prendeville, Kerry. "Pacific Regional Seminary Theses and Syntheses." *Pacific Journal of Theology* (Suva, Fiji) 2, no. 3 (1990).

Priest, Doug, Jr. *Doing Theology with the Maasai.* Pasadena, Calif.: William Carey Library, 1990.

Putnam, Robert. *Making Democracy Work: Civic Traditions in Modern Italy.* Princeton, N.J.: Princeton University Press, 1993.

Qadir, S. "Civilisational Clashes: Surveying the Fault Lines." *Third World Quarterly* 19, no. 4 (1998).

Queen, Christopher S. *Engaged Buddhism in the West.* Boston: Wisdom Publications, 2000.

Queen, Christopher S., and Sally King, eds. *Engaged Buddhism: Buddhist Liberation Movements in Asia.* Somerville, Mass.: Wisdom Publications, 1996.

Rahner, Karl, ed. *Encyclopedia of Religion*. London: Burns & Oates, 1975.

Rankin, Mary Backus. *Elite Activism and Political Transformation in China: Zhejing Province, 1865–1911*. Stanford, Calif.: Stanford University Press, 1986.

————. "The Origins of a Chinese Public Sphere: Local Elites and Community Affairs in the Late Imperial Period." *Etudes Chinoises* 9, no. 2 (1990).

————. "Some Observations on a Chinese Public Sphere." *Modern China* 19, no. 2 (1993).

Rauschenbusch, Walter. *A Theology for the Social Gospel*. New York: Macmillan, 1917.

Redding, S. G. *The Spirit of Chinese Capitalism*. New York: Walter de Gruyter, 1993.

Rengger, Nicholas J. "Culture, Society, and Order in World Politics." In *Dilemmas of World Politics,* ed. John Baylis and N. J. Rengger. Oxford: Oxford University Press, 1992.

Ringmar, Erik. *Identity, Interest, and Action: A Cultural Explanation of Sweden's Intervention in the Thirty Years War*. Cambridge: Cambridge University Press, 1996.

Robbins, Thomas, William C. Shepherd, and James McBride, eds. *Cults, Culture, and the Law*. Chico, Calif.: Scholars Press, 1985.

Roberson, B. A., ed. *International Society and the Development of International Relations Theory*. London: Pinter, 1998.

Roberts, R. H. "Globalized Religion? The Parliament of the World's Religions (Chicago, 1993) in Theoretical Perspective." *Journal of Contemporary Religion* 10, no. 2 (1995).

Robertson, Roland. "Globalization, Modernization, Postmodernization: The Ambiguous Position of Religion." In *Religion and Global Order,* ed. Roland Robertson and William R. Garrett. New York: Paragon House, 1991.

Rosette, Bennetta Jules, ed. *The New Religions of Africa: Priests and Priestesses in Contemporary Cults and Churches*. Norwood, N.J.: Ablex, 1979.

Rossiter, Clinton. *Conservatism in America: The Thankless Persuasion*. 2d ed. New York: Vintage Books, 1962.

Rowe, William T. *Hankow: Commerce and Society in a Chinese City, 1796–1889*. Stanford, Calif.: Stanford University Press, 1984.

————. *Hankow: Conflict and Community in a Chinese City, 1796–1895*. Stanford, Calif.: Stanford University Press, 1989.

————. "The Problem of 'Civil Society' in Late Imperial China." *Modern China* 19, no. 2 (1993).

Runzo, Joseph. "God, Commitment, and Other Faiths: Pluralism versus Relativism." *Faith and Philosophy* 5, no. 4 (October 1988).

Said, Edward. *Orientalism*. New ed. New York: Vintage Books, 1994.

Samartha, S. J. *One Christ, Many Religions: Toward a Revised Christology.* Maryknoll, N.Y.: Orbis Books, 1991.

Sampson, Cynthia. "Religion and Peacebuilding." In *Peacemaking in International Conflict,* ed. I. W. Zartman and J. L. Rasmussen. Washington, D.C.: U.S. Institute of Peace, 1995.

Sanders, E. P. *Paul and Palestinian Judaism: A Comparison of Patterns of Religions*. Philadelphia: Fortress Press, 1977.

Sanneh, Lamin. *Encountering the West*. Maryknoll, N.Y.: Orbis Books, 1993.

———. *Translating the Message: The Missionary Impact on Culture.* American Society of Missiology Series 13. Maryknoll, N.Y.: Orbis Books, 1989.

Sarvate, Sarita. "Whither to, the Indian Melting Pot? Is India Destined to Become a Big Brown Version of America?" *India Currents* 11, no. 5 (August 31, 1997).

Schleiermacher, Friedrich. *The Christian Faith*. Trans. H. R. MacKintosh and J. S. Stewart. Edinburgh: T. & T. Clark, 1928.

———. *On Religion: Speeches to Its Cultured Despisers.* Ed. Richard Crouter. Cambridge: Cambridge University Press, 1996.

Schreiter, Robert. *The New Catholicity: Theology between the Global and the Local*. Maryknoll, N.Y.: Orbis Books, 1997.

Schweiker, William. "Responsibility in the World of Mammon." In *God and Globalization*. Vol. 1: *Religion and the Powers of the Common Life,* ed. Max L. Stackhouse with Peter J. Paris. Harrisburg, Pa.: Trinity Press International, 2000.

"The Seventeen-Article Constitution of Prince Shotoku." In *Sources of Japanese Tradition*. Vol. 1. New York: Columbia University Press, 1958.

Shafiq, Muhammed. *The Growth of Islamic Thought in North America: Focus on Ishmail Raji al-Faruqi*. New York: Amana Publishers, 1994.

Sharpe, Eric J. *Comparative Religion: A History*. Chicago: Open Court, 1975.

———. *Karl Ludvig Reichelt*. Hong Kong: Tao Fong Shan, 1984.

Shen Yue. "'Shimin shehui' bianxi" (An investigation of 'townspeople's society'). *Zhexue janjiu* (Studies of philosophy) 1 (1990).

———. "Zichanjieji quanli ying yi wei shimin quanli" (Bourgeois right should be townspeople's right). *Tianjin shehui kexue* (Tianjin social sciences) 4 (1986).

Sherwin, Byron L., and Harold Kasimov, eds. *John Paul II and Inter-religious Dialogue.* Maryknoll, N.Y.: Orbis Books, 1999.

Shils, Edward. "The Virtue of Civil Society." *Government and Opposition* 26, no. 1 (1991).

Shriver, Donald. "The Taming of Mars: Can Humans of the Twenty-First Century Contain their Propensity for Violence?" In *God and Globalization.* Vol. 1: *Religion and the Powers of the Common Life,* ed. Max L. Stackhouse with Peter J. Paris. Harrisburg, Pa.: Trinity Press International, 2000.

Sizemore, Russell, and Donald Swearer. *Ethics, Wealth, and Salvation.* Columbia: University of South Carolina Press, 1990.

Smith, A. "Dangerous Conjecture." *Foreign Affairs* 76, no. 2 (1997).

Smith, Bardwell L. *Religion and the Legitimation of Power in Thailand, Laos, and Burma.* Chambersburg, Pa.: Anima Press, 1978.

Smith, Bardwell L., ed. *Religion and the Legitimation of Power in Sri Lanka.* Chambersburg, Pa.: Anima Press, 1978.

Smith, Wilfred C. "Idolatry: A Comparative Perspective." In *The Myth of Christian Uniqueness,* ed. John Hick and Paul F. Knitter. Maryknoll, N.Y.: Orbis Books, 1987.

———. *The Meaning and End of Religion.* New York: Macmillan, 1963.

———. *Towards a World Theology.* Philadelphia: Westminster Press, 1981.

Smock, David R., ed. *Perspectives on Pacifism: Christian, Jewish, and Muslim Views on Nonviolence and International Conflict.* Washington, D.C.: U.S. Institute of Peace, 1995.

Soumen Shen. "Afro-Brazilian Cults and Religious Change in Brazil." In *The Changing Face of Religion,* ed. James A. Beckford and Thomas Luckmann. London: Sage Publications, 1989.

———. "The Changing Face of Khasi Religion." In *The Changing Face of Religion,* ed. James A. Beckford and Thomas Luckmann. London: Sage Publications, 1989.

Spiro, Medford. *Buddhism and Society.* London: Blackwell, 1970.

———. *Burmese Supernaturalism.* Englewood Cliffs, N.J.: Free Press, 1967.

Spuler, Michelle. "Buddhism in the West: An Emerging Genre." *Religious Studies Review* 26, no. 4 (October 2000).

Stackhouse, Max L. *Christian Social Ethics in a Global Era.* Nashville: Abingdon, 1995.

———. *Creeds, Society, and Human Rights.* Grand Rapids, Mich.: Eerdmans, 1984.

————. General introduction to *God and Globalization*. Vol. 1: *Religion and the Powers of the Common Life,* ed. Max L. Stackhouse with Peter J. Paris. Harrisburg, Pa.: Trinity Press International, 2000.

————. "The Hindu Ethic and the Ethos of Development." *Religion and Society* (India) (December 1973).

————. "Observations on Globalization in India." In *Dialogue on Globalization,* ed. John Mohen Razu and Moses Paul Peter. Bangalore: SCM Press, 2000.

————. "Politics and Religion." In *Encyclopedia of Religion.* Vol. 11. Ed. Mircea Eliade et al. New York: Macmillan, 1987.

————. "Public Theology, Islam, and the Future of Democracy." In *The Church's Public Role,* ed. Dieter Hessel. Grand Rapids, Mich.: Eerdmans, 1983.

————. "The World Religions and Political Democracy: Some Comparative Reflections." In *Religion and Society* (India) 29, no. 4 (December 1982).

Stackhouse, Max L., et al. *Apologia: Contextualization, Globalization, and Mission in Theological Education.* Grand Rapids, Mich.: Eerdmans, 1988.

Standaert, Nicholas. "Christianity as a Religion in China." In conference volume of "Religion and Chinese Society." Hong Kong, May 29–June 2, 1999.

Strachey, Lytton. *Eminent Victorians.* New York: Harcourt, Brace & Co., 1918.

Strand, David. "Protest in Beijing: Civil Society and Public Sphere in China." *Problems of Communism* 39, no. 3 (1990).

————. *Rickshaw Beijing: City People and Politics in the 1920s.* Berkeley: University of California Press, 1989.

Su Shaozhi et al. "Zhongguo de gongmin shehui de fazhan qushi" (The development of Chinese civil society). In *Dangdai zhongguo de guojia yu shehui guanxi* (The relationship between state and society in modern China), ed. Zhou Xueguang. Taipei: Guiguan, 1992.

Su Wei. "Man tan Beijing de wenhua quanzi" (Some thoughts on the cultural circles in Beijing). *Zhuguo zhichun* (China Spring) (January 1992).

Takeuchi Yoshinori. *The Heart of Buddhism.* New York: Crossroad, 1991.

Tambiah, Stanley J. *Magic, Science, Religion, and the Scope of Rationality.* Cambridge: Cambridge University Press, 1990.

————. "Sangha and Polity in Modern Thailand: An Overview." In *Religion and Legitimation of Power in Thailand, Laos, and Burma,* ed. Bardwell L. Smith. Chambersburg, Pa.: Anima Books, 1978.

Thangaraj, M. Thomas. *The Crucified Guru.* Nashville: Abingdon Press, 1994.

Thomas, Scott. "Religious Resurgence, Postmodernism, and World Politics." In *Religion and Global Order,* ed. John Esposito and Michael Watson. Cardiff: University of Wales Press, 2000.

Tiele, Cornelius P. *Elements of the Science of Religion, Gifford Lectures 1896 and 1898.* Edinburgh and London: William Blackwood & Sons, 1897.

Tillich, Paul. *Christianity and the Encounter of World Religions.* Minneapolis: Fortress Press, 1994.

———. *Systematic Theology.* Vol. 1. Chicago: University of Chicago Press, 1952.

Tillman, Hoyt Cleveland. *Utilitarian Confucianism: Ch'en Liang's Challenge to Chu His.* Harvard East Asian Monographs 101. Cambridge, Mass.: Harvard University Press, 1982.

Ting, K. H. *Love Never Ends.* Trans. Janice Wickeri. Nanjing: Amity Press, 2000.

Tinker, George. "The Full Circle of Liberation: An American Indian Theology of Place." In *Ecotheology: Voices from South and North,* ed. D. G. Hallman. Maryknoll, N.Y.: Orbis Books, 1994.

Tracy, David. "Fundamental Theology, Hope, and the Mass Media: Can the Muses Still Inspire?" In *God and Globalization.* Vol. 1: *Religion and the Powers of the Common Life,* Ed. Max L. Stackhouse with Peter J. Paris. Harrisburg, Pa.: Trinity Press International, 2000.

Tu Wei-ming. "Cultural China: The Periphery as the Center." In *The Living Tree: The Changing Meaning of Being Chinese Today,* ed. Tu Wei-ming. Stanford, Calif.: Stanford University Press, 1994.

———. *The Way, Learning, and Politics: Essays on the Confucian Intellectual.* Singapore: Institute of East Asian Philosophies, 1989.

Twiss, Sumner B., and Bruce Grelle, eds. *Explorations in Global Ethics: Comparative Religion Ethics and Interreligious Dialogue.* Boulder, Colo.: Westview Press, 1998.

Udana: Solemn Utterances of the Buddha. Trans. Bhadragaka. Bangkok: Mahamakuta-Raja-Vidyalaya, 1954.

United Bible Societies. *World Report.* Reading, England: UBS, 1999.

———. *World Report.* Reading, England: UBS, 2000.

Vajirananavarorasa, Prince. *Vinayamukha.* Bangkok: Buddhist University of Thailand, n.d.

van der Leeuw, G. *Religion in Essence and Manifestation.* Vol. 2. New York: Harper & Row, 1963.

van der Veer, Peter. *Religious Nationalism: Hindus and Muslims in India.* Berkeley: University of California Press, 1994.

Verhey, Allen. "The Spirit of God and the Spirit of Medicine." In *God and Globalization.* Vol. 2: *The Spirit and the Modern Authorities,* ed. Max L. Stackhouse with Don S. Browning. Harrisburg, Pa.: Trinity Press International, 2001.

Waardenburg, Jacques. *Classical Approaches to the Study of Religion.* The Hague: Mouton, 1973.

Wach, Joachim. *The Comparative Study of Religions.* New York: Columbia University Press, 1958.

———. *The Sociology of Religion.* Chicago: University of Chicago Press, 1944.

Waever, Ole. "Four Meanings of International Society." In *International Society and the Development of International Relations Theory,* ed. B. A. Roberson. London: Pinter, 1998.

Wakeman, Frederic. "The Civil Society and Public Sphere Debate: Western Reflections on Chinese Political Culture." *Modern China* 19, no. 2 (1993).

Walls, Andrew. "African Christianity in the History of Religions." In *Christianity in Africa in the 1990s,* ed. Christopher Fyfe and Andrew Walls. Edinburgh: Center for African Studies, University of Edinburgh, 1996.

———. *The Missionary Movement in Christian History.* Maryknoll, N.Y.: Orbis Books, 1997.

Walzer, Michael. "The Idea of Civil Society," *Dissent* (Spring 1991).

Walzer, Michael, ed. *Toward a Global Civil Society.* Oxford: Berg Hahn Books, 1995.

Wan, Sze-kar. "Abraham and the Promise of the Spirit: Galatians and the Hellenistic-Jewish Mysticism of Philo." *Society of Biblical Literature 1995 Seminar Papers* 34 (1995).

Wang Shaoguang. "Pochu dui *Civil Society* de misi" (Breaking the fixation on civil society). In *Dangdai zhongguo de guojia yu shehui guanxi* (The relationship between state and society in modern China), ed. Zhou Xueguang. Taipei: Guiguan, 1992.

Wapner, Paul, and Lester Edwin J. Ruiz, eds. *Principled World Politics: The Challenge of Normative International Relations.* Lanham, Md.: Rowman & Littlefield, 2000.

Warren, Heather A. *Theologians of a New World Order: Reinhold Niebuhr and the Christian Realists, 1920–1948.* Oxford: Oxford University Press, 1997.

Watson, Adam. Introduction to *The Evolution of International Society.* London: Routledge, 1991.

Watson, Bradley C. S., ed. *Liberalism in the New Millennium.* Latrobe, Pa.: Center for Political and Economic Education, 2000.

Watt, Montgomery. *Muhammad at Mecca.* Oxford: Clarendon Press, 1953.

———. *Muhammad at Medina.* Oxford: Clarendon Press, 1956.

Weigel, George. "What Really Happened at Cairo, and Why." In *The Nine Lives of Population Control,* ed. Michael Cromartie. Washington, D.C.: Ethics and Public Policy Center, 1995.

"Welcome Vajpayee! A Strong Government Was Long Overdue." *News-India Times* 28, no. 13 (March 7, 1998).

Westerlund, David, ed. *Questioning the Secular State: The Worldwide Resurgence of Religion in Politics.* London: I. B. Tauris, 1996.

Whaling, Frank. *Theory and Method in Religious Studies: Contemporary Approaches to the Study of Religion.* New York: Mouton de Gruyter, 1995.

Wheller, Nicholas J., and Tim Dunne. "Hedley Bull and the Idea of a Universal Moral Community: Fictional, Primordial, or Imagined?" In *International Society and the Development of International Relations Theory,* ed. B. A. Roberson. London: Pinter, 1998.

Whitehead, A. N. *Religion in the Making.* New York: Macmillan, 1926.

Wight, M. "De systematibus civitatum." In *Systems of States.* Leicester: Leicester University Press, 1977.

Williams, Duncan Ryuken, and Christopher S. Queen, eds. *American Buddhism.* Richmond, England: Curzon Press, 1999.

Wilson, Edward O. *Consilience.* New York: Knopf, 1998.

Witte, Jr., John. "The Spirit of the Laws, the Laws of the Spirit: Religion and Human Rights in a New Global Era." In *God and Globalization.* Vol. 2: *The Spirit and the Modern Authorities,* ed. Max L. Stackhouse with Don S. Browning. Harrisburg, Pa.: Trinity Press International, 2001.

Wuthnow, Robert. *Christianity and Civil Society: The Contemporary Debate.* Valley Forge, Pa.: Trinity Press International, 1996.

———. "The Last Modern Century." *New Perspectives Quarterly* 8, no. 2 (1991).

———. "Understanding Religion and Politics." *Daedalus* 120, no. 3 (Summer 1991).

Xie Wen. "Zhongguo gongmin shehui de yunyu he fazhan" (The birth and development of civil society in China). In *Dangdai zhongguo de guojia yu shehui guanxi* (The relationship between state and society in modern China), ed. Zhou Xueguang. Taipei: Guiguan, 1992.

Xi Zhaoyong. " 'Shimin shehui bianxi' de bianxi" (An investigation of 'investigation of townspeople's society'). *Zhexue janjiu* (Research on philosophy) 5 (1990).

Xu Fuguan. "The Tragic Fate of Chinese Intellectuals in an Extraordinary Time." In *Intellectuals and China,* ed. Zhou Yangshan. Taipei: Shibao Wenhua Chuban, 1980.

Young, Richard F. *Perspectives on Christianity in Korea and Japan.* Ed. M. Mullins. Lewiston, N.Y.: Edwin Mellen Press, 1995.

——. *Resistant Hinduism: Sanscrit Sources on Anti-Christian Apologetics in Early Nineteenth Century India.* Vienna: Institüt für Indologie, 1981.

——. *Vain Debates: Buddhist Controversies of Nineteenth Century Ceylon.* Trans. G. P. V. Someratna. Vienna: Institüt für Indologie, 1991.

Zartman, I. W. *Collapsed States: The Disintegration and Restoration of Legitimate Authority.* Boulder, Colo.: Lynne Rienner, 1995.

INDEX

Abe, Masao, 264n.45
Aborigines, 159–60
Abu Bakr, 292, 294
Abu Talib, 289, 291
action, 70–71, 76. *See also* politics
Adams, James Luther, 187, 208
Advani, L. K., 236
Africa
    eschatology and, 165
    literacy's impact in, 166–67
    the Ten Commandments and,
        141n.2
    tribal religions and, 145–47,
        154–58
    See also African Religion
African Religion, 145–46, 154–
    58, 166–67
'Alawi, Shaykh al-, 305, 305n.16
Ambedkar, Babasaheb, 49–50,
    217
anatta, 263–64
Andrae, Tor, 275–76
anomie, 133n.43
anthropology, 79, 84
Apologia (Stackhouse et al.),
    172
Arabicity of Islam, 302, 303
ashrama dharma, 219, 220,
    221
Association of African Earth-
    keeping Churches, 156
associations
    civility and, 188–89
    and civil society in China,
        186–87

Confucianism and, 210
Hinduism and, 235–36
reasons for failure of de-
    velopment of, in China,
    207
attachment, 53, 244, 247
Augustine, St., 278
Australia, 159–60
avatars, 267
avijja, 246, 246n.17
Ayodhya, India, 218, 225

Babari Masjid, 218
Balibar, Etienne, 187n.37
barakah, 283, 284
Barth, Karl, 63n.8
Bastide, Roger, 143–44
Bellah, Robert, 174n.2, 189
Berger, Peter, 119, 186
Bharatiya Janata Party, 225–26
Bhikkhu Khemo, 264
Bible, the
    Catholic mission and, 192n.49
    in China, 192–93
    tribal religions and translations
        of, 168–69
bio-piety, 219–21, 227–29, 234,
    236
bodhisattvas, 256, 256n.35
Bozeman, Adda, 129n.37
Brahman, 216–17
Brazil, 142–44
Bretton Woods system, 125–26
Brook, Timothy, 182
Buber, Martin, 105

331

comparison of Buddhism and
Christianity on, 260–61
comparison of Christianity and
Islam on, 303
foolishness of the Christian,
258–59
Islam on politics and, 307–8
Kant on, 69–70
pluralists on, 96
the Qur'an on, 242–43n.10,
301
revelation and, 241–42
ruah and, 250
Schleiermacher on, 72–73
Goldblatt, David, 1
Goldenweiser, Alexander A., 84
grasping, 264n.45. *See also* greed
The Great Learning, 205
greed, 243n.11, 250, 251–52,
252n.28, 262, 269–70
Green, Ronald, 25
Greene, Theodore M., 68n.19, 71
Grelle, Bruce, 25
gurus, 47, 222
Gutiérrez, Gustavo, 9n.8

Habermas, Jürgen, 178n.9, 181,
186
Habits of the Heart (Bellah et al.),
189
hadith, 284, 285–88, 306
Haiti, 144
hajj, 293–94
Han, 20
Harvard School, the, 87, 91
Havel, Vaclav, 180
Hegel, G. W. F., 1, 78, 104
Heidegger, Martin, 86
Heiler, Friedrich, 89
Heim, S. Mark, 23n.16, 33, 34,
101n.77
Held, David, 1, 7n.5
hermeneutic theory, 90
hesed, 197–98

Hick, John, 93–94, 96
hijrah, 301–2
Hillers, Delbert, 191n.47
Hinduism
on *avatars,* 267
Buddhism and, 49
the caste system and, 20
a Christian theological
approach to, 229–36
Confucianism contrasted with,
45
future of, 236–38
globalization and, 221–29
as an "identity religion," 44–45
influence on the West, 47
Judaism and, 15n.13
nationalism and, 46–47
a new particularism and, 28–29
nonindigenous disruptions of,
46
overview of the history and
central teachings of, 213–21
universalism of, 48
Hindu Students Council, 225
Hindutva movement, 217–28,
225, 235
historical-critical method, 279,
299
history of religion, 22
house churches, 44
Huang, Peter, 186
Huang Dao, 178
Hughes, J. Donald, 152–54
human rights
in China, 174
developing countries' challenge
to the liberal view of, 116
the Five Precepts and, 263n.39
postmodern approaches to, 8
tribal religions and, 149–50,
161
Huntington, Samuel, 14n.11, 132,
175–76
Husain, M. F., 232

twofold attitude toward
  Muhammad and, 305–6
universalizing drive of, 53–54
women and, 20
See also Muhammad
Iwuchukwu, Father, 109, 109n.88

Jainism, 224
James, William, 104
Janzen, John M., 166
Jesus
  the cross and, 199–201
  as establishing a community
    reality, 258
  and the foolishness of God, 257
  the historical, 244
  the historical-critical method
    on, 279
  Kant on, 68, 71
  Muhammad and, 289–90
  Paul on love and, 196–98
  Schleiermacher on, 73–74
  Sufi commentary on, 304
  summary of what he offers
    other religions, 98–101
jihad, 298
John Paul II, Pope, 23n.17, 303,
  308
Judaism
  Buddhism contrasted with, 254
  covenant in, 193–94
  globalization and, 300
  revelation and, 242
  traditional religions and, 38–39
  tribal religions and, 15n.13
Jung, L. Shannon, 160
justice, 76, 94

Kant, Immanuel
  Christianity and, 71n.24
  on the concept of religion,
    68–71, 75–77
  conflict resolution and, 135

deontological principles
  articulated by, 25
and Enlightenment-based
  interpretations of non-
  Christian religions, 24
Green on, 25
influence of, 106–7
Lessing on, 68n.19
on mystery, 69n.21
phenomenology of religion
  contrasted with the approach
  of, 85, 86
Pietism and, 68n.18
the study of culture and, 60
Kardec, Alain, 142
karma, 247
Keane, John, 174n.2, 185n.30,
  186
Kelman, Rabbi Naamah, 300
kewu, 206
Khadijah, 290, 291
Kierkegaard, Søren, 262n.38
Kittivuddho, 267
Klostermaier, Klaus, 215, 236–
  37, 238
Knight, Kelvin, 128n.34
Knitter, Paul, 32–34, 94, 96
Korea, 20
Koyama, Kosuke, 52, 170
Kraemer, Hendrik, 63n.8, 304
Kristensen, W. Brede, 88–89
Küng, Hans, 27, 136
Kwok Puilan, 169

Lang, Andrew, 81
law
  Bozeman on, 129n.37
  and civil society in China, 185
  international society and, 117
Laws of Manu, 219, 221
Lessing, G. E., 68n.19
Lévi-Strauss, Claude, 187n.37
Levy-Bruhl, Lucien, 61, 61n.7,
  104

neoliberalism (continued)
  the international society
    tradition and, 121
  on the rationality of states as
    actors, 126–27
  shortcomings of theories of,
    130–33
  the Third World and, 114–15
neo-orthodox Christians, 63
neorealism
  assumptions of, regarding the
    state, 129–30
  basic assumptions of, 110–11
  functional understanding of
    international society held by,
    122
  inability to address problems in
    international relations, 111
  as an insufficient base for
    international order, 134
  the international society
    tradition and, 121
  on the rationality of states as
    actors, 126–27
  shortcomings of theories of,
    124, 130–33
Neuhaus, Richard, 186
new catholicity, the, 230–34
new world order, the, 125
Ng Kam Weng, 14n.10
NGOs, 136
Niebuhr, Reinhold, 125, 242,
  264, 264n.45, 270
Nietzsche, Friedrich, 80
nirvana, 247
nonresident Indians, 230–32,
  235, 236
nontheism, 260–65
nontranslatability of the Qur'an,
  302, 303
normlessness, 133n.43
no-self, 263–64
nuclear weapons, 225–26
numinous experience, 84

Obenchain, Diane B., 21–29
observation
  Buddha and, 250
  Buddhism and Christianity and,
    259–60
  dharma and, 249
  divine revelation and human,
    240–41
oral tradition, 166
organization, 129n.36
orthodoxy, 108, 232–34
Otto, Rudolf, 82, 83–84, 86, 89
Outka, Gene, 25
outsiders, 199, 200

Palamas, Gregory, 261
panchamas, 219
Paramahamsa, Ramakrishna, 233
Parliament of World Religions,
  27, 136
participation, 62
paticcasamuppada, 245–46
Paul
  on the body of Christ, 99–100
  on covenant, 193–201,
    194n.52, 195n.53,
    195–96n.54, 209–12
  on creation, 165
  on Jesus and love, 196–98
  on Judaic legalism, 194n.52
Peck, George, 101n.77
Pentecost, 301–2
people of God, the, 193–96
Pereira de Queiroz, Maria Isaura,
  142
Perraton, Jonathan, 1
phenomena, 85–88
phenomenology of religion
  Enlightenment-based
    scholarship and, 22
  faith and, 104–5, 108
  theology and, 102
  two approaches to, 82–91
Phumipol, 267